D1565854

THE LIFE AND WRITINGS OF THOMAS HELWYS

EARLY ENGLISH BAPTIST TEXTS

SERIES DESCRIPTION

The purpose of the series *Early English Baptist Texts* is to provide scholars, students, and church leaders with a contemporary, multivolume, scholarly edition of primary sources representative of English Baptists of the seventeenth century. While the series is intended to provide a valuable source to church leaders, it is also intended to make a long lasting contribution to scholarship in the areas of Baptists studies, the English Reformation, and the history of Christianity in general. It is anticipated that the series will consist of several volumes of primary source materials, the larger part of it never before edited. The selected works were penned by seven different English Baptists leaders, namely: John Smyth (d. 1612), Thomas Helwys (1550?-1616?), John Murton (d. 1625), William Kiffin (b. 1616), Katherine Sutton (1630-1663), Hanserd Knollys (c. 1599-1691), and Thomas Grantham (1634-1692). The collection aims to be diverse and inclusive, broad enough to transcend narrow confessional interests.

EDITORS

Rady Roldan-Figueroa, is Assistant Professor of Historical Studies, Department of Religion, Baylor University.

C. Douglas Weaver is Associate Professor of Religion and Director of Undergraduate Studies, Department of Religion, Baylor University.

PROJECTED TITLES

—*The Extant Writings of Thomas Helwys (1608-1612)*

—*Collected Works of John Smyth (d. 1612)*, including: *The Bright Morning Star: Or, The Resolution and Exposition of the 22 Psalm* (Cambridge, 1603); *A Pattern of True Prayer* (London, 1605); *The Differences of the Churches of the Separation* (Middelburg, 1608); *The Character of the Beast* (Middelburg, 1609); *Parallels, Censures and Observations* (Middelburg: 1609).

—*John Murton (d. 1625) and the General Baptists*, including: *Objections* (1615); *A Description of What God Had Predestined* (London, 1620); *A Must Humble Supplication* (1621).

—*Collected Works of Hanserd Knollys (1599-1691)*, including: *A Moderate Answer* (London, 1645); *Christ Exalted* (London, 1646); *An Exposition of the First Chapter of the Song of Solomon* (London, 1656); *The Parable of the Kingdom of Heaven Expounded* (London, 1674); *The Baptists Answer to Mr. Obed Wills* (London, 1675); *Mystical Babylon Unveiled* (London, 1679); *An Exposition of the 11th Chapter of Revelation* (London, 1679); *The Gospel Minister's Maintenance Vindicated* (London, 1689); *An*

Answer to a Brief Discourse Concerning Singing (London, 1691); *The Life and Death of that Old Disciple of Jesus Christ* (London, 1692); *An Exposition of Revelation* (London, 1689)

—*Katherine Sutton: A Christian Woman's Experience (1663)*

—*Collected Works of William Kiffin (1616-1701)*, including: *Observation upon Hosea* (London, 1642); *Confession of Faith* (London, 1644); *A Brief Remonstrance* (1645); *Confession of Faith* (London, 1652); *About Imposition of Hands* (London, 1654); *Letter to the Lord Mayor of the City of London* (London, 1660); *The Humble Apology* (London, 1660); *A Serious Answer* (London, 1692)

—*Thomas Grantham: Christianismus Primitivus (1678)*

SERIES FOREWORD

The series *Early English Baptist Texts* is inspired in the idea that a return to the sources, in the spirit of the Renaissance's ideal of *ad fontes*, can only inject new dynamism to Baptist theology. Serious engagement with historical Baptist sources can move Baptist theological reflection in the direction of robust ecumenical engagement as well as self confident contributions based on historical Baptist theological insights. In fact, what this series offers is the opportunity to discover *de novo* the historical complexity, the plurality of voices, and the significant diversity of views that informed early English Baptists. This discovery will allow us to think of Baptists in new ways, ways that will allow for a broadening of Baptist identity.

The series is modeled after very successful collections of primary sources that have become standard resources for scholars, pastors, and other students of Baptist history, intellectual history of the Reformation, and Christian thought in general. Among the collections in mind are *Ancient Christian Writers* (Newman Press), and *Library of Christian Classics* (Westminster Press). Perhaps more in proportion with the editors' intentions is the collection, *Classics of the Radical Reformation* (Herald Press). Richard Groves' editions of Thomas Helwys' *A Short Declaration of the Mystery of Iniquity* (1998) and Roger Williams' *The Bloudy Tenant of Persecution* (2001), both by Mercer University Press, also provide an outstanding model for the present series. However, the texts of the collection are not limited to topics of religious liberty. Instead, the texts are meant to provide readily available primary sources for the study of early English Baptist thought in its broader manifestations.

Early English Baptist Texts stands to fill an important void in contemporary Baptist scholarship. The great majority of texts authored by early seventeenth century English Baptists remain buried in obscurity, only accessible to the expert scholar in research libraries throughout England and the United States. While accessibility to these works has greatly improved thanks to scholarly services of the digital age such as Early English Books Online, their access is still limited to a reduced specialized readership. Access to these works is further limited due to the historical gap between a potential contemporary American audience and the historical context that provided the backdrop against which early English Baptists articulated their ideas and composed their writings. Finally, the works for which there are existing modern editions are few in number and these very editions are now rare and hard to find. *Early English Baptist Texts* will be the first collection of its kind in Baptist scholarship. Many of the texts that are included will be edited for the first time, adapted to modern English usage, and properly set in their historical context in light of the best contemporary scholarship available.

Works to be included in the series have been selected according to the following criteria. First, they are representative of the complexity and rich diversity of English Baptists' of the seventeenth century. The editors of the collection affirm the continuing validity of the traditional classification of early English Baptists into General and Particular Baptists. Hence, a conscious effort has been undertaken to include texts that are representative of these theological impulses of the movement.

Second, works have also been selected based on their potential to illuminate the social history of the movement. In this sense the collection will be more than just an "anthology of classics." Indeed, some of the volumes of the collection will be dedicated to longstanding and well established classics, such as the collected works of John Smyth. However, careful thought has been given to include works that have traditionally been considered marginal either for the content matter or due to the status or gender of the author. Finally, the editors have sought to include in the collection works that are representative of different literary genres. Accordingly, confessions, books of sermons, journals, and controversialist literature are included side by side with more formal theological treatises and biblical commentaries.

In closing, while the editors are aware of the natural appeal of the series to a primarily Baptist audience it has been their intention to produce a scholarly work attractive to a broader public. Accordingly, the editors have invited renowned scholars to write introductions and notes to each volume, as well as other reading aids. It is hoped that the quality of the work will also inspire new generations of scholars to explore the rich history of the Baptists.

The James N. Griffith Series in Baptist Studies

This series on Baptist life and thought explores and investigates Baptist history, offers analyses of Baptist theologies, provides studies in hymnody, and examines the role of Baptists in societies and cultures around the world. The series also includes classics of Baptist literature, letters, diaries, and other writings.

Walter B. Shurden
Series Editor

MERCER
UNIVERSITY PRESS

Endowed by
Tom Watson Brown
and
The Watson-Brown Foundation, Inc.

THE LIFE AND WRITINGS OF THOMAS HELWYS

Written and Edited by

Joe Early, Jr.

Early English Baptist Texts

MERCER UNIVERSITY PRESS
MACON, GEORGIA

MUP/H781

First Edition.

Books published by Mercer University Press are printed on acid free paper that meets the requirements of American National Standard for Information Sciences—Permanence of Paper for Printed Library Materials.

Mercer University Press is a member of Green Press initiative (greenpressinitiative.org), a nonprofit organization working to help publishers and printers increase their use of recycled paper and decrease their use of fiber derived from endangered forests. This book is printed on recycled paper.
Early, Joseph E. (Joseph Everett), 1970
[Selections. 2009]
The life and writings of Thomas Helwys / written and edited by Joe Early, Jr. -- 1st ed.
p. cm.
Includes bibliographical references and index.
ISBN-13: 978-0-88146-146-6 (hardback : alk. paper)
ISBN-10: 0-88146-146-6 (hardback : alk. paper)
1. Helwys, Thomas, 1550?-1616? 2. Baptists—England—Biography. 3. Baptists—Doctrines—Early works to 1800. 4. Baptists—History. 5. England—Church history—16th century. 6. England—Church history—17th century. I. Title.
BX6495.H44E27 2009
286.092--dc22
[B]
2009011282

In honor of James Leo and Myrta Ann Garrett

CONTENTS

FOREWORD TO THIS VOLUME

The question of Baptist identity has been a topic of ongoing interest for many generations. For the past century, numerous Baptist scholars have given serious attention to this task. Some have produced primers identifying key principles that are prominent in Baptist self-understanding. Others have sought to identify a single key idea that defines Baptists. Both approaches are useful.

Another major path to illuminating the question of identity is to listen to the original voices of the movement. What were the founders' visions of Christianity? What ideas did they cherish most? What notions of the church did they reject? What were their arguments for seeking change? The questions of origins and identity are not the same. Since their first generation 400 years ago, Baptists have added to their original convictions many important emphases, such as a strong commitment to missions. They have also developed a notable variety of Baptist denominations with sharply differing emphases. The question of identity is therefore complex, and answers to the problem are varied. Nevertheless, listening to original Baptist voices remains one essential path to assessing Baptist identity.

Thomas Helwys (c. 1575–c. 1614) was a leading Baptist founder. He came from English gentry, secured legal training at Gray's Inn in London, and returned to live in the family house at Broxtowe Hall in Nottinghamshire. He was drawn to radical religious ideas and joined the congregation of Separatist John Smyth. In order to escape persecution, Smyth and Helwys arranged transport for the congregation to Holland. There, they became the founders of the Baptist movement. Smyth became convinced that infant baptism was not scriptural. He baptized himself and then baptized his followers, thereby establishing the first Baptist church in Amsterdam. Soon, however, he abandoned this path and led his followers to join a Mennonite congregation. Helwys and approximately ten followers maintained their Baptist conviction and split with Smyth. They returned to England and established the first Baptist church in England at Spitalfields in 1612. Helwys was arrested and imprisoned and eventually died for his convictions.

Helwys shared key insights with Smyth. Separatists of the era attacked the Anglican Church as a false church. Their goal was to reconstitute a true church based on their understanding of Scripture. The Separatists did not agree on the Anglican Church's interpretation of what constitutes the true church. Therefore, in England, Presbyterians, Congregationalists, Baptists, Quakers, and other groups emerged, each with its own vision of true Christianity.

Helwys, who was an articulate writer, made very clear the basis for his differences not only with the Anglican Church, but also with the Congregationalists and Presbyterians. He held that the church was comprised of believers, and for this reason he rejected infant baptism. With regard to salvation, he followed Arminius and rejected Calvin's notion of predestination. He is perhaps best known for *A Short Declaration of the Mystery of Iniquity* (1612), in which he offers the earliest Baptist plea for full religious liberty. Helwys thus offers significant reflection and insight on the nature of the church, salvation, and the relationship of the church to the state—all themes close to the core of Baptist identity.

Joe Early renders a splendid service to readers who want to explore the origins of Baptist identity for themselves by assembling Helwys's key works in a single volume. Early offers an introduction to Helwys's life, and in the course of this biographical sketch he summarizes leading themes in Helwys's treatises. Helwys's letters and confessions are brief texts, but they provide important statements of his views. In his longer treatises Helwys develops his key concepts in much greater detail.

In this volume the reader has the opportunity of hearing firsthand one of the earliest Baptist voices. Some features of Helwys's writings may seem strange to our ears. How would his original audience have heard him and applied his ideas in the practice of the earliest Baptist church? How do we appropriate his ideas today? Exploring this extended range of Helwys's writings may allow readers to determine what was critical for Baptist identity at the outset of the movement. One could hardly do better in seeking to understand Baptist identity than begin the quest by reading the original works of the first English Baptist.

Bill Pitts
Baylor University
October 2007

INTRODUCTION

As the Baptist denomination approaches its 400th birthday in 2009, it has reason to remember and celebrate its history. Over these four centuries the denomination has grown from ten members to a worldwide membership of more than forty-three million. From the first Baptists in the early seventeenth century to the Baptists of the twenty-first century, all maintain some commitment to the Baptist distinctives of biblical authority, autonomy of the local church, priesthood of all believers, the two ordinances of baptism and the Lord's Supper, individual responsibility (soul competency), separation of church and state, and the two offices of pastor and deacon.[1] Some of these distinctives may not be maintained by all groups with as much diligence as in the past, but together these distinctives still differentiate Baptists from other Christian denominations. Nearly 400 years ago Thomas Helwys outlined these distinctives in his writings.

Thomas Helwys's life and writings demonstrate a desire for freedom of conscience and religious liberty. He lived in an age and in a country where everyone, under pain of imprisonment, exile, or death, was required to be a member of the Church of England as well as acknowledge and follow its doctrines and practices. Helwys's conscience would not allow him to do so; therefore, he and other Separatists moved to Amsterdam, Holland, where they could worship without persecution. After arriving in Amsterdam, problems began to arise within the Separatist community. Helwys and the other Separatist leaders soon found themselves at odds with each other over ecclesiological and soteriological issues. Several of Helwys's writings concern these issues. Helwys later came to believe that fleeing England had been a mistake. He had to return to confront King James I on the issue of religious freedom. To make his point to the king as clear as possible, Helwys wrote *A Short Declaration of the Mystery of Iniquity* in 1611. In this book, Helwys asked for religious liberty not only for his own church, but also for all Protestants, Catholics, Jews, Muslims, and even atheists. He believed that if one were a loyal servant of England, the crown had no right to infringe on one's religious affairs. King James was not moved, and Helwys was thrown into prison. Helwys may have died at the hands of an unsympathetic monarch, but *A Short Declaration* lives on and continues to inspire Baptists today.

Though *A Short Declaration* is his most famous work, one cannot comprehend the theological development and motivation of Helwys's adoption of the Baptist distinctives without examining all of his extant writings, which until the publication of the following collection have never appeared in one volume. Helwys wrote two confessions of faith: a Latin confession, *A Synopsis of Faith of the True English Church in Amsterdam* (1610)

---

[1] In a helpful acrostic, the first letters of each of these distinctives spell the word "Baptist."

and *A Declaration of Faith of the English People Remaining in Amsterdam, Holland* (1611). Some of the most enlightening and overlooked materials are his three extant letters. He wrote two other books, *A Short and Plaine Proof by the Word and Works Of God that God's Decree is Not the Cause of Any of Man's Sins or Condemnation* (1611) and *An Advertisement or Admonition unto the Congregations, Which Men Call the New Fryelers, in the Lowe Countries.* (1611). These confessions, books, and letters demonstrate that Helwys was not only a strong advocate of religious freedom, but that he maintained all of the Baptists distinctives, espe-cially separation of church and state and believer's baptism. An examination of these documents will place these Baptist distinctives in a historical and theological context and separate them from what some may assume about Baptist beginnings. While Thomas Helwys might not be comfortable in some of today's Baptist churches, he would fit in quite well in most.

The first permanent Baptist and founder of the first Baptist church in England, Thomas Helwys helped develop Baptist theology and ecclesiology. He died a martyr for his faith. Because of these contributions, Thomas Helwys deserves special recognition on his denomination's 400th birthday.

To honor and remember Thomas Helwys, I have written this book, a compilation of all of his known writings. The documents have been translated from either early modern English or Latin into modern English. In working with the original documents I found several incorrect biblical citations, and where these were obvious they were corrected. Others were not easily corrected as they appear to be a combination of several verses taken from various parts of the Bible. Still others appear to be generalizations of biblical texts. These were left as they appear in the original documents. Helwys's biography contains a delineation of his theology and ecclesiology. All footnotes concerning the writings of Thomas Helwys correspond with his works in the document section of this text.

I hope you are as inspired by the life of Thomas Helwys as I have been.

Joe Early, Jr.
Assistant Professor of Religion
University of the Cumberlands

ACKNOWLEDGMENTS

There are several people that helped me in the preparation of this book that I would like to acknowledge. First of all, Dr. Paul Gritz was invaluable in his assessment of the biographical and theological section of this work. I would also like to thank Drs. Robert Johnson, Leon McBeth, and Karen Bullock, who instilled in me a love of Baptist history. My father, Dr. Joseph Early, Sr., also deserves recognition. Even though he is a mathematician, he proved to be quite adept in helping me translate Helwys's old modern English texts into modern English. In researching this book, Mrs. Jan Wren, the head librarian at the University of the Cumberlands, was more than helpful. Without her help in tracking down many of these documents and acquiring them for me, this book would never have come to fruition. I would also like to thank the library staffs at the Bodleian Library at Oxford University and the Angus Library at Regent's Park for their assistance in my research.

SECTION ONE

THOMAS HELWYS

LIFE AND TIMES

THE ENGLISH REFORMATION AND
THE RISE OF PURITANISM

Since the arrival of Augustine at Canterbury in 596, England had been a Roman Catholic nation. With few exceptions, England and her kings adhered to the religious dicta set down by the pope. The VenerableBede praised the Christianity of England in his *Ecclesiastical History of the English People*, cathedrals and abbeys were built, and monastic orders flourished. Though early reformers such as John Wycliffe and William Tyndale published English Bibles and argued for religious change, the monarchy burned their books, declared the authors heretics, and England remained true to Rome by the power of the crown. By 1534, however, England was no longer aligned with the Roman Catholic Church and had formed its own state church with the ruling monarch as its head.

The primary incident that began the alteration of the religious landscape of England had little to do with the reformation that was taking place on the continent. The English Reformation, as it was called, had its roots in politics but was fought out in the realm of religion. The English Reformation began out of the desire of King Henry VII (1485–1509) and King Henry VIII (1509–1547) to perpetuate and strengthen their family's hold on the English throne. To accomplish this objective, Henry VII, the first of the Tudor kings, sought to form an alliance by means of a politically expedient marriage. Therefore, Henry VII arranged the marriage of his oldest son, Arthur (1486–1502), to Catherine of Aragon (1485–1536), the daughter of King Ferdinand (1479–1516) and Queen Isabella (1451–1504) of Spain. Prince Arthur and Catherine were married in 1501. Arthur, however, died six months later without an heir. There was considerable doubt as to whether the fifteen-year-old Arthur and the sixteen-year-old Catherine had ever consummated their marriage.[1]

To keep the alliance with Spain intact, Henry VII sought permission from Pope Julius II (1484–1513) to allow his second son, Henry, to marry Arthur's widow. If Arthur and Catherine had not consummated the marriage, it could be dissolved easily. If the marriage had been consummated, a papal

---

[1] Alison Weir, *The Six Wives of Henry VIII* (New York: Grove Press, 1991) 40.

dispensation was needed to remove the impediment of affinity. Catherine stated to the papal legates that she was still a virgin. This statement was made at the request of Ferdinand and Isabella, who wanted to ensure the validity of their daughter's second marriage. Pope Julius provided a dispensation in 1503, permitting Henry and Catherine to marry. However, Henry VII decided to wait and see if a more politically advantageous mate might appear for his son. When Henry VIII was crowned king in 1509 and no better candidates had appeared, he married Catherine of Aragon and made her his queen. Catherine bore him one child, a daughter, Mary, who lived to adulthood. As the Tudor line had so recently won the crown in the War of the Roses and England had had no semblance of a female monarch since Matilda's (1107–1167) questionable reign in the twelfth century, a son was needed to secure the dynasty. When Henry and Catherine failed to produce a son even after years of marriage, it appeared that the Tudor line would end.[2] To avoid such a catastrophe, Henry and his advisors decided to take drastic action.

It was decided that the marriage would be dissolved. If sanctioned by the pope, Henry could remarry and thus improve the likelihood of producing a male heir. Therefore, Henry asked permission from Pope Clement II (1523–1534) to divorce Catherine. He based his appeal on his stated belief that Arthur and Catherine had in fact consummated their marriage and that Leviticus 20:21 had forbidden him to marry his brother's widow. He claimed that God was condemning him for this sin and that the proof was his lack of a male heir.[3] Deuteronomy 25:5, however, required a man to marry his brother's childless widow. Despite these conflicting Scriptures, Henry VIII built his argument on Leviticus 20:21.

Since Henry had so recently been named "Defender of the Faith" by Pope Leo X (1513–1521) for his tome *Assertio Septem Sacramentorum* against Martin Luther,[4] he may have expected his divorce to be granted without any difficulty. Serious issues quickly arose, and a clean, non-controversial divorce was impossible. First of all, an earlier pope, Julius II, had provided Henry

---

[2] Since Henry had sired an illegitimate son, he faulted Catherine for failing to bear a male heir.

[3] Weir, *The Six Wives*, 144.

[4] A. G. Dickens, *The English Reformation*, 2d ed. (University Park: Pennsylvania State University Press, 1989) 116.

with a papal dispensation to marry Catherine in 1503.[5] Reversing a papal dispensation was no simple task, and no pope wanted to do it. In addition, Catherine was the aunt of the emperor of the Holy Roman Empire, Charles V (1519–1558), who in a recent military campaign had taken control of Rome and taken the pope prisoner.[6] The emperor did not want to see his aunt disgraced and cast aside. Therefore, Pope Clement could not afford to antagonize Charles V.

Henry and his advisors decided that England would separate from the Roman Catholic Church. To fill this religious void, Henry and the newly appointed archbishop of Canterbury, Thomas Cranmer (1489–1556), and a lawyer named Thomas Cromwell (1485–1540) created the Anglican Church, or the Church of England. In order to make his will uncontestable and thus protect his heir, Henry passed the 1534 Act of Supremacy that named the king, in this case himself, as the head of the Church of England.[7] All ties with Rome were now broken. Henry was then able to divorce Catherine and marry Ann Boleyn (c. 1501–1536). Henry would remarry five more times.[8]

Henry had moved away from the Roman Catholic Church, but the doctrines and practices of the Church of England remained very similar to those of traditional Roman Catholicism. In the Six Articles of 1539, Henry demanded that anyone who denied the Roman Catholic teachings of transubstantiation; private masses; confession; celibacy for priests, monks, and nuns; or offered Communion in both kinds would be put to death.[9] It was obvious to all that Henry's break with Rome was political, not spiritual. He did, however, allow the publication and dissemination of a Bible in the English language, the Great Bible of 1539.

Henry VIII died in 1547. His son, Edward VI (1547–1553), came to the throne when he was nine years old under the regency of William Seymour (1587–1660), the duke of Somerset. Whereas Henry had been inclined to

---

[5] Ibid., 154–56.

[6] Ibid., 127.

[7] "Act of Supremacy," in Henry Bettenson, *Documents of the Christian Church*, 2d ed. (Oxford: Oxford University Press, 1963) 227.

[8] For an excellent overview of the English Reformation, see Eamon Duffy, *The Stripping of the Altars: Traditional Religion in England, 1400–1580* (New Haven: Yale University Press, 1992).

[9] "6 Articles," in Gerald Bray, ed., *Documents of the English Reformation* (Minneapolis: Fortress Press, 1994) 222–32.

keep many of the Roman Catholic practices intact, Edward's religious polices, and those of the duke of Somerset, were tilted toward the reformed side of Protestantism, in particular the thought of Heinrich Bullinger (1504–1575) and John Calvin (1509–1564).[10] During Edward's reign, the Church of England was led by the archbishop of Canterbury Thomas Cranmer, who installed *The Book of Common Prayer* (1549) and the Forty-two Articles in 1553 as the church's doctrinal standard. *The Book of Common Prayer* set down in precise terms how morning and evening services were to be held and how the sacraments should be administered, settling all issues of church polity. Because it kept so many Roman Catholic practices, such as the wearing of vestments, the prayer for the dead, and the invocation of the Holy Spirit at the Prayer of Consecration, it was held in disdain by many of the more Protestant-minded members of the Church of England.

A more reformed edition of *The Book of Common Prayer* was issued in 1552. The book did away with the prayer for the dead and exorcism, allowed for the wearing of the surplice but no other priestly vestments, and omitted all reference to the Mass. As sanctioned by Parliament, the "Black Rubric," as it was called, required that the laity kneel at Communion but not adore the host. The Forty-two Articles of 1553 denounced the pope, denied God's real presence in the Eucharist, and established doctrine along a more Protestant basis.[11] Protestantism was now in full bloom, and anything resembling Roman Catholicism was disregarded. All images were removed from churches, crosses were taken down, altars were replaced by wooden tables, members of the clergy were permitted to marry, and the laity was allowed to receive the cup during Communion. Edward, however, was a sickly king; thus, he died, leaving no male heirs and, of course, no brothers.

With no other male heir, the crown was passed by default to the eldest female heir, Mary Tudor (reigned 1553–1558), daughter of Henry VIII's first wife, Catherine of Aragon. Mary had been passed over in favor of her half-brother Edward upon the death of their father. In much the same vein as her mother, Queen Mary was a staunch Roman Catholic and realized that her future was tied to Rome. If England returned to Roman Catholicism, she

---

[10] Bard Thompson, *Humanists and Reformers: A History of the Renaissance and Reformation* (Grand Rapids: Eerdmans, 1996) 592; Dickens, *English Reformation*, 222–24.

[11] "42 Articles," in Bray, *Documents of the English Reformation*, 284–311.

would be perceived as a legitimate queen as the daughter of Henry VIII and Catherine of Aragon. If England remained Protestant, Mary would be perceived as illegitimate and a pretender to the throne. She quickly removed all the Protestants from political office, sent some 800 "Marian exiles" fleeing to the continent, and burned over 300 Protestant leaders at the stake,[12] including Thomas Cranmer, earning her the nickname "Bloody Mary." All the acts enacted by Edward that favored Protestantism, such as *The Book of Common Prayer* and the Forty-two Articles, were rescinded. She then invited the Roman Catholic clergy back from exile to resume their previous positions. Catholic services were reinstituted, and persecution against Protestants became the order of the day.[13] To make the situation even worse for the Protestants, she then married the future king of Spain, Phillip II (1556–1598). Once England's ally, Spain was now England's strongest enemy and a devout Roman Catholic country. Mary, however, was also ill. After a failed attempt at motherhood, she died childless, and Roman Catholicism in England perished with her.

The next monarch was Elizabeth Tudor (1558–1603), the daughter of Henry VIII and his second wife, Ann Boleyn. Elizabeth I, who had been imprisoned by Mary, was much like her father in her support of the Church of England. Protestantism was again reinstated, *The Book of Common Prayer* was returned to all the churches in England, and Roman Catholic clergy were exiled. Elizabeth feared Roman Catholicism for the same reason Mary had feared Protestantism. If Roman Catholicism remained, Elizabeth was nothing but the illegitimate child of Henry VIII and Ann Boleyn.

With Elizabeth now on the throne, the Marian exiles returned from the continent. These exiles were strongly in favor of a broader reformation. In effect, they sought to purify the Church of England from all vestiges of Roman Catholicism. For this reason, these Calvinistic Marian exiles became known as Puritans. The Puritans, however, were quickly disappointed with Queen Elizabeth. They despised the 1559 version of *The Book of Common Prayer* and its Roman Catholic tendencies, such as genuflecting, kneeling at Communion, bowing at the name of Christ, wearing the surplice, the marriage and ordination liturgies, and the office of bishop. The Puritans believed that these rites did not have a scriptural basis and therefore should be removed. The

---

[12] Diarmaid MacCulloch, *The Reformation: A History* (New York: Penguin Books, 2003) 285.

[13] Ibid.

only satisfaction the Puritans received was the removal of the "Black Rubric." The Puritans preferred the 1556 *Genevan Book of Order.* By 1560 they were also using their own Geneva Bible instead of the Great Bible. Elizabeth, however, was quite content with the current Church of England and rejected the new directions of the Puritan clergy.

Parliament once again passed the Act of Supremacy in 1559. It declared England's complete independence from Rome and named its ruling monarch, Elizabeth, the "Supreme Governor of the Church of England." The Act of Uniformity was passed in 1563,[14] mandating the use of *The Book of Common Prayer* and making attendance at parish churches compulsory. Anyone failing to comply faced severe penalties. Elizabeth also instituted the Thirty-nine Articles in 1563. A revision of Cranmer's original Forty-two Articles, the Thirty-nine Articles were pro-Protestant. These articles affirmed Scripture as the final authority in matters of salvation (6) and denied that the Virgin Mary was sinless (15). They also denied transubstantiation (28), the sacrifice of the mass (31), and allowed ministers to marry (32).[15] All clergy were required to subscribe to the Thirty-nine Articles.

Together, these acts became known as the Elizabethan Settlement. They were intended to create a *via media* between the old and new religions of England that would allow them to unite in the Church of England. They also allowed the Church of England to claim Protestantism and a separation from the pope's authority and Roman Catholicism, while retaining many of the liturgies and sacraments and the pomp of the Roman Catholic Church, which Elizabeth adored.

For many Puritans, the Elizabethan Settlement, particularly *The Book of Common Prayer,* was too similar to the Roman Catholic Church in its practices. Many Puritans refused to acquiesce, worshiping in private or attempting to incite reform from within the Church of England. To block this new movement, in 1593 Elizabeth passed An Act for Retaining the Queen's Subjects in Due Obedience,[16] making it illegal for Puritans not to attend Anglican churches. Those who refused to conform and were caught faced

---

[14] "1563 Act of Uniformity," in Bettenson, *Documents of the Christian Church,* 235–38.

[15] "39 Articles," in Bray, *Documents of the English Reformation,* 284–311.

[16] "An Act for Retaining the Queen's Subjects in Due Obedience," in Bettenson, *Documents of the Christian Church,* 242–73.

imprisonment. Those who continued to defy were given the choice of exile or death. In spite of these acts and edicts, by 1603, when Elizabeth died, the Puritan movement was strong and growing.

Like her siblings who had risen to the crown, Elizabeth died with no children. The Tudor line died with her, and the Stuart family claimed the crown. James I of Scotland (1603–1625) was the new king. He was an advocate of the Calvinistic, Presbyterian system promoted by the Scottish reformer John Knox. With a more Reformed monarch ruling England, the Puritans hoped they might finally be permitted to purify the Church of England, remove *The Book of Common Prayer*, or least suggest changes without the threat of persecution. They presented the court with the Millenary Petition,[17] asking the king for an audience. They were granted a meeting with the king at the Hampton Court Conference on 14 January 1604.[18] The Puritan complaints were delivered by John Reynolds, president of Corpus Christi College, Oxford. Reynolds stated, "That the doctrine of the church might be preserved in purity, according to God's Word. That good pastors might be planted in all churches to preach the same. That the church government might be sincerely ministered, according to God's Word. That *The Book of Common Prayer* might be fitted to more increase of piety."[19] After listening to their arguments for Presbyterian Puritanism, James declared that if this were to happen, "then Jack, and Tom, and Will, and Dick shall meet, and at their pleasure, censure me and my council and all our proceedings."[20] The Church of England would remain in its current state, and persecution of dissenters would not cease.

At the conclusion of the conference, James stated that he would "make the Puritans conform or hurry them out of the country." And he was true to his word. During his reign, 300 Puritan clergy members were exiled. The only concession the Puritans received from King James at the Hampton Court Conference was the decision to prepare a new translation of the English Bible.[21]

---

[17] Pauline Croft, *King James* (New York: Palgrave-Macmillan, 2003) 156.

[18] MacCulloch, *The Reformation*, 514.

[19] J. R. Tanner, ed., *Constitutional Documents of the Reign of James I, A.D. 1603–1625, with an Historical Commentary* (Cambridge: Cambridge University Press, 1930) 62.

[20] Ibid., 67.

[21] Croft, *King James*, 157.

SEPARATISM

Many Puritans came to the conclusion that the Church of England was no longer a true church and chose to separate from it. These people became known as Separatists. Baptist historian Barrington White lists four reasons why the Separatists left the Church of England. First, many of its members had made no personal confession of faith and therefore might not have been true Christians. Second, the church ministry was not based on the apostolic model of presbyters and deacons. Third, *The Book of Common Prayer* was closer to the teachings of Roman Catholicism than the Bible. Fourth, Separatists wanted a say in matters of their own church government.[1]

A large number of Separatists left the Church of England with the hope of returning after it had been purified. Baptist historian Leon McBeth has indicated that these Separatists were more pragmatic.[2] It was practical to leave the Church of England until it had rectified its errors. Though it did not appear so in his early ministry, Robert Brown (1550–1663) is a prime example of this breed of Separatism. Others, however, realized that the Church of England was beyond repair and had no intention of returning. McBeth calls these people "principled Separatists."[3] Instead of attempting to purify the Church of England, they formed their own illegal churches. Because they believed that all authority within the church rested with its members, they became known as Congregationalists. They did, however, believe that the state should support true religion and suppress false religion. These first Separatists were not proponents of freedom of conscience. Men such as John Greenwood (d. 1593), Henry Barrow (1550–1593), and John Penry (1559–1593) are included in this group.

A student at Corpus Christi College, Cambridge University, in 1572, Robert Brown was the fountainhead of the early Separatist movement in

---

[1] Barrington R. White, *The English Separatist Tradition* (Oxford: Oxford University Press, 1971) 71.

[2] H. Leon McBeth, *The Baptist Heritage: Four Centuries of Baptist Witness* (Nashville: Broadman Press, 1987) 25.

[3] Ibid.

England.[4] After becoming imbued with Puritanism, he left Cambridge and began to establish Separatist churches in the Norwich area. These churches were based on the premise that baptism alone did not make one a member of a true church. Because of pressure from the Church of England, he and many of his followers left England in 1582 for Middleburg, Holland, where they established their churches in safety. In *A Treatise of Reformation, Without Tarrying for Anie*,[5] Brown taught that true Christians should come together and form their own churches, that membership should be based on a covenant, and that churches should elect their own officers. For this reason, Brown is often credited with being the father of Congregationalism.

After claiming that his congregation had disparaged him, Brown returned to England and was reconciled with the Anglican Church in 1691. He was later ordained into its priesthood. While serving as a rector for the Church of England at Achurch cum Thorpe in 1617, Brown again turned on *The Book of Common Prayer*. For this action and further altercations with the Anglican Church, Robert Brown was excommunicated in 1631 and executed in 1633.[6] Despite his apostasy against the Separatist cause, Robert Brown had a great influence on other Separatists such as John Greenwood, Henry Barrow, and John Penry. With these men, the headquarters of the Separatist movement shifted from Cambridge to London.

John Greenwood was a student at Corpus Christi College, Cambridge University, from 1577 to 1581.[7] While at Cambridge he became a radical Puritan with strong Separatist inclinations. After his school days, he was appointed chaplain to Lord Rich, an influential Puritan at Rochford, Essex. Greenwood came to the belief that the Church of England was beyond redemption and made a complete break from the Puritans and became a Separatist. In 1586 he moved to London, where he became a leader in the Separatist community. He helped organize and taught at a Separatist church that frequently met in the St. Paul's Cathedral Churchyard. This church later

[4] Michael Watts, vol. 1 of *The Dissenters: From the Reformation to the French Revolution* (Oxford: Clarendon Press, 1992) 27–31.

[5] Robert Brown, *A Treatise of Reformation, without Tarrying for Anie,* in Robert Harrison and Robert Brown, *The Writings of Robert Harrison and Robert Brown,* ed. L. H. Carlson and Albert Peel (London: George Allen and Unwin, 1953).

[6] F. L. Cross and E. A. Livingstone, eds., *The Oxford Dictionary of the Christian Church,* 3rd ed. (Oxford: Oxford University Press, 1997), s.v. "Robert Brown."

[7] Watts, vol. 1 of *The Dissenters*, 34–35.

became known as the Ancient Church. It relocated to Amsterdam and became a haven for many alienated Separatists. Greenwood was also a writer and disseminator of pamphlets that were very critical of the Anglican Church. He was arrested in 1587 and thrown in the Clink Prison in Southwark for promoting sedition and starting dissenter churches. When tried by the high commission, Greenwood remained firm in his convictions and, along with his fellow Separatist Henry Barrow, was hanged on 6 April 1593.

Henry Barrow had attended Cambridge University from 1566 to 1572. In 1580 he heard a Puritan sermon that led him to retire to the country to mediate on what he had heard. When he emerged he was a strict Puritan. He soon met and became friends with John Greenwood, who introduced him to Separatism. While Barrow was visiting Greenwood in prison, he was arrested and charged with writing and publishing seditious books. His books, A *True Description of the Visible Congregation of the Saints* and *A Broad Discovery of the False Church*, promoted the belief that all authority in the church was vested only in its membership. He remained in prison until he was hanged with Greenwood on 6 April 1593.[8]

John Penry was a Separatist of Welsh descent who attended Peterhouse College, Cambridge University, from 1580 to 1584 and St. Albans, Oxford University, where he earned an MA in 1586. He ran afoul of the Church of England for his constant espousal of Puritan beliefs.[9] His most famous 1587 work, *Equity of an Humble Supplication in the behalf of the Country of Wales, that some Order may be taken for the preaching of the Gospel among those people*, criticized the episcopal system of the Church of England. Penry attributed the rampant idolatry and superstition in Wales to restrictions placed on its clergy. Instead of speaking to the issues at hand, Welsh clergy were required to use set prayers and homilies as dictated in *The Book of Common Prayer*. The publication infuriated Archbishop John Whitgift (1530–1604), and he promptly accused Penry of authoring the pro-Puritan and anti-Episcopal *Marprelate Tracts*. These widely popular tracts assailed the episcopal system and advocated Puritanism. Even though they were written by Job Throckmorton, Penry feared Whitgift and fled to Scotland in 1589. He relocated to London in 1592, joining Greenwood and Barrow in the Separatist community. Within a year he was arrested for treason and hanged on 29 May

[8] Ibid., 35–37.
[9] Ibid., 38–39.

1593. Baptist historian Earnest Payne believed that John Penry was the first person to suggest to the Puritans and Separatists the possibility of immigrating to America to escape persecution.[10]

Francis Johnson (c. 1562–1617) was another important Separatist. Johnson was a 1581 graduate of Christ's College, Cambridge, where he became a Puritan and served as a Fellow from 1584 to 1589. Johnson's most famous student was John Smyth (c. 1570–1612), in whom he instilled a love of Puritanism.[11] After advocating a presbyterian rather than episcopal church government, he lost his fellowship in April 1589 and spent the next five months in jail. He was allowed to leave England in 1590 and went to Middleburg, Holland, where he served as minister to pro-Puritan English nationals.[12] As Johnson was a Puritan and had no love of Separatism, the English government asked him to gather and burn the writings of Barrow and Greenwood. He was more than happy to do so. In order not only to destroy but also refute their teachings, Johnson kept two copies of *A* Plaine Refutation of the Claims of the Establishment. *After examining it, he became intrigued by its arguments. Johnson decided to go to London to confer with its authors, who were in prison. After meeting with Barrow and Greenwood, Johnson was won over to their cause and became a Separatist. He was named pastor of the Separatist Ancient Church in London in 1592.*[13] *He was immediately arrested and spent the next five years in jail.* After the martyrdoms of Greenwood, Barrow, and Penry, the Ancient Church realized that it could not survive in London and moved to Amsterdam.[14] Henry Ainsworth (1571–1622) served as pastor until Johnson rejoined them in 1597. Johnson remained one of the primary Separatist leaders in Amsterdam until his death in 1617.

---

[10] Ernest A. Payne, *The Free Church Tradition in the Life of England* (London: SCM Press, 1951) 34.

[11] Walter Burgess, *John Smyth the Se-Baptist and Thomas Helwys and the First Baptist Church in England with Fresh Light upon the Pilgrim Father* (London: James and Clarke and Co., 1911) 30, 235.

[12] Watts, vol. 1 of *The Dissenters*, 38.

[13] Burgess, *Smyth and Helwys*, 34.

[14] William R. Estep, *The Anabaptist Story: An Introduction to Sixteenth-Century Anabaptism*, 3rd ed. (Grand Rapids: Eerdmans Publishing Company, 1996) 284.

THE HELWYS FAMILY

Thomas Helwys was born into an old English family that could trace its lineage to the thirteenth century. From its earliest days until the early seventeenth century the family remained in the vicinity of Nottinghamshire, where they made a successful living as gentlemen farmers. Until the time of Edmund Helwys, Thomas's father, little distinguishes the Helwys family from the majority of the landed gentry in Nottinghamshire.

During the 1590s, Edmund Helwys had built a large manor called Broxtowe Hall in Nottingham and purchased other lands in Northampton and Lincoln. Though trained as a lawyer, Edmund considered himself something of a theologian and wrote an apocalyptic tract in 1589 titled *A Marvel Deciphered*. In this exposition of Revelation 12, which was clearly inspired by England's defeat of the Spanish Armada in 1588, Edmund makes a veiled reference to the woman dressed in the sun as Queen Elizabeth and the dragon as the pope. Twenty-six years later, Thomas Helwys, in his most famous work, *A Short Declaration of the Mystery of Iniquity*, came to a similar conclusion about the pope.[1]

---

[1] Walter Burgess, "The Helwys Family," *Transactions of the Baptist Historical Society* 3 (1912): 18–30.

THOMAS HELWYS

The eldest son of Edmund and Margaret Helwys, Thomas Helwys was born at his family's ancestral home of Broxtowe Hall in Nottingham. His date of birth is unknown, and no records exist of Thomas's life prior to the death of his father in 1590, at which time he inherited Broxtowe Hall. As Thomas was either ill prepared or too young to assume the sizeable duties he had inherited, Sir Thomas Stanhope and Edward Stanhope, his uncles, were entrusted with the Helwys property.[1]

To ready Thomas to be the proprietor of a large estate, his uncles sent him to Gray's Inn, the most prestigious of the four Inn's of court, in London to study law.[2] Gray's Inn was a logical place for a son of the gentry to attend. It was not steeped in ecclesiological law, as were Oxford and Cambridge, but rather common law, which would help him better administrate his business affairs.[3] Gray's Inn was widely respected. Francis Bacon and Thomas Cromwell had been among its students. Moreover, another of his uncles, Geoffrey Helwys, was a wealthy and well-connected merchant living in London and would be available to help Thomas if a need arose. Fifteen years later, Geoffrey would become sheriff of London. Thomas enrolled at Gray's Inn in January 1592 and remained there until late 1594.

In matters of religion, there is no reason to doubt, prior to his arrival at Gray's Inn, that Thomas had been anything other than a loyal member of the Church of England. During his years as a student in London, however, he would have been introduced to Puritanism and its radical offshoot, Separatism. It is reasonable to assume that he knew of the execution of Separatists John Greenwood and Henry Barrow at Tyburn and John Penry at Southwark in 1593.[4] These executions would have been the talk of London

---

[1] J. Glenwood Clayton, "Thomas Helwys: A Baptist Founding Father," *Baptist History and Heritage* 8 (Jan 1973): 3.

[2] W. T. Whitley, "Thomas Helwys of Gray's Inn and Broxtowe Hall, Nottingham," *The Baptist Quarterly* 12 (1934–35): 241.

[3] Ernest A. Payne, *Thomas Helwys and the First Baptist Church in England*, 2d ed. (London: The Baptist Union, 1966) 2.

[4] Payne, *Thomas Helwys*, 2.

and especially the students of Gray's Inn, as Henry Barrow had attended Gray's Inn in 1576.

After completing two years of study, Helwys left London in early 1595 and returned to Nottingham to manage the family estate. On 3 December of the same year, he married Joan Ashmore in the Billborough Parish Church, and the couple took up residence in Broxtowe Hall.[5] No records from the next few years have survived, but one may assume that Helwys, like a typical member of the landed gentry, would have spent much of his time managing his estate and raising his seven children. We do know that Helwys was close friends with the vicar of Worksop and Puritan sympathizer Richard Bernard (1568–1641).[6] Helwys soon began to allow Bernard and other Puritans to hold services in Broxtowe Hall. Although there is no way of knowing who attended these services, the Nottinghamshire region was densely populated with Puritans, so one can imagine that they were well attended. The more Helwys came into league with Puritan sympathies, the more his home became a haven for Puritan teachings.

John Smyth, a Christ's College, Cambridge, graduate in 1594 and Fellow from 1594 to 1596, was the most influential person to enter Broxtowe Hall. John Smyth had been ordained by the bishop of London in 1594 and was the city lecturer of Lincoln (1600–1602), only a few miles from Broxtowe Hall. Though Anglican, he became a Puritan while studying under future Separatist leader Francis Johnson at Cambridge. Smyth believed that the Anglican Church had not achieved a true reformation. Too many of its practices resembled Roman Catholicism. Smyth met Helwys around 1600 and was soon preaching at Broxtowe Hall.

Smyth's preaching was not pleasing to the Anglican authorities. He frequently denounced ecclesiastical authority, infant baptism, the spiritless nature of the Anglican Church, and the Roman Catholic elements that remained in the Church of England. Evidently he had been "preaching at men

---

[5] Ibid., 3.

[6] Henry Martyn Dexter and Morgan Dexter, *The England and Holland of the Puritans* (Boston: Houghton, Mifflin and Co., 1905) 378. Initially a friend to Smyth and Helwys, Bernard later turned on them when members of his church began to join the Smyth church. As evidenced by his dubbing Smyth the "se-Baptist," Bernard's criticisms continued even after Smyth moved to Amsterdam. W. T. Whitley, "Biography of John Smyth," in vol. 1 of *The Works of John Smyth, Fellow of Christ's College, 1594–1598* (Cambridge: Cambridge University Press, 1915).

of this city" and was dismissed from his post as Lincoln city lecturer on 13 October 1602. Later that year, his license to preach was revoked.[7] Smyth then supported himself as a physician.[8]

Smyth frequently attended the parish church at Basford in 1606. One day the regular minister, Jerome Phillips, failed to show up. As the congregants were preparing to leave without holding a service, in order for them to have some manner of worship, Smyth read, briefly preached from the psalms, and prayed. He then dismissed the service. Three days later, the vicar and church wardens of Basford were cited before the archdeacons' court for allowing Smyth to preach without a license or the bishop's permission.[9] Smyth did not deny that he had preached, but insisted that it was only because Phillips had been absent. Smyth's account of the service was substantiated by members of the church who wrote the bishop, but to no avail. This may have been the event that led Smyth to his first consideration of Separatism.

In 1606, while visiting Helwys, Smyth, a chronic suffer of tuberculosis, became quite ill and it appeared he might die. Helwys took him into Broxtowe Hall and over several months slowly nursed him back to health.[10] Even though there are no known accounts of the sickbed conversations between Helwys and Smyth, one must assume that many of them were theological. Historian Earnest Payne believed that this was when Smyth and Helwys came to the conclusion that the Anglican Church was beyond reform and moved on to Separatism.[11] By the time Smyth had recovered, he and Helwys had become very close friends.

In 1606 Smyth became the pastor of a Separatist church in Gainesborough, Nottinghamshire. Future Separatist leaders John Robinson (1575–1625) and Richard Clifton (d. 1616), the former rector of Babworth, were his assistants. As the members were spread across the Lower Trent Valley, the church also met at Scrooby in north Nottinghamshire. The membership

---

[7] Michael Watts, *The Dissenters* (Oxford: Clarendon Press, 1978) 1:41.

[8] A. C. Underwood, *A History of the English Baptists* (London: The Baptist Union Publication Department, 1947) 34.

[9] Payne, *Thomas Helwys*, 4.

[10] Whitley, "Thomas Helwys of Gray's Inn," 247; William R. Estep, "Thomas Helwys: Bold Architect of Baptist Policy on Church-State Relations," *Baptist History and Heritage* 20/3 (July 1985): 27–28; Payne, *Thomas Helwys*, 4.

[11] Payne, *Thomas Helwys*, 4.

of this church was composed of believers who freely signed a covenant that bound them to each other, not to any outside authority.[12] The Gainesborough Church was a very important church, as many of its members sought refuge in America aboard the *Mayflower* and became known as the Pilgrim Fathers.

Smyth believed that his church was a true representation of New Testament principles. This action was the very epitome of Separatism. Helwys followed Smyth and became a member of the Gainesborough church. By this time, Smyth was not only Helwys's pastor, but also his theological mentor. Over the next two years Smyth became a strong advocate of religious liberty, and Helwys once again followed his pastor.

Less than a year later, it was becoming obvious to Smyth and Helwys that they would not be able to hold services for much longer in Gainesborough. The ecclesiastical authorities were enforcing Elizabeth's 1593 Due Obedience Act,[13] and the vocal Smyth was becoming a high-profile problem. The first step the Separatists took was to split into two congregations. The first group was led by Smyth and Helwys, who continued to meet at Gainesborough, and the second was led by Richard Clifton at Scrooby Manor in north Nottinghamshire. Clifton's assistant was John Robinson. Even though the church was now two distinct congregations meeting in different locations, the two congregations remained under the same covenant and considered themselves one church.

In order for their members to be able to worship without fear, Smyth decided to move the group to Amsterdam, Holland. In the preface to his 1611 *Declaration of Faith of the English People Remaining in Amsterdam,* Helwys explained his rationale for leaving England: "Would we not have lost all we had?... Would we not have laid down our lives?... Have we not neglected ourselves, our wives, our children and all we had and respected him [Smyth]? And we confess we had good cause to do so in respect of those most

---

[12] Whitley, "Biography of John Smyth," in vol. 1 of *The Works of John Smyth, Fellow of Christ's College,* 1594–1598 (Cambridge: Cambridge University Press, 1915) lxii.

[13] *An Act for Retaining the Queen's Subjects in Due Obedience* was Queen Elizabeth's way to stop illegal Puritan meetings and enforce conformity with the Anglican Church. "Anyone of the age of sixteen who refused to attend church for a month, or who attempted to persuade others not to attend church, or who attended unauthorized meetings, was to be committed to prison. If the offender did not conform within three months he was to be given the alterative of exile or death," Watts, *Dissenters,* 1:39.

excellent gifts and graces of God that did abound in him. And our love was too little for him and not worthy of him."[14] The Smyth-Helwys group left England and arrived in Amsterdam in 1607. Helwys had left England in order to worship in peace and, perhaps more personally, to follow Smyth.

Anxious to go to Amsterdam, Helwys took the lead and may have paid both congregations' travel expenses. Affirming Helwys's eagerness, John Robinson said, "The truth is, it was Mr. Helwisse [sic] who above all, either guides or others, furthered this passage into strange countries: and if any brought oars, he brought sails, as I could show in many particulars, and as all that were acquainted with the manner of our coming over can witness with me."[15]

The group left just in time. Helwys's wife, Joan, who did not leave for Amsterdam with her husband, was arrested for breaking the Due Obedience Act and thrown into York Prison. At the time of her arrest, her husband was already in Amsterdam searching for a home for the church. Evidently, she was apprehended before she could join him. She spent three months imprisoned in York Castle and was released. No evidence suggests that she ever agreed to return to the Anglican Church.[16]

In the seventeenth century, Holland had no state religion, and all religions that were not considered disruptive were permitted. The Anabaptists were the most despised of all religious groups, despite their freedom to worship in Holland. Holland's plan of Rhegius proclaimed that if "Anabaptists would keep their errors to themselves they should be left alone."[17] By the time of Smyth's and Helwys's arrival, the city was full of religious dissenters who had either fled or been exiled from various European

---

[14] Thomas Helwys, *A Declaration of Faith of the English People Remaining in Amsterdam in Holland* (Amsterdam: n.p., 1611).

[15] John Robinson, *Of Religious Communion Private, & Publique with the Silenceing of the Clamours Raysed by Mr Thomas Helvvisse agaynst Our Reteyning the Baptism Receaved in Engl: & Administering of Bapt: vnto Infants. As Also a Survey of the Confession of Fayth Published in Certain Onclusions by the Remainders of Mr Smithes Company* (Amsterdam: n.p., 1614) 41.

[16] Burgess, *John Smyth, the Se-Baptist, Thomas Helwys and the First Baptist Church in England* (London: James Clarke, 1911) 116.

[17] W. T. Whitley, *A History of British Baptists*, 2d ed. (London: Charles Griffin and Co., 1923) 33–34.

countries. Smyth's former Cambridge professor Francis Johnson was already there, pastoring the Separatist Ancient Church.

The group had little trouble finding a location to worship and live. They moved into the two-story East India Bake House and four small buildings surrounded by a wall and owned by Jan Munter (1570–c. 1620), a Waterlander Mennonite.[18] The Bake House served as the home and the center of worship for the Gainesborough congregation, but not for Johnson's Ancient Church or even their brethren in the Scrooby Manor congregation. These Separatist groups remained apart, and as time passed they became more and more estranged from each other.

There were several reasons why the three Separatist churches in Amsterdam did not unite. The first reason was church ministry. Francis Johnson's Ancient Church followed the Calvinistic model of a threefold presbytery of pastors, teachers, and two types of elders. Smyth and Helwys believed in a uniform ministry with only the offices of pastor and one type of elder. The officers in this twofold ministry were to be indistinguishable.[19] Smyth was perceived by his congregation as first among equals.[20]

The second reason was Smyth's peculiar belief concerning books. All books were set aside during times of spiritual worship, which included praying, tithing, prophesying, the singing of psalms, baptism, and partaking of the Lord's Supper.[21] For Smyth, books used in spiritual worship were anathema because they were similar to *The Book of Common Prayer*, which he believed "quenched the spirit."[22] During the parts of the service such as preaching and expositing the text, the Hebrew and Greek translations could be

---

[18] Whitley, "Biography of John Smyth," lxxvi. The Waterlanders were an Anabaptist sect that broke away from the rigid German Mennonites in the sixteenth century. The majority of their theological tenets were consistent, but less strict than traditional Mennonite doctrine. They maintained a threefold ministry of teacher, bishop, and deacon and an Arminian soteriology; they rejected original sin; magistrates could not be members of their churches; and they maintained Hoffmanite Christology. They derived their name "Waterlander" because many of the churches, including those in Amsterdam, were in the north Holland region of Waterland.

[19] John Smyth, *The Differences of the Churches of the Separation*, in Whitley, vol. 1 of *Works*, 307–14.

[20] James R. Coggins, *John Smyth's Congregation: English Separatism, Mennonite Influence, and the Elect Nation* (Waterloo, Ontario: Herald Press, 1991) 51.

[21] John Smyth, *The Differences*, 276–80.

[22] Ibid., 277.

used and translated by voice. No translations into the vernacular could be employed. Only the original Greek and Hebrew texts were considered to be inspired.

Third, the Smyth and later Helwys church differed from the Ancient Church in matters of finance. Smyth maintained that tithing was an ordinance. Therefore, since the unredeemed were not permitted to partake in the ordinance of the Lord's Supper, they should not be permitted to tithe.[23] The Ancient Church was not so particular in matters of finance. They frequently accepted contributions from friends in England.

In a letter written to his family back in England on 26 September 1608, Helwys reiterated Smyth's rationale as to why their congregation failed to join one of the other Separatist congregations of Amsterdam. Helwys wrote,

> We differ in part in ministry, worship, government, and treasury. Their ministry consists of pastors and teachers or of pastors only, and we approve of no other officers in the ministry but that of pastors. As part of worship, they read chapters of texts to preach on and Psalms out of the translation. We lay aside the translation in praying, prophesying, and in the singing of Psalms. We suppose that we will yet prove the truth that all books even the originals themselves must be set aside in the time of spiritual worship. Yet, we still retain the readings and interpretations of scripture in the church for the preparation of worship, judging of doctrine, deciding of controversies as the ground of faith and of our whole profession. And thus we refuse to use the translations, holding them much inferior to the originals. And this we profess and I desire that you take notice, and to give notice to as many as possible you can know that this is the true cause of our controversy, whatsoever you hear to the contrary. And assure yourselves in this if you think there is any truth in me. Now concerning the government, they hold that the presbytery consists of pastors, teachers, and ruling elders. We hold that it consists of pastors only. The treasury with which they suffer makes them unable to help those who are unable to communicate with them. They do not sanctify their alms with prayer. We separate our alms from the gifts of strangers which we thankfully receive. And we sanctify the whole action by

---

[23] Ibid., 318.

prayer, before and after, as all the ordinances of God should be. Concerning these things, if God permits, you shall hear a great deal more about later.[24]

The Ancient Church had troubles of its own. McBeth noted three problems plaguing the Ancient Church. First, Johnson could not determine if he had the right as pastor to discipline his members. This question may have arisen over his wife, Thomasine, who offended the other members for wearing an extravagant amount of lace, ruffs, and rings. She was rumored to be a heavy drinker and on some Sundays remained in bed until nine o'clock. In Thomasine's defense, her first husband, Edward Boyes, had been a rich trader and her attire and manner were proper for his vocation.[25] However, she was now married to the pastor, and her decorum seemed immodest. This controversy was so serious that Johnson's brother and father were excommunicated over their criticism of Thomasine and the manner in which Johnson was handling her discipline, or lack thereof.[26] Second, the church was grappling with the true nature of baptism. Questions such as how it was to be performed, who may receive it, administer it, and what it signified abounded. Third, Johnson was constantly struggling over the nature of church government. He was convinced of the truths of the presbyterian system, while many of his members, such as Henry Ainsworth, believed in a more congregational approach.[27] Johnson and the Ancient Church lost several members over this issue. According to Henoch Clapham, a contemporary witness, while the Ancient Church was fighting over these issues, it was losing members to the Anabaptists.[28]

Even though the Scrooby Manor congregation had formed a covenant with the Gainesborough congregation and were in actuality a single church, they did not unite into one body in Amsterdam. John Robinson was now the

---

[24] Thomas Helwys, "Letter on Church Order," 26 September 1608, ms. 709, fol. 117, recto and verso, in Lambeth Palace library.

[25] Watts, *Dissenters*, 1:40.

[26] Benjamin Brook, vol. 2 of *The Lives of the Puritans*, 3rd ed. (Morgan PA.: Soli Deo Gloria Publications, 1996) 102.

[27] McBeth, *Baptist Heritage: Four Centuries of Baptist Witness* (Nashville: Broadman Press, 1987) 29.

[28] Champlin Burrage, vol. 1 of *Early English Dissenter* (Cambridge: Cambridge University Press, 1912) 156.

pastor of the Scrooby faction, and it appears that Smyth's rigidity in the aforementioned differences was also too much for him. In effect, the Scrooby congregation sided with the Ancient Church against its own Gainesborough brethren. With this action the Gainesborough congregation became the Smyth church. Within six months and to avoid problems with the other Separatist churches, Robinson had taken what could now be called his church to Leyden.[29]

Other than these peculiarities, the Smyth-Helwys church worship services were similar to those of most Separatist churches in Holland and England. Hughe and Anne Bromheade, members of the Smyth church, sent a letter to their cousin, Sir William Hammerton, in which they described one of their typical services. The letter reads,

> The order of the worship and government of our church is 1. We begin with a prayer, after someone reads one or two chapters of the Bible given the sense thereof, and confer upon the same; that done we lay aside our books, and after a solemn prayer made by the speaker, he propounds some text out of the Scripture, and prophesies out of the same, by the space of one hour, or three Quarters of an hour. After him a second speaker stands up and prophesies out of the said text in the like time and space; some time more some time less. After him the third, fourth, and the fifth and as time will give leave. Then the first speaker concludes with prayer as he began with prayer, with an exhortation to make contributions to the poor, with a collection being made and then concluding with prayer. This morning exercise is observed in the afternoon from two of the clock until five or six of the clock. Last of all the execution of the government of the church is handled.[30]

The most dramatic move taken by the Smyth church was the adoption of believer's baptism. Smyth came to the conclusion that one must confess Christ before accepting baptism. This nullified the baptism he had received by the Church of England and, in actuality, all infant baptism. Moreover, Smyth

---

[29] Coggins, *John Smyth's Congregation*, 58.

[30]"Letter of Hughe and Anne Bromheade," cited in Leon McBeth, *A Sourcebook for Baptist Heritage* (Nashville: Broadman Press, 1990) 22.

argued that the Church of England was not a true church; therefore, it could not dispense the true ordinances. For Smyth and Helwys, the true church was a local, visible church composed of two or three members bound by a confession of their personal faith followed by baptism.[31]

Though there were several dissenter churches in Amsterdam, Smyth and Helwys did not believe a true church existed there. Therefore, the Gainesborough Church was compelled to take another dramatic step. Scrooby pastor John Robinson described what happened next: "Mr. Smith [sic], Mr. Helwys and the rest having utterly dissolved and disclaimed their former Church, state, and ministry, came together to erect a new Church by baptism, unto which they ascribed so great a virtue, as that they would not so much as pray together before they had it. And after some straining of courtesy, over who should begin...Mr. Smith baptized first himself, and next Mr. Helwys, and so the rest, making their particular confessions."[32]

How Smyth came to believer's baptism has been a widely disputed topic. According to Baptist and Anabaptist historian W. R. Estep, he either came to believer's baptism after personal study or he was introduced to it by the Waterlander Mennonites, who practiced it. Since Smyth had been in Amsterdam in quarters rented to him by a Waterlander for a year prior to his acceptance of believer's baptism and since he appeared to embrace Waterlander soteriology, it is logical to assume that he was introduced to believer's baptism by the Waterlanders. Smyth, however, did not ask the Waterlanders to baptize him. Therefore, he may have reached believer's baptism on his own. This question may never be answered.

Smyth's se-baptism met immediate opposition from many of his Separatist colleagues. In defense of his decision, he stated in the *Character of the Beast* that finding the truth is always better than remaining in error: "That we should fall from the profession of Puritanism to Brownism, and from Brownism to true Christian baptism, is not simply evil or reprovable in itself, unless it is that we have fallen from true religion. If we therefore, having formerly deceived in the way of pedobaptistry, now do embrace the truth in

---

[31] Estep, *The Anabaptist Story: An Introduction to Sixteenth-century Anabaptism* (Grand Rapids MI: Eerdmans Publishing Co., 1996) 287.

[32] John Robinson, vol. 3 of *The Works of John Robinson, Pastor of the Pilgrim Fathers with a Memoir of Annotations by Robert Ashton, Secretary of the Congregational Board, London* (Boston: Doctrinal Tract and Book Society, 1851) 168.

the true Christian Apostolic baptism, then let no man impute this as a fault unto us."[33]

With this action, Smyth brought the first Baptist church into existence in 1609. Within ten years, Thomas Helwys, under the guidance of John Smyth, had taken a spiritual journey from the Anglican Church to Puritanism, then to Separatism, and finally to a new church founded on believer's baptism.

Despite Smyth's best efforts to defend his self-baptism and his congregation's recent baptism, questions, complaints, and condemnations continued to inundate his church by members of other Separatist churches. Richard Clifton informed Smyth that if everyone self-baptized, then churches could be composed of individuals, leading to nothing short of chaos. Smyth replied that no true church in Amsterdam practiced believer's baptism, so he had been forced to take this unprecedented action. Whitley stated that it was John Hetherington, one of Smyth's friends, who wrote and questioned him about why he did not seek baptism from the Mennonites. Hetherington wrote, "It was [a] wonder that you would not receive your baptism first from one of the elders of the Dutch Anabaptists."[34] After some investigation Smyth came to realize that the Waterlander Mennonites, of whom their landlord Jan Munter was a member, might meet these qualifications and thus be a true church. Within a year, he had determined that the Amsterdam Mennonites constituted a true church and had a true baptism and he had erred by not approaching them for baptism. Therefore, Smyth and thirty-two members of his congregation desired "to unite with the true church of Christ as quickly as possible."[35]

Thomas Helwys objected to the idea of joining the Mennonite Church. He believed that they had finally come to the end of their search for a true church. He maintained that if they were to seek baptism from Mennonites, then the baptism they so recently received was invalid and an error. Helwys may have also realized that if the English church became a part of the Waterlander Church, it would lose its identity and never return to England.[36]

---

[33] John Smyth, *Character of the Beast,* in Whitley, vol. 2 of *Works,* 564.

[34] Whitley, vol. 1 of *Works,* xcviii.

[35] "Application for Union with the Waterlander Church in Amsterdam," in Whitley, vol. 2 of *Works,* 681.

[36] William R. Estep, "Thomas Helwys: Bold Architect of Baptist Policy on Church-State Relations," *Baptist History and Heritage* 20/3 (July 1985): 27–28.

Smyth apparently believed that their immigration to Amsterdam was permanent and his group had no desire to return to the persecutions in England. Helwys clearly believed that their self-imposed exile was temporary and they would return home when there was a possibility of greater religious toleration. Therefore, Helwys and ten followers refused to follow Smyth and the majority into the Waterlander fold.

Helwys's pleas were ignored, and Smyth and his followers moved ahead in their bid to join the Waterlanders. Smyth sent the Waterlanders *A Short Confession of Faith in XX Articles* written in Latin. He hoped that the Waterlanders would see the similarities in their belief systems and quickly accept them. To slow down the process, Helwys sent the Waterlanders a letter written in Latin that warned them of being too quick in accepting the Smyth church into their congregation. Helwys told the Waterlanders that Smyth and his followers had been "justly excluded" and were impenitent in their sin. Despite this unequivocal statement, Helwys does not define the nature of this sin. He also told them "not to receive such things [the Smyth church] by which you may be defiled, whereby it is best that you know little of corrupting the entire mass that may be corrupted."[37] The tone of the letter is congenial. He was not castigating the Waterlanders for considering Smyth, but rather attempting to explain what Helwys and his followers had done to Smyth and his adherents. Along with this letter he sent them his *Synopsis of Faith*, a nineteen-article Latin confession of faith. Much can be inferred from the fact that both Smyth and Helwys wrote their first documents in Latin. Since neither was fluent in Dutch and Latin was a language known by most scholars, it was the easiest way for both men to communicate with the Dutch-speaking Waterlanders.

The examination of both confessions shows that Helwys had been deeply affected by Smyth. Fifteen of the twenty articles in Smyth's *Confession* are almost identical to Helwys's *Synopsis of Faith*. The wording may differ, but the theological meaning is the same. They are in complete agreement concerning the Trinity, the creation of man, a rejection of infant baptism, church officers, and the Lord's Supper. The effects of the novel system of Holland's own Jacob Arminius (c. 1559–1609) and living in a Waterlander community can also be perceived in the theology of Smyth and Helwys. They had moved away

---

[37] Thomas Helwys, "Letter to the the [sic] Consistory of the United Mennonite Church at Amsterdam," 1610.

from the Puritan soteriology that had been grounded in Calvinism and embraced a more Arminian soteriology. Helwys, however, does give less importance to free will than Smyth.

Significant theological differences are found in Articles 7 and 10 of Smyth's *Confession*, which correspond to Articles 6 and 7 of Helwys's *Synopsis*. Smyth's Article 7 and Helwys's Article 6 concern Christology. Smyth states "that Jesus Christ, as pertaining to the flesh, was conceived by the Holy Spirit in the womb of the Virgin Mary, afterwards was born, circumcised, baptized, tempted, etc."[38] While not overt, it does appear that Smyth is espousing, or at least not refuting, the Hofmannite Christology that was prevalent among the Mennonites.[39] Hoffmanite Christology stressed that Jesus did not have a human body but was a purely divine being with celestial or angelic flesh. Jesus' body passed through the Virgin Mary as water passes through a pipe. Helwys eliminated the Hofmannite concept by stating "that Jesus Christ manifested in the plenitude of time, in flesh, made from woman, conceived and born from her, etc."[40] Helwys made it clear that Jesus had human flesh.

Smyth's Article 10 and Helwys's Article 7 concern justification. Smyth states "that the justification of man before the divine tribunal (which is both the throne of justice and mercy), consists partly of the imputation of the righteousness of Christ apprehended by faith, and partly of inherent righteousness, in the holy themselves, by the operation of the Holy Spirit, which is called regeneration or sanctification; since any one is righteous, who does righteousness."[41] Helwys states "that the redemption of man before God can only consist of obedience to Christ and justice through faith, it is dead if it is understood as excluding works."[42]

Articles 12, 14, and 17 of Helwys's *Synopsis* are independent of Smyth. Article 12 pertains to relationships within the church. Helwys is concerned

---

[38]John Smyth, *Short Confession of Faith in XX Articles*, cited in Lumpkin, 100.

[39] Estep, "Thomas Helwys," 27.

[40]Thomas Helwys, *Synopsis Fidei, Verae Christianae Ecclesiae Anglicanae*. [A Latin "synopsis" of faith of the "true English Christian Church" at Amsterdam under the leadership of Thomas Helwys, delivered (probably between February and 12 March 1610) to the Waterlanders there, with thanks for the teaching they had given them.] (Amsterdam: n.p., 1610) 61.

[41] Smyth, *Short Confession*, 101.

[42] Helwys, *Latin Synopsis of Faith*, 61.

that churches may become so large that all the members cannot know each other and properly care for each other's needs. He stressed that in order for the elders to perform their ministries properly, they must know each member of the church.[43] Article 14 reflects Helwys's Puritan understanding of the Sabbath. He maintained that on each Sabbath, all the members must refrain from secular work and gather together in the worship of God.[44] In Article 17, Helwys states that no arbitrary dictums should be forced on the church or members of the church.[45] All church teachings were to be grounded in Scripture and not in caprice.

In a letter sent to the Waterlanders on 12 March 1610, Helwys claimed that succession was the most important obstacle to the reconciliation of the disparate churches. Helwys now insisted that "the whole cause in question being succession (for it is indeed and in truth) consider we beseech you, how it is the anti-Christ's chief hold, and that it is Jewish and ceremonial, an ordinance of the Old Testament and not the New."[46] Succession is the belief "that there should be an orderly transmission, elders ordaining elders, and baptism only to be received only from people already baptized."[47] Even though this letter followed closely on the heels of his *Synopsis*, Helwys had made no previous reference to succession. According to Helwys's *Synopsis* (Article 9)[48] and Smyth's *Confession* (Articles 12 and 13),[49] they both held to local autonomy and the gathered church principle. Helwys believed that the baptisms performed by Smyth and himself were valid and did not need the approval of any other church. Helwys must have believed that the Waterlanders and Smyth were advocating their own version of Roman Catholic apostolic succession.

Evidently, Helwys's letter led to a conference among the Waterlander elders, Smyth, and himself on 23 May 1610. There are no records of the activities of this conference. James Coggins, a leading Smyth biographer, believes that the Smyth church's application to join the Waterlanders was

---

[43] Ibid., 62
[44] Ibid., 62-63
[45] Ibid., 63
[46] Thomas Helwys, "A Vindication of the Position Assumed by the English Baptists."
[47] Whitley, *Thomas Helwys*, 249.
[48] Helwys, *Latin Synopsis of Faith*, 62
[49] Smyth, *Short Confession*, 101.

accepted at this time. Other historians believe the meeting was inconclusive. Whatever the outcome, Helwys was not pleased with it.

By 1611 Helwys had come to the understanding that the Smyth church had no intentions of backing off their attempt to join the Waterlanders. He may also have believed that the differences between his church and Smyth's church were now too stark for reconciliation to be possible. These realizations seemed to launch Helwys into a frenzy of writing. In 1611 he wrote a new confession of faith and three books. The first work was his *Declaration of Faith of the English Church Remaining in Amsterdam*. This declaration is the first true English Baptist confession of faith and reveals the maturation of Helwys's stance in the wake of his definitive break from Smyth.

Helwys also penned *An Advertisement or Admonition unto the Congregations, Which Men Call the New Fryelers, in the Lowe Countries*.[50] In this work, which was dedicated to Hans de Ries, a Waterlander who was trying to help the Smyth congregation, Helwys outlined four major problems with Smyth's and the Mennonites' theology. These objections concerned Hoffmanite Christology, Sabbath observance, the magistracy, and succession. These four issues would continue to surface in many of Helwys's writings. Despite their differences, Helwys thanked the Waterlanders for pointing out diverse errors among them.[51] Helwys, therefore, acknowledged the influence of the Waterlanders on his own thought.

Helwys also wrote *A Short and Plaine Proof by the Word and Works of God that God's Decree is not the Cause of Any Man's Sins or Condemnation*.[52] In this work, Helwys moved away from his attacks on Smyth and the Waterlanders and took aim at the high Calvinists. Helwys demonstrated the weaknesses in the Calvinistic tenets of predestination, particular election, and the damnation of infants. Helwys dedicated this works to Isabel Bowes, the wife of William Bowes. While in Coventry, Lady Bowes had allowed theological discussions to be held in her home and had been present when Smyth had debated other Puritans over whether or not to separate from the Church of England. He may

---

[50] Thomas Helwys, *An Advertisement or Admonition unto the Congregations, Which Men Call the New Fryelers, in the Lowe Countries* (Amsterdam: n.p., 1611).

[51] Ibid., 94.

[52] Thomas Helwys, *A Short and Plaine Proof by the Word and Works of God That God's Decree Is Not the Cause of Any Man's Sins or Condemnation and That All Men Are Redeemed by Christ. As Also. That No Infants are Condemened* (Amsterdam: n.p., 1611).

have believed that she was a kindred spirit and would render them some manner of aid, but the Lady Bowes was dedicated to the Puritan cause of reforming the Church of England. Helwys's appeal came to naught.[53]

The differences in Helwys's *Synopsis* of 1610 and his post-*Synopsis* writings, in particular his 1611 *Declaration of Faith*, are significant. The *Synopsis* had been largely dependent upon Smyth. The *Declaration, A Short and Plaine Proof, An Advertisement*, and *A Short Declaration of the Mystery of Iniquity* demonstrate that Helwys had moved away from Smyth in some areas and was beginning to form his own positions. In Article 2 of the *Declaration*, Helwys affirmed original sin, saying that "his sin was imputed to all; and so death went over all men."[54] He continues his discussion on original sin in Article 4, where he states that "men are by nature the children of wrath and born in iniquity and in sin conceived.... Yet God giving grace, man may receive grace or may reject grace."[55] Whereas in Article 5 of his *Synopsis* he had not renounced free will, he now repudiated it by removing it all together from his *Declaration*. In fact, in his *Short Declaration of the Mystery of Iniquity*, he called free will "that most damnable heresy."[56] Helwys delineated his position concerning free will in the conclusion of his *A Short and Plaine Proof by the Word and Works Of God that God's Decree is Not the Cause of Any of Man's Sins or Condemnation*:

> If their meaning is free will in Christ and that we have free power and ability through Christ to work out our salvation and that through Christ we are made able to do every good work, such a free will we hold. But that man has any free will or power in himself to work his own salvation or choose life, we utterly deny having learned that of the apostle (Ephesians 2.8.9). "That by grace men are saved through faith and not of themselves, but it is the gift of God not of works less any man should boast of himself." But this grace of God, (which is his mercy by Christ) God has given to all, but all do not receive it. (John 1.10.11) "He was in the world and the world did

---

[53] Whitley, vol. 1 of *Works*, lvii–lviii.
[54] Helwys, *A Declaration of Faith*, 68.
[55] Ibid.
[56] Helwys, *An Advertisement*, 152.

not know him. He came to his own, and his own did not receive him."[57]

In Article 8 of the *Declaration,* Helwys denounces Hoffmanite Christology but in much stronger language than in Article 6 of the *Synopsis.* He states that Jesus was "manifested in the Flesh, being the seed of David, and of the Israelites, according to the Flesh. The Son of Mary the Virgin made of her substance."[58] He reiterates his defense of the body of Christ in *An Advertisement.* With very strong biblical precedents, Helwys demonstrated that

> now in that Christ's body was mortal and died, it was not a heavenly, glorious, spiritual, powerful body, but it was an earthly, natural weak body, and had the same infirmities that our bodies have (sin excepted, as showed in Hebrews 4.15). We do not have a high Priest that cannot be touched with the feeling of infirmities, but was tempted in all things in like sort, yet without sin. Also in Chap. 5.2 we see that he is succinctly able to have compassion on them that are ignorant and that are out of the way, because he is also compressed with infirmity. And his infirmities appear in that he was hungry (Matthew 4.2). He was weary (John 4.6). He was troubled, and his soul was in great heaviness (Mark 14.33.34). He confessed his flesh was weak (Matthew 26.41). All of these infirmities or any infirmity could not come from heaven because in heaven there are no imperfections or imperfect things. We demand can heavenly bodies be weary, can they be hungry, can they be troubled, and can their souls be in heaviness, or are they weak and mortal?[59]

Prior to his death in 1612, Smyth wrote his *Last Book.* While discussing the nature of Christ, Smyth insinuated that Helwys misunderstood his teachings because he did not have the medical knowledge that Smyth had

---

[57] Helwys, *A Short and Plaine Proof,* 91
[58] Helwys, *Declaration of Faith,* 70.
[59] Thomas Helwys, *An Advertisement,* 96.

acquired as a practicing doctor.[60] Smyth stated that all children receive their nature from their father and are only nourished by their mother.[61] In Article 19 of Smyth's *Defense of the Short Confession*, Smyth claims to not have denied the physical nature of Christ coming from Mary but stressed his spiritual nature more frequently because it was more important. Even though Smyth claimed that his interpretation of the nature of Christ was different from that of the Waterlanders, he did not deem it worthy of making it a test of fellowship.[62]

Articles 11 and 12 of the *Declaration* are expanded from *Synopsis* Article 9 and are a repudiation of succession. Helwys strengthens Article 9 of the *Synopsis* in Article 11 of the *Declaration* by elaborating on the concept of the gathered church as constituting the true church. He stated that "though they are but two or three," they have Christ with them and may "administer the holy ordinances."[63] Article 12 of the *Declaration* claims that no church has Christ alone, but rather every church has Christ.[64]

Succession was the primary topic of *An Advertisement*. His descriptions of succession allege that the practice was nothing but Roman Catholicism in disguise. A key to Helwys's defense was the question of where true baptism began. He noted that to "come to your ground, this is the sum of that which you say. Baptism was once raised up by one unbaptized person, after this act, none did. It is neither lawful for any unbaptized to baptize, but all must have it from him, and so you follow on with your proportion from baptism, to the church and ministry."[65]

Helwys then pressed the question of whether after the first baptizer, John the Baptist, performed his task, anyone else had been permitted to perform the ordinance. Answering his own question, Helwys stated that John was "unbaptized (or rather not being of any other first baptized). If his example is a particular example for one man only (as you say) then was it abolished when your predecessor had once begun to baptize. So is that example now of no

---

[60] Smyth, *Last Book*, in Whitley, vol. 2 of *Works*, 758; Burgess, *John Smyth, the Se-Baptist, Thomas Helwys and the First Baptist Church in England* (London: James Clarke, 1911) 265–66, Coggins, 124.

[61] Smyth, *Last Book*, in Whitley, vol. 2 of *Works*, 758.

[62] Ibid., 759.

[63] Helwys, *Declaration of Faith*, 70-71.

[64] Ibid., 71.

[65] Helwys, *An Advertisement*, 118.

use?"[66] If the Waterlanders were correct, every person who was truly baptize[...] then must somehow be able to trace the lineage of those in the baptismal line back to John the Baptist. In Helwys's opinion, this was no different from having to be baptized by a priest standing in apostolic succession for one to be a member of the Roman Catholic Church.

Helwys maintained that if succession was true, then no new churches could be formed without the permission from an established church with elders who could baptize them and approve of their church. Therefore, everyone must come to that church, in this instance the Waterlander Church, for acceptance. Helwys perceived this as unbiblical and impossible. He noted that the Waterlanders would

> have all people, and nations, and tongues come to you, and your beginnings for the ordinances of Christ: No people may have power to administer in the holy things except they first join themselves to you, and be one with you and receive power and all the holy things from you. Herein do you with the man of sin exalt yourselves above all that are called of God, and you take to yourselves above all that are called of God, and you take to yourselves that preferment under the gospel that God gave only to the Jews under the law.[67]

Helwys believed that to hold succession in such a manner was arrogant. It was as if they were saying, "All people and nations must then come to you, and receive all the holy ordinances from you."[68]

Invalidating succession was very important to Helwys, but in all actuality he may have been reading too deeply into Smyth's desire to be baptized into the Waterlander Church. In his *Last Book*, Smyth stated that he never believed in succession. He believed that he had erred by performing his own baptism when a true church, the Waterlanders, had been present. He only sought baptism to maintain some semblance of order within the church.[69]

---

[66] Ibid., 111.
[67] Ibid., 104.
[68] Ibid., 108.
[69] Smyth, *Last Book*, in Whitley, vol. 2 of *Works*, 756–57.

It must have been a shock to Helwys's church in London when they learned that the Smyth congregation had finally been admitted into the Mennonite church in 1615 and their baptisms were accepted as valid. No rebaptism was required.

In Article 20 of the *Declaration*,[70] Helwys adjusted *Synopsis* Article 13[71] by adding elders to serve along with deacons as the officers of the church. Smyth made no similar adjustment.

Completely new to the *Declaration* is Article 24, concerning the magistracy. Helwys added this article because Smyth discussed the magistracy in his second version of the *Short Confession*,[72] which was issued soon after Helwys's *Synopsis*. Following the Waterlander belief, in Article 35 Smyth states that Christ has not "called his disciples or followers to be worldly kings, princes, potentates, or magistrates.... This then considered (...does not fit the crucified life of the Christians)...so hold we that it beseems not Christians to administer these offices."[73] Helwys disagreed with this interpretation. Helwys states in Article 24 of the *Declaration* that magistrates "may be members of the 'Church of Christ' retaining their magistracy, for no one Holy Ordinance of God debars any from being a member of Christ's Church."[74] Helwys continued his defense of allowing magistrates membership in the church in his *An Advertisement*:

It is made most plain that the power and authority of the magistrates is the holy ordinance of God. They are further called, the ministers of God, and their administration is set down to take vengeance of those that do evil, and to praise those that do well. And the instrument that is used to punish evil doers is the sword. And in all this they are the ministers of God for good and for the good of God's children. Therefore they are commanded to pray for them. Thus their power (being of God) is holy and good being (as it is showed here by the Apostle) appointed of God for good, who does,

---

[70] Helwys, *Declaration of Faith*, 72.

[71] Helwys, *Latin Synopsis of Faith*, 62.

[72] Most historians believe that this confession was actually written by Waterlander leader Hans de Ries (1553–1638). See William L. Lumpkin, *Baptist Confessions of Faith* (Philadelphia: Judson Press, 1959) 102.

[73] John Smyth, *A Short Confession*, in Lumpkin, 111–12.

[74] Helwys, *Declaration of Faith*, 73.

nor can appoint nothing but that which is holy and good, and pleasing to him. God is holiness and goodness, and he cannot appoint anything that is contrary to himself.[75]

When comparing Helwys's 1610 *Synopsis* to his 1611 *English Declaration* and his other post-*Synopsis* works, it is apparent that his rupture with Smyth was complete. Helwys repudiated every tenet of Waterlander theology that Smyth now maintained and that had been included in his *Synopsis*. He now affirmed original sin, the magistrate's ability to be a member of the church, and oath taking. He denied free will and Hoffmanite Christology. Helwys's soteriology was now a mix of Calvinism and Arminianism. In matters of original sin and the will, he became more Calvinistic than Arminian. Yet, in matters of atonement and the perseverance of the saints, Helwys remained strictly Arminian. Helwys was making a clear statement that his group was different from both Smyth's church and the Waterlanders.

There may have also been some personal differences between Smyth and Helwys. In Smyth's *Last Book*, he took offense to Helwys's allegations that he had not given his share of money to the Amsterdam congregation and had been living off the common fund. Smyth replied that "concerning a secret imputation, which Mr. Helwys by way of intimation suggests as though I had received much help of maintenance from his company or from that company of English people that came over together out of the north parts with me, I affirm this much: that I never received of them all put together the value of forty shillings."[76]

While Helwys was debating Smyth, he concluded that it was wrong to have fled persecution. He knew he had to return to England. As all of Helwys's 1611 writings were penned in Amsterdam, he could not have returned to England before the end of 1611. The more probable date is early 1612, when he organized the first Baptist church in England in Spitalfields outside the city walls of London.[77]

Knowing that they faced certain persecution, what then was the impetus behind the Helwys church's decision to return home? There are several

---

[75] Thomas Helwys, *An Advertisement*, 129.
[76] Smyth, *Last Book*, in Whitley, vol. 2 of *Works*, 759.
[77] Payne, *Thomas Helwys*, 1.

possibilities. First, he had left behind his wife, Joan, and their children. Joan had probably been imprisoned in York Castle by the authorities because they had failed to catch Thomas. Joan was now free, but her persecution continued and she was facing it without her husband.

Second, Separatists in England were berating their brethren in Amsterdam for fleeing to safety rather than trying to make changes at home. Enoch Clapham was one of the lead antagonists of the Separatists who fled to Holland. In 1608 he wrote a tract titled *Errors on the Right Hand, Against the Several Sects of Protestants in Those Times*, which attacked those who fled to the Netherlands and those who hid their faith in England.[78] When discussing those in Holland, Clapham wrote that they had been wrong to flee their homeland to start a church among those of another language for the sake of safety.[79] He believed that they were in error in that "they alleged in the defense Elijah's fleeing in time of persecution, and our Savior's advice to his disciples, if they were persecuted in one city to flee into another."[80]

In his final and most famous work, *A Short Declaration of the Mystery of Iniquity*, which he penned and published in late 1611 before he left Holland, Helwys all but acknowledged Clapham was discussing him in the conclusion. Helwys used virtually the same words to describe the Robinson congregation that had chosen to remain in Leyden. Echoing Clapham's description of Helwys, Helwys declared, "But these men flee to cities to which they cannot preach the Gospel, being of a strange tongue, neither have they any intent nor meaning to preach the Gospel to those cities."[81] Clapham may have made Helwys feel guilty for abandoning his home country.

Helwys was also in contact with Separatists who were living in Suffolk. They spoke out strongly about fleeing persecution, calling it "eating blood and running."[82] The Suffolk group's position on fleeing persecution, therefore, may have influenced Helwys's decision to return.[83]

---

[78] Enoch Clapham, *Errors on the Right Hand, Against the Several Sects of Protestants in Those Times*, in Joseph Ivimey, vol. 1 of *A History of the English Baptists* (1811; reprint, Paris AR: Baptist Standard Bearer, 2005) 86.

[79] Ibid.

[80] Ibid.

[81] Helwys, *A Short Declaration*, 302.

[82] Lawne, *A Prophane Schism*, in Burgess, *Smyth and Helwys*, 289.

[83] G. Hugh Wamble, "The Concept and Practice of Christian Fellowship: The Connectional and Inter-Denominational Aspects Thereof, among the 17th Century

Though *A Short Declaration of the Mystery of Iniquity* is primarily known as a defense of freedom of religion, it is also quite apocalyptic. Helwys believed the beasts from the book of Revelation had been revealed and that "the days of greatest tribulation spoken of by Christ wherein the abomination of desolation is seen to be set in the holy place."[84] Helwys goes so far as to say that the first beast was the Roman Catholic Church. He believed the power wielded by the Roman Catholic Church in both spiritual and temporal matters was unbiblical, spiritually binding, and malevolent. In this vein, Helwys stated,

> A spiritual power setting up a Pope or Bishop by virtue of his office with a triple crown, kings and princes bowing to him, and serving him, and (by virtue of his office) carrying a bloody sword, and his hands full of blood. This is part of his outward pomp and power. He bears spiritual names of blasphemy claiming to be the head of the church and Bishop of the universal flock. He takes upon himself the power to cast soul and body to hell, and to send to heaven whoever he will, to make spiritual laws and decrees as he will, and to bind men's consciences to the obedience thereof.[85]

The second beast was the Anglican Church because its hierarchy was unbiblical and merely aped that of Rome. Helwys disparagingly wrote,

> We call all of you to witness whether the second beast is not as plainly seen in the hierarchy of arch bishops and lord bishops and whether it is possible that there should be made so lively an image of the first beast as is in the hierarchy in all titles and names of blasphemy, in all pomp, and in all power throughout. It begins with their book worship, with the conformity belonging to it, and so going through all their offices, and officers, courts, canons, and decrees. If all these things are not the image of the first beast, conceived in his bowels, and brought out of his bosom, let heaven

---

English Baptists" (unpublished Th.D. thesis, Southern Baptist Theological Seminary, Louisville, Kentucky, 1955) 58–59.

[84] Helwys, *A Short Declaration*, 159.

[85] Ibid., 168.

and earth witness, and let all the men on the earth deny if they can, and show any other image of the first beast.[86]

Helwys also railed against the Puritans who clung to the Church of England even when they knew it was a false church. Helwys caustically stated,

> In your many books you cry out about the things that are amiss among you, and sue and supplicate, and still continue in your former ways. You testify hereby against yourselves that you are unreformed, and that there is a way of reformation, wherein you would be, if you might have leave or license to enter into it. Seeing that you cannot obtain it, you justify it lawful to walk in an unreformed profession of religion upon this ground because you may not have leave by act of Parliament to reform. What more false a profession can be found on earth than this of yours, who profess that you know a way of much truth in which you would walk, but you do not, because you cannot by superior power be permitted.[87]

The fourth group that Helwys attacked was the Brownists, who refused to renounce the false baptism they had received at the hands of the Church of England. Helwys found this action hypocritical and self-persecutory, saying, "The Brownists approve of the baptism and baptizing of those who parents persecute their own children for walking in their way. Are these the seed of the faithful?"[88] In other words, the Brownists believed the baptism they received from a false church that was now persecuting them remained a valid baptism.

Helwys hoped to warn the people of his own country before they were devoured by the beasts or led astray by false prophets who claimed to reform. He believed that there were few people in England who could prepare the church for the times that were approaching. Helwys reserved most of his vitriol for his former friend, John Robinson, whom he condemned by name for insisting upon infant baptism. In regard to Robinson's retaining infant baptism, Helwys stated, "God has not promised anywhere to accept to salvation of the parents' faith for their children, nor to condemn them for their

---

[86] Ibid., 179.
[87] Ibid., 219.
[88] Ibid., 271.

parents' infidelity. This is but one among many of Mr. Robinson's doctrines of devils which he has heaped upon his tedious book."[89]

A second reason for Helwys's castigation of Robinson was his desire to stay in Leyden even though Helwys believed Robinson was having no evangelistic success. Few Dutch people spoke English, and few of the English spoke Dutch. Moreover, those who could understand the evangelistic endeavors of Robinson's congregation had turned a deaf ear to the foreigners. When discussing Smyth's congregation, Helwys stated,

> We put these seducers in remembrance that our Savior Christ gives this rule also to his disciples, that if they will "enter into any house or city that will not receive them, nor hear his word, when they depart from there, they will shake off the dust of their feet as a witness against that house or city." But when will these men, according to this rule of Christ, shake the dust off their feet for a witness against Amsterdam or Leyden, who neither receive them nor the word they bring, otherwise they receive Turks and Jews, and all sorts who come only to seek safety and profit?[90]

Helwys maintained that if the Dutch refused to listen, Robinson's church had the responsibility to "shake the dust off their feet" and move to a new location or perhaps return home to witness to their own English brethren.

Helwys also criticized Robinson for refusing to return to England for no other reason than fear for his personal security. Instead of working for change in his own country, he chose to publish his works in the safety of Holland and have them sent to England. Helwys stated that even he had been misled initially by Robinson's motivation to move:

> We hold ourselves bound to acknowledge, and that other might be warned, to manifest how we have been (through our great weakness) misled by deceitful hearted leaders who have and do seek to save their lives, and will make sure not to lose them for Christ. Therefore, they flee into foreign countries and free states, and draw people after them to support their kingdoms, first seeking their own safeties, and then

---

[89] Ibid., 280.
[90] Ibid., 306.

publishing (as they pretend) the Gospel, or seeking the kingdom of heaven, and publishing, as far as they may with their safety.[91]

The Separatists who remained in Holland, particularly John Robinson, resented Helwys's comments concerning their permanent removal from England and their inability to minister to the native Dutch. Robinson stated that he had "so preached to others in those cities, as that by the blessing of God working with us, we have gained more to the Lord than Mr. Helwys' church consists of."[92] Robinson also noted that Helwys had been one of the first people to advocate the move from England to Amsterdam and even paid the passage of fellow Separatists who could not afford it.

Helwys realized that when he returned to England he could end up either with other religious dissenters in Newgate Prison or executed at Smithfield. The majority of Separatists, dissenters, Anabaptists, and other non-Anglicans were placed in this prison until they capitulated, were executed, or died from the prison's terrible conditions.

Richard Bancroft (1544–1610), the archbishop of Canterbury, had been responsible for the mistreatment of many of the Separatists. Bancroft died in 1610, and George Abbot (1562–1633), a lackey for King James I, became the archbishop of Canterbury. Thus, the execution of Separatists for heresy continued. King James considered himself a theologian and would not allow heretics safe harbor in England. Accused and found guilty of Arianism, Bartholomew Legate was executed at Smithfield on 18 March 1611.[93] The Legates had family among the Mennonites in Amsterdam and had remained in touch with them. It is reasonable to assume that the English refugees in Amsterdam would have known what had happened to Bartholomew Legate and what might face those who returned.[94]

Edward Wightman (1566–1612) was condemned by the bishop of Litchfield and Coventry for being a Baptist and executed on 11 April 1612.[95]

---

[91]Ibid., 302.

[92] John Robinson, *The Works of John Robinson, Pastor of the Pilgrim Fathers,* 3 vols. (London: John Snow, 1851) 3:159.

[93] Joseph Ivimey, *A History of English Baptists,* 4 vols. (London: printed for author, 1811) 1:75.

[94] Payne, *Thomas Helwys,* 11–12.

[95] W. T. Whitley, *A History of British Baptists* (Kingsgate: Charles Griffen and Company, 1923) 29.

The notice of condemnation stated that he was being executed for holding "that the baptizing of infants is an abominable custom; that the Lord's Supper and baptism are not to be celebrated as they are now practiced in the Church of England and that Christianity is not wholly professed and preached in the Church of England, but only a part."[96] These charges must have made Helwys nervous, as these beliefs were similar to his own. Helwys also rejected infant baptism and even went beyond Wightman in asserting that the Church of England was the second beast from Revelation.

Helwys must have heard about the execution of these dissenters. Still, he turned his face toward England and declared, "Let none think that we are altogether ignorant what building and warfare we take in hand and that we have not sat down and in some measure thoroughly considered what the cost and danger may be, and also let none think that we are without sense and feeling of our own inability to begin and our weakness to endure to the end the weight and danger of such work, but in all these things we hope and wait for wisdom and strength from the Lord."[97] Helwys was returning home to save his fellow Englishmen from the "mystery of iniquity" and was ready to endure any persecution to do so.

John Robinson believed that Helwys had other reasons for returning to England. He claimed that life had proven too hard for Helwys's congregation and quipped that it "neither is likely, if he (Helwys) and the people with him at Amsterdam could have gone on comfortably, as they desired, that the unlawfulness of flight would have ever troubled him." Now, Robinson believed that Helwys was merely seeking "vain glory, and with courting persecution by challenging the king and the state to their faces."[98]

Helwys and his contingent arrived in London in 1612. Rather than move inside the London walls, Helwys moved his little church of Baptists into Spitalfields on the outskirts of the city.[99] Of this first Baptist church on English soil, Walter Burgess wrote, "It was a church led and officered by laymen. It had been tested by the trials of exile and the fires of controversy.... It was deprived almost at once of its chief leaders by imprisonment, but it still

---

[96] Ivimey, *History of English Baptists*, 1:75.
[97] Helwys, *A Short Declaration*, 307.
[98] Robinson, vol. 3 of *Works*, 160.
[99] Whitley, *A History of British Baptists*, 34.

held together. These brave men and women were dignified by the greatness of the cause they espoused."[100]

When Helwys arrived in England, he already had copies of *A Short Declaration* in hand. He probably paid for the publication of his book by selling Broxtowe Hall in 1610.[101] W. T. Whitley believes that in this book Helwys made the first appeal in the English language for complete religious liberty.[102] Helwys argued that forcing people to be members of a church by swearing an oath did not make them loyal to the church and was identical to the practices of Roman Catholicism.

One of the most surprising statements in *A Short Declaration* may have been Helwys's demand for universal religious toleration. Helwys was not only asking for religious freedom for his little contingent, but for Presbyterians, Puritans, Roman Catholics, and even for non-Christians such as Jews and Muslims. Helwys wrote,

> If they be true and faithful subjects to their king for we do freely profess, that our lord the King has no more power over their consciences than over ours, and that is none at all: for our lord the King is but an earthly King, and he has no authority as a King but in earthly causes, and if the King's people be obedient and true subjects, obeying all humane laws made by the King, our lord the King can require no more: for men's religion to God is between God and themselves; the King shall not answer for it, neither may the king be judged between God and man. Let them be heretics, Turks, Jews or whatsoever, it appertains not to the earthly power to punish them in the least.[103][

A declaration this sweeping had never been spoken before in the English language.

---

[100] Burgess, *Smyth and Helwys*, 282–83.
[101] Ibid., 130.
[102] Whitley, *A History of British Baptists*, 33.
[103] Helwys, *Short Declaration*, 208.

Unlike many dissenters, Helwys publicly disseminated the book and hoped it would promote discussion among the dissenter community. He used the book to announce his arrival and aspiration to discuss religious liberty with James I and the Anglican authorities. Out of a desire to converse with the one person in England who could aid his cause, he sent an autographed copy to King James I. Only four original copies of this book have survived. One of the copies is in the Bodleian Library at Oxford University and may have been the copy Helwys sent to King James. In what is believed to be in Helwys's own hand, this copy contains a personal note to the king:

> Hear, O King and do not despise the counsel of your poor and let their complaints come before you. The King is a mortal man and not God, therefore he has no power over the immortal souls of his subjects to make laws and ordinances for them and to set spiritual lords over them. If the King has authority to make spiritual lords and laws, then he is an immortal God and not a mortal man. O, King, do not be seduced by deceivers to sin so against God who you should obey or against your poor subjects who should and will obey you in all things with body, life and goods or else let their lives be taken from your earth. God save you the King.[104]

Helwys wanted James to realize that he was still a loyal Englishman and a supporter of the monarchy. At the beginning of one of his strongest appeals for religious freedom, he told James,

> Let it suffice our lord the king and let it not seem a small thing, that the God of Gods has made our lord the king a mighty earthly king over diverse nations and has given our lord the king an earthly power to make laws and ordinances (such as the king in his own wisdom will think best, and to change them and alter them at his own pleasure) to rule and govern his people by, and to appoint governors and officers to execute the king's will. All of the king's people are bound of conscience to God and duty to the king to obey the king with their goods, bodies and lives in all service of peace and war. Whosoever will resist the king

---

[104] Helwys, *A Short Declaration*, 156.

herein; they resist the ordinance of God and will receive judgment
from God, besides the punishment with the sword of justice which
God has given to the king to punish evildoers that transgress the king's
laws. God has also honored the king with titles and names of majesty
that are due but to himself (Psalm 82.1, 6; Daniel 5.18) and has
commanded honor to be given to the king (1 Peter 2.17). God has
commanded all his people specially to pray for the king. (1 Timothy
2.2) Let this kingdom, power and honor fully satisfy our lord the
king's heart, and let it suffice the king to have all rule over the people's
bodies and goods.[105]

King James was impressed neither with the straightforwardness of the
personal appeal nor with his claim of loyalty. He particularly resented being
told that he did not have the right to command all aspects of his subjects,
body and soul. James believed in the divine right of kings. On one occasion,
he stated, "Kings are justly called gods, for they do exercise a manner or
resemblance of Divine power upon the earth, for, if you will consider the
attributes of God, you shall see how they agree in the person of the king."[106]

King James's reaction was predictable. In his view, Helwys had
committed treason by speaking out so boldly, telling the king how he should
or should not rule, and for attacking the Church of England of which he was
the supreme governor. He immediately threw Helwys into Newgate Prison,
where he spent the rest of his life. Appeals were made to gain his release, but
the king was unmoved. Perhaps Helwys hoped his uncle, Geoffrey Helwys,
the sheriff of London, would intervene for him. There is no evidence that
Geoffrey made any attempt to aid his nephew. He did, however, provide ten
pounds to Thomas's wife, Joan, who is described in Geoffrey's 1616 will as
the "widow of Thomas Helwys."[107] Helwys had therefore died in Newgate
Prison before or in 1616, prior to the death of Geoffrey Helwys.

Baptist historian Thomas Crosby believed that a note dated 1613 and
found in the library of the House of Commons may have been written by

---

[105] Ibid., 200.
[106] Richard W. Leopold, Arthur S. Link, and Stanley Corbin, eds., *Problems in American History*, 2d ed. (Englewood Cliffs NJ: 1957) 3.
[107] Whitley, *A History of British Baptists*, 35.

Thomas Helwys.[108] It addressed the Right Honorable Assembly of the Commons-house of Parliament. The note reads as follows: "A most humble supplication of diverse poor prisoners and many others the king's majesty's loyal subjects read to testify by oath of allegiance in all sincerity, whose grievances are lamentable, only for the cause of conscience…by his majesty's faithful subjects most falsely called Anabaptists."[109] The note insists that the only reason the prisoners had been separated from their families and livelihood was because of their desire not to go against their conscience in matters of religion. At the bottom of the note appear the words "rejected by the committee." The note is signed "H. H." Since the note was signed H. H., not T. H., and Geoffrey Helwys's 1616 will explicitly confirms that Helwys was already dead, it is highly doubtful that this note was written by Thomas Helwys.

After the death of Helwys, the mantle of leadership fell to John Murton. Like Helwys, Murton had also been thrown into Newgate Prison in 1613. Murton spent the final thirteen years of his life in Newgate, where he died in 1626. While in prison, Murton continued to press for cause of freedom of conscience and religious liberty in his 1615 book *Objections Answered by Way of Dialogue*. This book was later republished under the title *Persecution for Religion Judged and Condemned*.[110] He penned a second book on freedom of conscience in 1620, *A Humble Supplication*.[111] Roger Williams, the father of American Baptists, reported that Murton had written the book on the paper

---

[108] Thomas Crosby, vol. 1 of *The History of the English Baptist from the Reformation to the Beginning of the Reign of King George I* (London: n.p., 1738–1740) 275–76.

[109] The Third Report of the Historical Manuscripts Commission, 14.[

[110] John Murton, *Persecution for Religion Judg'd and Condemn'd: in a Discoure [!], between and Antichristian and a Crhistian [!]. Proving by the Law of God and of the Land, and by King James His Many Testimonies, That No Man Ought to Be Persecuted for His Religion, so He Testifie His Aallegiance by the Oath Appointed by Law. Proving Also, That the Spiritual Power in England, Is the Image of the Spiritual Cruel Power of Rome, or That Beast Mentioned, Rev. 13…to Which Is Added, a Humble Supplication to the Kings Majesty* (London: by author, 1615).

[111] John Murton, *A Humble Supplication to Many of the King's Majesty Loyal Subjects, Ready to Testify All Civil Obedience, by the Oath of Allegiance, or Otherwise, and That of Conscience: Who are Persecuted (Only for Differing in Religion), Contrary to Divine and Human Testimonie* (London: By the Author, 1620).

stoppers that came with his daily jug of milk.[112] In spite of the imprisonment of their leaders, their church grew and spawned four more General Baptist churches in London: Lincoln, Sarum, Coventry, and Tiverton.

---

[112] Roger Williams, *The Bloody Tenet of Persecution for Cause of Conscience Discussed in a Conference between Peace and Truth. Who, in all Affection, Present to the High Court of Parliament, (as the Result of Their Discourse) These (among Other Passages) of Highest Consideration* (London: n.p., 1644). Edited and reprinted by Richard Groves (Macon GA: Mercer University Press, 2001) 32.

HELWYS'S CHURCH IN SPITALFIELDS

By examining the theological, soteriological, and ecclesiological content of Helwys's confessions, letters, and books, and assuming the church would hold the same beliefs as its pastor, a picture of the Spitalfields church comes into focus. In most theological matters, the Helwys church was consistent with other seventeenth-century Christian denominations. When discussing the Father, Son, and Holy Spirit, they maintained the standard Trinitarian interpretation. When discussing Jesus, Helwys tightened his Christology to ensure that no Hoffmanite inclinations could be construed and the full humanity of Christ was preserved.

The soteriology of the Baptist church at Spitalfields was an amalgamation of Calvinism and Arminianism. They clearly held to a general atonement and thus were dubbed "General Baptists." They maintained that Christ elected to salvation those who chose to follow him,[1] believed that a Christian could fall from grace, yet denied free will. Helwys may have denied free will out of the fear that he would have been seen as holding general redemption.[2] Helwys and his church claimed to believe in original sin, but it appears that Helwys may have held to the belief of actual sin. This allowed Helwys to claim that infants were freed by the grace of Christ. Justification occurred because of the work of Christ and the obedience of man.

In matters of ecclesiology, the Spitalfields church was formed on the basis of believer's baptism (by affusion, not immersion), not a church covenant. Believer's baptism was essential to salvation. Infant baptism merited punishment. Helwys wrote, "If you will have infants baptized, that is, washed with water and certain words, then you bring in a carnal rite, which does not purge the conscience (for you do not hold that the infants' consciences are purged by it), and so you make the new covenant and ordinances carnal, like to the old, which may not be, unless you will directly oppose the evident word of the Lord, as you have long herein done, to your utter destruction, unless

---

[1] Michael J. Walker, "The Relation of Infants to Church: Baptism and Gospel in 17th Century Baptist Theology," *The Baptist Quarterly* XXI (April 1966): 247.

[2] J. Glenwood Clayton, "Thomas Helwys: A Baptist Founding Father," *Baptist History and Heritage* 8 (Jan 1973): 13.

you repent."[3] Two or three believers could come together and form a church and execute the ordinances. They did not need to rely on baptism from any elder of another established church to authenticate their own. Each church was autonomous. A line of succession was not only unnecessary, but Roman Catholic. The Sabbath was also important to Helwys. In fact, the keeping of the Sabbath was almost perceived as an ordinance. If possible, one was to refrain from worldly activities and gather with the church in the worship of Christ.

The church officers at Spitalfields would have been elders or deacons elected by the local church. A person's ordination was good only in the church that ordained him, and a person had no right to enforce his beliefs in another church. His task was to help the members of the church in their spiritual and physical needs. Women played a prominent role and could serve as deacons. If a church was without officers, it was still a church and could administer the ordinances.

Magistrates could be members of the Spitalfields church. Helwys believed that magistrates were divinely appointed to their offices to protect those who did good and punish those who did evil in civil matters. The magistrate could retain his office and be a member of the church. Helwys also maintained that oaths could be taken to settle a dispute.

Under the guidance of Thomas Helwys, these doctrines and distinctives became the foundation for the first Baptist church in England. They were maintained by Helwys's descendants, such as John Murton and Leonard Busher, and became the hallmarks of the General Baptists.

---

[3] Thomas Helwys, *A Short Declaration of the Mystery of Iniquity* (Amsterdam: n.p., 1611), 275.

A LASTING LEGACY

Thomas Helwys was not the first Baptist. This honor belongs to John Smyth, and he rightfully holds a distinguished position in denominational history. Smyth was the first Baptist and the founder of the first Baptist church, but his time as a Baptist lasted less than a year. He is more accurately described as a seeker. He was always looking for further light, and his time as a Baptist was an intermediate step in his search. Had he not died in 1612, he would have likely moved from the Waterlanders at some point as he continued his faith journey. Perhaps the most important contribution Smyth made to the Baptist denomination was in bringing Thomas Helwys into the Baptist fold.

Thomas Helwys was a member of John Smyth's church and became a Baptist with him in 1609. Like his friend and mentor, Helwys was a seeker. Unlike Smyth, however, when Helwys found what he believed to be the true church, his search was over and he could not be moved from his convictions. Helwys remained a Baptist for the rest of his short life. He solidified his beliefs and was an ardent defender of his well-reasoned positions. His contributions to the Baptist denomination cannot be overstated. If it were not for Thomas Helwys and his comprehensive writing in defense of his beliefs, these first Baptists may have vanished under the pressure of persecution or been absorbed into the Waterlander community of Amsterdam.

Smyth and Helwys established the core principle that separated Baptists from many other Protestant denominations when they formed their church on the ordinance of believer's baptism in 1609. Moreover, they stressed the importance of baptizing only believers as a prerequisite for membership into their first Baptist church. Their insistence upon confession before baptism made the first Baptist church a church of believers. After Smyth left the Baptists for the Waterlander Mennonites, Helwys and his congregation maintained believer's baptism and carried it with them to England in 1612. His excellent defense of believer's baptism and biblical arguments against infant baptism provided the members of his church and the generations that followed with an apology for its most identifiable distinctive and first ordinance.

Thomas Helwys founded the first Baptist church in England in 1612 and rooted it in the principles of his *Declaration of Faith*. This church was distinctly Baptist, based on the Scriptures, congregationalism, believer's baptism, autonomy, the office of pastor and deacon, and religious liberty. From this little church outside the walls of London in Spitalfields, the Baptist denomination took root in England. By 1626 the church had spawned five other churches built on the same principles. Despite persecution from the ecclesiastical authorities and fellow dissenters who rejected the novel idea of believer's baptism, these churches grew and more were added to their number. From this humble beginning, the General Baptists were born and have continued to exist, though in small numbers, well into the twenty-first century. Helwys's teachings, however, have continued to inspire all Baptists.

In his *Short Declaration of the Mystery of Iniquity*, Helwys made the first appeal in England for complete religious liberty for Christians and non-Christians. Never before had someone dared to stand up to the English monarchy and the established church in such a manner. He insisted that the crown had no business attempting to impose its religious convictions on anyone. He believed that the king could make civil law but that he had no authority over man's relationship to his God. He also believed that the church and the state were separate spheres with neither having the right to force its will on the other. Helwys paid for his convictions with his life. When he perished in Newgate Prison, he became a martyr not only for Baptists but for all people who believe in freedom of conscience and the freedom to practice their religion without the fear of persecution. Baptists have continued Helwys's fight for freedom of religion for almost 400 years. To this day, no Christian denomination has worked harder for religious liberty and the separation of church and state more than the faithful descendants of Thomas Helwys.

SECTION TWO

EXTANT HELWYS DOCUMENTS

1. LETTER ON CHURCH ORDER

Helwys's first letter was written on 26 September 1608, prior to his split with John Smyth. Written to their friends and family back in England, Helwys informed them as to why they were having problems with and why they had not joined the other exiled English Separatists (Francis Johnson's and John Robinson's congregations) in Amsterdam. Helwys stated that their differences were ecclesiological in nature, centering on church officers, style of worship, participation with the government, and tithing. As a result, this letter provides an adequate depiction of worship in the Smyth-Helwys church.

A note sent by Thomas Helwys one
Of the elders of the Brownest
Church, sent to his brethren.

I desire to verify some things to you concerning how matters are going here (Amsterdam) with us, and concerning the differences between some brethren and us. We differ in part in ministry, worship, government, and treasury. Their ministry consists of pastors and teachers or of pastors only, and we approve of no other officers in the ministry but that of pastors. As part of worship, they read chapters of texts to preach on and Psalms out of the translation. We lay aside the translation in praying, prophesying, and in the singing of Psalms. We suppose that we will yet prove the truth that all books even the originals themselves must be set aside in the time of spiritual worship. Yet, we still retain the readings and interpretations of scripture in the church for the preparation of worship, judging of doctrine, deciding of controversies as the ground of faith and of our whole profession. And thus we refuse to use the translations, holding them much inferior to the originals. And this we profess and I desire that you take notice, and to give notice to as many as possible you can know that this is the true cause of our controversy, whatsoever you hear to the contrary. And assure yourselves in this if you think there is any truth in me. Now concerning the government, they hold that the presbytery consists of pastors, teachers, and ruling elders. We hold that it consists of pastors only. The treasury with which they suffer makes them unable to help those who are unable to communicate with them. They do not sanctify their alms with prayer. We separate our alms from the gifts of strangers which we thankfully receive. And we sanctify the whole action by prayer, before and after, as all the ordinances of God should be. Concerning these things, if God permits, you shall hear a great deal more about later.

    T H

2. LETTER OF THOMAS HELWYS AND CHURCH TO THE CONSISTORY OF THE UNITED MENNONITE CHURCH AT AMSTERDAM

The following undated letter was obviously written by Helwys after his break with Smyth. It is apparent that Helwys was not pleased with Smyth's congregation's attempt to become a part of the Waterlander Mennonite community. In both letters Helwys warns the Mennonites that Smyth and his followers are confused in their beliefs and vacillate from position to position. Therefore, they should not be accepted into their fellowship without a careful examination of their doctrine. This letter accompanied Helwys's 1610 Confession of Faith of the True English Church.

Grace and peace to you from God our Father and our Lord Jesus Christ. Dearest brothers, our bond of faith (in which we have come here) obliges us at the same time to advance by the same rule, and we avow to demonstrate this in all things towards you, this measure of knowledge and grace which God has given us or which will be given to us. Furthermore, we expect you to make the decision that you should make. Wherefore we have judged it to be in our interest (as statements were heard at the time from some of the very persons who used to be part of us, but now, due to their impenitence for their sin, are not part of our church of Christ and do not have the power of receiving and ejecting members, whereas the holy judgment of Christ and his Church have been granted to us; and from communion with everything holy they are justly excluded, and now try to join themselves to you) to make sure that you, may you be warned, do not receive such things by which you may be defiled, whereby it is best that you know little of corrupting the entire mass that may be corrupted.

And we beseech you in the fear of God, that you yourselves may wait and be judged innocent, and not be condemned as wicked by poor advice or reason, from which crime we implore you to abstain so that God may turn you towards Him in highest prayer.

But we are persuaded of better things from you, and assiduously expect that you will put your work into stubborn reforms rather than into corroboration of your sins, and, besides that, that you will invest your assistance in building, not destroying us.

And here we hope that you keep the word of God and the rule of your direction in all your things, the second profession of your faith, and we commend you to be followed by God and the very word of Grace which may be built upon and give you that which you may inherit by law and possess with all sanctified things. Fare ye well.

3. A VINDICATION OF THE POSITION ASSUMED BY THE ENGLISH BAPTISTS

This letter, dated 12 March 1610, is an attempt to explain to the Mennonites of Amsterdam that Helwys and his faction are no longer a part of the Smyth congregation. Helwys states that the sole reason for the schism is Smyth's embrace of successionism. Helwys makes no mention of Smyth's endeavors to merge with the Waterlanders. This letter, therefore, was written soon after their split.

Beloved in the Lord, your approved care, diligence and faithfulness in the advancement of God's holy truth, being the good experience (to god be given the glory) well known unto us, makes us desire that we can do no less than, with our best hopes, hope that through the grace of God (his word and spirit directing you) we will find you still. And therefore we are with much gladness and willingness stirred up to write to you, praying you, as you love the Lord and his truth, that you will take wise counsel and that from God's word how you will deal in this cause between us and those who are justly for their sins cast out from us. And the whole cause in question being succession (for so it is in deed and truth), consider, we beseech you how it is the Antichrist's chief hold, and that it is Jewish and ceremonial, an ordinance of the Old Testament, but not of the New. Furthermore, let it be well considered that this Succession, which is founded upon neither the times, person, nor place, cannot be proven by any man's conscience. So, wherein should we ground our faith? We cannot tell upon whom nor when nor where. We beseech you consider how we can in faith forsake the evident light of God's truth to walk in such darkness?

And this is our warrant from the word of truth. First, we will discuss baptism. John the Baptist being unbaptized preached the baptism of repentance and they that believed and confessed their sins he baptized. And whosoever will now be stirred up by the same spirit to preach the same word, and men thereby being converted, may, according to John's example, wash them with water and who can forbid it? And we pray, that we may speak freely herein, how dare any man or men challenge to themselves a preeminence herein, as though the spirit of God was only in their hearts and the word of God now only to be fetched at their mouths and the ordinances of God only to be had from their hands—unless they were apostles. Has the Lord restrained the spirit, his sword, and Ordinances as to make particular men lords over them or the keepers of them? God forbid! This is contrary to the liberty of the Gospel, which is free for all men at all times and in all places: yes so our Savior Christ does testify—where so ever, whosoever, and when so ever two or three are gathered together in his name there he is in the midst of them.[1] And thus much in all Christian love we do advertise to you, that this ground of truth is and will be maintained against all the world and that by the great adversaries of our faith in diverse other main points who will be glad to have such an advantage against you if you will publish or practice any things against this ground in the xviii chapter of Matthew. The professors of Christ will sustain much reproach by it; and therefore we earnestly entreat you, even by the love of Christ that is in you, that you will be well advised what you do in these things.

And now for that other question—that elders must ordain elders. If this is a true perpetual rule, then from whom does your eldership come? And if one church might once ordain then why not all churches always? O, that we might be thought worthy to be answered in these things or that the poor advice of so few, so simple and weak might prevail with you to cause you to look circumspectly to your ways in these things! The Lord that knows all hearts knows ours towards you. We desire that there may be found no manner of errors in you, but that you and we might walk uprightly in the ways of God, casting utterly away all the traditions of men, and this we are persuaded is your unfeigned desire also. Now fulfill our persuasion herein and try your standing in these points and do not respect how many hold these things with you but respect from what grounds of truth you hold them.

Thus we beseech the Lord to persuade your hearts that your hands may not be against his truth and against us, the Lord's unworthy witnesses. We take leave commending you to the gracious protection of the Almighty and to the blessed direction of this word and spirit, beseeching the Lord to do you according to the great love and kindness that you have shown to us. Grace and peace be with you. Amen. Your brethren in Christ.

"Amsterdam this 12th of March 1610."
Tho. Helwsys [sic]

---

[1] Matthew 18.20

William Piggott
Thos. Seamer
John Murton

"P.S.—We have written to you in our own tongue because we are not able
to express our minds in any other and seeing you have an interpreter"

4. Confession of Faith of the "True English Church"

Following the separation of the Smyth and Helwys congregations in 1610, Helwys sent a confession of faith, outlining his church's beliefs, to the Waterlander consistory of Amsterdam. Helwys's 1610 Confession of Faith of the True English Church is an attempt not only to delineate the teachings of his congregation but also to point out the errors in Smyth's congregation. Written in Latin, the nineteen-article document is a prototype of his 1611 A Declaration of Faith of English People Remaining in Amsterdam. In this confession, Helwys pays special attention to the body of Christ, the Sabbath, and the autonomy of each church.

Under thomas helwyss [*sic*] at amsterdam in nineteen articles presented to the waterlanders, with thanks for their already given information and recommending themselves for the future.

(Archives of the Amsterdam Mennonite Congregation, No. 1350. 3 pages folio).

Synopsis of the testaments of faith of the Anglican Church of the Belgian Church of Amsterdam:

1

That there are three who bear witness in the heavens,
The Father, the Son [the Word] and the Holy Spirit,
And these Three are one God, by whom all things on earth and in heaven
Have been created and preserved.

2

That this God created in His own image Man,
Who sinned and by whose disobedience all sinners were made;
But who will all be redeemed by the obedience
Of Jesus Christ.

3

That God imposes the necessity of sin on no one.

4

That there is no sin passed through generations, from our parents and their parents.

5

That God wants all men to be saved and to come to a knowledge of truth,
And does not want the death of the dying.

6

That Jesus Christ manifested himself in the plenitude of time,
In flesh, made from woman, conceived and born from her,
The Holy Spirit watching over her, the fruit of her womb,
The seed of Abraham, Isaac, and Jacob and the second flesh of David.
And this true man was circumcised, and baptized and prayed,
And was tempted, and was afraid, and was inexperienced in Jewish law,
And hungered, and thirsted, and was exhausted,
And ate, and drank, and rested his eyes in sleep,
And grew in stature and cognition,
And was crucified and died,
And rose from the grave, and ascended to heaven,
And exists as the only King, Priest and Prophet,
Omnipotent in the sky and on the earth given to him.
And he is one person, true God and true man.

7

That the redemption of Man before God can only consist of obedience to Christ and justice through faith, it is dead if it is understood as excluding works.

8

That Man has the possibility of redemption by the grace of God through Christ (by the Holy Spirit acting in Him through the prayers of the Evangelical), of recovering his senses, of believing, of returning to God and persevering to the end; and nevertheless in Man there exists the possibility of resisting the Holy Spirit and turning away from the Lord.

9

That the Church is the assemblage of the faithful, baptized in the name of the Father, the Son and the Holy Spirit, where at times their faith and sins are confessed; that the Church has the power of Christ, the function of prayer, baptism, and is the Sunday assemblage for administrating, selecting and removing its ministers, receiving and ejecting its members, as well as possessing the canons of Christ.

10

That baptism is the external sign of a remission of sins and mortification, and is a renovation of life and for that reason does not extend to children.

11

That the Sunday assemblage is an external sign of the communal spirit of Christ and of reciprocal faith and charity.

12

That one and every member of the congregation should know one another in order that they may offer each other all gifts of fraternal charity, in mind as well as in body, so that practicing Presbyterians should know the entire congregation, in which matter the Holy Spirit constitutes the Episcopacy.

13

That the Churches are ministries or Episcopacies to whom the power of praying, baptizing and administrating Sunday assemblage has been granted by the Church; or Deaconships, men and spouseless women who see to the needs of the poor and sick brothers on behalf of the Church.

14

That the Church should (as an example by the side of Christ of the Disciples and the first Churches) convene on the first day of the week for prayer, sermons, celebrating God, breaking bread, and offering all the gifts of communal spirit which pertain to religious education, mutual edification and preservation of the members of the faith of religion and piety in the Church;

and, for that reason, that the Church should take upon itself the ordinary labors of our vocations which can impede us.

15

That brothers impenitent in sin, after a third warning administered by the Church, are to be ejected by excommunication from the community of the Church

16

That the excommunicated are not fugitives with respect to civil society.

17

That adiaphora are not of the Church nor are imposed upon any member of the Church, but are a Christian liberty to be preserved in this manner.

18

That the dead return (and change instantaneously into the living), their bodies the same in substance but different in quality.

19

That all men after the Resurrection are to be compared by works before the tribunal of Christ, to be judged by virtue of their works, so that the pious may be redeemed and enjoy eternal life, and the impious condemned in Gehenna enduring eternal torture.

And through this we mentioned the mercy of God, and Christ, in a word His second, although we ourselves are unknowing, simple and ignorant, ready with all reverence and humility to be instructed by God through His instruments in the way in which Our Lord has called us forth for our greater information in truth, and by God we are thus blessed by the best means which have been provided by you in abundance to us, supplicating and invoking Our Lord Jesus Christ so that he may guide you and us in all truth through His Spirit.

Thanks be to you and peace from God Our Father and from Our Lord Jesus Christ.

5. A DECLARATION OF FAITH OF ENGLISH PEOPLE REMAINING AT AMSTERDAM IN HOLLAND

After breaking with John Smyth in 1610, Thomas Helwys wrote A Declaration of Faith of English People Remaining at Amsterdam in Holland in 1611. Recognized by the majority of Baptist scholars as the first true English Baptist confession of the faith, the purpose of A Declaration of Faith *was to differentiate the beliefs of Helwys's congregation from that of Smyth's. The confession contains twenty-seven articles. Despite their separation, the confession illustrates Smyth's and the Mennonites' influence on Helwys's doctrine in the denial of limited atonement and the ability for a Christian to fall from grace. A significant difference from Smyth and the Waterlander Mennonites, however, is discernable in Helwys's Calvinistic insistence on original sin and what was referred to in his time as "free will." Other differences include Helwys's denial of succession, which he referred to as Old Testament doctrine, his acceptance of some oaths if they did not compromise one's Christian life, the bearing of arms in self-defense, and the ability for a church member to participate in the government. The only original copy known to exist is in the York Minister Library.*

Before presenting his Declaration of Faith, *Helwys provided his readers with several pages of prolegomenon to explain the reasons for his actions. Many of these pages were not accessible, and the pages that are included are quoted from Walter Burgess's 1911 work* John Smyth the Se-Baptist, Thomas Helwys and the First Baptist Church in England with Fresh Light Upon the Pilgrim Fathers *(London: James Clarke & Co., 1911), 205–11.*

Our purpose—they say—being to publish our faith with its warrant. Let it not seem strange that our writing does not bear that proportion that writings usually do, in that we are simple men, destitute of art to order and bewtifie[1] our writings withal, which is one special cause that makes us with all unwillingness write, but we trust the truth of God will not be less regarded of its lovers because of our simplicity....

---

[1] To render beauteous or beautiful; to make fair or lovely; to adorn, embellish, decorate.

We hold—say they—that Adam being fallen and in him all mankind, the Lord being equally just and merciful has by Christ redeemed Adam and in him all mankind (not restored him), yet all actual transgressors must repent and believe and by faith in Jesus Christ be justified or else perish in their transgressions. Now hereby we hold...that the Lord creates no man to damnation but that men bring it upon themselves by their own sins (Ezekiel 18.20) and that therefore all infants as well as any dying before they have committed actual sin are redeemed by Christ, their estates and conditions being all one. We beseech all that fear God to weigh seriously what grievous cause of offense there is in this.

Secondly, we hold that men confessing their faith and sins are only to be baptized and that infants not being capable of the word of God nor of faith and repentance are also incapable of the baptism of repentance. And we pray the wise-hearted advisedly to consider to what end should infants be washed with that water, it is not commanded or practiced.... Why should men make a ceremonial ordinance of a substantial ordinance, for certainly if it must be administered upon infants it is only a ceremony or shadow, for the infants are not then truly mortified and sanctified, and, it may be, never will. You men of understanding, fearing God, look to your judgments and practices in these things, and in all things walk by the rule from the word of truth. What rule or warrant can be produced that you should take the word of God and holy ordinances of the New Testament, which are all real and substantial, and administer them to or upon a young infant and so make them of no effect? Why are you so carried away with the traditions of men? You have begun to go towards reformation, you have cast away the cross, you have put by sureties, but the father (if he will) may answer and take charge. Go on but one step further and let the party baptized answer and take charge of himself, and then there will be comfort in administering and comfort to whom it is administered. Let nothing be wanting that the Lord requires in his word lest you be reproved with the young man in the gospel. We trust the Lord in time will give you to see these things, and not so only, but both you and us to see further things of which we are ignorant (for none have attained to it), if we will but see our ignorance and in humility willingly seek knowledge....

We hold that God in his first promise concerning Christ was merciful to all mankind alike, all mankind being under one and the same transgression.

You do not hold this.

We hold, with the apostle (1 Timothy 2.6), that Christ gave himself as a ransom for all men and that he is the savior of all men, but especially of those that believe, (1 Timothy 4.10); and that "he is the reconciliation not only for the sins of the faithful but for the sins of the whole world" (1 John 2.2).

You hold otherwise.

Again, we hold that as our Savior Christ commanded, (Matthew 28.19)—Men must teach and baptize.

You hold they may baptize and not teach. Or thus:—We hold those that believe may be baptized (Acts 8.37).

You hold, they that do not believe.

Where is this so great cause of offense? Why do you displease yourselves so much at us, especially you who are called the "Separation" as to alienate your affections, estrange your speeches, and change your countenances as though we were monsters or at the least wild men?...

Whereas formerly it has been thought and reported that we held these things, being seduced by Mr. Smyth, we being now, through the great grace mercy and favor of God towards us (though through the cruel malice of Satan against us, and the spirit of error in him), divided from him, we pray a change of that judgment. We trust we will approve unto all men that we hold our faith of conscience to God from the ground of the scriptures. And yet let no man think that we could not willingly have undergone that reproach and far greater to have still enjoyed them. Yes, what would we not have endured or done? Would we not have lost all we had? Yes, would we not have plucked out our own eyes? Would we not have laid down our own lives? Does God not know this? Do men not know this? Does he not know it? Have we not neglected ourselves, our wives, our children, and all we had and respected him? And we confess we had good cause to do so in respect of those most excellent gifts and graces of God that then did abound in him. And all our love was too little for him and not worthy of him. And therefore let none think and let him not think but that our souls have and do mourn for the loss of such a man and if the Lord had taken him away from us we might have cried out (bear with our foolishness) the chariot and the horsemen from Israel. But he has forsaken the Lord's truth, he his fallen from grace. And though the fowler had spread his net and laid it, the net is broken and we are escaped blessed and praised be our God. Yet had he fallen alone our grief would have been full enough, but in that so many near and so dear to us are fallen with him that he has out of his own measure enlarged his own sin and our grief.

But our comfort is in the Lord alone and in his holy truth and if the Lord had not now held us up we would have surely fallen. And we trust we will be established, for God is able to make us stand. Do not let all these things distaste any man of the truth nor keep him back from any of it, but rather encourage men to it, in that the Lord has so mercifully preserved a poor remnant. And let men look to the cause and not to the accidents, and yet if they do look to the accidents they will see the like in the churches of God (the apostolic churches of primitive times) where men were baptized confessing their faith and their sins....

If you believe or profess anything because it is the judgment or exposition of Mr. Calvin, Mr. Beza, Mr. Perkins, or any other never so highly respected among you either dead or living, you hold the glorious gospel of Christ in respect of persons....

All this is not written to take away from the holy ordinance of teaching, but to inform the people of God that they must have their knowledge out of the word of God by the teaching of the spirit of God that they may be able to try the teaching of their teachers and not be tied to understand the scriptures as they expound them. But that they may be able to say with good consciences, we believe it not because you our teachers teach us thus, for we know you are also ignorant and subject to error, but we believe it because we know it to be the truth of God and that our own knowledge from the word of God by the testimony of the spirit of God. This knowledge everyone must have that will be saved....

We beseech you (teachers or preachers) therefore in the bowels of compassion, if there is any compassion or mercy in you do not be so confident in your former understandings, which in many things you have but by tradition and from the writings and practices of other men. Hear us with patience. We speak in the uprightness of our hearts to you, for the advancement of God's glory, the overthrow of your souls and of the souls of the poor people of God that depend on you too much; for whom we wish that we could shed rivers of tears because we know that they have many excellent things in them and that they have the zeal of God, but not according to knowledge. They are our natural countrymen and diverse of them are our loving kindred in the flesh, and some of our most worthy and dear friends to whom we owe the best fruits of our lives and the entire affections of our hearts. Therefore do not blame us is we use all the means that we can by the word of God to draw them to the sight of the sin of ignorance which does so overshadow all men for which sin all men must perish if they do not repent....

To read the scriptures acknowledging your ignorance and ask understanding of God. This is a way by which the most simple souls that seek the truth in sincerity may attain to the knowledge of salvation contained in the word of God....

A
Declaration of Faith
of
English People
Remaining at Amsterdam in Holland

Heb. 11.6
Without faith it is impossible to please God. Hebrews.11.

Romans 14.23
Whatsoever is not of faith is sin.

To All the Humble minded who love the truth in simplicity, Grace and peace.

A Declaration, Etc.
We Believe and Confess

1. There are THREE which bear record in heaven, the FATHER, the WORD, and the SPIRIT. These THREE are one GOD in all equality, 1 John 5.7; Philippians. 2.5, 6. By whom all things are created and preserved, in Heaven and in Earth. Geneses[SIC OR TYPO? PERIOD AFTER GENESES?]. 1.

2. That this GOD in the beginning created all things from nothing, Genesis. 1.1. and made man from the dust of the earth, Chapter 2.7, in his own image, Chapter 1.27, in righteousness and true Holiness. Ephesians 4.24. Yet tempted, fell by disobedience. Chap. 3.1–7. Through whose disobedience, all men sinned. Romans 5.12–19. His sin was imputed to all; and so death went over all men.

3. By the promised seed of the woman, JESUS CHRIST, and by his obedience, all are made righteous. Romans 5.19. All are made alive, 1 Corinthians 15.22. His righteousness being imputed to all.

4. That notwithstanding this, Men are by nature the Children of wrath, Ephesians 2.3. Born in iniquity and conceived in sin. Psalm 51.5. Wise to all evil, but they have no knowledge of good. Jeremiah 4.22. *The natural man does not perceive the things of the Spirit of God.* 1 Corinthians 2.14. And therefore man is not restored to his former estate, but that as man, in his estate of innocence, having in himself all disposition to good and no disposition to evil, yet being tempted might yield, or might resist: even so now being fallen, and having all disposition to evil, and no disposition or will to any good, yet GOD giving grace, man may receive grace, or may reject grace according to that saying; Deuteronomy 30.19. *"I call Heaven and Earth to record. This day against you, I have set before you life and death, blessing and cursing. Therefore chose life, so that both you and your seed may live"*

5. That before the Foundation of the World GOD Predestined that all who believe in him will be saved, Ephesians 1.4, 12; Mark 16.16. and all that do not believe will be damned. Mark 16.16. all of which he knew before. Romans 8.29. And this is the Election and reprobation spoken of in the Scriptures, concerning salvation, and condemnation, and that GOD has not Predestined men to be wicked, and so to be damned, but that men being wicked will be damned, for GOD would have all men saved, and come to the knowledge of the truth, 1 Timothy 2.4. and would have no man perish, but would have all men come to repentance. 2 Peter 3.9. and does not will the death of him that dies. Ezekiel 18.32. And therefore GOD is the author of no man's condemnation, according to the saying of the prophet. Hosea 13. Your destruction O Israel is of yourself, but your help is from me.

6. That man is justified only by the righteousness of CHRIST, apprehended by faith, Romans 3.28. Galatians 2.16. Yet, faith without works is dead. James 2.17.

7. Men may fall away from the grace of GOD, Hebrews 12.15. and from the truth, which they have received and acknowledged, Chapter 10.26. after they

have tasted of the heavenly gift, and were made partakers of the HOLY GHOST, and have tasted of the good word of GOD, and of the powers of the world to come. Chapter 6.4, 5. And after they have escaped from the filthiness of the World, may be tangled again therein and overcome. 2 Peter 2.20. A righteous man may forsake his righteousness and perish Ezekiel 18.24, 26. Therefore let no man presume to think that because he has, or once had grace, therefore he shall always have grace. But let all men have assurance, that if they continue to the end, they will be saved. Let no man then presume; but let all work out their salvation with fear and trembling.

8. That JESUS CHRIST, the Son of GOD is the second Person, or substance in the Trinity, in the Fullness of time was manifested in the Flesh, being the seed of David, and of the Israelites, according to the Flesh. Romans 1.3 and 8.5. the Son of Mary the Virgin, made of her substance, Galatians 4.4. By the power of the HOLY GHOST overshadowing her, Luke 1.35. and being thus true Man was like us in all things, sin only excepted. Hebrews 4.15. being one person in two distinct natures, TRUE GOD, and TRUE MAN.

9. JESUS CHRIST is the Mediator of the New Testament between GOD and Man, 1 Timothy 2.5, having all power in Heaven and in Earth given to him. Matthew 28.18. He is the only KING, Luke 1.33, PRIEST, Hebrews 7.24, and PROPHET, Acts 3.22. Off his church, he is also the only Law-giver, has in his Testament set down an absolute, and perfect rule of direction, for all persons, at all times, to be observed; Which no Prince, nor any whosoever, may add to, or diminish from, as they will avoid the fearful judgments denounced against them that will do so. Revelation 22.18, 19.

10. The church of CHRIST is a company of faithful people 1 Corinthians 1.2. Ephesians 1.1, separated from the world by the word and Spirit of GOD. 2 Corinthians 6.17. being knit to the LORD, and one to another, by Baptism. 1 Corinthians 12.13. Upon their own confession of the faith. Acts 8.37. and sins. Matthew 3.6.

11. That though in respect of CHRIST, the Church is one, Ephesians 4.4. yet it consists of diverse particular congregations, even so many as there will be in the World, every congregation, though they are but two or three, have CHRIST given to them, with all the means of their salvation. Matthew 18.20.

Romans 8.32. 1 Corinthians 3.22. They are the Body of CHRIST. 1 Corinthians 12.27. and a whole Church. 1 Corinthians 14.23. And therefore may, and should, when they come together, to Pray, Prophesy, break bread, and administer all the holy ordinances, although as yet they have no Officers, or that their Officers should be in Prison, sick, or by any other means hindered from the Church. 1 Peter 4.10 and 2.5.

12. As one congregation has CHRIST, so do all, 2 Corinthians 10.7. And that the Word of GOD does not come out from any one, neither to any one congregation in particular. 1 Corinthians 14.36. But to every particular Church, as it does to all the world. Colossians 1.5.6. And therefore no Church should challenge any prerogative over any other.

13. That every Church is to receive in all their members by Baptism upon the Confession of their faith and sins wrought by the preaching of the Gospel, according to the primitive Institution, Matthew 28.19. And practice, Acts 2.41. And therefore Churches constituted after any other manner, or of any other persons are not according to CHRIST'S Testament.

14. That Baptism or washing with Water, is the outward manifestation of dying to sin, and walking in newness of life. Romans 6.2, 3, 4. And therefore in no way appertains to infants.

15. The LORD'S Supper is the outward manifestation of the Spiritual communion between CHRIST and the faithful mutually. 1 Corinthians 10.16.17. They are to declare his death until he comes. 1 Corinthians 11.26.

16. That the members of every Church or Congregation should know one another so that they may perform all the duties of love one towards another both to soul and body. Matthew 18.15. 1 Thessalonians 5.14. 1 Corinthians 12.25. And especially the Elders should know the whole flock, of which the HOLY GHOST has made them overseers. Acts 20.28; 1 Peter 5.2, 3. And therefore a Church should not consist of such a multitude that they cannot have particular knowledge of one another.

17. That the Brethren who are impenitent in one sin after the admonishment of the Church are to be excluded from the communion of the Saints.

Matthew 18.17. 1 Corinthians 5.4, 13. Therefore the committing of sin does not cut off any from the Church, but it is the refusing to hear the Church to reformation.

18. Excommunicants in respect of civil society are not to be avoided, 2 Thessalonians 3.15. Matthew 18.17.

19. That every Church should (according to the example of CHRIST'S Disciples and primitive Churches) upon every first day of the week, being the LORD'S day, assemble together to pray, Prophesy, praise GOD, and break Bread, and perform all other parts of Spiritual communion for the worship of GOD, for their own mutual edification, and the preservation of true Religion, and piety in the church. John 20.19. Acts 2.42 and 20.7, 1 Corinthians 16.2. They should not labor in their callings according to the equity of the moral law, which CHRIST did not come to abolish, but to fulfill. Exodus 20.8, &c.

20. That the Officers of every Church or congregation are either Elders, who by their office do especially feed the flock concerning their souls, Acts 20.28, 1 Peter 5.2, 3. or Deacons, Men and Women, who by their office relieve the necessities of the poor and impotent brethren concerning their bodies, Acts 6.1–4.

21. That these Officers are to be chosen when there are persons qualified according to the rules in Christ's Testament, 1 Timothy 3.2–7. Titus 1.6–9. Acts 6.3.4. By Election and approbation of that Church or congregation whereof they are members, Acts 6.3.4 and 14.23, with Fasting, Prayer, and Laying on of hands, Acts 13.3 and 14.23. And as there is but one rule for Elders, therefore there is but one sort of Elders.

22. That the Officers of every Church or congregation are tied by Office only to that particular congregation where they are chosen, Acts 14.23 and 20.17. Titus 1.5. Therefore they cannot challenge by office any authority in any other congregation whatsoever except they would have an Apostleship.

23. That the scriptures of the Old and New Testament are written for our instruction, 2 Timothy 3.16 and that we should search them for they testify of

CHRIST, John 5.39. Therefore they are to be used with all reverence, as containing the Holy Word of GOD, which is our only direction in all things whatsoever.

24. The Magistracy is a Holy ordinance of GOD, that every soul should be subject to it not for fear only, but for conscience sake. Magistrates are the ministers of GOD for our wealth, they do not bear the sword for nought [sic]. They are the ministers of GOD to take vengeance on them that do evil, Romans 13. It is a fearful sin to speak evil of them that are in dignity, and to despise Government. 2 Peter 2.10. We should pay tribute, custom, and all other duties. We are to pray for them, for GOD would have them saved and come to the knowledge of his truth. 1 Timothy 2.1.4. And therefore they may be members of the Church of CHRIST, retaining their Magistracy, for no Holy Ordinance of GOD debars any from being a member of CHRIST'S Church. They bear the sword of GOD,—this sword in all Lawful administrations is to be defended and supported by the servants of GOD that are under their Government with their lives and all that they have according to the first Institution of that Holy Ordinance. And whosoever holds otherwise must hold, (if they understand themselves) that they are the ministers of the devil, and therefore not to be prayed for nor approved in any of their administrations,—seeing all things they do (as punishing offenders and defending their countries, state, and persons by the sword) is unlawful.

25. That it is Lawful in a just cause for the deciding of strife to take an oath by the Name of the Lord. Hebrews 6.16. 2 Corinthians 1.23. Philippians 1.8.

26. That the dead shall rise again, and the living being changed in a moment,—having the same bodies in substance though diverse in qualities. 1 Corinthians 15.52 and 38. Job 19.15–28. Luke 24.30.

27. That after the resurrection all men will appear before the judgment seat of CHRIST to be judged according to their works, that the Godly will enjoy Eternal life, the wicked being condemned will be tormented everlastingly in Hell. Matthew 25.46.

6. A Short and Plaine Proof by the Word and Works of God That God's Decree Is Not the Cause of Any of Man's Sins or Condemnation

Thomas Helwys published A Short and Plaine Proof *in Amsterdam on 2 June 1611. The book is dedicated to Lady Bowes, who was the benefactor of the Puritan Richard Bernard and in whose home Helwys had witnessed John Smyth debate Puritan divines. Helwys had hoped that Lady Bowes would take up his cause and promote his teaching as she had done with Bernard. Bowes, however, rejected Helwys's Arminian doctrine and remained firmly grounded in the Calvinism of the Puritans. A Short and Plaine Proof is a short treatise against high Calvinism, particular election, Pelagianistic free will, and fatalistic predestination. He builds the majority of his arguments on his concept that if Adam had chosen not to eat in the Garden of Eden, death would have never entered the world.*

Colossians 2.8
Beware unless any take you captive through philosophy and vain deceit.

Psalm 119.113
I hate vain intentions but the law I do love.

To the Lady Bowes, Grace and wisdom from above.
Worthy Lady, when I began to consider to whom I might best commend the care of this so great a cause, my heart could conceive of none so fit as you, and for two causes so that the third may not be wanting. The first is, because I know your faithful, unfeigned love of God and his truth and that you stand in many things according to knowledge. The second is because I know that there is no one in the land that has better means to procure a cause of religion that can be handled according to the judgment of the best. The third is the faithful, reverend, loving respect I bear to you and that from your own worthy deserts in the best things and in all your good to me. I pray and beseech you by the love of God that has been in you for a long time (that which I wish may abound in you more and more) that you will not fail my hopes which are: That you will either plainly see an upright, conscionable, sound answer

from the word of truth to this ground here propounded, or else give glory to God and receive it for the blessed truth of God. The ground is easily and plainly set down which is that God gave Adam free will and power in himself not to eat of the forbidden fruit and live or to eat and die. God could not in his eternal decree ordain or appoint him to life or death for then his free will would have been overthrown. If Adam had not eaten and sinned (which was of his own power) then death would not have entered. Therefore God did not decree that death should enter. Thus God's decree cannot be the cause of man's condemnation. I now pray you Lady, with all the love of my soul that you will entertain this great cause of God in your thoughts. Let it take up your best meditations so that good will be produced and you may continue to be an instrument to advance the gospel of Jesus Christ. You will be sure of a high recompense of reward at the hands of the most high in heaven, and your remembrance will be blessed among the saints upon the earth. Thus praising the Lord to bless you and to give you his Holy Spirit with a gracious, wise, understanding heart, to discern what is right in the things in which we may differ. I take leave with all the grace and faithful honesty of my heart (as I have cause) desiring your best good.

June 2, 1611 Tho: Helwys

Psalm 111.2
The works of the Lord are great and should be sought out by all them that love them.

To all that wait for salvation by Jesus Christ, Grace and Peace from God.

Whereas we formerly in a little treatise entitled A Declaration of Faith of the English People Remaining at Amsterdam have in the fifth article in short set down our faith of election and reprobation concerning salvation and condemnation. There has been some private opposition since we wrote it. The love of God and of his truth constrained[1] us to speak much more than we were able for the maintenance of this clear light of truth that God in his eternal decree has not appointed some particular men to be saved and some particular men to be condemned and so has redeemed but some. But that Christ is given as a ransom for all men, yes, even for the wicked who brings swift

---

[1] Throughout his writings, Helwys uses "constrained" to signify force.

damnation upon themselves, denying the Lord who bought them (2 Peter 2.1). It may and will seem strange that we of all others should take it in hand to deny man's cause of so deep a controversy and so deep a mystery. We answer that it concerns us as much as any. Therefore, though we are not able as we desire we were, yet because we should, we are ready to show ourselves willing to go forward with our best ability, since it is a deep mystery (as the whole truth of God is) we had more need to search into it that by the grace of God we might find the depth of it so far as God has revealed in his word, as all men should do. We pray to God that the reader will not be deceived by that old deceit of the mystery of iniquity, the man of sin, who tries to persuade us that it is too high a point and too deep a mystery for us to enter into. For by this deceit the mystery of iniquity has prevailed and to this day does prevail among thousands and ten thousands who do not search into any part of the scriptures at all, but rest on the faith of the church, and through it many (blessed by God) may be broken out of that depth of darkness. Yet they have not come to that clear fountain of light to know, profess, and practice what the Lord requires at their hands to search into and know his whole truth revealed in the scriptures. And for this mystery at hand let it be plain to you that you should know that a Savior is sent. Then you should also know to whom he is sent. If you think to satisfy yourself in that you know he has sent a Savior to you, you do not seek the glory of God, nor the good of your brother, and then the love of God is not in you. Therefore cast away all excuses and apply your heart with all careful diligence and faithful uprightness to search and find out the depth of this high point and mystery so that you may give glory to God for sending his son as Savior for all men.

We pray that the God of light makes this truth break forth and increase among you (blessed be his name) as it has done and does daily break forth and increase in these parts and among those who you account the best reformed churches. We require your loving patience to bear with our wants and your conscionable consideration of that which is spoken to you from the word of God and whose spirit be upon you. Amen.

Among the rest of the fearful works of the mystery of iniquity, which is not the least, (if not the greatest) is that men who are seduced by Satan and sin (through ignorance) are grown to such a height of evil that they call the Creator (who is spirit) to account. They will have a natural reason for all his works. In one particularity, they will try to reason as to how sin came and who or what was the first cause of it. The word of God cannot restrain these men. They will not be kept within its bounds. But they will enter into the secret counsels of God and by their vain philosophy measure God's thoughts by their own thoughts and his ways by their ways. They will find the cause of sin before the world was created. They find that the Almighty had decreed all things that come to pass, and that of him, and through him all things are. They will and do conclude most blasphemously that God had foredecreed that sin should come to pass. Not being content to stay here, they run on with a high hand and they see that sin enters by action and that God is the moving cause of all things "For in him we live, move, and have our being" (Acts 17.28). These men by their nature and from their carnal hearts that must and do necessarily conclude that God is the moving cause in the action of sin. Yet by the craft and subtlety of Satan who lies in wait to deceive them under a cullor,[2] they say that God is not the author of sin or the actor of sin. He is, however, the author and actor of every action and they then distinguish between the action and the sin. They will have God's providence in every action, although the action is sinful, but not God's providence in the sin of the action, as in Adam's eating of the forbidden fruit. He is the author, actor, and moving cause in the action of eating, but not in the sin. They do not see that the action was the sin.

They walk by their own imaginations and intents, deceiving, and being deceived, pretending not to lay sin upon God when (indeed in truth) they directly make God the author of sin. Our best thoughts of them are that they do it ignorantly. The Lord gives them hearts to repent and all of whose conversions will be the joy of our souls.

To deal in this high point and mystery of godliness who is more unfit than we to deal with these men. Of all we are the most unfit. Yet to show ourselves faithful with the talent that God has given us, we have through the grace of God, taken it in hand to do our best service for the Lord, hoping for his assistance and acceptance.

And first this much, we desire to demonstrate their reasons and conclusions to show where we differ from them and they digress from the truth.

---

[2] Under a pretext or pretenses, under the mask or alleged authority of someone or something

We confess that God has decreed all the good that comes to pass and that of him and through him are all good things. The Lord is the author, actor, and moving cause in every good action and his providence is in every good action. (But God has not decreed that any evil should come to pass, neither is he the author, actor, or moving cause to or in any action that is evil, neither is his providence over, or in, any action that is evil) (James 1.13–18). All these forealleged reasons and collections (and how many more we do not know) are brought to maintain that fair glorious deceiving opinion of particular election, and particular reprobation, and so of particular redemption which (to speak to the understanding of the simplest) is that God out of his eternal decree and will, especially chose and has appointed some particular men to be saved and they must be saved. Out of his own forepurpose and will, he has cast away some to be damned which would not and should not be saved, and they out of necessity must be damned and so he has particularly redeemed some, and left others to perish.

To conclude, and utterly destroy under one ground of truth these and all other distinctions, conclusions, and devices produced to maintain this opinion, we will (by the grace of God) take the most plain, easy, and short way that by the direction of his spirit our hearts can devise, which is a way most fitting our own capacities, and (we hope) will be most profitable for the upright-hearted reader.

To proceed to this we will first set down what is the cause of condemnation, and that is shown in these words of the apostle (Romans 5.12) "Death entered by sin" and (verse 18) "by this offense the fault came upon all men to condemnation." Therefore, it is proven that sin is the cause of condemnation, which all will grant that know God. All that fear God might grant here and search no further that if sin is the cause of condemnation then God's decree is not the cause. We know this will not give them satisfaction. But to give full satisfaction we must seek to find out who, or what, is the first cause of sin, and this must be found out by the first sin in the first sinner. In that passage (by the grace of God) we will labor, with all our poor endeavors, to show that the Almighty has cleared himself by his word and works. He did not decree, nor was the author, actor, nor moving cause, in, or of the first sin and then of no sin. After this is proven, we hope it will appear to all who do not either willingly or negligently shut their eyes, that no man is condemned because God has decreed him to condemnation. It is proven that man's sin is the cause of condemnation and the holy one was no cause of man's sin.

To prove that God did not decree, nor was the author, actor, or moving cause in, or of the action of sin, let us be guided by the holy word and works of God. Both of which will prove this so evidently as it shall never be gainsaid with any cullor or show of truth.

First then we come to a due consideration of God's work in the creation of Adam, which though all men know, yet it appears that few men do thoroughly consider.

"God created him a perfect man according to his own image and likeness" and (Genesis 1.26.27) "in righteousness and true holiness" (Ephesians 4.24). God gave him free power over his own will, as is proven when he said "You will eat freely of every tree in the garden but of the tree of knowledge of good and evil you will not eat from it. For when you eat of it, you will die the death" (Genesis 2.16–18). Thus God gave him free power over his own will and body to eat or not to eat. Yet the Lord restrained him of the forbidden fruit by his commandment and threatening judgment, but not by his omnipotent power.

This perfect holy work of God and this perfect holy word of God is not to be gainsaid. God did not decree that Adam should sin. Therefore God was no author, actor, or moving cause in, or of the action of sin.

We have no purpose (because we think we have no need) to stand upon any other ground for the whole trial of this great and weighty cause. We will strive to make it as plain as possible as we can, by God's assistance, that in these few words it will be proven that God did not decree that Adam should sin. Thus then we proceed.

It is proven here that God gave Adam free will and power to eat, or not to eat, and this all men do confess. How then can it be said, with any spiritual understanding, that God decreed he should sin? For God's forecouncil and decree must come to pass as the prophet David showed (Psalm 33.11) "The council of the Lord will stand forever and the thoughts of his heart are throughout all ages."

The Lord cannot be prevented by men or angels, but what in his eternal decree before all the beginnings he has decreed must come to pass. Therefore it could not be the decree of God that man should sin seeing that he gave him free will and power not to sin. If man had not sinned, as it was in his own free choice, then God's decree had been prevented, which cannot be. Therefore out of necessity it must be yielded that God did not decree that man should sin, unless any will deny that man did not have free will, and that is to speak directly and plainly against the holiness of God, which though men do, (in maintaining this opinion that God has appointed of his own will, some to condemnation) they do under a cullor.

Is it not then plain that everyone who has an eye may see that to give Adam free will not to sin and an eternal decree of God that man should sin can never stand together in the almighty, who is one and the same and "has no variableness and no shadow of turning" (James 2.17).[3] Can men make freedom and bondage in one and the same action, all in one man, and at the same time? How will men be able with any good conscience make things so contrary hang together?

Moreover, we see how the Lord by his commandment commanded Adam that he should not sin. Will anyone not withstanding this say that it was God's eternal purpose and will that Adam should sin? Does God command anything against his eternal will? In the fear of God let men take heed how they go about (by subtle arguments) to prove God contrary to himself, which they plainly do when they say it was the eternal will of God that man should sin and yet God commands that he should not sin.

Thus, it appears by the excellent, perfect, and holy work of God in man's creation that God has freed himself from decreeing that Adam should sin. Moreover, by his holy word he commanded him not to sin and lays death before his eyes as judgment if he sinned. What more could the Lord do for Adam than he has done? He made him a perfect man in righteousness and true holiness. He blessed him and gave him his commandment with power and ability in himself to keep it. And will men for all this say that God decreed he should sin and be condemned or that God was any actor, author, or moving cause in, or to his sin.

And if men will deny and say that they do not hold that God has decreed or was the author, actor, or moving cause in Adam's sin, then let them also deny their opinion that God has decreed any man especially to condemnation. For if God decreed man not to sin God then decreed no man to condemnation in that sin is the cause of condemnation. For if sin had not been, there would be no condemnation.

This is then the decree of God concerning condemnation: God decreed that if man sinned he should die the death, but God in no way decreed that man should sin. We have been shown this both by the word of God and by

---

[3] James 1.17

the works of God, which we wish men to hold to themselves, if they will not contradict it and not run after vain inventions.

We will now set down the fairest deceiving show that all the contrary-minded have for their opinion. They say that God has decreed and appointed some to condemnation and they must be condemned. This makes God's decree the cause of their condemnation. Let it always be remembered that it is proven by the word of God that sin is the cause of condemnation and not God's decree.

This is then the whole substance of what they say. God has decreed to forsake and leave those that he has appointed to condemnation to themselves. He has withheld his grace from them leaving them to sin and so to perish for their sin. We will not ask them to prove this because we know they cannot, but we will show by the mercy of God that it is an old conceived imagination and has no ground of truth.

In this their feigned ground, we must understand those who hold that God leaves and forsakes man first. And this we have utterly disproven already in that we have shown and proven that God did not leave Adam first, who was the first to fall under condemnation and by whose offense the fault came on all men to condemnation. This will seem strange (but let God have the glory) that God has decreed no man's condemnation no more than he decreed Adam's condemnation. For both God's mercy and his justice in all things and particularly concerning salvation and condemnation is one and the same for all mankind as it was to Adam after his fall. For God's decree was before the world was.

To make this plain and so by the grace of God to bring an end to all of it, let us consider with holy and upright hearts and with a willingness to be informed from the word of God, by the meanest earthen vessel, that God will stir up for the witnessing of any part of his truth. Let us, I say, consider the state of Adam after his fall.

First he was fallen and by him all mankind (Romans 5.12.18). He was under the condemnation of God which was pronounced against him (Genesis 2.17). Can any man devise or imagine that any of his posterity, who were still in his loins, and had not yet sinned, after the same manner of transgression, fell further under the condemnation of God than he? It could not be that any should. Although it may be that some may imagine that they did fall further, but it could not be that any should fall further under the decree of condemnation than he, in that he fell under the deepest judgment of God's decree of condemnation which God had declared by his word. We know no deeper decree of judgment than the decree of condemnation. It was under this that Adam fell and this judgment went over him and over all by his transgression.

When Adam fell, and of his own free will first forsook God, did God leave him? No! Such was the mercy of God (everlasting glory and praise be given to his name) as he would not yet leave Adam, but gave him freely of his own grace and deliverance the promised seed (Genesis 3.15). And, as the apostle has shown (Romans 5:12–21) that by Adam's sin the fault came upon all to condemnation. In the same chapter and verses he equally shows with equal like words and reasons, yes with self same words and reasons, that as by the offense of one (that was Adam) the fault came on all to condemnation. Even so by the justifying of the one (that is Christ Jesus) the benefit abounded towards all men to the justification of life. As sin reigned to death even so might grace also reign by righteousness unto eternal life by Jesus Christ. The Lord by the unspeakable evidence of his truth has provided to men's consciences, to those that will believe his word, that he did not leave and forsake Adam, nor for his sin was any of mankind placed under that condemnation which by Adam's offense went over all. But by grace in Christ has freed Adam and in him all mankind from the sin of Adam.

We want to make it even plainer that as Adam was freed from that sin, so all mankind was also freed. And as the promise of Christ, the promised seed, was made and sent to Adam, even so was he promised and sent to all the world for the same end which was to save him as the Lord has shown by his own words (if he may be believed and may the Lord give men hearts to believe him). (John 12.47) "I came not to judge the world but to save the world." And (John 3.17) "God did not send his son into the world that he should condemn the world, but that the world through him might be saved." Now let the godly hearted reader judge whether the promised seed Christ was not promised and sent to all the world for the same end which he was promised and sent to Adam, which was to save the world. And as he was promised and sent for the same end to all the world as to Adam, so he was also promised and sent under the same condition to all the world as he was promised and sent to Adam.

The condition was that Adam should believe and under the same condition Christ was promised and sent to the entire world as is shown by Christ's own words (John 12.46) "I come as a light unto the world that whosever believes in me should not abide in darkness." And (John 3.16) "God so loved the world that he has given his only begotten son that whosoever believes in him should not perish but have everlasting life." Now where is this conceived device that God should decree to leave and forsake some so that they might perish? Who has told men of such a decree that God has or does withhold his grace from anyone and leaves them to sin and to perish for their sins? Where have they found it out and learned it so perfectly? The word of God has not taught it to them and the works of God have not shown it to them to teach men that the Lord's decrees and ways are unequal either in his justice or in his mercy. They judge and teach that God has decreed (for Adam's sin) to forsake and leave some and to withhold his grace from them so that they will perish and has decreed to save some others by giving them grace. They would then make the Lord more just to some than to others in condemning and more merciful to some than others in saving and all for one and the same sin. The Lord complained of Israel because they say his ways are unequal (Ezekiel 18). The whole chapter through shows them how unjustly they accused him in using the Proverb "The fathers have eaten sour grapes and the children's teeth are set on edge."[4] They charge the Lord to punish the child for the father's fault. The Lord in that whole part of his word ever strives to prove his ways equal in punishing the soul that sins. "And that the son will not bear the iniquities of the father."[5] Furthermore, he says "that he has no desire that the wicked should die but that they should return and live."[6]

If the Lord had a great cause to complain of Israel for this so unjust accusation which they laid upon him, how much greater a cause he has to complain of all of you who charge him to have condemned all the souls that are condemned from the beginning of the world to the end for Adam's sin. You say that God decreed to leave them under Adam's sin and not to give them a Savior and to withhold his grace that they might perish making Adam's sin the cause of all their condemnation. Since it was this cause that the Lord left and forsook them, it is then the cause of their condemnation. Under this condemnation are brought so many thousands of millions of poor infants that die "before they have done good or evil" (Romans 9.11) as the Holy

---

[4] Ezekiel 18.2
[5] Ezekiel 18.20
[6] Ezekiel 18.23

Ghost testified to be their condition. And our Savior Christ (Luke 18.16) while commenting on the condition and quality of babes, said "Suffer the babes to come to me, for of such is the kingdom of heaven." And he says (Matthew 18.3) "Unless you are converted and become as little children you will not enter into the kingdom of heaven." (Verse 4) "Whosoever therefore will humble himself as this little child the same is the greatest in the kingdom of heaven." In all this it shows that the children of Christ's Kingdom must be of such humble quality and condition as infants. I hope none will deny, but all infants are of one quality and condition, even the infants of the Turks. Our Savior Christ speaks of all infants in a general way, and will men yet judge some infants condemned?

And of such infants the Lord showed his great compassion when he said to the Prophet Jonah (Jonah 4.11) "Should I not spare Nineveh that great city where there are six score thousand people that cannot discern between their right hand and left and also many cattle?" In this the Lord showed that they had not sinned and neither were they guilty of their father's sins. Will you yet charge the Lord to condemn so many infants and all for Adam's sin? Are your ways not unequal to say and teach men to hold and think of God in this way? Does the Lord not say that "the soul that sins shall die"?[7] Yet, men still dare to say that the souls of infants will die who have neither done good nor evil. Upon these rocks and many more your opinion of particular redemption casts you. You know so little of the mystery of iniquity in this point. And who does know the depth of the mystery of iniquity in this matter? Yet, give us leave to show you some high degrees of the mystery of iniquity in your opinion.

First, it makes God's decree the cause of sin and condemnation and this makes God the author and cause of condemnation and sin which is high blasphemy against the holy one. And by this all the sin in the world (that has been, is, and will be committed) is laid upon God, which is high iniquity and the sin of sins.

Secondly, it restrains the love of God to the world in giving his son for a Savior. Our Savior Christ said (John 3.16) "God so loved the world that he gave his only begotten son that whosoever believes in him should not perish but have eternal life." This opinion of particular redemption says that God did not so love the world, but he loved some few particular persons and he gave his son for them and only they will believe and be saved. The greatest part of

---

[7] Ezekiel 18.20

mankind God did not love, but he decreed that they will be damned and he has not given his son for them but has left them to perish. Thus denying the greatest part of the world to have any means of salvation and that there is no Savior for them. And so it was to no end that our Savior Christ commanded his disciples (Mark 16.15) to "Go into the entire world and preach the gospel to every creature." Whereas our Savior Christ says (Matthew 10.14.15) "Into whatever city or town you enter, if they do not receive you or hear your words, shake the dust off your feet. Truly it will be easier for those of the land of Sodom and Gomorrah on the Day of Judgment than for that city." And he also says (John 16.8)[8] that "when the comforter comes he will reprove the world of sin, because they did not believe in me." In all these places and throughout the entire gospel it is shown that the judgments will be increased on those that do not receive Christ or his word. And yet this lamentable opinion of particular redemption and reprobation says that they can have no part or portion in Christ. Their judgment is enlarged for not receiving Christ with whom they have nothing to do. Thus, they make Christ offer himself to those who would not have received him and of whom he has decreed will not receive him, nor believe in him and make the words of the Lord feigned and words of dissimulation. In Deuteronomy 5.29, where he wished concerning all Israel, "that there was such a heart in them to fear me and to keep all my commandments always so that it might go well with them and with their children forever." And also those words of our Savior Christ (Luke 13.34) where he speaks with such unfeigned earnestness, "O Jerusalem, Jerusalem which killed the Prophets and stoned those that were sent to you, how often would I have gathered your children together as the hen gathered her brood under her wings and you would not." What impiety is this to account these words as feigned? If any will say they do not account them feigned then they must be forced to confess that God decreed that all Israel and all their posterity had an uprightness of heart, feared him, and kept his commandments so that it might go well for them forever. So he did not decree that any of them or their posterity were condemned. If our Savior Christ's words were not feigned words then he would have gathered the children of Jerusalem together who would not be gathered and so he would have had them believe in him when they would not. And yet they that hold this fearful opinion hold that God would not have some men, yes, most men believe, but has decreed their

---

[8] John 16.8–9

condemnation. Though the Holy Ghost says (Acts 1.30)[9] that "now God admonishes all men everywhere to repent." Yet those of this opinion that hold God has decreed some to reprobation say he would not have all, but some to repent. If they would speak plainly and not halt between opinions, they must say that God would have some to be unbelievers, and wicked, and disobedient. That is the highest blasphemy. It is above "the wickedness of the fool that says there is no God."[10] It is to say there is a wicked God that has decreed wickedness.

Furthermore, this opinion does exceedingly diminish and lessen that great work of grace wrought by Christ's redemption. It makes Christ a particular, private redeemer for some private men. This highly dishonors Christ in that his great sufferings are not accomplished and are not sufficient to take away Adam's sin and so he has not utterly broken, but only bruised the serpent's head. This makes Adam's sin abound above the grace of God by Christ, overthrowing the word of God. (Romans 5.20) "Where sin abounded grace abounded much more," speaking of Adam's sin.

Moreover, this opinion that God has by his decree elected some particularly to salvation and that there neither is, nor ever was, nor can there ever be condemnation to them works presumptions in men. For if men can but once persuade themselves that God has elected them then they are secure. They do not need to work out their salvation with fear and trembling. God decreed them to be saved and they must be saved. They have no need to fear. If they increase and grow in knowledge and grace, it is well, but if they do not it is all one, for it is decreed that they must be saved and this causes slothful, careless, and negligent professions. These are those who will say "We have by your name prophesized, cast out devils and have done many great works" (Matthew 7.22). "We have eaten and drunk in your presence, and you have taught in our streets." But for all their presumption it will be said to them, "I do not know you, depart from me all you workers of iniquity" (Luke 13.26–27).

And this opinion that God has decreed and rejected some to be damned and that there neither is nor ever was salvation for them by Christ, (for they were as you say decreed to condemnation before Adam fell) makes some utterly despair in thinking there is no grace for them and God has decreed their

---

[9] Acts 17.30
[10] Psalm 53.1

destruction. It makes others desperately careless, holding that if God has decreed they will be saved, then they will be saved. If God has decreed that they will be damned, they will be damned and so in a desperate carelessness run headlong to destruction.

To conclude this opinion, the fall of man (in respect of the world which is held not to be redeemed) is all one with the fall of the devils. And the Gadarenes (Matthew 8.29) might have said with the devils, "Jesus son of God, what have you to do with us?" Here all the faith in preaching the gospel to the world is destroyed. For what faith can a man have to preach the gospel to such when (by this opinion) he has more cause to suspect that God has otherwise decreed them to condemnation? What faith can there be to preach the gospel when we do not know whether Christ belongs to them or not? All faith in praying one to another is overthrown. For how can a man of faith pray for any man when he cannot know whether God has decreed him to condemnation? He may be praying against God's decree. In deed and in truth holding this opinion that God has particularly by his decree decreed some particular men to condemnation and they cannot be but condemned does not allow man to have faith in his own salvation when he cannot have faith in another man's salvation that brings forth as good or better fruits than himself. How can he have faith in his own salvation, seeing that he may fall away as any other, and can know no more of God's decree concerning himself than concerning another? So a man's soul comes to distress between fear and doubting, as the holy prophet David's did many times. In Psalm 40 he says, "My sins have taken such a hold upon me that I am not able to look up. Yes, they are more in number than the hairs of my head. Therefore, my heart has failed me."[11] If you fall under such an estate and condition (which the godliest do) where will your comfort be, in the mercies of God? Why? You do not know whether God has decreed to show mercy on you or not. Will you say you know God has decreed to show mercy on all that believe as we say? But how do you know that God has decreed that you are one of those that will believe after seeing? You have much more cause to fear that you are not one of them. You may imagine yourself to be one, but this opinion that God has decreed some especially to be saved and some particularly to be condemned overthrows your faith utterly. You cannot know with certainty and then you cannot believe it. And let this be well observed by all that all have any

---

[11] Psalm 40.12

understanding or love of God's truth in that this opinion sets faith before knowledge. You must first believe that Christ is given as a Savior for you before you can know that he is a Savior for you. It cannot be that a man should believe what he does not know. (Romans 10.14) "How will they believe in him of whom they have not heard?" If a man must first know that God has sent his son as a Savior for him before he can believe it, which if men are not void of all religion they must then confess, then let thy mystery of iniquity of that man of sin himself devise (whose devising is this particular redemption) how any man can know by the word of God that Christ has given a Savior for him unless he can show his name set down in the word. Those that do not see this (let it not offend) are blind and cannot see at noon day. These are some of the fearful, proper fruits of this opinion, that God has decreed some particular men to salvation and they cannot be but saved, and some particular men to be damned and they must be damned and cannot be saved because God has decreed their condemnation. We have spoken enough of this.

Now we will endeavor to show what understanding God has given us in this high mystery and great work of redemption. If we can prove by plain evidence of scripture that Christ by his death and sufferings has redeemed all men, then this whole cause is at an end.

First we seek to prove that the first promise concerning Christ was general to all and this is evident. (Genesis 3.15) Where the promise of Christ is made of Adam and Eve, who were all mankind and in whom all mankind had sinned and for the taking away of the condemnation due for that sin, Christ was there promised and given, and not for a part. Which is further proven (1 John 2.2) "He is a reconciliation for our sins (speaking of all the faithful to whom he wrote) and not for our sins only, but also for the sins of the whole world." How is it possible that the Holy Ghost should speak more plainly to show that Jesus Christ is the reconciliation for the faithful which are not of the world and for the unfaithful which are the world? Moreover, (2 Corinthians 5.15) the apostle reasoned to prove that all were dead, in that one was dead for all. If one is dead for all then all were dead and he died for all. And (verse 19) "God was in Christ and reconciled the world to himself not imputing their sins unto them." (1 Timothy 2.5.9)[12] "There is one God and one mediator between God and man, the man Christ Jesus, who gave himself as a ransom for all men." Thus we see that Christ is a reconciliation for the

---

[12] 1 Timothy 2.5–6.

sins of the faithful and not only for some, but also for the sins of the whole world. All were dead, and he is dead for all. God in Christ reconciled the world to himself in that Jesus Christ gave himself as a ransom for all men. This might be sufficient to satisfy every upright heart, but yet let us see further.

The Holy Ghost by the apostle Peter (2 Peter 3.9) speaks to those mockers who said where is the promise of his coming? The Lord of that promise "is not slack (as some men count slackness) but is patient towards us. He would have no man perish, but would have all come to repentance." Here the apostle shows that it is not slackness in the Lord that he does not come to bring judgment, but it is his patience. The reason for the Lord's patience is that he would have no man perish but would have all come to repentance. Therefore, he has certainly redeemed all. (1 Timothy 2.4) "God wills that all men shall be saved and come to the acknowledgement of the truth." (Colossians 1.20) "Through the peace made by the blood of his cross he reconciled to himself and through himself all things both which are on the earth and which are in heaven."

Why should we need to allege any more grounds of scripture to prove that Christ has redeemed all men and that he would have no man perish? These will suffice. O that they might suffice what gladness should come to our souls to see men tractably minded to submit themselves to the word of truth which is so evident in this point. Far be it for any who fear God either from a froward[13] or negligent mind to pass by this great point, though many are led by so weak means, by reason of our exceeding weakness, we are not able to the full desire of our souls to discover the depth of the mystery of iniquity in the opinion of particular election and reprobation, and also of particular redemption. Nor are we able to show forth the great mystery of godliness in the true and holy understanding of universal or general redemption of all by Christ. Yet, let us in a few words show you how greatly the mercy of God is towards mankind and is advanced by Christ's redeeming of all.

When man had of his own free will (being tempted) yielded to the temptation of the serpent and neglected the commandment of his God and Creator, he brought condemnation upon himself and all mankind. God in his infinite mercy would not leave Adam and in him all mankind to perish under that condemnation. But, he sent a Savior to redeem Adam and all mankind

---

[13] Obstinate or stubborn

from that sin. In this he showed himself equally merciful and equally just to all, being no respecter of persons, by not pardoning Adam and giving him a Savior and condemning the greater part of Adam's posterity for his sin. But he gave his son as a Savior for all. If through unbelief they do not deprive themselves of him.

And what a comfortable doctrine is this to all when every poor soul may know that there is a grace and salvation for him in Christ. That Christ has shed his blood for him, that by believing in him he may be saved. God does not want him to die, but that he should repent and live. Thus all despair is taken away "For the grace of God that brings salvation to all men has appeared" (Titus 2.11). All careless presumption is cut off "for he that will not believe is damned" (Mark 16.16). (Revelation 2.25)[14] "Hold fast to that which you have already accepted until I come. For he who overcomes and keeps my works to the end, to him I will give power over nations." (Hebrews 3.14) "We are made partakers of Christ if we keep sure to the end that beginning of which we are beholden."

What gracious heart can ever disapprove of this understanding that Christ has redeemed all? It is most strange that men who fear God should be so full of indignation against it. Why should men think it is too much that Christ should be a Savior for all men, as well as for them, especially as it is so agreeable to the whole word of God and being a doctrine that does so magnify and set forth the mercy of God to all mankind in giving a Savior that to all who believe in him might be saved? This also advances the justice of God in condemning unbelievers seeing he has left them without excuse in that he has given them a Savior, in whom because they do not believe, they are justly condemned.

Much more might be said for the advancement of the great mystery of godliness in this point of Christ's general redeeming of all men, but we especially desire that the true ground of the cause may prevail with you. We do not doubt that comfort will follow abundantly. If we may have led you in anything from the first ground, we have utterly gone beside our purpose. The sum of all of what we have purposed to speak is this: That Adam having free will (which no man who knows God to be holy may deny) then God could not decree any man particularly to be saved or any man particularly to be condemned, for life and death, salvation and condemnation were in the free

---

[14] Revelation 2.25.26

choice of Adam and did not depend on God's decree, but upon Adam's own will. God gave Adam power in and over himself to choose life or death. He did not decree him either to life or death. For if God had decreed him either to life or death, then his free will had been taken away. For God's decree must come to pass. Therefore it is most easy and plain to understand that Adam, having free will and power, not to have eaten of the forbidden fruit could have lived forever. God did not decree he should die. Adam had free will and power in and over himself to eat of the forbidden fruit and die. God did not decree that Adam should live. This then is the decree of God (as he has declared in his word to Adam); obey and live, disobey and die. This is the law of works. Adam had free will and power in himself from God perfectly to keep the law. God did not decree (as we have shown) that he should obey or disobey, live or die. And let it be well observed that all the decrees of God concerning life or death to man and mankind were made with Adam. Therefore we produced him for all. We have shown that as Christ, the promised seed, was given and sent to Adam to be his Savior, for the same end he was given and sent to the entire world under the same condition, which was that he should believe in him. For if Adam had not believed, he must have been condemned and if the entire world had not believed, the world must have been condemned. And as Adam believing in the promised seed was (through the grace and mercy of God in Christ) saved, even so all the world who believe in the promised seed were through that grace and mercy of God in Christ also to be saved.

And as the Holy Ghost, (Romans 5.14–15) speaking of infants said "That death reigned also over those that have not sinned after the like manner of the transgression of Adam. Yet the grace of God and the gift by grace which is by one man, Christ Jesus, has abounded much more to them." Thus it is further confirmed that all infants are freed by the universal redemption of Christ from that condemnation, which you (by your opinion of particular redemption) would cast upon most of them, as has been shown before.

Whatever else has been spoken of and the word of God has forewarned us of, we earnestly beseech all that fear God, and love his truth, with the holiest thoughts of their hearts to consider all this. May the Lord give you all understanding hearts. Our hearts desire and our prayer to God for you all is that you might be saved and come to the acknowledgment of the truth.

It is a custom among men to conclude that free will must follow this understanding of universal redemption. If their meaning is free will in Christ and that we have free power and ability through Christ to work out our salvation and that through Christ we are made able to do every good work, such a free will we hold. But that man has any free will or power in himself to work his own salvation or choose life, we utterly deny having learned that of the apostle (Ephesians 2.8.9) "That by grace men are saved through faith and not of themselves, but it is the gift of God not of works lest any man should boast of himself." But this grace of God, (which is his mercy by Christ) God has given to all, but all do not receive it. (John 1.10.11) "He was in the world and the world did not know him. He came to his own, and his own did not receive him." And (Acts 13.46) Paul and Barnabas spoke boldly and said, "It was necessary that the word of God should first be spoken to you, but seeing that you put it from you and judge yourselves unworthy of ever-lasting life, lo we turn to the Gentiles." And Stephen said (Acts 7.51) "You are stiff-necked and of uncircumcised hearts and ears, you have always refused the Holy Ghost."

Thus Christ offers himself and man has the power and does reject Christ. He has put the word of God from him who resists the Holy Ghost and freely of his own will works his own condemnation. But he does not have the power at all to work out his own salvation. We say this only to clear ourselves from that gross and fearful error of free will from which the Lord in his great mercy has freed us.

The End

7. AN ADVERTISEMENT
OR ADMONITION
TO THE CONGREGATIONS,
WHICH MEN CALL THE NEW FRYELERS,
IN THE LOWECOUNTRIES,
WRITTEN IN DUTCH
AND PUBLISHED IN ENGLISH.

Thomas Helwys wrote An Advertisement or Admonition unto the Congregations, Which Men Call the New Fryelers, in the Lowe Countries, Written in Dutch and Published in English *in 1611 while living in Amsterdam. This work was written to repudiate several Waterlander doctrines that had been embraced by John Smyth. Though generally addressed to all the congregations of Fryelers in the Low Countries, it was particularly addressed to Hans de Ries. A Waterlander elder and theologian, De Ries was helping the Smyth congregation gain acceptance into the Waterlander community. In this work, Helwys points out what he perceives to be four major flaws in the Waterlander theology. First, Helwys rejects the Hoffmanite Christology of the Waterlanders, which maintained that Christ had celestial or angelic flesh. Helwys argued that Christ received his flesh from the Virgin Mary or he could not truly have been a man. Second, he insisted that the first day of the week be kept as the Sabbath or day of rest. Of all the arguments he makes in* An Advertisement, *the Sabbath argument receives the least treatment. Third, Helwys argued against the Waterlander doctrine of succession, which held that the ordinances can only be performed by someone who is a member of the true church. This argument was personal to Helwys as he and Smyth had baptized each other with no link to an established church. Helwys argued that a true church is where two or more are gathered in Christ's name. Therefore, he discerned no need to go to the Waterlanders for another baptism as if they were the only true church in Holland. Fourth, Helwys disagreed with the Waterlanders over the magistracy. The Waterlanders believed that if a person was involved with the government, he could not be a member of the truth church. Helwys argued that the magistracy was a holy ordinance and debarred no person from church membership.*

Wherein is handled four principal points of religion.

1. That Christ took his flesh from Mary having a true earthly, natural body.
2. That a Sabbath, or day of rest, is to be kept holy every first day of the week.
3. That there is neither succession nor privilege to persons in the holy things.
4. That the magistracy, being a holy ordinance of God, debars no one from being a part of the Church of Christ.

After these follow certain demands
Concerning God's decree of Salvation
And condemnation.

Prov. 9:8
Rebuke the wise and they will love you.

Prov.29:1
They that harden their neck when they are rebuked will suddenly be destroyed and cannot be cured.

Printed 1611

To Hans de Ries, Reynier Wybrantson
And the Congregations
Wherever they are.

Having long desired to publish our faith to this nation and in particular to those congregations where you are (as we have formerly done in our own nation) and also to make known the things in which you and we differ and are opposite. We have now, through the mercy of God, thus far brought our desires to pass, being only unsatisfied for our own insufficiency that we are no better able to manifest your errors to you. We have diverse causes from good grounds to do that which we have done. First because we are bound to discover the mystery of iniquity by all good means that we can, and in the cup that she has filled to us, to fill her to the double. Secondly that we might through the grace of God (if your minds are willing) be instruments of good unto you and also because you have been instruments of good in discovering the diverseness of our errors, which we acknowledge to the praise of God and with thankful hearts to you. We have done this by way of opposition and public reproof, which you have done by private instruction. For our defense, we answer you. You came publicly among us and advanced your error of succession and order from a proportion of the scriptures and have destroyed the faith of many who for sincere respect were willing to follow you. We have dealt diverse times with many of you privately, but you have lightly regarded our loving admonitions esteeming all of what we said as nothing. Some of you go on in your sin seeking to make these people one with you, who are justly cut of from God and his people for falling away from grace. We have written privately to your whole congregation to prevent you in that evil. We have written particularly to you H. de R. but all is in vain in that you esteem the truth we profess and us as vain. Thus, we are constrained[1] (for the deference of the truth of God we profess and that we may not seem to justify you in your evils, and to make it known to all that we have good cause to differ from you) to publish these things in the manner that we do. We desire that it may appear to all of your consciences that we have strong grounds for these things where we differ from you, though we are weak in the maintenance of them. If any will oppose part or all of what we have written here, we do desire this equal kindness that it may be set over into English for all our understandings, as we have caused this to be set over into Dutch for all your people. If there is cause for reply, we will by the assistance of God, answer it with all the ability that God will make us able. Farewell to you. Peace and love, with the faith from God, and from our Lord Jesus Christ, be with all of those that are in Christ Jesus. Amen.

Thomas Helwys

The holy writer John in the second chapter of Revelation, writing to the Church of Pergamum, one of the seven churches in Asia, writes (verse 14) "I have a few things against you because you have those among you who maintain the doctrine of Balaam." And (verse 15) "Even so you also have those among you that maintain the doctrine of the Nicolatians," which things I hate. And writing to the church of Thyatira (verse 20) he says "I have a few things against you that you suffer the woman Jezebel." In all such things, the holy

---

[1] Helwys often uses "constraint" in a manner to convey the Holy Spirit's desire to move him to action.

man of God teaches that this is a great impiety for any church of Christ to suffer any false teachers or any false doctrine that are maintained by any that are among them. If they do and do not repent, the Lord who hates wickedness as much now as ever, will certainly come against them with the same judgments that are threatened in his word. Therefore, we in love forewarn you who profess yourselves to be the church of Christ and yet have (hear us with patience) so many doctrines of devils that are professed and maintained among you, that you must repent or the Lord will rise up in wrath against you. We do not speak by reports, but of our own knowledge, having heard with our own ears and seen with our own eyes the things of which we by God's assistance will speak.

Of Christ's Flesh

The first matter we will speak to you is (in which your iniquity greatly abounds) that you have among you those that deny Christ took the flesh of Mary. Some of you hold that he brought it from heaven and some do not know from where he brought it. Both of these destroy the faith of Christ. The apostle (2 Peter 2.1) speaks of those who secretly bring in damnable heresies, even denying the Lord that has bought them.

We will now say something to the first that hold that he brought it from heaven so that the grossness of their black error may appear. The ground of scriptures testify that that which is from heaven is heavenly, therefore, if Christ brought his flesh from heaven then he must have had a heavenly body in that nothing can come from heaven but that which is heavenly. The apostle (1 Corinthians 15) says that the heavenly bodies are glorious, they are not weak, but are powerful, they are spiritual, and they are immortal. Now in that Christ's body was mortal and died, it was not a heavenly, glorious, spiritual, powerful body, but it was an earthly, natural weak body, and had the same infirmities that our bodies have (sin excepted). As shown (Hebrews 4.15) we do not have a high Priest that cannot be touched with the feeling of our infirmities, but in all things was tempted in like sort, yet without sin. Also (Chapter 5.2) we see that he is sufficiently able to have compassion on those that are ignorant and that are out of the way because he is also compassed with infirmity. And his infirmities appear in that he was hungry (Matthew 4.2). He was weary (John 4.6). He was troubled and his soul was in great heaviness (Mark 14.33.34). He confessed his flesh was weak (Matthew 26.41). All of these infirmities or any infirmity could not come from heaven for in heaven there are no imperfections or imperfect things. We demand can heavenly bodies be weary, can they be hungry, can they be troubled, and can their souls be in heaviness, or are they weak and mortal? If so there is misery in heaven which cannot be. Therefore, it is concluded, never to be denied by any that have grace, that Christ did not bring his flesh from heaven, in that there was infirmity and weakness (which is imperfection) in his flesh. Here (having so fit an occasion) let us speak a word to those in whose sin death and hell has consented to say that God was turned into or made flesh. How is it that God could be made of weak flesh which was full of infirmities, as has been shown by the scriptures of Christ's flesh? Some of these say that all that Christ suffered and did in the flesh was but in show. It will be given to them according to their faith. If they do not repent they will have a Savior but in show. Although the willful perverse stiffness of these men promise little hope, yet let us say, what by the grace of God we are in any way able, if we might by our best endeavors stop men from running so violently to condemnation in this accursed judgment that they hold, which says all the Christ suffered and did hear upon earth was but in show.

For this purpose we will commend the Godly disposed reader to the xv chapter of the first letter to the Corinthians where the apostle declares to them again the gospel which he had formerly preached and which they had received and in which they were saved, unless they had believed in vain.[2] He showed that first of all he had delivered to them that Christ died for their sins, and that he was buried, and rose again on the third day. "So we preach and so you have believed"[3] said the apostle, not withstanding all this, some of the Corinthians were fallen to say that there was no resurrection of the dead, with whom the apostle (because he knew that they had received and believed that Christ died and was raised again) reasoned as follows. If there is no resurrection of the dead then Christ has not risen. If Christ has not risen then our preaching is in vain, and your faith is also in vain. We are also found as false witnesses of God for we have testified of God that he has raised up Christ, whom he has not raised up, if the dead are not raised. For if the dead are not raised then Christ is not raised, and if Christ is not raised your faith is in vain and you are still in your sins. Those that are asleep in Christ have perished. If only in this life we have hope in Christ "we are of all men most

---

[2] 1 Corinthians 15.2
[3] 1 Corinthians 15.11

miserable."[4] The apostle by these undeniable arguments and reasons proved Christ's death and resurrection. First, that Christ died (Verse 3). And for proof of that he takes the testimony of the scriptures. By the same proof and warrant of the scriptures he proves that he was buried and rose again. For further confirmation of his being raised from the dead the apostle produced the witness and testimony of Cephas who saw him, and of the twelve, and he was seen by more than five hundred brethren at once, and after that by James, then all of the apostles, and last of all himself. He added for further proof their preaching. So we preached, said the apostle, and appealed to their own consciences for this truth of Christ's death and resurrection in saying to them so you have believed.[5]

Here the apostle, that they might be brought to the sight of the depth of the iniquity of this their error, declares to them what must follow if there is no resurrection, Christ cannot be raised from the dead. And first concerning us the apostle says[6] (you say there is no resurrection and so Christ has not risen from the dead) this follows, you make all our preaching vain, and we are preachers of vain things. You also make us false witnesses of God for we have testified that God raised Christ from the dead and this reproach you cast upon us. And so you bring this evil upon yourselves in saying there is no resurrection and that Christ has not been raised from the dead. Your own faith is then in vain. You have a vain faith and you are yet in your sins. All your sins rest on you. Furthermore by this your saying you bring this judgment upon all that are dead in Christ so that they have all perished and all the faithful in Christ that are living, you make them "of all men the most miserable."[7] You have laid before them all evil in saying that there is no resurrection. He concluded, "But now Christ has risen from the dead, and was made the first fruits of those that sleep."[8]

To turn all this evil that the apostle has here shown to the Corinthians (that said there was nor resurrection where by it followed that Christ was not risen) upon all those that say Christ died but in show, and so did not die at all in truth, it is most plain that all this evil comes upon their heads. In saying

---

[4] 1 Corinthians 15.19
[5] 1 Corinthians 15.1–11
[6] 1 Corinthians 15.14–19
[7] 1 Corinthians 15.19
[8] 1 Corinthians 15.20

that Christ died but in show, they must say he did rise again but in show and so there was no resurrection in truth. And here they (most miserable men that they all are) make the apostles preaching most vain, for then they are preachers of vanities and shadows if Christ is dead but in show. So they make them false witnesses of God for they have testified that God raised Christ from the dead whom he has not raised. If so it is that he had not died. Then the faith of the faithful is in vain and their sins are yet on them. If Christ is not dead and risen again then all those that are asleep in Christ have perished and all the faithful who are living are of all men most miserable. But we conclude against all those that say Christ died but in show with the same words that the apostle concludes against the Corinthians. "But now Christ died, and is risen again from the dead, and was made the first fruits of those that sleep."[9] Therefore, the apostle's preaching is not in vain and neither are they false witnesses of God. The faith of the faithful is not in vain and neither is any part of their sins abiding or remaining yet on them. The faithful that are asleep have not perished and neither are the faithful in this life of all men most miserable. But all this is in their portion who say Christ died but in show (which is not at all), their preaching is in vain and they are preachers of the most vain things. They are false witnesses of God in that they testify that Christ did not die, and so God did not raise him up from the dead. Their faith is vain and they are still in their sins, and all who are dead in their false faith have perished and thus their estates are most miserable.

What is sufficient to speak against this wicked blasphemous opinion of theirs which says Christ's sufferings and death were but in show? These are those that in the highest degree deny that Christ came in the flesh. For if they did confess and believe that Christ came in the flesh then they must be forced to confess that he died, for all flesh must die and be changed, as is shown (1 Peter 1.24) "All flesh is grass, and all its glory is as the flowers of the field," and all the glory of man is as the flower of grass which withers and falls away. All the disciples of Christ never made question of his death, for they saw and were sure he was dead and therefore they began to doubt of his resurrection through infidelity of which there had been no cullor[10] for them to doubt if they had been of these men's opinions that he died but in show.

---

[9] 1 Corinthians 15.20
[10] Under a pretext, pretense, or mask of something with alleged authority

All that is spoken of the resurrection of the dead is spoken of Christ. It would not be amiss to further consider what the Holy Ghost by the apostle showed (1 Corinthians 15) concerning the resurrection of the dead for by his resurrection his death will appear. This is what the apostle set down here concerning Christ's death and resurrection and concerning his natural and earthly body and his spiritual and heavenly body. The apostle shows first of all (verse 3) that Christ died. (Verse 20) That Christ was raised from the dead and (verse 35) there is a question concerning how the dead are raised up. To that question the apostle answered that he was speaking of the dead bodies in general, and of Christ's dead body in particular (whom he had shown in verse 20, to be the first fruits of those that sleep). That which you sow (says the apostle) is not quickened unless it dies teaching as he had shown before that Christ's body did die, and all bodies must die first, or else cannot be quickened, that is raised from the dead (verse 36). Then it is most evidently proven from the scripture that Christ was raised from the dead. It is evidently proven here that he must and he did first die for (the apostle says) it could not be quickened unless it first dies. The apostle having answered that part of the question in showing how the dead are raised then proceeded to the second question, which is, with what bodies do they come forth? To this question he answered (verses 37.38) "You do not sow what that body will be, but God gives it a body at his pleasure, to every seed his own body." Here the apostle shows that Christ's body and all bodies that are of Christ (for those bodies are the only ones he speaks of (verse 23) are not raised in the resurrection with those bare bodies that are sown, but God gives a body at his pleasure even to every seed its own body, that is to the seed of man, all one body (to those which are raised in Christ) for there is but one flesh of men. The apostle having here first shown that the same bare body that is sown will not be raised up again, he then shows in what manner of body it will be in the resurrection, and how it will differ from that which was sown and died. (Verse 40) The apostle says, "There are heavenly bodies, and earthly bodies," and (verse 49) "we will bear the image of the heavenly." Here is set down with what manner of bodies the dead are raised and Christ, being the first fruits of the dead, was raised with such a body. He then follows with how the heavenly body and the earthly body do differ in glory. The earthly body is corrupt, dishonorable, weak, natural, and mortal. The heavenly body is incorrupt, glorious, strong, spiritual, and immortal. We have the image of the earthly body from the first Adam, which was made (says the apostle) a living soul that is natural and earthly. Those that are of Christ will have the image of the heavenly body. From the last Adam a quickening spirit, that is a spiritual, heavenly body which is the image of Christ's glorious body after his resurrection. Thus we see the whole drift and intent of the apostle in all this scripture is to prove the resurrection of the dead, and how the dead rise, and with what manner of body. All of this is by Christ's death and resurrection because he died and rose again in the same order (verse 23) with the same body (verse 49) and all who are of Christ will rise again, proving that Christ had a natural, earthly, and mortal body, sown in corruption, in dishonor, and weakness, raised in incorruption, in glory, in power, a spiritual, heavenly, and immortal body. What can be more plainly set down if men that have eyes would see and would not wink with their eyes? Why will men pervert the scriptures to their own destruction? They take a piece of a sentence from here and a piece of a sentence from there and never look to the scope and sense. According to our small talent, we will show the error of those that have fallen to so deep a destruction as to say God was turned into flesh and so his death and all his sufferings were but a show and stay those (if by the grace of God it may be) that have not fallen so far.

And now we speak to those that do not know from where Christ received his flesh. They see that is proven that it could not have been from heaven for then there could not possibly have been any infirmities in it. They see further, or through the grace of God might see, that Christ had a natural, earthly, mortal body, and that there is but one flesh of men. Will they still remain ignorant and doubting as to where Christ received his flesh? Then they still remain in sin. Let them, therefore, leave their doubting (which is through their ignorance) if they look for salvation by Christ. Let them know and believe from God's scriptures that Christ is of the seed of David and of the Israelites according to the flesh (Romans 2.3[11]; 9.5). He is the son of Mary, the virgin and made of her substance (Galatians 4.4). And so this does agree with the first promise made concerning Christ (Genesis 3.15) where it is spoken by God that the seed of the woman will break the serpent's head without which knowledge and faith no man will ever be saved. There is no salvation but by Christ, the promised seed of the woman. Those, therefore, among you that will not know and believe that Christ is the seed of the woman, conceived in her womb, by the power of the most high

---

[11] Romans 1.3

overshadowing her, will never be saved by Christ the promised seed of the woman. This is then your great sin that many among you suffer and maintain a false faith concerning where Christ had his flesh. You approve and allow some that hold and maintain no faith concerning where Christ received his flesh, and so you approve and maintain them in their sin. Whatsoever any hold or maintain that is not of faith is sin. To be ignorant of any part of what the scriptures have manifested is sin and to determine to remain ignorant and so to continue to the end is death, for without repentance any one sin is death as the apostle James showed (James 2.10) "Whosoever will keep the whole law and yet fails in one point is guilty of all." Do not deceive simple souls by nourishing them in their sin, which you do in saying it is not needful to salvation to know where Christ received his flesh as though there were any part of the law or gospel not needful for salvation. And if there is any part of the law not needful then Christ did not need to come to fulfill the whole law, which he did as he said in Matthew 5.17. And if there is any part of the gospel of salvation (which Christ has purchased with his blood (Ephesians 1.13.14)[12] not needful to salvation then Christ purchased more than is needful. In the fear of God, do not walk by your own inventions, leading and suffering simple souls to walk in the ways of death and condemnation.

Of the Day of Rest

Our second complaint is that many among you (and how far you are all polluted we do not know but have great cause to fear) do not profess and practice keeping the seventh day a day of rest and holy to the Lord, abolishing the law which was given on the mountain out of the midst of the fire on the day of the assembly, and which was written in the Tables with the finger of God, as shown (Exodus 20.8–11; Deuteronomy 9.10) all of which was the whole law, as our Savior Christ says (Matthew 5.17.18) "I have not come to destroy the law, but to fulfill it. For truly I say to you until heaven and earth perish not one jot or tittle of the law will escape until all things are fulfilled." Not withstanding all that was spoken by God the Father, and Jesus Christ his Son, many of you with a high hand raise out and destroy one of these Ten Commandments written by the finger of God (Exodus 34.28) and you will have but nine. You have rent asunder the law of God and cast away what is not pleasing to you. You do not hold the examples of the disciples of Christ as a

---

[12] Ephesians 2.13

sufficient rule of direction for you as has been shown (Acts 20.7; 1 Corinthians 16.1.2) that on the first day of the week they came together to break bread. On every first day of the week when they came together Paul ordered in the churches that everyone should lay aside for the necessity of the saints that there might be no gathering when he came.

How will you be able to stand before the Lord? He has established a law "which it is easier that heaven and earth should pass away, than one tittle of the law should fall" (Luke 16.17). Are you now able to show (which God forbid that any should be so wicked as to enterprise) that all these words were not spoken and written by God himself? If "Remember the Sabbath day to keep it holy,"[13] is no part, jot, nor tittle of this law then you have some cullor for the evil you practice and profess. Does any mouth of blasphemy dare speak it or can any hand of blasphemy write it? We hope not. Why not then give glory to God, and repent of your sin, and pray to the Lord that if it is possible the thoughts of your hearts, the blasphemy of your mouths, and the wickedness of your hands may be forgiven you. Do not sin as you do against God in turning your feet away from the Sabbath of the Lord and doing your own wills on his holy day in which you also do wrong to man, and beast, to whom the Lord has in mercy given a special day of rest. But yet we will further show you that which you will never be able to answer. Our Savior Christ (Matthew 24.20) speaking of the destruction of Jerusalem (which was to come to pass, and did, long after his death) said "Pray that your flight will not be in the winter, nor on the Sabbath day." He shows undeniably that there should still remain a special day of rest for the people of God to worship him on. Christ bids them to pray that their flight will not be on the Sabbath so that they will not be forced to flee when they should rest and worship God. And if our Savior Christ had meant that his disciples should have been of your judgment, it would have been all one and it would not matter on what day their flight would had been. God give you grace to see your great error that you may not still be hateful to God, and men, and beasts. We have spoken enough of this unless further occasion is offered. We omit showing you all the confusion you bring into the church if there will is no certain day when the disciples should come together to edify one another, to break bread, to pray, and to gather for the saints. If your rule is true (which is as false as God is true) they may choose whether they will come at all, unless you have authority

---

[13] Exodus 20.8

to make a law to bind them, which we are sure you do not have from God. Even so you confound all due proceeding in the rule of admonition by the church if there is no certain day when the church is bound to meet. But we will pass by this hoping you will fall under the former ground and then you will easily see (through the grace of God) all these things and many more which accompany your error that utterly destroys all godliness, religion, and the holy communion of saints. Therefore, repent and forsake your error, for if you do this you destroy the laws of God and there can be no religion of God in you.

Of Succession
Thirdly you have among you (and your leaders are guilty as well) those that maintain a succession and that from your own beginnings you will have all people, and nations, and tongues come to you, and your beginnings for the ordinances of Christ. No people may have power to administer in the holy things unless they first join themselves to you and be one with you and receive power and all the holy things from you. Here you with the man of sin exalt yourselves above all that are called of God and you take to yourselves that preferment under the gospel that God gave only to the Jews under the law. Their preferment says the apostle (Romans 3.1.2) "was much in every manner of way." Chiefly, because to them were credited and committed the oracles of God. And will you thus (as you do) take this honor to yourselves and set up your preferment as much in every manner of way? Are the oracles of God committed to you of credit to be kept? Show by what prophesy [sic] of scripture you challenge these things if you can. On this ground (which proceeds from great pride and arrogance, but yet of ignorance we hope) you account yourselves Jerusalem and the kingdom of heaven. Indeed, (we confess) if you could prove yourselves Jerusalem and the kingdom of heaven then all are bound to come to you and all the holy things must proceed from you. The Holy Ghost in the scriptures speaks of Jerusalem leading us from the earthly Jerusalem to the heavenly Jerusalem, which you call yourselves. Then people are called to worship you and fall down before you, as we will prove some do. By drawing them to it, it is to your shame in suffering and to their everlasting destruction in so doing and suffering themselves to be so drawn. Thus, the Holy Ghost speaks of the heavenly Jerusalem in the scriptures (Isaiah 2.3) "And many people will say come and let us go up to the mountain of the Lord to the house of the God of Jacob, and he will teach us his ways, and we will

walk in his path, for the law will go forth from Zion, and the word of the Lord from Jerusalem." In like manner the prophet David speaks (Psalm 110.2) "The Lord will send the rod of his power out of Zion." Are these prophecies meant of you? If the law and the word of the Lord come forth of and from you, then are you this Zion? Are you this Jerusalem? The apostle Paul taught the Corinthians not to think so of themselves when he said (1 Corinthians 14.36) "Did the word of the Lord come out from you? Did it come to you only?" Be taught of the apostle and be humbled, and humble yourselves you high minded people (we speak only to those that are thus minded) and confess your sin and repent.

If this will not yet suffice, let us show you further by the word of truth that you can in no spiritual sense be called Jerusalem. (Psalm 122.3.4) The holy prophet says "Jerusalem is built as a city that is compacted together in itself, to this city even the tribes of the Lord go up to give their testimony to Israel and to praise the name of the Lord." And (Psalm 125.1) "Mount Zion cannot be removed, but remains forever." Are you this city so compact together in yourselves? If you are the city, then you are none of the tribes, but the tribes must come to you. Might you not, by the grace of God, see your great ignorance in that you cannot discern between the city and the people, but you will be the city. We demand of you, who will be the people? Are you Mount Zion which cannot be removed? Will you remain forever? If you can promise this of yourselves, you go beyond all the excellent churches that are spoken of in the New Testament. There remains no mention of these churches at this day to be seen but only that the scriptures testify that such churches there were, but not one of them have remained to this day. Therefore, none of them were Mount Zion. Will you lift up your horn on high and be more than all of them? This is the "foolishness of folly."[14] Bear with our rudeness. The Lord knows we seek his glory and your good, although our infirmities may too often appear. It is your turning from these evils that we desire for God's glory and the salvation of your souls. Therefore, we will, through God's grace, endeavor yet further to show you your error in this point.

The Prophet in Psalm 48.2.3 speaks this way of Mount Zion. It is northward in situation and "It is the joy of the whole earth and the city of the great king." In this palace of God it is known as a refuge and (verse 8) "God will establish it forever, Selah." To add to this glorious description so at large

---

[14] Proverbs 14.24

set down by John, (Revelation 21.10.14) where he "saw that great city that holy Jerusalem descending out of heaven from God whose wall had twelve foundations and on them the names of the twelve apostles of the Lamb." "This city has no need of either the sun or of the moon to shine in it for the glory of God lights it, and the Lamb is the light of it" (verse 23). "And the nations that are saved will walk in the light of it" (verse 24). "And the nation and the kingdom that will not serve it will perish and these nations will utterly be destroyed" (Isaiah 60.12). Now, see yourselves how unlike you are to this city. Are you the joy of the whole earth? Sorrow is the joy that we the poor wine less of Christ have in you for our part, as you will further hear. Do the people that are saved walk in your light and will the nation, and kingdom that will not serve you perish? God forbid. Be content and glad to have this city as your joy, and to be citizens of this city, and to walk in the light of it, and to serve it or else you will perish and be destroyed. But this city cannot perish nor be destroyed, but you may be, and therefore you are not this Jerusalem. The world knows that you are not the earthly Jerusalem. Do not wink with your eyes but see and do not stop up your ears but hear how the word of God convinces you in this your error.

We now beseech the upright hearted among you to be willing to hear what the apostle Paul shows Jerusalem to be and not to follow your own inventions. The apostle to the Galatians (4.22–26) showed that Abraham had two sons, and two wives, one son by a servant, and one by a free woman. He who was born of the servant was born after the flesh. He that was of the free women was born by promise. By these things another thing is meant (says the apostle) for these mothers are the two testaments. The one is Hagar or Sinai that is a mountain in Arabia and it answers to Jerusalem which is now in bondage with her children. But the Jerusalem which is above is free and is the mother of us all. Thus, the apostle as plainly as possible (for the understanding of all) teaches that Hagar, the bond woman, signifies the old Jerusalem which is the Old Testament, with all the carnal ordinances of it. And by Sarah, the free woman, is meant the new Jerusalem, the New Testament, with all the spiritual ordinances of it. And this spiritual mother, Sarah, the free woman, the new Jerusalem, the New Testament, is mother of all that are born after the spirit. They are her children, as the apostles said of himself and others (verse 31). Now will you be this Jerusalem, the mother of all the faithful? Will it not suffice you to be children, but must you be the mother of all? Do you not see how you agree with the antichrist of Rome that claims to be the mother of all churches? How far contrary is this to all the rest of your profession, who profess such humbleness of mind in all things. Yet, you seek this height to advance yourselves above the poor servants of God. Through his grace and mercy by the power of his word and spirit you are born children of the free woman. Though weak children you are born as free as any. What great evil is this (in so many of you as would) to seek to bring us in bondage to you when you cannot (by any warrant of God's word) have any more freedom in any holy thing or to any holy thing than we if we are the children of one mother, for then we are brethren. Thus, do not sin against God, and do not wrong us by seeking to tread us under your feet which you do in advancing yourselves over us to bring us into subjection, who are born as free as you.

The word of God makes it clear that neither you nor any church or congregation or people are Jerusalem. It will easily follow that you or any church, congregation, or people are not the kingdom of heaven. This is because the heavenly Jerusalem and the kingdom of heaven are all one, as all that have any understanding agree and know. Therefore, it will not be needed to use many more words in this cause. Let us in short, therefore, show what the scriptures speak of the kingdom of heaven. Our Savior Christ (Luke 4.34)[15] says, "Surely I must also preach the kingdom of God to other cities for therefore I am sent." This kingdom cannot in any understanding be meant of any people, for it must be preached to all people and this agrees with that which was spoken before of Jerusalem which is, that it is the New Testament. And thus speaks our Savior Christ (John 3.5) "Unless a man be born of water and of the spirit, he cannot enter into the kingdom of God." It is as plain as anything can be that no people are the kingdom of God, but people should enter into the kingdom of God and when they have entered, then they are of the kingdom of God and children of the kingdom (Matthew 13.38). Therefore, we pray that the Godly reader will consider that there is a difference between the kingdom and the people. Otherwise where was the kingdom before your first beginning? Was there no kingdom for your first beginners to enter into? Did they make a kingdom and enter into it all of themselves? Then surely it was not the kingdom of God. It stands upon you to look for it before they set up a new kingdom. They did not enter into Christ's kingdom, for Christ's kingdom was and is an everlasting kingdom and cannot be shaken, as

---

[15] 1 Corinthians 4.43

the author of Hebrews showed (Hebrews 12.22) while speaking of Mount Zion, the city of the living God, the Celestial Jerusalem. (Verse 28) "Seeing we receive a kingdom that cannot be shaken, let us have grace, and we may serve God so that we may please him with reverence and fear."

We have endeavored with the best of our abilities (which you may see are small) to speak to the larger of this point because we ourselves have been formerly misled by error that the Church is the kingdom of heaven and Mount Zion. Because we know some others are strongly possessed in it, who do not hold succession, but indeed it is the ground of all succession. For if the church is Jerusalem then there must be a succession for there must be a due proportion of all things between the type and truth, between the old Jerusalem and the new Jerusalem and between shadow and substance. Since there is a succession in the Old Testament, therefore, there must certainly be succession in the New Testament. If, therefore, you can prove that you are Jerusalem, we yield to you all the prerogatives of Jerusalem. All people and nations must then come to you and receive all the holy ordinances from you. All sacrifices must then be offered up to you. Those that are not in you are not in Christ. All that are born of water and of the spirit must enter into you and all that are saved must walk in the light of you. And then you are the joy of the whole earth. You must then be preached to other cities and you cannot be shaken for Christ's kingdom is an everlasting kingdom which will never be taken away nor destroyed (Daniel 7.14). But you may be shaken, taken away, and destroyed though you were as excellent a church as Corinth, Ephesus, Philippi, Thyatira, Smyrna, and Philadelphia. For all of these churches were shaken, taken away, and destroyed, though they were more excellent churches than you, even so may you be much more. Therefore, you are not the kingdom of heaven or the heavenly Jerusalem and so those privileges do not belong to you, which you challenge, and some wretched men have given you (whose condemnation does not sleep) and all under the cullor of your being Jerusalem.

Now let us bring to trial your other ground concerning this cause. You say the ordinances of Christ were (as you call it) when once raised up again, they are not to be raised up anymore, but all men must fetch them from those who raised them up or from those that received them at their hands by succession. First we say to you that which some of you could not or will not ever be able to answer while the world endures. How do you know of faith that he, or they, or from whom you received your beginnings were the first? This can never be proven to any man's conscience, that has any conscience, unless you can show particular prophecies of scripture that such a man should first raise up (to speak your own words) the ordinances of Christ and that he has done it and that you have it from him. All these you must prove by scripture if your rule is true and men must have faith in it. But you cannot prove any of these by scripture and, therefore, your rule is not true and no man can have faith in it and it should not be held and practiced by any that wait for salvation by Jesus Christ in whom they must have faith in all that they hold, profess, and practice, or else they sin. Without faith it is impossible to please God (Romans 11.6). Let us, by the mercies of God entreat all of you that profess the name of Jesus not to stand on such uncertain and unsound grounds. How will you ever be able to prove that he or they are from whom you (by succession) have your beginnings were the first? No man can ever prove it. The world is too wide for man to comprehend or know all that is done in it. It is a vain invention. Cast it away. There is no warrant in God's word to warrant it to you that he or they were the first.

And if he or they were the first, what then? Must all of the world come to them? By what rule of God's word do you do this? There must be a special command for him or those to begin and a restraint or forbidding command to all men from doing it afterwards. God is as merciful to his people now as ever he was, and he has not left them without rule or direction that they should sin and fall. The Lord was so careful for his people Israel (for whom he had wrought so great wonders and they were continually rebellious against him) and gave Moses two warnings at one time. (Exodus 19.21.24) "Go down and charge the people not to break through to gaze on the Lord or many of them will perish." And again "do not let the priests and the people break to come up to the Lord or they will be destroyed." The Lord most carefully appointed Aaron and his sons to those several offices and services about the tabernacle as is shown (Numbers 4) when the Lord charged Moses and Aaron that they should not cut off the tribe of the family of the Kohathites. The Lord said to do this to them so that they may live and not die. Let Aaron and his sons come and appoint everyone of them to his charge lest they touch or see those holy things they should not touch and see and die. The Lord out of his great grace, mercy, and love was so careful with his people to give such straight rules of direction for them so they would not come near, handle, or see those things which did not appertain to them to handle, or see and to sin and die. Has the Lord been less gracious now in leaving his people neither directions nor directors to appoint them to their office to show them what is commanded and what is forbidden? Surely you will not say so? The Lord is as merciful to rebellious Israel as ever he was. We then require you to show where the Lord has now commanded some especially to begin and meddle with holy things and forbidden all others, except by their appointments of which they are permitted and appointed to it. If you will set up a special temple and priesthood of your own, show your warrant from the word of truth, which seeing you cannot possibly do, let God have the glory, and see your own shame and humble yourselves, and repent of this error. Will you now with your patience suffer us a little to declare and try your best ground for these things which we have received from some that are the greatest among you? We could repeat diversities of your arguments and reasons, but we will spare you. We will take your strongest ground, which if we can by the ground of truth show to be most unsound, we will hope that those among you that seek the Lord in singleness of heart will forsake it. First know this and let all know that you have never been able at any time to produce any one scripture and maintain it for your succession. Although we have had diverse conferences with the chiefest among you, yet you reason by similes and proportions of your own devisings for the most part.

To come to your ground, this is the sum of what you say. Baptism was once raised up by one unbaptized person, after this none did, neither was it lawful for any unbaptized to baptize, but all must have it from him, and so you follow on with your proportion from baptism, to the church, and ministry. And this is the way you run, not knowing where it leads you. We pray you mark what the wise man said (Proverbs 4.19) "The way of the ungodly is as the darkness, they do not know where they will fall." Even so, you know so little about what pit you will fall into or on what rock you cast yourselves and others in this your way. First where you say that when baptism was once (by one unbaptized) raised up or begun, none after being unbaptized did or might. Neither John nor any apostle taught you this. We do not know where you have learned it, but you are strong in it, and say it is the course and order of the scriptures. But we require you with godly consideration to consider that here under a cullor of binding to the due general course of the matter and manner of the scriptures (which all should follow) you bring men to a due particular course of purpose, which none are bound to follow unless any dare say of themselves, as that excellent and worthy apostle Paul said (Philippians 2.17)[16] "Brethren, be followers of me." In short, see, if you would not be so blind, where your rule leads you. You tie the word and ordinances of God to men. First concerning baptism, you must bring a man prophesied of as John was that will be able to answer as John did to those who asked him, "Who are you that we may give answer to them that sent us, what do you say of yourself?[17] Why do you baptize?"[18] John answered, "I am he that the prophet Isaiah prophesized of. I am the voice of him that cries out in the wilderness make straight the way of the Lord."[19] Thus John proves his office and ministration to be lawful and therefore Jerusalem and all Judea who are of faith might come forth to him to be baptized. This man was sent in the power of the spirit of Elijah. Therefore, whatsoever he did in his ministry was true and warrantable so that men might safely join themselves to his baptism. Neither could men learn baptism and the manner of it but of John, and of those that received it from him. Will you now on behalf of your first beginner answer us who asks you who you are that baptizes and says all men must have their baptism from you? What do you say of yourself? Where is your warrant? Will you answer us as you have done, that John's example is your warrant? We will answer you (as we have often done) by the same example. And we say further, that John's example and all the examples and rules in the scriptures that are to be followed are general. There is not one particular example or rule in all the New Testament that is only to be imitated and observed by any one man, any two, ten, twenty, or a hundred. But whatsoever example may be found in the scriptures any one man may follow, and whatsoever rule or commandment any one man may observe and keep. Even so another man may follow the same example and keep the same commandment, and so of two men, ten, twenty, or a hundred and the like may be said of time and place. There is no example or rule in the New Testament that is only proper or appertaining to any one person, or person's time, or times, place or places for the New Testament is the covenant of grace which Christ has purchased with his blood. There is no part of it that can be abolished until he comes for judgment. But if any part of it, any example, or rule in it is tied to any particular person, or persons, time, or times, place or

---

[16] Philippians 3.17
[17] John 1.22
[18] John 1.25
[19] John 1.23

places, these all may be abolished before Christ's coming. Therefore no part of the New Testament can be particularly tied to any one of them.

To show for example the question in hand of John's example of baptizing, being unbaptized (or rather not being of any other first baptized). If his example is a particular example for one man only (as you say), then was it abolished when your predecessor had once begun to baptize? If this is so, is his example now of no use? It may be so for anything you know or can ever know that he was not the first. If your rule is true then how wretched is your case that challenges a prerogative that by your own rule does not appertain to you. Your best advantage is, that you can but imagine that you are the first and you would have us imagine so with you.

Well, we beseech you to consider thoroughly this one point especially. That the New Testament or any part of it neither rule nor example does particularly appertain to any one person, or serve only one person, or serve only for any one time or place. If you deny it you abolish Christ, and the testament purchased with his blood and make it a carnal covenant for no spiritual covenant can ever be abolished. If you confess that the New Testament and all the rules and examples in it are general to all, then all men may, in all places where the Lord by his word and his spirit will stir up and imbue them with gifts and graces, preach the gospel, and when men are converted, baptize them, and so your succession has fallen to the ground. And in that you have no loss, if you love the Lord and his holy truth, for in doing so the holy ordinances of Christ are set at liberty which you have kept in bondage to the great dishonor of God and to the utter confusion of the diverse souls whose blood will be required at your hands (though they have perished in their own sins) if you do not repent.

Moreover as we have shown before, John came in the power and spirit of Elijah, therefore whatever he did in his office and ministry was warrantable and according to the truth and he could not err in it. No man that knows any truth will deny this and we speak to men of understanding. Did your first beginner come in the power of the spirit in this measure? Was all warrantable and according to the truth that he did in his ministry? Will any affirm that all he did was warrantable? Can any affirm it? Could he not err? God forbid that any who fear God should be so foolish. No, he was not a man coming forth in some small measure out of the deep mist of the mystery of iniquity who was much in error and ignorance. Yes, even in the administration of baptism oils you have been his unprofitable disciples. Would you tie all the world from the east to the west to come fetch the holy ordinances of Christ from him and you his successors through all your errors, ignorances, and grievous corruptions, of which we know of so many, and have cause to be jealous of you for many more? What truth, piety, or godliness is there in this? You seek to make men either presently swallow up all your errors ignorantly, to be washed by you with water, or else stay until they have learned them. Otherwise they must not be baptized at all. Furthermore men must be forced to learn your language, and so until the poor disciples of Christ that would follow him (English men or any other nation) can speak Dutch, they are debarred from the holy ordinances of God, the means of their salvation by your rule, a fearful mystery of iniquity.

By this you have wrought such wickedness among us, and brought such desolation upon us the poor people of God that as we have cause to wish that in our heads there were floods of water and our eyes were fountains of tears that we might power out a complaint against you for this your abomination which you have set up and by which you have wrought such destruction and ruin in the church of God, seeking to pull it down to build up yourselves. You have glorified your church and set her up to sit as a queen, taking to yourselves all power and authority. Yes even to shut the gates of the holy city, the heavenly Jerusalem, saying that none may enter but by your authority. O that you could see your great sin and the lamentable evil that you have wrought. First, you sin against God in destroying his temple which is built truly (though exceedingly weak) on the foundation of the word of God. You have caused the enemies of God to blaspheme, and to make a mockery of the profession of Jesus Christ. You have caused those who were more indifferently minded to double their doubting and step backward rather than come forward. Thus, you have sinned with a high hand against the God of heaven, who is able and will fill you double for this your inequity if you do not repent. And to us you have brought much sorrow, grief and vexation of soul and spirit upon us. The Lord knows we speak the truth and great has been our cause of grief to see the church of Christ, which is his body, of which we are (though we are unworthy members) rent and torn into pieces. We and our profession have been made a scorn of men who have wished and wanted our overthrow. They have taken it upon themselves to foretell of these evils that have come upon us, which are coming to pass according to their foretelling. They have triumphed against us and blessed themselves as though their fore sayings must come to pass. Thus our enemies have rejoiced at our miseries, but the Lord has wounded them on their right eye and made them a rejoicing to their enemies.

Were this all our woe it would be full enough, but you have by this your great sin brought a further evil on us. You make our enemies rejoice over us. You have made our friends our enemies. Yes our familiar friends with whom we took sweet counsel and went together to the house of God. Such is the enmity between us and them (of which you have been the chief instruments) and it can never have an end while any of us live. It is that enmity which the Lord put between the seed of the woman and the seed of the serpent which can have no end unless we fall into the same destruction. There is no place of repentance to be found for their transgression. They were once enlightened and had tasted of the heavenly gift and were made partakers of the Holy Ghost. They had tasted of the good word of God and of the powers of the world to come and are now fallen away. It is impossible that they should be renewed again by repentance seeing that they crucify again to themselves the son of God and make a mockery of him (Hebrews 6.4–6). Now, we will show how they were once enlightened. First, Mr. John Smyth (on whose head the blood of all these people will be) has by his profession and in all his practice, and by word, and in his sundry writings, with such force of argument and strength of protestation with ground of truth, (as his writings show) manifested himself to be enlightened with this truth of God.

"Wherever two, or three, are gathered together into Christ's name, there Christ has promised to be in the midst of them" (Matthew 18.20). Therefore, they are the people of God and church of Christ and have a right to Christ and all his ordinances and have no need to seek to be admitted by men to the holy things, but may freely walk together in the ways of God and enjoy all holy things. He has fallen from this truth of God of which he was enlightened by the denying the words of our Savior Christ, that says "Wherever two or three are gathered together etc." They hold that the first two or three that are gathered together only they have the right to Christ and all his ordinances and after that all men must come to them. They restrain the words of Christ, which are general, from any two or three to only to the first two or three. In doing so, they have set up a succession against that which he has formerly by all words, writings, and practice set himself with all detestation. And this man, like Balaam, has consulted with you, and has put a stumbling block before the people of God, who were also enlightened, and so many of you have fallen with him to the same sin and are under the same condemnation. And Mr.

Jarvis Nevill having witnessed not only this but diverse other truths for that which he has been long imprisoned and condemned to perpetual imprisonment and is in an expectation of death for the same. Yet, not withstanding all his former fidelity and constancy of which his bonds were famous throughout the whole land, he fell with M. Smyth upon this your blind succession (forsaking the rock on which he stood). He has now returned beyond his vomit exclaiming against your succession and strives to build up the succession of Rome, which he has formerly with all zeal and holiness pulled down. In doing so he has become an hissinge[20] of men, and a reproach to all the godly, and is made a scorn of the wicked, a just reward for all that fall away.

Moreover this wicked man Mr. Smyth has professed and maintained with all manifestations of faith and confidence that Christ took his flesh of Mary. Affirming that the entire world was not able to answer that place (Hebrews 2.14) where it is said "As the children are partakers of flesh and blood, and, he also himself, likewise, took part with them," and also (Genesis 3.15) The seed of the woman will break the serpent's head, but now he is fallen from this, following a device of some of you. He cannot find in all the scriptures where Christ had the first matter of his flesh. But the second matter is his nourishment that he had of Mary, saying further, that if he had the strength of many men he would labor to cast the contrary out of the church for being an article of faith, and he has taught that Christ's miracles, sufferings, and death, yes, even his hanging on the cross, were all typical and carnal. He compares Christ's flesh to his garments, and therefore not to be striven about. So likewise he is fallen from the faith of justification by Christ's righteousness only to inherit righteousness in himself. So he will be justified partly by his own righteousness, either not standing need of all of Christ's righteousness, or else not holding his righteousness sufficient for him. And he is also fallen from the faith in the point of magistracy, professing he did not know that he differed from you in anything.

Furthermore this wicked man Mr. Smyth has professed and taught and his confederates have learned from him that God is a spirit, and that he will be worshiped wholly in spirit and truth. And he and they knew that the apostle (1 Corinthians 14.14–16) said "If I pray in a strange tongue my spirit prays, but my understanding is without fruit. I will pray therefore with the spirit,

---

[20] Laughingstock, object of derision

but I will also pray with understanding. I will sing with spirit, but I will also sing with understanding. Or else how will they that do not understand, say amen." And (verse 11) "Unless I know the power of the voice, I will be like him who speaks as a barbarian."[21] This man not withstanding, when he had himself but a little understanding of your language, and the rest of his confederacy of which some had no understanding to be spoken of and diverse none at all, neither have they yet come to worship with you, being barbarians to you and say amen (or else what do they do there) not knowing whether you bless or curse.

The ignorant papists will stand up in judgment against these men. Yes the idolatrous heathens who have not known and heard the things that these men have known and heard. Of such men as these and they that are fallen with him, the apostle Jude says "A woe to them for they have followed the way of Cain and are cast away by the deceit of Balaam's wages, and perish in the gainsaying of Korah" (Jude 11). Having your persons in admiration because of advantage, which you might all right well see, and we do not doubt but that some of you do see, for you know their understanding in your language, and for what cause can you imagine that they should run to gaze at you? The apostle (1 Corinthians 14.19) says, "I had rather speak in the church or congregation five words with my understanding that I might also instruct others than ten thousand words in a strange tongue." Does the apostle not teach here that it is better to hear five words in the church or congregation with understanding than ten thousand words in a strange tongue? But these men, with an assortment of women that are void of understanding, had rather hear in your church or congregation five words without any understanding than ten thousand words with understandings in a congregation or church gathered together by the preaching of the gospel of Jesus Christ, and baptized into his name upon the confession of their faith and sins.

They knew this was our beginning, but your beginning they did not know and neither can they know. If you had any other beginning it is not according to God's word, but it is all one to them. They have not regarded how you began in the faith, nor how you stand in the faith which (if they had not forsaken all religion) they would have had regard of. Religion was not, nor is it their mark that they aimed at as you may easily discern by these their willful blind courses. This is where you have led them by your blind

---

[21] Foreigner

succession. Now, between you and us, and let all the Godly on earth consider whether you have walked uprightly or not and whether you have sought for yourselves and not the glory of God nor our building up in the faith. And thus we have left the succession of your baptism, putting you in the remembrance that we have showed you that by your opinion you make John's baptism and example a particular example for one man, but for what man you cannot tell. But whosoever came with the first light of it, he has preeminence. You imagine this was your first beginner, which you will never be able to prove unless you can know all things that are done under the sun. All that is in you is "vanity of vanities"[22] as we trust many of you will easily see and wish all may. And for those people who have run after your inventions, of whom we would not once have made mention, but the better to bring you to the sight of the greatness of your sin and to set them out as an example so that others might be warned, which we desire that they may be. When they will hear of such people whose knowledge, gifts, and graces were great, and who walked and professed to walk strictly by the rules of Christ and are under his yoke, they are now Belial. They walk by no rule of Christ and are not under his yoke. They have disclaimed themselves for having any power to the holy things and have given it all to you. All their religion is to only come and gaze at you who speak to them in a strange tongue, "which is not given as a sign to those that believe but to those that do not believe" (1 Corinthians 14.22). They are left in confusion neither knowing nor caring where to go. We have cause to magnify the name of God in that he has confounded them in their ways that would have confounded his way of truth. We have cause to bless God who has prevented you and kept you from making them one with you, in which you would have strengthened them in their evil and enlarged your own sin exceedingly.

Let us now proceed to the succession of your church and ministry. We cannot conceive which way you will be able ever to make any show or cullor that this unbaptized man should have commission to do all things if your rule of particular proportion is good. There is no such course or proportion in the scriptures. John's example will not serve your turn, since John planted no churches. If you will have planters of churches and that all men must come to them, then they must be endowed with like gifts as the first planters were, speak all languages as the apostles did, work miracles, and not err in doctrine

---

[22] Ecclesiastes 1.2

for the Lord's hand is not shortened, nor is his grace and mercy lessened to his church and people. But if he sends men with the same office and authority that he sent his apostles, he will for the honor of his own name, the advancement of his truth, and the good of his people, give them the same gifts and not bring his truth and people into bondage to men full of errors, ignorance, and blindness, as you and all men are. Therefore be content to be builders upon the foundation laid and do not forbid others to build on it, but let every man take heed how he builds on it (1 Corinthians 3.10). This may suffice for this point. So we now come to that which the best approved among you have had no word of answer yet, and we know you can say nothing for it, holding your own rule of succession according to your course and proportion, unless you will be very unadvised as to hold proportion in one thing and no proportion in another. What we intend to speak to you about is your ministry.

How can you raise a ministry? Where is your particular example? Your rule is that elders must make elders and none but elders must administer in the holy things. You raise baptism after John's examples, but how will you do it in ordaining elders? Seeing you have no such example and when you have done it what device will you have to keep this authority to yourselves? This is your ground for your succession, as all had baptism from John the first baptizer, so all must have baptism from your first baptizer. As all churches proceeded from the first church at Jerusalem, so all churches must precede from Jerusalem your first church. As elders proceeded by ordination from the first elders, so all elders must proceed by ordination from your first elders. Here is your proportion. But how did your elders come by their ordination? Did they ordain themselves? Where is your example and proportion for that? Did the church ordain them? Your proportion is then gone for the first elders were not so ordained. Thus you are overtaken in your ground not seeing where it leads you. Forsake it. It will not be a disgrace to forsake your error. In that you will show that the true grace of God is in you by denying yourselves and your own ways and advancing the way of the Lord. Hold to yourselves the perfect rule that all gainsayers are not able to withstand which was given by the law giver. And that is "Where two or three are gathered together into my name, there I am in the midst of them and whatever they bind on earth, will be bound in heaven, and whatever they loose on earth will be loosed in heaven" (Matthew 18.20.18). (1 Corinthians 3.16.21.) "Do you not know that you are the Temple of your God? Let no man rejoice in men for all things are yours." And (2 Corinthians 6.15–18) "What concord has Christ with Belial, or what part has the believer with the infidel, and what agreement has the temple of God with idols? Wherefore you must come out from among them and separate yourselves says the Lord and touch no unclean thing and I will receive you, and I will be a father to you, and you will be my sons and daughters" says the almighty Lord. These three places of scripture prove the following. First, that wherever two or three are gathered together in Christ's name, Christ is in the midst of them and they have power to bind and loose which is to receive in and cast out, to appoint officers and to discharge, and to administer in all holy things, for having Christ they have with him all things. Also (Romans 8.32) which states that Christ's power cannot be divided from him, therefore where he is his power must also be. He is a king and where he is he gives power to his servants to serve him in all his ordinances.

The second alleged place confirms where it is said, "Let no man rejoice in men, for all things are yours."[23] In verse 5 of 1 Corinthians 3 the apostle said "Who is Apollos? What is Paul? They are only the ministers in whom you believed," showing the Corinthians that they were not the temple of God. They did not have interest in all things because of their persons, but because they believed their doctrine. And wherever a company of men now will believe their doctrine, even they are the temple of God, and all things are theirs, as well as all things were the Corinthians.

The third place fore alleged, proves who they are that Christ has promised to be in the midst of. They are those that separate themselves from Belial, (which are men without a yoke) from unbelievers, from idols, and who touch no unclean things. These are the ones God will receive, and among whom he will dwell and walk and he will be their God and father and they will be his people and children. They will not need to respect the persons of men as has been shown because by the free gift of God's grace and through their faith in Christ all things are given to them. Will any man not withstanding all this say that any people or congregation separated from all uncleanliness may not enjoy Christ and all the holy ordinances unless they are admitted there by other men? Did the apostle Paul disclaim both for himself, and Cephas, and Apollos all privilege to their persons and teach the Corinthians that their persons did not give them interest into the holy things but it was their doctrine through their own faith? Does any dare challenge

---

[23] 1 Corinthians 3.21

privilege to their persons and so take away the authority of the apostle's doctrine and ministry that is still in as good a force and authority as ever in the scriptures? All the ministries and doctrines that people believe today are theories. It should be by faith in the scriptures, not by succession.

Here we desire that all men that have any uprightness of heart would enter into a due consideration of the depth of this error of succession, from, or by the persons of men. And through God's assistance we will endeavor to speak what we are able for the discovery of this error, which is so great and dangerous, and of the sharp bitter fruits of which we have deeply tasted and our wounds are yet fresh and green. But not withstanding by the grace of God, we will not be provoked to speak beyond the bounds of sobriety. We proceed by the most easy, plain, and evident way of our best understandings.

We entreat you and all men with all holy advisedness to consider what the wall of separation was between the Jew and the Gentile. The apostle (Romans 3.1.2) declares plainly what was in these words, "The preferment of the Jew and the profit of circumcision is much more in every manner of way. Chiefly, because to them the oracles of God were committed." This was the division wall which the Lord had set up between the Jews and the Gentiles. He gave his statutes and ordinances to Israel to keep, not debarring the Gentiles at all from enjoying the benefit of his statutes and ordinances as the Lord showed, (Exodus 12.49) "One law will be to him that is born in the land, and to the stranger that dwells among you." This then was the preferment and the division wall, the Jews kept the oracles and the Gentiles must have them at their hands. If the Gentiles had possessed the land of Canaan, and the holy city, and the temple, and all the holy things, they would have all been polluted in their hands. But when the Jews had possession of all the holy things, and communicated them to the Gentiles, they were holy to them. Thus Gentiles could have no benefit of the holy things unless they came to the Jews and received them from them, and so enjoyed them under them. This is as plain as anything can be. The partition wall between the Jew and Gentile was in respect of the privilege that belonged to the person of the Jew in that to the person of the Jews the oracles were committed to be kept. As we have shown there was the same law of ordinances for the Gentile as for the Jew, but the Gentile must receive them from the Jews, and they must come up to Jerusalem to worship with the Jews (Acts 8.27; John 4.20). Christ has broken down this stop of the partition wall "That he might reconcile both to God in one body by his cross, and slay hatred in doing so and make peace"

(Ephesians 2.16.15). Thus the Lord has of himself made peace both with the Jew and Gentile. Now he does not prefer any one people above another in giving his oracles to them to keep, but has made his covenant with all, both Jew and Gentile, "They that are far off, and they that are near" (Acts 2.39; Ephesians 2.17). "To every man that does good there will be glory and honor and peace, to the Jew first and also to the Greek, for God is no respecter of persons" (Romans 2.10.11). By God's appointment, "there are now no more strangers and foreigners but through Christ, all both Jew and Gentile have an entrance to the Father by one spirit" (Ephesians 2.19.18) not standing in need of admittance by men. And whatever people, either Jew or Gentile are "built on the foundation of the Apostles and Prophets, Jesus Christ himself is the chief cornerstone, in whom all the buildings are coupled together, and grown into a holy temple of the Lord. They are built together to be the habitation of God by the spirit" (Ephesians 2.20–22). Therefore no people are bound to seek men to be built into a habitation of God, but the doctrine of the apostles by the work of the spirit is sufficient. All this proves that the partition wall is broken down, which is, that the oracles are not now committed to any people of credit to keep that all should be forced to come to them as the Gentiles were of necessity constrained to come to the Jews. Christ has slain that hatred says the apostle, and has reconciled the Gentiles to God, and so God is equally favorable to them both, that is to all men (for all were either Jews or Gentiles).[24] God does not favor anyone in the respect of the committing of his oracles to be kept. They are now left free to all that come according to that prophecy of scripture (Isaiah 55.1) "Everyone who thirsts come to the waters, and you that have no silver come buy and eat. Come I say buy wine and milk without silver and without money."

This then is confessed by all (that have any knowledge in the religion of God) that the separation wall is broken down, and being rightly understood also that the separation wall was a personal privilege to the particular nation of the Jews by genealogy. They were to keep the oracles of God by succession among themselves from generation to generation. The Gentiles who were without could not be admitted to the holy things but by them, this being the division wall, and this being broken down, and the Gentiles let in, and the door set open for all, and freedom and liberty proclaimed. "By the blood of Jesus Christ we may be bold and enter into the holy place, by the new and

---

[24] Ephesians 2.16

living way which he has prepared for us through the veil that is his flesh" (Hebrews 10.19.20). Thus all succession is abolished, all privilege and preferment to particular persons in keeping the holy oracles is taken away, and they are free for all men, (that believe) to possess and enjoy, "for we are all the sons of God by faith in Christ Jesus."[25] "There is neither Jew, nor Greek. There is neither bond nor free. There is neither male nor female. We are all one in Christ Jesus" (Galatians 3.26–28). Now those that will set up a succession and will have all the oracles of God committed to them and that all men must receive the ordinances of Christ from them, they build up the partition wall again and challenge for themselves the preferment meant of the Jews. They stop the entrance into the holy place by the new and living way which Christ has made by his blood. They deny that any people built on the foundation of the apostles and prophets by the spirit can be the habitation of God. They will not permit men to be the sons of God by faith. All these things are nothing and not available unless men come to them and are admitted by them. Men cannot have Christ unless they have them nor be joined to Christ unless they are joined to them nor may they put on Christ unless they put on them. Let all the godly equally judge between you and us whether this does not set up the partition wall again, which gives a special privilege and preferment to one people more than another and that none may enjoy the holy things but from their persons. We desire that this may yet be better observed and well understood that you or whatever people who maintain succession or will have a privilege or preferment in the possession of the holy things, it does appertain and is tied to your persons. The power and authority you challenge is in your persons. It is not in your gifts and doctrine set by your persons. Do not tie us to them. We will prefer the gifts and doctrine of the apostles before yours and we will be directed by them. And the authority and preference you challenge is not in your office or set by your persons or personal preference who sends precepts and rules by the authority of your office. And we and all that fear God will cast away your authority and office and the authority and office of all others with the precepts and rules made by their power. We will only submit ourselves to the office and authority of the apostles and to the precepts and rules that they have set down by the power of their office, which power and office they received from God, not from men, nor by man (Galatians 1.1). Thus may you and all men see

---

[25] Galatians 3.26

that what people, church, or congregation challenges to themselves any privilege or preferment in keeping the holy things and that they are the only ones who may dispose of them to others, such privilege and preferment must be proper to their persons only. All such privilege to these persons as we have before shown Paul, Cephas, and Apollos disclaimed although they were the ministers by whom the Corinthians believed. And will you or any people or church challenge privilege and preferment to your persons over all men? Although by your ministry they do not believe. All your warrant for this is because you say you are the first.

If you will yet stand for privilege by your being first (as you imagine) hear what our Savior Christ says to you for your instruction. (Matthew 20.13.14) "Friend I do you no wrong, take that which is your own and go your way. I will give to the last as much as to you." These men thought because they came first into the vineyard they should have had more wages than those that came last, although their wages were agreed upon. So you think you are worthy of more authority than those that came last because you suppose you were the first. But our Savior Christ teaches you in this place that the honor and reward is all one to the last, as to the first. And take heed, lest by your sin (if you had no other) the Lord passes this sentence against you and says to you "The first will be the last."[26]

Now we will draw to an end this point that the gospel has come unto the entire world alike (Colossians 1.6). "For God show no partiality."[27] And therefore the entire world should receive it, believe it, and obey it alike. In so doing, all have free liberty to enjoy and administer all the holy ordinances alike. For of whomsoever the Lord requires obedience of all his ordinances, they obeying, he gives to them the privilege and benefit of all his ordinances. Then whatsoever people receive, believe, and obey the gospel as truly as another people do, they have as much privilege and liberty to enjoy the gospel and all the ordinances as any other people. "God is no acceptor of persons, but in every nation, he that fears him and works righteousness is accepted by him" (Acts 10.34.35). If any will now fear God, and fast, and pray as Cornelius did, their prayers and alms will come up in remembrance before God and the spirit of God will direct them to hear what Peter said, and to be directed by Peter, and the rest of the apostles. Do not bid them to send for you, or go to

---

[26] Matthew 20.16
[27] Acts 10.34

you, or any people to make them perfect, for the word of God is all sufficient to teach them and instruct them and make them perfect to every good work, as is shown. (2 Timothy 3.16.17) "The whole scripture was given as inspiration by God and is profitable to teach, convince, correct, and to instruct in righteousness so that the man of God may be absolute, being made perfect to all good works." Here may you and all learn and understand that the word of God is all sufficient to make the people of God absolute and perfect to every good work: to pray, to preach, to baptize, to break bread, to administer in all the holy things and to walk in all the ways of God without the help of any man or men. If any man should be so unwise as to think that the meaning of the Holy Ghost here is only to make a man perfect to every good work in himself, it is a great weakness, seeing that the Holy Ghost testified that "the manifestation of the spirit is given to every man to profit withal" (1 Corinthians 12.7). (1 Peter 4.10) "Let every man as he has received the gift minister to the same to each other as good disposers of the manifold graces of God." To make this plain that he who runs may read it and understand that Christ and all things are given to every faithful people, although they are but two or three according to Christ's own words (Matthew 18.20). Christ is their king (Luke 1.33). "He is their mediator" (Hebrews 9.15), by whose blood they may be bound to enter into the holy place. "He is their high priest who with one offering has consecrated forever those who are sanctified" (Hebrews 10.21.14). He made them kings and priest to God's rule (Revelation 1.6). "They have come to Mount Zion and to the city of the living God, the celestial Jerusalem" (Hebrews 12.22) "whose gates are not shut by the day and there is no night" (Revelation 21.25). We conclude, therefore, with those heavenly words of comfort spoken by the Holy Ghost to every faithful man and men though they may be but two or three (Revelation 22.17), "Both the spirit and the bride say come. Let him that hears, say come, and let him that is thirsty come, and let whosoever will, take of the water of life freely."

Now away with yourselves and let all men consider whether this is not all sufficient. Here is the king, the mediator, the high priest, and the city of Jerusalem with her gates open. The spirit of God is bidding all to come freely. And all the faithful will be made kings and priests of God. What should keep the faithful from entering in and offering sacrifices, and administering in all the holy things before the Lord, seeing they are appointed there by God? (1 Peter 2.5 and 4.10).

If the Jews coming out of captivity had had Solomon as their king, Moses their mediator, Aaron their high priest, Jerusalem their city with her gates open and their God bidding them to come, who should have forbidden them from bringing their sacrifices and administrating them before the Lord freely? If Pharaoh should hinder them all the plagues of Egypt would fall on him. And though Tobiah despised them, and Sanballet conspired against them, yet they prayed to their God that their enemies' shame would be turned upon their own heads and the Lord would bring their councils to nought [sic] (Nehemiah 4). God has promised to do no less for his people now against his and their enemy the mystery of iniquity, the man of sin. "He will consume him with the spirit of his mouth and abolish him with the brightness of his coming" (2 Thessalonians 2.8). "And he will smite the earth with the rod of his mouth and with the breath of his lips and he will slay the wicked" (Isaiah 11.4).

Now take heed and let all people take heed how they go about to hinder the people of God that have freedom and liberty to administer before him, "being a holy priesthood to offer up spiritual sacrifices acceptable to God by Jesus Christ" (1 Peter 2.5). We say take heed as to how you go about to hinder them by setting up your own inventions and abominations, and bringing swift judgment on yourselves. And so we leave this point praying that you do not lightly pass by it though we have handled it weakly. But let all that desire unfeignedly in the truth of their souls to see the profession of Jesus Christ flourish in purity and sincerity and in the light of all truth set their own hearts and teach others to seek Christ in his word. And to follow him in all worship and service according to the examples, rules, and precepts in the scriptures that are written for us to that end. "For whatsoever these things are aforetime written, they are written for our learning" (Romans 15.1).[28]

Let all men therefore that in uprightness desire to walk in the ways of God according to true direction seek to be taught of God by the scriptures and not to be led by the examples and precepts of men. For if a people though but two, or three, by reading and hearing the scriptures and by the work of the spirit, come to the faith of the gospel and must be compelled to join to any or some people that formerly professed Christ, then they must be forced to profess as they profess, and walk in their steps with them. And so they are brought in subjection to all their errors, and are polluted by joining with

---

[28] Romans 15.4

them in all their corruptions. So they cannot nor must not be led forward towards perfection as they should be (Hebrews 6.1). But they must be led forward or go backward or out of the way, or stand still as the people to whom they join will lead them. This destroys all pure profession of the gospel and keeps men back from walking in the clear light of it. If two or three will in the honesty of their hearts desire to walk honestly with the Lord and keep themselves unspotted of error, this woeful rule of succession debars them so that they may not do so. It constrains them to join to some people, denying them liberty to walk after the rules and examples in the scriptures and so to follow Christ. It binds them to follow Christ with them, as they follow Christ. Hence it comes that the pope says, "Lo here is Christ,"[29] and seeks to force all to follow Christ with him. And the bishops say "Lo here is Christ" and they seek to compel all to follow Christ with them. The Presbyterian says "Lo here is Christ," and they constrain all others to follow Christ with them. We pass by the most ungodly and unwise familiasts and scattered flocks that say he is in the desert as that is nowhere to be found in the profession of the gospel according to the ordinances until their extraordinary men (they dream of) come, which will not occur until there comes a new Christ and a new gospel. And you to whom we especially write, you say, "Lo here is Christ" and you would have all to follow Christ with you. Now in these troublesome days, which our Savior Christ has foretold, and are now coming to pass of which if it were possible that the very elect would be deceived.[30] Let all the godly stay themselves upon the blessed counsel of our Savior Christ who said to all that will follow him, "Take heed, behold I have shown you all things before," (Mark 13.23) which is by his word. Therefore we must only go this way and follow no men. We pray that all of you (that would have men follow Christ with you) to remember how our Savior Christ reproved his disciples for their evil disposition, who when they saw one casting out devils in Christ's name they forbid him because he was not following Christ with them. Jesus utterly disapproved them saying, "Do not forbid him, he that is not against us is with us" (Luke 9.49).[31] So if our Savior Christ would not suffer his disciples to challenge to themselves this privilege nor would he also restrain that disciple for professing his name although he did not follow Christ with them,

[29] Mark 13.21
[30] Mark 13.22
[31] Luke 9.50

why should any challenge to themselves or why should the people of God think they are bound to give to anyone this prerogative?

Let all the people of God everywhere know that they have liberty to follow Christ by themselves, which if God's people would practice with fear and reverence, relying only on the direction of God's word and spirit, it would make them most wary and careful of their ways, lest they should run into error and so be justly reproved by all while all men's eyes are on them. Contra wise, if of necessity they are bound to go and join another congregation, they walk securely because the walk of that people is their warrant. Whatsoever they find among them must be received as approved and good. And this makes those who often receive many good motions of the spirit quench those provocations of the spirit because they think they must join to some people and can see none that walk so uprightly and holy with whom they may have comfort to join. This is a chief cause of all this evil in that many are blinded with this error that you, and all the forenamed people, do stand so stiffly upon, that they must join to the church. And so this liberty is hidden from their eyes (you all that teach that doctrine being instruments of it) that they may join themselves together in the covenant of the New Testament, and so be the church and the temple of God themselves as well as you or any people. And through the gracious blessing of God which he has promised will be on those who do and walk in his ways. They may and will grow to be a most holy people and a house for the most-high God to dwell in. The word and the spirit of God are fully sufficient to build them up and they edify one another in their most holy faith according to the rules of the Holy Ghost in the New Testament. And all this is without the authority or admittance of any people professing before them, but all this you hide from their eyes.

O that the children of God were as wise in their generation in all things, and in this, as the sons of men then they would lose no part of that liberty in which Christ has made them free. Then every people called of God would run of themselves "the race set before them, and follow hard toward the mark for the price of the high calling of God in Christ Jesus" (Philippians 3.14). Unto those called of God by the word of his spirit, raise up your hearts and strive with all zeal and holiness to run one before another in the profession of truth. Until these gracious affections and holy endeavors possess the hearts and spirits of men there can be no hope to see the glorious light of God's truth in their profession flourish and grow. While some church or congregation is settled in dregs of error and are overtaken with a secure, cold, frozen profession of the gospel and some other church or congregation is carried away with a headstrong blind zeal into many errors and will have all men come and follow Christ, or rather go out of their way or be frozen with them. While men think they are to give them this preferment, what hope is there of the growth of pure religion? We therefore earnestly beseech all people, by the mercies of God (in whom there is any faithful love of God's truth) not to respect any men neither to follow Christ with them as your example, but follow Christ as you are taught in his word and as you have holy men's examples, whose holiness is approved in the scriptures. In all love we exhort you to be so minded by the name of Jesus.

Although this that has been manifested from the scriptures and may give full satisfaction to every faithful holy professor of the gospel (that Christ by his presence gives all power to every congregation, as well as to any one people or congregation that has gathered together in his name, though they may be but two or three, whether they are the first gathered or the last gathered, or whether there are elders, or no elders among them, with God it is all one). Yet because among all (almost) who profess Christ there is so much a do about ordination or laying on of hands, as though elders' hands were the only ones sanctified to that use, we pray the godly reader will receive full satisfaction from Acts 13.1–3 where it does evidently appear that the church or congregation at Antioch, (where there were no apostles or elders) by the direction of the Holy Ghost, with fasting, praying, and laying on of hands, separated Paul and Barnabus [sic] to the work of their ministries where the Holy Ghost had called them. And Paul did not go to the apostles in Jerusalem that were there before him to consult with them (Galatians 1.17) but after they were separated from the church, being sent forth by the Holy Ghost, they came down to Seleucia (Acts 13.4). From this time they first began to administer in the office of their apostleship. In all this let it be observed, that it is here set down expressly in the scriptures that they were called to their office by God and set forth by God, and the church did only ordain, or separate them to that work. Therefore this does nothing to contradict Galatians 1.1 where it is said "Paul an apostle, was not of men, neither by man" for he was called and sent of God. Thus, it is proven that the church or congregation has power (with fasting and prayer) to lay on hands and to separate and ordain the men chosen to administer. This is the ordination set down in the scriptures which most men make so great an idol. And we hope we will not need to prove particularly that the church or congregation has power to elect or choose their officers seeing that it is so plainly set down (Acts 14.23; 6.3.5).

Of Magistracy

The fourth matter that with the assistance of God we purpose to speak to you of is to prove to you, and all that are contrary minded, that the king, prince, and magistrates, ruling and governing by the power of God with the sword of justice may be members of the church of Christ while retaining the magistracy. For proof, the apostle Paul (Romans 13.1.7) first shows (speaking of the highest powers) that "all powers are ordained of God."[32] And whoever resists the power resists the ordinance of God. By this it is made most plain that the power and authority of the magistrates is the holy ordinance of God. They are further called the ministers of God and their administration is set down to take vengeance on those who do evil and to praise those that do well. The instrument that is used to punish evil doers is the sword. And in all this they are the ministers of God for good and especially for the good of God's children. Therefore they are commanded to pray for them (1 Timothy 2.12).[33] Thus their power (being of God) is holy and good and their office and administration is holy and good (as it is shown here by the apostle) appointed by God for good, who does, nor can appoint anything but that which is holy and good, and pleasing to himself, for he is holiness and goodness itself, and he may not nor cannot appoint anything that is contrary to himself.

God then has ordained and appointed this holy ordinance with the end, and use of it, and manner and administration of it. The magistrates are to apply themselves to the same thing. They obey the holy commandments and will of God and are pleasing and acceptable to the Lord in their obedience by applying themselves to it. The Holy Ghost intends and shows that there is a required diligent, willing, faithful obedience in their administration, and not a forced constrained obedience, as the devils obey God, whose obedience is not acceptable and well pleasing to him. Furthermore, he is well pleased in showing the power of his own might in that commanding them they must obey him. The devils do not willingly obey God in anything. They do not willingly know God which is apparent (Matthew 8.29) when they cried,

---

[32] Romans 13.1
[33] 1 Timothy 2.1.2

"Jesus, son of God, what have we to do with you." Although they believe there is one God, yet they do it unwillingly because they tremble (James 2.19). Their faith increases their fear. We say all this to make it plain to the simplest. First, there is an obedience which God commands by the word and works of his power in which they that obey do not please God as when he commanded the unclean spirits to come forth and they obeyed him. And thus Pharaoh obeyed when he let the people of Israel go to serve the Lord, as Moses and Aaron said in Exodus 12.31. This was not willing obedience and therefore not acceptable to God. Secondly, there is an obedience which God commands by the word and works of his grace, wherein and whereby, they that obey please God and are acceptable to him. This is the "obedience that is better than sacrifice."[34]

This is the obedience that God requires of kings, princes, and magistrates, a diligent, willing, faithful obedience, as is showed from these words. They are ministers of God and are applying themselves for the same thing. And let us with all grace and holiness to God and reverence to his holy ordinance consider what it is they are to apply themselves to. It is to punish evil doers with the sword and to reward or praise those that do well. These words might convince you all of your error on this point and they will condemn you all if you do not repent of your teaching and by stiffly maintaining that those ministers of God, retaining this their office from God, may not be members of the church of Christ. Hearken to their office or ministry again. It is to punish evil doers and to reward or praise those that do well. In this their holy administration they are like God. In applying themselves faithfully to the task they do the work that is proper of God. The divine property and work of God is to execute justice on the wicked and show mercy to those that do well. So far as the Lord has committed authority to magistrates to administer in these things, they do the proper work of God. Therefore the Holy Ghost by the prophet David, speaking of the magistrates, says in Psalm 82.6 "I have said you are Gods," speaking in respect of the great honor that is due to them by their holy office where he has appointed them.

The some and scope of that which is here set down in this point is to show you that the apostle teaches that the office and ministry of magistrates is a holy office appointed of God. And that the Lord requires of the magistrates a diligent, willing, faithful, obedience, which is pleasing to the Lord. Of which

---

[34] 1 Samuel 15.22

obedience they perform uprightly, though weakly, and failing in many things as the apostle confessed he and all the children of God did (James 3.2). Yet, believing the gospel of Jesus Christ and repenting of their sins, how can it be denied that they are to be admitted as members into the body of Christ? Is this a good exception, because they are magistrates? Why then do you have exception against them? They are the holy ministers of God and do his will in faithful obedience. What a doctrine of devils this is that any should be denied to be members of the body of Christ for executing a holy office appointed by God. For further proof that it is a holy ordinance or office pleasing to God it is shown that we are commanded to obey one's conscience and that is only that which is holy and good. For God forbid that his children should be tied of conscience to obey anything that is unholy and not good. The apostle shows here that the Holy Ghost intends no such thing as he said in verse 3[35] that magistrates are not to be feared for good works. (1 Peter 2.17) "Fear God, honor the king," and therefore if magistrates will command anything against God or godliness, the people of God are not bound to obey. And for this cause, the apostles when they were commanded by the rulers and elders of Israel that in no way should they speak or teach in the name of Jesus, they answered, "Whether it is right in the sight of God, to obey you, rather than God, you judge."[36] All this gives still further proof that the magistracy is a holy ministry or office appointed by God only for good. Therefore, none bearing that office or ministry is for that cause to be debarred from being members of the body of Christ, which is his church. Unless men for executing an office commanded by Christ should be debarred from Christ, which is more than madness for any that profess Christ to affirm.

Furthermore, God has by reason of that high power and authority which he has given to magistrates commanded such fear, such obedience, and so great an honor to be given to them by all men. Will they who have been so greatly honored by God with such authority, dignity and power, for bearing this honor which God has put on them, will they for this be accounted unworthy to be members of Christ's church? This is to bring the greatest dishonor that can be possible before God and his people and on that ordinance and its ministers of which and upon whom the Lord has put much honor. It is a most miserable, wretched, and dishonorable ordinance, office, or

---

[35] Romans 13.3
[36] Acts 4.19

calling that debars men from being members of Christ's body. And let all know, who have any understanding in the mystery of godliness, that if magistrates should not be members of Christ's church they cannot be children of the kingdom of Christ. If they cannot be children of the kingdom then they cannot be heirs of the promise. For those that are worthy to be heirs of salvation must first be children of the kingdom begotten by the immortal seed of the word and born anew (1 Peter 1.23). All are worthy to be members of Christ's Church. Therefore if you understand yourselves see that this is the end of your opinion. If you deny the magistrates, and hold them unworthy to be members of Christ's Church, you much more deny them to be worthy of salvation. If by reason of their office they are unworthy to be of the communion of saints on earth, they must be much more unworthy to be of the communion of saints in heaven. And thus by this your opinion you hold and maintain that God has appointed an ordinance and that they are his ministers of it (by his own appointment) and are by their office and ministry debarred of salvation. Your sin is no less than blasphemy against God in that you charge the most holy to have appointed an ordinance by the execution of which debars men from salvation. We hope you and your leaders do it ignorantly. Do not let the antiquity of your error make it precious to you, but rather vile. Do not sin by tradition after the doctrines of men, but be brought to try your ways by the word of God and let his spirit be your teacher and leader into all truth. Do not be led by men for all men have gone out of the way and are full of ignorance and error.

And to make it appear how you are misled in this bewitched opinion, we will come to some of your chief holds such as Mathew 20.25.26, Luke 22.24–26, and Mark 10, 5.45.[37] There arose strife among Christ's disciples over which should be the greatest. He said to them "the kings of the gentiles reign over them and they that bear rule over them are called gracious lords, but for you it will not be so. Let the greatest be as the least and the most chiefly as him that serves."[38] From this you gather that kings and magistrates that bear rule in the world may not be in the church. We wish that you would come (by the gracious direction of the spirit of God) into a due understanding of this scripture. We must first seek to know where the disciples of Christ did seek to be greater one than another, and if they did strive for worldly

---

[37] Mark 10.42.43
[38] Mark 10.42.43

preferment, then your ground may prove partly true. But if they did not strive for preferment in the world or worldly preferment, then there is no cullor that your collected ground should be true. In his speech our Savior Christ put and end to their strife and if they did not strive for worldly preferment or who should be the greatest in the world, then our Savior Christ did not speak at all concerning worldly superiority and rule. Although he did bring an example from the world, that is most usual in the scriptures. We hope this controversy may then easily come to an end if you are not utterly given up to your own ways and in all things. If the ignorant will not still be ignorant, they may by the grace of God see here most evidently the ground and cause of this strife among the disciples.

Zebedee's sons desired of our Savior Christ that they might sit one at his right hand and the other at his left in the kingdom, not speaking of the world. Our Savior first reproved them sharply and told them they do not know what they asked. And when he saw that this desire of superiority wrought disdain among them all, Jesus called them to him and taught them to know that although the kings and lords of the Gentiles and they that were great among them had dominion and authority and bore rule over them, in his kingdom it should not be so. He did not come to set up and establish such a kingdom in which men should seek to be one greater than another and bear rule one over another. Therefore he taught his disciples another lesson, telling them that whosoever will seek to be great or chiefest among them in his kingdom will be the servant of all.[39] That is the meanest of all, for that pride or arrogance in seeking to be chief and bear rule in the kingdom of Christ makes one the least. Because God rejects and will cast down the proud and will exalt the humble. Now as our Savior Christ taught his disciples here by an example from kings and rulers and great men that it should not be so among them in his kingdom. So also upon the same occasion of this strife and question of who should be the greatest (Matthew 18.1.4; Mark 9.34–36; Luke 9.46.48) our Savior Christ took a little child and sat him in their midst and taught them by the example of a child to be humble and lowly. He said unless they are converted and "become as little children they will not enter into the kingdom of heaven. And whosoever will humble himself as a little child, that person is the greatest in the kingdom of heaven."[40]

---

[39] Mark 10.36–45
[40] Matthew 18.3.4

From the first of these examples of kings and rulers and great men our Savior Christ said, "It will not be so among you."[41] You will not be like that in my kingdom, that is, to reign and rule and be great one over another.

From this first example you conclude that kings, rulers, and great men may not be of the kingdom of Christ. That you may better see the error of your collection and conclusion, we will collect and conclude the like from the other example which our Savior Christ made of a little child.

He said the disciples of his kingdom must be like little children, humble, not seeking to be greater one than another. Therefore little children may be of the kingdom of Christ because our Savior Christ said they must be like them. We know you can easily discern the error of this collection and conclusion, but why can you not discern the error of the other? We pray that as you love God and his truth, you will not be so partial to yourselves. We will still endeavor to show you the equal like of these conclusions that you may of conscience (denying the one) deny the other also.

Our Savior Christ said that the kings and rulers and great men of the Gentiles reign and rule over them, but it will not be so among you, the disciples of my kingdom. Therefore (you say) kings and rulers and great men may not be of the kingdom of Christ. In like manner may it be said (our Savior Christ speaking on the same occasion, little children are humble and do not desire to be one greater than another. It will be so among you the disciples of my kingdom therefore may any as well say) little children may be of the kingdom of Christ. Seeing you are confident (and according to that truth) that this last statement is not a true collection and conclusions, so also of conscience acknowledge that the first which you made is not true. As in the last both you and we do understand that Christ (speaking of his kingdom which is spiritual) did teach his disciples by the example of a little child, that by reason of its young years, was in quality and condition humble. So he would have them be humble in spirit. Our Savior does not teach here that little children are spiritually humble, and therefore may be of his kingdom. Because infants are born of the flesh they must be born again of the spirit in order to enter the kingdom of Christ (John 3).[42] Therefore, our Savior Christ here speaks of the quality and condition of children which is to be humble, not teaching that they may be of his kingdom. Even so our Savior Christ in the other example

---

[41] Matthew 20.26
[42] John 3.5

(speaking of the power to rule and authority of kings, rulers, and great men) taught them that in his spiritual kingdom among his disciples he will not have them as kings, rulers, and great men to reign one over another or one to be greater than another in his kingdom. Not teaching that kings, rulers, and great men may not be a part of the kingdom of Christ, but that his disciples may not (as kings, rulers, and great men) reign one over another in his kingdom.

In all this our Savior Christ speaks of his kingdom which is spiritual. He speaks against spiritual power and authority and will not have his disciples seek to be greater one than another not excepting against, nor disapproving the power and authority of earthly kings and princes. This is his own holy ordinance, but that they may be of Christ, retain their power and authority and administer in their office, and should to have due honor and obedience. But if they or any will seek to have spiritual power, rule and authority in this kingdom and make themselves greater than the rest of the disciples of Christ, that is what our Savior is speaking altogether against and of what he disapproves. In this respect, he teaches his disciples to be humble as little children and not to seek spiritual power and authority to be greater one than another. If they do, he who strives to be greatest will be least. But how is this rule of Christ (in which he so carefully and so often instructed his disciples) trodden under foot and utterly abolished by those that profess to be his disciples? Not to speak of the pope and all his confederates who in the height of all iniquity has exalted himself. What might we say to the lord bishops who so directly oppose Christ in this matter? How will they be able to stand before him with their spiritual, gracious lordships and so-called dignities which are so directly against his word and will? O that these things were not hidden from their eyes. Those that profess a Presbytery, though they do not bear such high names and titles as the rest, yet by their ruling power and authority (which by all means they seek to enlarge) if they do not take heed of their sins against this rule of Christ they will be found only a little less than any. And if we speak sparingly of you that profess an eldership, you should not think nor let it be thought by any that we do it either because we are partial or because your deserts are not fully evil enough. For the Lord knows and we know in part, and we wish to God you knew yourselves, that your iniquity is great here in your seeking and holding superiority over your congregations of which you belong, and partly by the authority and partly by the humbleness of a mind seeking to bear rule over the people of God. If by this our loving advertisement any or all of you whom we have spoken are provoked to evil, you will greatly increase your own judgments. For the Lord knows we do not speak it to provoke you to evil, but to provoke you to repentance before the great and evil day comes. On this day (for as all sin, but particularly and especially for this sin) the Lord will have a strict account if there is no repentance. We say especially for this sin because this sin of seeking superiority, rule and authority has and does utterly destroy all sincere and holy profession of the gospel. It keeps in captivity and bondage the consciences of men. It overthrows the strongest that resist and treads the weak under foot stopping up the way of life by men taking upon themselves to have in their hands the only keys to the kingdom of heaven. To return particularly to you who we first intended to speak, take heed lest while you set yourselves (by your opinion) against magistrates being of the kingdom of Christ, you have in the mean time set up a power and authority of your own, and so your second error is as evil as your first.

To put to an end to your first ground by this example which our Savior Christ brings of kings, rulers, and great men, because he said it will not be so among you,[43] that is, you will not be like them. If from these words you will yet hold that magistrates may not be of the kingdom of heaven and of the church, then you must also hold (unless you will show yourselves void of all understanding) that our Savior Christ in the same cause and on the same occasion brought an example of a little child and said it will be so among you, you will be like this little child, you must then hold that little children may be of the kingdom of Christ and of the church. If Christ had said, do not be like or debar out those who are brought for this example, rather than where he says be like and must admit in those that are brought for the example. So then those that are of this ground will admit infants in. Let them see (if they have any sight) that they debar magistrates out. And you that debar magistrates out by this ground must admit infants in. They are the examples of direct contradictions produced for one and the same thing. Therefore, those that debar both and those that admit both make things that are in direct contradiction to be alike. This is the most unjust and false understanding that can be in men. Let us, therefore, rather prevail with you to look at your ways and reconcile yourselves to the word of truth. And mark well the words of our Savior Christ concerning this point (Matthew 18.4) "Whosoever will humble

---

[43] Matthew 20.26

himself as this little child, the same is the greatest in the kingdom of heaven." And (verse 3) "They that are converted and become as little children will enter into the kingdom of heaven." There is no exception of persons. Kings and princes and all great men, if they are converted and become as little children and humble themselves, they may enter in and be the greatest in the kingdom of heaven. They do not enter by their princely power, but by their humility. We unfeignedly wish that all kings, princes, and rulers would see that their greatness, power, or authority does nothing at all to advance them to, or in the kingdom of heaven, but it is only their conversion and humility. But your opinion leads you to this; they cannot be converted unless they first cast away their magistracy. This is the truth of your ground, a most woeful ground if you could see its footsteps. If it is so that they cannot be converted unless they cast away their magistracy, then their magistracy is sin. If their magistracy is a sin then all their administration in which they administer by the power and virtue of it is also a sin. Who will be able to contradict this? Which way will all the devices of men and angels be able to avoid it? If magistrates cannot be converted to God (that is repent and believe) unless they cast away their magistracy, then their magistracy is sin. There is nothing but sin that hinders faith and repentance.

Do you (that hold this fearful opinion) see into what straights it has brought you? You have no way to turn yourselves. If there is any grace or love of God in you humble yourselves to the dust before the Lord and his people and proclaim your repentance. So that you may yet further be provoked to see the height of your sin, as far as we in our great weakness are (by the mercy of God) able to show you by reason of our so great weakness, we must have exceedingly failed and come up short. But yet by the uttermost grace of God we will endeavor to be faithful to God and you. We demand, cannot magistrates repent and believe and so be received or enter into the kingdom of heaven unless they cast away their magistracy? You profess and hold that they cannot. Why then is their magistracy sin and all they do by their power a sin? If this is so, why then has the most holy, righteous, merciful, and just God, the God of all power, given power from himself, and appointed an ordinance of the magistracy, by virtue of the power that was given by God, for magistrates to administer and who are commanded by God to provide righteous judgment? They are to punish the wicked in justice and to reward or praise the well doers in mercy, and all this you say is sin. In this God gives them power and authority and commandment to do. In all this they are his ministers doing his will, yet not withstanding all this is sin, for if by reason of their magistracy (retaining it) they cannot be converted, that is to repent and believe, then their magistracy is sin and then all they do by virtue of their magistracy, which is sin, must also be sin. In this you charge the most high God to ordain and give power from himself to magistrates to sin. So you make it a sin for them to punish those that do evil and to praise or reward the well doers. Although they do it by the power and commandment of God, you maintain that God gives power and commandment to sin. What a fearful estate and condition your error has brought you (Matthew 5.25). How will they answer it, those that do so strictly maintain and teach this error? Is this the least commandment that they break and teach men? To blaspheme the name of God in making him the author of sin saying the holy ordinance of magistracy, which he has ordained, is sin and maintain that magistrates may not be of the kingdom of heaven nor admitted to the church unless they first cast away their magistracy. There is nothing to be cast way to enter into the kingdom of heaven but sin. If there is no entering for magistrates but by casting away their magistracy, then it must be said that magistracy is a sin. We often go over this point that we might move you with careful advisedness to consider it, which we beseech you by the love of God to do, and not to dishonor God and your profession by such errors.

This is what the apostle writes to the Romans in chapter 13 and that which is spoken from that place might suffice for this whole cause of the power, authority, and administration of the magistracy. But it must yet be opposed on another ground that is held and strongly maintained against the magistracy, by which the most simple hearted are deceived and that is, "The weapons of our warfare are not carnal, but mighty through God to cast down holds" (2 Corinthians 10.4). From this scripture, diverse as some of magistrates may be in their holds to end causes and questions, you do not hold that they may make war nor put men to death. It is to be lamented with tears of men's souls to see the simple hearted so misled. They are deceived under a dangerous cullor, and a great show of holiness, not seeing the deceits of Satan who transforms himself into an angel of light. What holy heart will not easily be brought to think that war is an unchristian like thing where there is so much slaughter and bloodshed and which is accompanied with so many calamities and miseries and which is followed and maintained by so great force and violence by the of army of flesh. So likewise is it a lamentable thing that men should be executed and put to death, by sentence of law for offences.

These magistrates you will admit in no case. We pray that you will consider how should such magistrates as some of you would allow would order and determine causes of controversy without the sword of justice? Who would obey their orders and decrees if they had no power to constrain? Would evil doers be persuaded by words to do well? Would wrong doers by persuasion do right? If they would not, then were all your magistrates labor lost? They are but weak imaginations to imagine in your minds that there can be such magistrates, but let us come to your ground. The apostle says (2 Corinthians 10)[44] "The weapons of our warfare are not carnal." The ground and cause of the apostle's speech is this. There were certain false apostles (2 Corinthians 11.13–20) who crept in among the Corinthians who made a good show and exalted themselves. They had brought the people into bondage to uphold themselves in their exaltation. They sought to disgrace the apostle Paul. Because his writings were of great power and authority, they could not lessen the authority of them. Therefore, they sought to disgrace his person (2 Corinthians 10.10) "His letters (one says) are fore and strong, but his bodily presence is weak and his speech is of no value." To this the apostle answered (verse 7) "Do you look at things after their appearance?" And (verse two) do you esteem us as though we walked after the flesh? Though we walk in the flesh, we were not after the flesh, for the weapons of our warfare are not carnal." In all this showing and teaching them that they should not esteem of him according to the outward appearance in the flesh, for he did not come to make a great outward boasting show, and to subdue and bring men in bondage by such means, but by the power of the spirit. The apostle said "the weapons of our warfare are not carnal but are of faith."[45] The Apostle said (2 Corinthians 13.2) [46] "Seeing that you seek the experience of Christ that speaks in me let them know that they have sinned, and all others that if I come again I will not spare them." All this and much more of this sense he said to the Corinthians. And to him that spoke those things he said, (2 Corinthians 10.11) "Let him think, as much as we say in words by letters when we are absent, so much we will indeed do when we are present." Thus, the apostle labors to show them that his ministry was spiritual by the power from which he came among them. But seeing that they sought to disgrace his ministry by disgracing his person,

---

[44] 2 Corinthians 10.4
[45] 2 Corinthians 10.3.4
[46] 2 Corinthians 13.3.2

they should see that he would be the same in his deeds when present that they confessed him to be in his writings when absent. With what understanding can men gather from this that there may be no other weapons used in the world other than the weapons the apostle Paul used in his ministry of apostleship against false apostles? We have written much of this so that you might see how you are seduced by misapplying the words of scripture from the sense which is too usual among you.

Well, in this place we have learned from the apostle what his weapons were in the ministry of his apostleship. He taught the disciples to use only such weapons in their ministry.

Now let us also for a full finishing of this point at hand be taught of the same apostle (teaching with the same spirit and authority) concerning what weapons magistrates must administer in the office of their magistracy. And that is shown in (Romans 13.4) "They who bear the sword do not bear it for no reason. They are the ministers of God who are to take vengeance on those who do evil."

Here the words and sense of the scripture are given together and that evidently without any condition God has given magistrates power from himself and a sword to punish and take even vengeance on all evil doers. They may take vengeance of one, then of ten, and of ten thousand, this God has appointed, ordained, and commanded. God is a gracious, merciful God, and full of pity and compassion. Yes, he is more compassionate than all men can be. Therefore do not let men pretend holiness in their compassionate and pitiful disposition that would not have magistrates administer with the sword. For Satan deceives you in this and makes you more pitiful than God and thus you sin more grievously when you rejoice in yourselves and think you do exceedingly well. But the thing that misleads you all is that you can see no sword, but the sword of the spirit, and no armor but spiritual armor in the kingdom of Christ. Therefore the disciples of that kingdom (you say) must have no other weapons nor put on any other armor. There then can be no putting to death, nor any war, neither should there be, but all is spiritual. Suffer our foolishness if we seem as fools to speak to you. Even so in the kingdom of Christ, there is no treasure but spiritual treasure and no bags but spiritual bags (Luke 12.33). No buildings, but spiritual buildings. No apparel but spiritual apparel (1 Peter 3.3). No meat but spiritual meat (Romans 14.17). If then you will cast away all weapons and armor but such as the disciples of Christ use in his kingdom, you must also cast away all your bags and treasure, and all your buildings and houses, and you must wear no apparel but spiritual apparel, and eat not meat but spiritual meat. If all this is to be answered that in the New Testament the lawful use of all these things may be allowed, we answer even so is the lawful use of the magistracy to punish evil doers with the sword allowed and approved in the New Testament as is proven from Romans 13, which no man with any good conscience will ever be able to gainsay. To conclude we in love beseech you to see what an extreme strait you are brought into, (we mean all those that hold that magistrates may not be members of Christ's Church, and restrain their magistracy) that you must say that the magistracy is not a holy ordinance of God and that all that is done by their power and authority is sin. Therefore magistrates may not be admitted into the church of Christ unless they cast away their magistracy. If you confess that it is a holy ordinance of God, and that the administration and execution of it and whatsoever is done by the power and authority of the same according to the word of God in the punishing of evil doers and praising and rewarding the well doers is good and holy and just in the sight of God, then magistrates may be of the church of Christ and retain their magistracy. For no man may be debarred out of the church of Christ for doing that which is holy, just, and good.

We will deal yet more plainly with you so that the uttermost depth of your error may be discovered so that you and all men may utterly detest and abhor it. If you will say that magistrates are not otherwise the ministers of God, but are as the devils, one of our own countrymen, the forenamed Mr. Jarvase Nevile (falling on this and your other errors) most blasphemously has affirmed it. Unless you will also hold the same (which God forbid that any child of God should do) you can never deny magistrates being members of the church of Christ. For if you confess that they are the holy and good ministers of God applying themselves to their task, then how can you deny that they are unfit to be member's of the church of Christ? It is only because the holy and good ministers of God retain their ministry office and calling where they are appointed by God.

And now may you see that we had just cause in the beginning of this question to endeavor to show that the Lord requires a diligent, faithful, willing obedience of the magistrates. The devils obey by force and against their wills. God never makes them ministers of his mercy to any. But we see here that God has ordained magistrates as his ministers for good, both in mercy and justice, as well to reward the well doers and to punish the evil doers. Of all the people on the earth none have more cause to be thankful to God for this blessed ordinance of the magistracy than you and this whole country and nation. In that God has by his power and authority given to you magistrates who have so defended and delivered you from the hand of a cruel destroyer. Will you continue his holy ordinance and account it as a vile thing? Far be it from you to continue in this your so great evil sin.

Do not think that in the handling of this point, we seek to bring your persons into question or contempt with the higher powers. The Lord knows we have no such intent. We know their worthy patience in bearing with your great weakness, but only to bring this error into contempt among you so that you might forsake it. That is what we seek. We seek that the simple hearted might not be betrayed with it as they are. We do not know how far that deceitful opinion leads them, and all under a show of godliness. Much more might be said than we are able to say and we would willingly have said something more of this point and of others, but it is so difficult to get it set over into your language. Give us leave to say more to you to provoke you to tread under foot this unholy disposition that seems to be so holy, and makes you flatter yourselves, and think yourselves most holy, and that is that you would not have evil doers punished with the sword. You greatly please yourselves in your pitiful dispositions and that you think you please God when it is most evident that you sin grievously in it. For it is the good will, pleasure, and commandment of God that evil doers should be punished by the sword, and to that end he has given power and authority to magistrates. And you, contrary to the good will and pleasure of God, would not have evil doers punished with the sword. Is this not your great sin to be contrary minded to God? Take heed lest by this your disposition you could also wish or desire that wicked men dying in their sin might not be damned in which you should utterly dishonor God for then the enemies of God would triumph over him. They would then laugh at God holding him in scorn and derision. "God will laugh at their destruction and mock them when their fears come" (Proverbs 1.26). And all the saints of God will rejoice with him (Revelation 18.20). If the saints in heaven rejoice and praise God when he punishes and takes vengeance on the wicked, should the saints who are on the earth not also rejoice and praise God when they see or hear that the evil doers are punished here on earth by the powers and authorities God has appointed? And they are to praise God even more seeing that the Holy Ghost testifies that it is for their wealth. What a great sin of ingratitude and unthankfulness this is in all of you that so disapprove of magistrates and of their punishing of evil doers by the sword. If it were not for this ordinance all the godly on earth would be destroyed and the most godly first. Now we know that God is able to defend his own without the sword, but he has appointed this holy ordinance of the magistracy for the preservation and defense of all good men and for the subduing and keeping under and cutting off the evil doers. Let none make themselves more wise and more holy than God, which you all do that disapprove of the magistracy. Repent, for you are sinning with a high hand in dishonoring God by disapproving of his holy ordinance of magistracy which he has commanded should be honored with all godly fear, reverence, and obedience. If you repent and truly obey God then you must (being commanded by the authority of the magistracy) be ready with your own persons and all that you have to support and defend that sword of justice which they bear and by which they administer by that power and authority they have from God. Who are fitter to support and maintain the holy ordinance of God than those who profess to be children of God? Who are fitter to fight just and good battles than good and just men? What simplicity is this to think that it is more lawful to hire men to fight a battle than to fight it themselves? The people of Israel, that were the people of God, never did so, but they fought the battles of the Lord themselves and the Lord went forth with their armies and gave them victory over their enemies and put their adversaries to flight. If the magistracy is a holy ordinance of God now as it was then, it is as lawful for them to defend their countries and people now as it was then. It is as lawful now for the servants of God to be commanded by the magistrates to go to war as it was then. The servants of God might with better consciences and more comfort go to battle themselves (being commanded by the higher powers that are of God) though they died in battle than to hire men to be slain for them to whom the cause does not belong. There is no religion in this that magistrates by reason of your unwillingness to go to battle for the cause of God and for your own safeties and preservation should be forced to hire men to fight for you (although you pay for it) and in all this you pretend religion and conscience. But it is evident by the word of God that if the magistracy is a holy ordinance of God, it is to be supported by all holy and good men and means. If it is not a holy ordinance of God then magistrates are but ministers of God as are the devils. They are neither to be obeyed for conscience sake nor to be honored. We are not bound of conscience to honor and obey the power, authority, and ministry of the devils, but to refuse it. The apostle Paul's doctrine (Romans 13) and in the apostle Peter's letters on doctrine (1 Peter 2.3.17) are all made false and erroneous. But far be it for any that have any truth of true godliness deny the holy ordinance of the magistracy and so to overthrow the holy doctrines of the apostles. Let the godly beware of such. The apostle Peter foretold of them and of their manner of proceeding.

First he showed that there will be false teachers whose privilege will bring in damnable heresies; even denying the Lord that has bought them. Their followers will speak evil of the way of truth. These are those who despise government and are bound and stand in their own conceit and do not fear speaking evil of those that have dignity (2 Peter 2.1–10). Let us apply this to the persons and cause at hand. These men that most stiffly stand against the magistracy, have they not brought in damnable heresies? Do they not deny the Lord that bought them? Are they not those that deny the true humanity of Christ, denying that he had a true earthly natural body with which he bought them? They deny or are ignorant that he had a true natural earthly body, and in doing so they deny and are ignorant that the Lord bought them. We will not now speak to the rest of their damnable heresies, but will come to the one that despises government and speaks evil of those that are in dignity. Can there be greater despisers of government than those that deny it is lawful to punish evil doers with the sword? If the sword is taken away where is government? Will evil doers be governed with a rod of reed? Do we not daily see that many fears are not of the sword? If the sword of justice is taken away all government would be overthrown. Can there be greater despisers of government than those that would altogether overthrow it? They speak evil of those that are in dignity and authority. Do these men not speak evil of them when they teach and condemn them as evil doers in their execution of justice against offenders? Can they speak a greater evil than to say they are such evil doers as not worthy to be members of the church of Christ? What greater evil and contempt can be cast on them both before God and his people for they are absolutely denied to be the ministers of God, but are as the devils. Can there be a greater evil spoken of than this? To make it plainer that you who teach these things against the magistracy are these false teachers spoken of by the apostle Peter, there is one special mark and it is that you do it secretly. Can false teachers teach more secretly than you who teach this? Be sure you do not understand that teaching secretly is to be done in corners and secret places. The apostle shows that that is not his meaning when he speaks of bringing in heresy secretly in the teaching of doctrines. Is this heresy against the magistrates not most quietly brought in under a cullor? From our Savior Christ's own words where he said, "It will not be so among you."[47] And the apostle says "the weapons of our warfare are not carnal."[48] Is this not secretly done? You wrest the scriptures so deceitfully from a show of words leaving the true sense of that place and concluding most secretly and deceitfully that the magistrates who bear the sword may not be of the kingdom of Christ or his Church. Let what we said before suffice of the misunderstanding of these scriptures. And see further how under this first damnable heresy of denying magistrates to be of the church that this heresy is brought in secretly that the magistracy is utterly unlawful and all this is done by the power and authority of sin. For as we have shown there is nothing but sin that debars any from being members of Christ's Church. They then that hold that the magistracy debars men from being members of the Church of Christ must hold that the magistracy is a sin and magistrates, by the reason of their office and authority, are sinners. Although a magistrate should manifest never so great a faith and repentance, but these men will not yield that he may be of the church of Christ unless he casts away his magistracy. His faith and repentance is nothing. This unholy office and unsanctified authority does utterly overthrow faith and repentance. Let it not displease you that we write so plainly. If it is a holy office and a sanctified authority then it cannot debar any from being members of the church of Christ.

Thus may you and all see that there are those among you who teach that the magistrates may not be of the church and that is not lawful for them to punish evil doers with the sword, nor by the sword to maintain war for the preservation of their countries and people. These are those who secretly bring in damnable heresies, despising government and speaking evil of those that are in dignity and authority in that they seek the utter overthrow of all government. They account the authority of the magistracy as most vile because evil doers are punished by it, which you teach should not be, but it is sin and wickedness that is to be done. And if all men in these provinces under the government of the lords and states general were of your minds, as you would have them, where would governments and magistrates be? Is it not all in the dust? Thus it is evident that you would have kings, princes, and magistrates

---

[47] Matthew 20.26
[48] 2 Corinthians 10.4

utterly abolished. Is this the heresy not secretly brought in under so great a show of godliness to destroy the holy ordinance of God? How many of you understand that this heresy leads you to account magistrates, who are the ministers of God, the same as the devils? We hope there are thousands of you that have no such thoughts. Yet, it is most evident, and cannot be avoided, but it is the end of your ground and rule. Is this not secretly brought it? Therefore do not be deceived by fair and humble speeches. We profess to you by this that has already been said, and does it not appear plainly to any indifferent reader, that your ground leads you to this, that all that magistrates do (by virtue and power of their office in punishing evil doers) is sin. If any think it is good to oppose this, we will by God's assistance make it most clear to all that all who will see and not wink their eyes. If you, therefore, like to hold that magistrates are not otherwise the ministers of God, but are as the devils, then you must also leave your hold that magistrates by reason of their magistracy are to be debarred from the kingdom or church of Christ. And also it will appear that your ground does evidently overthrow all magistrates on the whole earth. For if God would have all kings and princes saved and come to the knowledge and profession of his truth, which the apostle said they would (1 Timothy 2.4) and you confess the same, and if they cannot come to the knowledge and profession of the truth unless they cast away their magistracy (as you say and hold) then all the magistrates must be cast away in the whole world. For God would have all the kings, princes, and magistrates upon the earth come to the knowledge of the truth and be saved. And if you do not want to overthrow all magistrates and magistracy on the earth, then leave your hold that they may not be of the kingdom and church of Christ.

The apostle speaks of one other mark that shows that you are the false teachers. It is that you stand in your own conceit. We have found this in some of you. We require that we may not find it in all of you for then it will appear and be evident to all men.

Thus we have in these points in which we differ from you spoken as far as God has enabled us. We beseech you all with singleness of heart to try your standing in these things we have spoken of and that you would not hold these opinions because you have held them so long, but you are lovingly advised to search the scriptures and see whether you have any good warrant to hold and profess and teach men so. Now, approve yourselves to us and to all men that you do not walk blindly in the steps of those who have gone before you. Rather that you desire and endeavor to walk by true sanctified knowledge from the scriptures and that you do not so much seek to heap multitudes together and build up great churches and congregations as to gather together a holy people and build up pure churches in the profession of the true faith so that you may be approved of God. Neither you nor any people can ever do this unless you first make sure that your doctrine is pure and undefiled. Though a people should never so much excel in all holiness of conversation, but they should excel in works, love, and service, in faith, and patience and that their works should be more at the last than at the first (Revelation 2.19). Yet if they suffer false doctrine and false teachers, they are impure and a polluted church "for a little leaven leavens the whole lump" (Galatians 5.9) and the Lord will not approve of them, but will certainly come against them "with the sword of his mouth"[49] and he "will remove their candlesticks out of there places."[50]

This is what the Lord says, but who believes the word of the Lord. If churches and congregations did believe the words of the Lord it would make them try their doctrines by the word of the Lord and go upon sound grounds with knowledge and understanding from the word of truth that is testified to them by the teaching of the spirit of God. They will not receive doctrines upon the good opinion they have of their teacher's knowledge, holiness, and faithfulness, although they should excel in all these things. Neither would the people of God be carried away after any doctrines by the strong working affections of their minds, judging it to be the working of the spirit of God when it is nothing but the spirit of their own affections. "They may have great emotions and feelings with much zeal but not according to knowledge" (Romans 10.2). Therefore we are commanded not to believe every spirit, neither in ourselves nor in others, but first try whether the spirit is from God. And by this we will know the spirit of the error. If we hear God's word (1 John 4.6) we must search and try everything by it.

O that churches and congregations would look at their ways, and not hold error for company's sake, nor walk in paths by affections. It is better to hold the truth alone and to walk in its ways, contrary to all affections of the heart which is deceitful. This is a hard doctrine. Who is able to hear it? It is a pleasing thing to walk in a profession of religion with a multitude, especially if some of the grounds of their faith agree with men's minds. This overthrows the first beginnings of the religion of God when men will choose to walk with

---

[49] Revelation 1.16
[50] Revelation 2.5

that people and in that profession of faith that best pleases their minds, not so much regarding the truth of their faith nor their holy walking in it. Although they may not like some things, but if it pleases some of them well, they will not differ over small matters. When they are once gathered and knit together in a multitude, then though error after error is discovered, and sin after sin committed, there will no breaking upon any conditions. This overthrows all growth of religion. We with you and all great congregations ask you to look at yourselves to see that you are not more careful to maintain your multitudes than the Lord's truth. A multitude in error and sin cannot please God. No, a few walking together in the truth with holiness will be acceptable in his sight. If there are but "two or three, he will be in their midst."[51] Therefore, do not please yourselves in your multitudes by walking in so many errors as you do. If you do not repent of these errors of which we have made mention, and all of your other errors and false doctrines maintained among you, the Lord will assuredly make you desolate. For this he has threatened and executed his judgment on Pergamos and Thyatira because they did not repent. He threatens and will execute the same judgment on you whose sin is in a like manner of transgression, if you do not repent. And your gifts and graces are many less than the gifts and graces of those churches and your false doctrines and sins are already many more and greater, and more speedily will his judgment be on you if you do not repent, which we unfeignedly desire that Lord will give you the grace to do. Be warned you that are leaders while it is today and do not harden your hearts. Why should you perish in your sins and lead so many simple souls to destruction with you?

We are praying that all the gracious hearted among you will remember what the wise man said. "Open rebuke is better than secret love, and the wounds of a lover are faithful" (Proverbs 27.5.6). And we will hope that though we reprove you, we will at length find more love (which is all we require of you) than they that so flatter you with their tongues. The grace of our Lord Jesus Christ be with you. Amen.

Cant. 4.8.

Come from Lebanon, even come from Lebanon, and look from the top of Amanah, from the top of Shenir and Hermon, from the dens of the lions, and from the mountains of the leopards.

---

[51] Matthew 18.20

To all the most worthy Governors
Learned teachers, and Godly people
Of all estates and conditions in these united
Provinces. Grace and peace from God the
Father, and our Lord Jesus Christ.

We among the rest of the people of God that profess the gospel of Jesus
Christ have a great cause to praise the Lord for the freedom and liberty that we
have in these provinces, to profess and speak in the name of Jesus. We are
bound and do with all humbleness of heart thankfully acknowledge it. And we
beseech the Lord in mercy to recompense it sevenfold into the bosom of those
that are in authority, by whose great favor we enjoy this blessed and
comfortable liberty. This liberty that we have we do not have the least of
thoughts to abuse and neither (by the grace and mercy of God) will ever
willingly do. And we humbly crave now, that we may with favor and good
acceptance use this Christian liberty to propound one ground of religion by
way of a question and demand. We do not doubt (through the grace of God)
but if it will be thoroughly and faithfully debated and tried by the godly,
wise, and learned, it will put a short end to that long continued controversy of
God's eternal decree of life and death to salvation and condemnation. And
thus with reverence and due respect to all degrees of persons we proceed.

Our first question and demand is.
1. Whether God did not decree, that if Adam did obey, he should live?

Our Second.
2. Whether God did not, according to his decree, create Adam in his
own image (Genesis 1.17)[52] and in righteousness and true holiness
(Ephesians 4.24) and gave him free will and power, in and of himself, that he
might obey and live?

Our Third.
3. Whether God did not according to his decree and work of creation
give Adam his commandment to obey and live (Genesis 2.16.17)?

---

[52] Genesis 1.27

Our Fourth.

4. God then decreeing that if Adam did obey he should live, and giving him free will and power in and of himself that he might obey and live, and commanding him to obey and live. Our demand is, with what manner of understanding can it be held or said that God decreed that Adam should disobey and die? Does this not make God in his decree, his works, and in his commandments contrary to himself? Does God decree that if Adam did obey he should live and decree that if he should disobey he would die? Did God create Adam after his own image with power and will to work righteousness and decree that he should work unrighteousness and sin? Does God command Adam to obey and decree that he should disobey? We demand to know how these things can agree.

Our Fifth.

5. Whether God ever made any other decree with mankind concerning life and death, salvation, and condemnation but the one he made with Adam? (Romans 5.12). Then if God did not decree that Adam should sin, by whom then did sin enter? Adam, by whose sin condemnation came upon all men, is not to be condemned (Romans 5.18). How then can it be said that God has decreed any man to sin or any man to condemnation?

Our Sixth.

6. Whether God's decree was not from before all beginnings? (Genesis 2.17). If Adam disobeyed and sinned then should he die? How then is it said that it was God's decree that he should disobey and die? Both of these decrees cannot stand. Can the first then be denied?

Our Seventh.

7. If any should through unadivisedness [sic] not knowing God or of willful wickedness, deny before his fall that Adam had free will and power to work righteousness, we demand of them was his understanding not holy and his will holy? Were not all faculties and powers of his soul and body holy? Did he not have the power to use them in a holy manner? If all these things were not so, how is it that what God said is true? "In the image of God he created him" (Genesis 1:26).

Our Eighth.

Before his fall did Adam not use all the faculties and powers of his soul and body in a manner wholly to God's glory? When the Lord brought to him all the foul of heaven and every beast of the field to see what he would call them, and he gave names to all cattle, and to the fowls of heaven, and to every beast of the field.[53] Also when the Lord brought the woman he had made to Adam, Adam said, "This is now bone of my bone and flesh of my flesh. She will be called woman because she was taken out of man."[54] We demand whether it is not most evident and plain that Adam had free power over his understanding, will, and affections, when he did these things to the glory of God?

Our Ninth.

Adam then having free will and power from God in and by his creation to obey and live, how can it be possibly said that God in his eternal decree decreed him or any man to condemnation?

We desire a godly careful consideration and reviewing of these things, for upon this ground depends the whole cause of predestination and God's decree concerning salvation and condemnation. If Adam had free will and power to obey, which no man that ever knew God can deny, then how could God decree any man to condemnation? If Adam did not have free will and power to obey, then God decreed he should disobey and sin, and then how can it be denied but that God has decreed men to condemnation. Is universal redemption utterly overthrown? For how could Christ redeem all, and God decree some to be condemned? But if Adam had free will and power to obey then God decreed no man to condemnation. And if God decreed no man to condemnation before the beginning of the world, then the Lamb that was slain from before the beginning of the world must have been given as a redeemer for all men. And then all men are bound to glorify God in that he has given them a Savior and means of salvation. But if he has not given a Savior for all men, then the greatest part of men in the world have no cause to glorify God. We demand whether this does not greatly rob God of his honor?

And let us yet require one thing more at your hands that baptize infants. Do you not in faith baptize them as being redeemed by Christ in that you

---

[53] Genesis 1.19.20
[54] Genesis 2.23

declare them (as appeared in your form of baptism) to be sanctified in Christ and therefore they should be baptized as members of the Church, which is the body of Christ? Surely it cannot be but that you faithfully believe that all the infants you baptize are redeemed by Christ or else you would not baptize them in the name of Christ and acknowledge them as members of his body. If you do hold that all the infants you baptize are redeemed by Christ, then if your rule of particular redemption and particular predestination is a true rule, you must also hold that all Dutchland must be saved and not one of them can be condemned. And so you most hold the like opinion of all England, all France, all Scotland, and generally of all the nations of whose baptizing of infants you approve. And in that you approve of the baptizing of all the Turks and all the heathens whosoever and their infants, if they should come to the acknowledgement of the faith of Jesus Christ, which we hope none can say. You do most plainly show that you hold that Christ redeemed them also. Thus you hold that Christ has redeemed the entire world if you would but rightly understand yourselves in your own ground, which we beseech you to endeavor to do so. So you will be able (through God's grace) to give a good reason of your faith.

O that we might on Christ's behalf require that you with godly careful advisedness consider thoroughly these few things so simply and plainly set down. So that all the honor and praise that is due to Christ for his great work of redemption might freely be given to him. And that none that profess and fear his name would strive to lessen his unspeakable work of mercy. In this they do not only lessen the honor and praise due to him for that his so gracious work of redeeming all without respect of persons, but they also deprive the people of God of the true understanding of God's equal grace and mercy to all, being all but under one and the same transgression in Adam, by whose sin only condemnation went over all, the sin in which Christ was given was for Adam. It then must be given to all his posterity as God does not punish the child for the father's sin, but especially forgives the father who sins. Let men beware how they take from the word of God, and so flee the vengeance that is to come on all those that will do so.

Grace be with you Amen.

As it is suspected that those who hold universal redemption do, or must hold free will, we desire to testify to all for the clearing of ourselves from the suspicion of that most damnable heresy that God in his mercy has so far given us grace to see that whoever holds universal redemption by Christ cannot hold free will, if they have any understanding. Free will utterly abolishes Christ and destroys faith and sets up works. Free will is to have absolute power in a man's self to work righteousness and obey God in perfect obedience. And such men do not need Christ, and if any will be as blind as to think that Christ restored man into his former estate of innocence, then there must be a new tree of knowledge of good and evil. For there is no other way shown in the scriptures for a perfect man that is restored to Adam's state to sin but by eating of that tree. If man is restored to perfection or if all men did not fall in Adam, as the scriptures testify they did (Romans 5.12.18), then man has power in himself to obey and then some may obey and stand in no need of Christ.

We do not know any certainty of these men's opinions. Therefore, we will not enter into them. Only one man once told us that he had free will, but we found him to hold so many other horrible opinions in which he was so obstinate that we had no faith to have any further conference with him. To these men only do we say this much, the word of God says (Genesis 5.2)[55] that "God created Adam in the likeness of God, he made him." (Verse 3) "Adam lived for one hundred and thirty years and begat a child in his own likeness after his image." Cannot men see here that Adam did not begat a child in the likeness of God, but in his own likeness? The likeness or image of God, which is perfection, righteousness, and true holiness, does differ and is clearly contrary to the likeness and image of sinful Adam, of whom when he begat Seth, his son, who was an imperfect, unholy, and an unrighteous man. If they cannot see this then they are void of all knowledge of God. And we leave this as a remembrance to all those who stand for free will; that they may look back to whose image and likeness they are begotten. If their fathers begat them in the image of God, then they are certainly perfect, holy, and righteous, and so have free will. But if their fathers begat them in their own image and likeness, as Adam begat his son Seth, then let them with David cry out and confess "Behold I was born in iniquity and in sin my mother conceived me" (Psalm 51.5). And if they confess that they were born in iniquity and conceived in sin as the holy man David was, how the devil does bewitch them to make them think that they are perfect and have free will.

For ourselves we confess with the apostle (Romans 7.18) that we know that "Nothing good lives in me." And Christ has taught us (John 3.6) "that

---

[55] Genesis 5.1

which is born of the flesh is flesh" and therefore must do the works of the flesh. "That which is born of the spirit is spirit." Therefore, all which are born of the flesh must be born again before they can become spiritual. And we confess with the same apostle (1 Corinthians 1.30) that we are of God only through Jesus Christ who of God is made to us, "wisdom, and righteousness, and sanctification, and redemption." (Ephesians 2.8.9) "By grace only we are saved through faith and not of ourselves but of the gift of God not of works." Let it be here observed that faith is a created quality in man, as knowledge is, which being sanctified by the spirit of grace is knowledge to salvation and faith to salvation. Therefore, our Savior Christ[56] showed that knowledge is not sufficient faith. "It is not the knowers of my will but the doers that are justified."[57] And the Holy Ghost (speaking of faith) said, "Faith without works is dead," (James 2.17) showing that the devils believe. Therefore faith is not a new gift. It is grace in Christ which the apostle said in this place is the gift of God by which men's knowledge and faith are sanctified to salvation and so are saved by grace only, through faith sanctified by the grace of God in Christ. And this grace of God, which is his mercy by Christ, God has given to all, for by that grace God brought salvation to all men (Titus 2.10).[58] But all have not received it, as Paul and Barnabus[SIC OR TYPO?] testified against the Jews. (Acts 13.46) "You have put out from you the word of God and have judged yourselves unworthy of everlasting life." And Stephen said to them (Acts. 7.51) "You have always resisted the Holy Spirit." Now we pray that this great iniquity of such as (by the deceit of Satan and sin) are carried into these errors we before spoke of, and we do not know how many more grievous and damnable there are, may they not be stumbling blocks to hinder any gracious heart from fearing, seeking after, and embracing any truth of God they hold. Let the blessed truth of God never be the less beloved and liked, because many that profess it hold fearful errors. Rather embrace it and use all godly diligence to bring them out of their errors, if it is possible, or they will perish in them, which is to be greatly feared by many of them.

The End

Tho. Helwys

---

[56] These are Paul's words.

[57] Romans 2.13

[58] This verse doesn't appear in the Bible.

8. A SHORT DECLARATION OF THE MYSTERY OF INIQUITY

Thomas Helwys wrote his most famous and influential work, A Short Declaration of the Mystery of Iniquity, *while living in Amsterdam in 1612. Only four copies of this work are known to be in existence. The copy in the Bodleian Library at Oxford University contains a personal handwritten note to King James that is believed to have been written by Helwys. In this note he reminds the monarch that while all Englishmen have a duty to be loyal to the king, the king is not God and must not interfere or attempt to rule the consciences of his people.*

The first major section of A Short Declaration *concerns religious liberty. It is the first book in the English language to call for the king to grant complete freedom of conscience in religious matters. Helwys does not ask only for freedom of religion for his own church, but for all people. He makes this clear in his most famous quotation: "Let them be heretics, Turks, Jews, or whatsoever, it does not appertain to the earthly power to punish them in the least measure."*

The second section of A Short Declaration *is very apocalyptic. Helwys believed that he was living in the last days as noted in the book of Revelation 13. * A Short Declaration *is laced with apocalyptic language and interpretations of prophecies as he viewed them coming to pass in England. Helwys described the errors of four different groups whom he believed were promoting the abomination of desolation. The first section is written against the pope and the Roman Catholic Church, whom Helwys considered the first Antichrist, mentioned in Revelation 13. The second section is a diatribe against the Anglican Church, whom he believed was composed of an unspiritual and unscriptural hierarchy and merely aped the Roman Catholic Church. He believed the Anglican Church was the second beast of Revelation 13. The third section is an attack of the Puritans. Helwys believed the Puritans had lost their way because they continued to cling to a false hope that the Anglican Church would reform. The final section is a personal attack against the Separatists in general and his old pastor, John Robinson, in particular. Helwys's main argument with the Separatists and Robinson was because they insisted that their infant baptisms, which took place in the Church of England, were still valid.*

Helwys concludes his book with an explanation of why he decided to return to England and why he decided that fleeing persecution was wrong. He also castigated John Robinson and the other Separatist congregations in Holland for not returning to England to help their English brethren and, if need be, lay down their lives for the truth.

Jeremiah 51.6
Flee out of the midst of Babel, and deliver every man his soul, do not be destroyed in her iniquity, for this is the time of the Lord's vengeance. He will render to her a recompense.

Hosea 10.12
Sow to yourselves in righteousness, reap after the measure of mercy. Break up your fallow ground, for it is time to seek the Lord, until he comes and rains righteousness on you.

Anno. 1612
Hear, O king and do not despise the counsel of the poor and let their complaints come before you.

The king is a mortal man and not God, therefore he has no power over the immortal souls of his subjects, to make laws and ordinances for them and to set spiritual lords over them.

If the king has authority to make spiritual lords and laws, then he is an immortal God and not a mortal man.

O king, do not be seduced by deceivers to sin so against God whom you should obey nor against your poor subjects who should and will obey you in all things with body, life, and goods or else let their lives be taken from the earth.

God save you the king.
Tho: Helwys
Spitalfields near London…

To the Reader

The fear of the almighty (through the work of his grace) having now at last overweighed in us the fear of men, we have thus far by the direction of God's word and spirit stretched out our hearts and hands with boldness to confess the name of Christ before men. We are to declare to the prince and people plainly their transgressions, that all might hear and see their fearful estate and standing, and repent, and turn to the Lord before the decree comes forth, before the day of their visitation passes, and that the things that belong to their peace are altogether hidden from their eyes. In this writing we have with all humble boldness spoken to our lord the king, our defense for this is that we are taught by God especially to make supplications, prayers, intercessions, and give thanks for our lord the king.[1] And we are taught that the gracious God of heaven (by whom the king reigns) desires that the king will be saved and come to the knowledge of the truth. Therefore, we the king's servants are especially bound by all the godly endeavors of our souls and bodies to seek the salvation of the king although it puts our lives in danger. If we saw our lord the king's person in danger either by private conspiracy or open assault, we are bound to seek the king's preservation and deliverance even if it meant the laying down of our own lives. If we did not, we should be readily and most worthily condemned as traitors. How much more are we bound to seek the preservation and deliverance of our king's soul and body as we see him in such great spiritual danger as we now do? If any are offended by us for doing so, they do not love the king. If our lord the king should be offended at us his servants for doing so, the king does not love himself. If all men and the king should be offended with us (which God forbid) yet in this matter we are sure that our God will be well-pleased with us in that we have with our best strength and faithfulness obeyed him who commands and teaches us to admonish all men everywhere to repent. This is our sure warrant and our assured hope and comfort.

Now as we have (according as we hold ourselves bound) thus far confessed Christ's name before men by writing, so we will (with the Lord's assistance) be ready, as we hold ourselves bound to confess Christ before men by word of mouth, not fearing (through God's grace) those that kill the body

---

[1] 1 Timothy 2.1.2

and after that are not able to do any more. In this duty to God and his people, we must confess that we have to this point greatly failed, but we will now be ready, with the Lord strengthening us, rather to be sacrificed for the publishing of the gospel of Jesus Christ, and for the service of your faith than to fail as we have done in both our duties to God and you. This we readily vow to God and promise to you. The will to do good is present in us, but we find no means in us to perform this duty and service. We saw a law in our flesh that was strongly rebelling against the laws of our minds, but our assured truth and confidence is that God's grace alone is sufficient to make us able in every way to do these things to which we ourselves are in no way able. Yet we will say with the apostle Paul, "If God is on our side who can prevail against us? Who will separate us from Christ's love? Will tribulation, or anguish, or persecution, or famine, or nakedness, or peril, or the sword? No. The Lord we trust in these things will make us conquerors."[2] And "though our outward man should perish"[3] or may suffer afflictions, (which were most foolish if we should not wait for), yet let the people of God look to the truth we witness and consider with holy and wise hearts whether we do not have good warrant. Yes, we have a direct commandment to do that which we do, though we are unfit and unworthy for such a service. Will we hear the Lord say, "Come out of her my people?"[4] Will the spirit of God that commands him that hears say "Come" and will we not say come? "Will the word of the Lord command archers to come against Babel and all that bend the bow to besiege and encircle it, and let none escape, and to recompense her double"[5] (Jeremiah 50.29; Revelation 18)? Will we spare our arrows though they are weak? Will the Spirit of God say, "All you that are mindful of the Lord do not keep silent" (Isaiah 62.16)?[6] Will we hold our peace because we are not eloquent? No, no, we have rejected our duties for too long. Now through God's grace we dare do so no longer. Therefore we cry to you the people of God saying "Babylon is fallen. She is fallen."[7] "Come out of her. Come out of her. If you continue to partake with her in her sins, you certainly will be

---

[2] Romans 8.31.35.37
[3] 2 Corinthians 4.16
[4] Revelation 18.4
[5] Jeremiah 50.29
[6] Isaiah 62.6
[7] Revelation 18.2

partakers of her plagues."[8] Therefore we say "Let him who is thirsty, come. Let whosoever will, take of the water of life freely come."[9] We call to all the valiant archers who bend the bow to come to the siege against the great city. We pray that all who are mindful of the Lord will not keep silent or give the Lord rest until he repairs and sets up Jerusalem as the praise of the world. Our continual prayers to the Lord are, and will be, that the Lord will enlighten your understandings, and raise up all the affections of your souls and spirits so that you may apply yourselves to these things as far as his word and spirit directs you so that you may no longer be deceived and seduced by false prophets who prophesy peace to you when war and destruction are at the door which the Lord allows both you and them to see, that you may all flee to the Lord for your deliverance and salvation. Amen.

Tho: Helwys

THE PRINCIPLE MATTERS HANDLED IN THE BOOK

The declaration will prove that these are the days of greatest tribulation, spoken of by Christ (Matthew 24), where the abomination of desolation is seen to be set in the holy place.

That there has been a general departing from the faith and an utter desolation of all true religion.

That the prophesy [sic] of the first beast (Revelation 13) is fulfilled under the Romish spiritual power and government.

That the prophesy [sic] of the second beast is fulfilled under the spiritual power and government of archbishops and lord bishops.

How kings will hate the whore and make her desolate.

What great power and authority, honor, names and titles God has given to the king.

That God has given to the king an earthly kingdom with all earthly power against which none may resist but must in all things obey willingly, either to do, or suffer.

That Christ alone is king of Israel, and sits upon David's throne, and that the king should be a subject of his kingdom.

---

[8] Revelation 18.4
[9] Revelation 22.17

That none should be punished either with death or bonds for transgressing against the spiritual ordinances of the New Testament, and that such offences should be punished only with the spiritual sword and censures.

That as the Romish hierarchy says in words that they cannot err, so the hierarchy of archbishops and lord bishops show by their deeds they hold that they cannot err and in this they agree as one.

The false profession of Puritanism (so-called) and the false prophet is discovered.

Their two deceitful excuses for their undergoing of all those things they cry out against are made manifest.

The false profession of Brownism (so-called) is plainly laid open with their false prophets, and with their false supposed separation from the world.

The vanity of their most deceitful distinction between a false church and no church (upon which their whole false building stands) is made evident.

Some particular errors of Mr. Robinson's book concerning the justification of separation is laid open.

That no man justifying any false way, or any one error, though of ignorance, can be saved.

The perverting of those words of our Savior Christ (Matthew 10) "When they persecute you in one city, flee to another,"[10] is contrary to all the meaning of Christ is plainly showed....

---

[10] Matthew 10.23

BOOK 1

What godly reader can without mourning affections read of the great destruction and overthrow of Jerusalem with the house and people of God prophesized by the prophet Jeremiah? And what heart is not much affected to see the exceeding great sorrow of the prophet, when he uttered this prophesy [sic] and declared the sins of the people? (Jeremiah 9). And when all these came to pass (according to the word of the Lord), the prophet saw it with his eyes, who could not yet sit down and lament to hear the most grievous lamentations that he pours out for that so great desolation and destruction, of which the Lord had destroyed and made desolate his own city, house and people? (Lamentations 1–3). No, they gave no regard to the words of the Lord spoken by the prophet concerning these things (Jeremiah 37.2). Yet when they saw the prophecy accomplished a deep sorrow took a hold of them. Then, "the elders of the daughter of Zion sat upon the ground, and kept silent, and cast dust on their heads and they girded themselves with sackcloth and the virgins of Jerusalem hung their heads down to the ground" (Lamentations 2.10). Whosoever reads it cannot deny, but that there was a just cause of all this sorrow. And therefore the prophet might say, "Behold and see if there is any sorrow like my sorrow" (Lamentations 1.12). If it cannot be denied, but that the hearing and seeing of this prophesy [sic] of so great a desolation fulfilled was a just cause of this great sorrow. Where then are the eyes and the ears of men that might hear and see far greater tribulations and desolations than these that were prophesied by a greater prophet than Jeremiah, and even now fulfilled in the fierce wrath of judgment by the most high, and that in the sight of all men? Yet, who considers it? Who takes up a lamentation for it? Are all men utterly void of mourning affections? Or are they destitute of understanding in the cause of sorrow? Do men think the danger has past? Surely, one of these must be the cause or else men's hearts would abound with sorrow and their eyes would pour out floods of tears and they would utter with their tongues and pens lamentations of great woe.

Now if it can be shown by the word of truth that a deep error of darkness possesses the last two, that is, those who through ignorance think in themselves there is no such cause of sorrow and those that through ignorance think the danger is already past, then the first that cannot mourn must fall under the sharp censure of a great hardness of heart and an insensible deadness of all affections.

We in the humility of our souls confess that this work is too great for our abilities, but our strength is in the Lord who is able to make us sufficient for these things. If we by faith in Christ depend upon him, even though our faith is so full of infidelity, it must follow that our strength is full of weakness which would beat us to the ground for the undertaking of this or any such work of the Lord. But the word of God compels us. It commands us to show ourselves faithful in little (Matthew 25.19–30), from which ground (by the grace of God) we have be drawn to do that little that we have formerly done and undertake (through the Lord's gracious assistance) now to do that which we will do, beseeching, and trusting of his mercy towards us in this matter, that all the praise may be given only to the glory of his name.

First we desire to show those their error, that through ignorance they do not see and that there is a great cause of lamentation and woe. We require them to turn their ears to the prophesy [sic] of that great prophet Christ Jesus (Matthew 24.4–28; Luke 21.8–31) where he foretells of a time when men will see the abomination of desolation spoken of by Daniel the prophet set in the holy places, then there will be a great tribulation such as was not seen from the beginning of creation to this time nor will be. And unless those days are shortened, no flesh will be saved. Has the like prophesy [sic] ever been heard of? Or can there be any desolation like this desolation in which no flesh will be saved? No, from the beginning of the world there has never been the like, nor will be, say our Savior Christ. Who can remain ignorant of these days and times and what ignorance it is not to know that these even now are the days and times prophesied of? Have not wars and rumors of wars been heard of? Has nation not risen against nation and realm against realm? Have there not been famines, pestilence, and earthquakes in diverse places? Have many not been offended and betrayed one another and hated each other? Have there not arisen many false prophets? Does our Savior Christ not say these are the beginnings of sorrow? Now all these things have come to pass, which must be the beginnings of sorrow. It must be that the days of the height of sorrow have arrived. Do men not see the abomination of desolation set up in the high places? Is it not a deep error of ignorance then for men not to see that this is now the greatest cause of sorrow and lamentation that ever was?

We next want to show in a few words the error of those that think the danger of the days has passed. Let them look upon the words of our Savior

Christ when he spoke of the shortening of the days. He says in Matthew, "Then, if any will say, 'Lo here is Christ, or lo there is Christ,' do not believe it."[1] And in Luke, "Take heed and do not be deceived for many will come in my name, etc."[2] Is it not in this instant these days? Have there ever been so many saying "Lo here is the Christ, lo there is the Christ?" Have there ever been so many false professions of Christ and false prophets showing great signs and wonders as if it were possible to deceive the very elect?[3] Who then can deny but that these are the deepest days of danger of which Christ gives such warnings to take heed? Therefore, they may easily see here their error into whose hearts that imagination has once entered to think that these dangers here prophesied of have past. Then if the end of these sorrows has not passed and the beginnings have passed, as is shown, then it must be confessed that the days of the great tribulation are present. But who considers these things? Who regards the words of this great prophet? If men did consider and carefully behold these things, what heart could conceal enough sorrow and what head could contain tears, or tongue has sufficient words to express and utter the sorrows fitting these days? If Jeremiah complained for the want of tears and could not be satisfied with sorrowing for the slain of the daughter of Zion that perished by the sword and famine (which was but bodily death), how much more cause have men now to sorrow, to see men poisoned with bitter waters, killed with fire, smoke, brimstone, stung with scorpions and hurt with serpents, (Revelation 9.5; 8.11) and cast into the great winepress of the wrath of God (Revelation 19.20), which is the everlasting destruction of soul and body in hell to suffer all the plagues, torments, and judgments of wrath forever? Were the famines of bread and the sword of Nebuchadnezzar, and the seventy years of captivity a fully sufficient cause to make Jeremiah's eyes fill with tears, his bowels swell, his heart turn within him, and his liver to be poured upon the earth?[4] Were not all these woes uttered by the seven angels from the sound of seven trumpets, of an angel fleeing through the mist of heaven who said with a loud voice, "Woe, woe, woe, to the inhabitants of the earth, from the sounds remaining of the trumpets of the three angels, which

---

[1] Matthew 24.23
[2] Luke 21.8
[3] Mathew 24.24
[4] Lamentations 2.11

yet must blow their trumpets?"[5] And have not these three angels blown their trumpets? And is not the sound not still sounding in our ears? Are not all these woes yet in the sight of our eyes? Are all these woes (which are woes of everlasting death and destruction) not sufficient to break men's hearts all to pieces? What stony hardness of heart possess men in these days that their hearts do not melt for these woes.

A main and general reason for all of this is because this prophesy [sic] is of spiritual desolations, destructions, and woes that cannot be understood but with spiritual hearts, nor seen but with spiritual eyes. The hearts and eyes of men are natural and carnal, and therefore these things cannot affect them (1 Corinthians 2.14).

Another special reason is because men do not consider how far these things concern themselves, but every nation, every people, and every man puts these days far from them as in no way appertaining to them. If we therefore could prevail (O that we might prevail) by all the fear and love of God to persuade men and by the compassionate pity of the salvation of their own souls move them with deepest consideration to consider how near those things are that concern them, unless they are under these woes and not aware of them, which men may easily be by reason of the great ignorance that is in all men, particularly in the understanding of the prophecy of the book of Revelation which most men (though otherwise accounted mighty in the scriptures) do pass by, seldom or never touching them in their teachings or writings. They are tainted (we do not doubt) with their own insufficiency, which if they would acknowledge, it would be commendable (their acknowledgment we mean, not their ignorance). Yet their course is much more commendable than those who have busied themselves to bring forth so many imaginary expositions of that holy writ. We say imaginary expositions because they are for the most part but according to vain imaginations and fancies of men's minds because they are without the warrant of the word and spirit.

We confess in humility to our own shame. We are better able to reprove this than to correct it, acknowledging unfeignedly and groaning daily under the burden of our own great ignorance and blindness in the understanding of the prophesy [sic] of that book. All this may further provoke us with you, and you with us to take heed lest we be under any part of this desolation and woe, under which whosoever is, and remains, must perish. By the grace of God, we

---

[5] Revelation 8.13

will make it evidently appear from the scriptures. Therefore, let all people, and nations, and tongues take heed and beware.

And first to proceed in this cause, we will endeavor to prove by the witness of the undoubted word of truth that all nations and peoples upon the earth that have or do profess Christ (for of them only is this prophesy [sic]) have been under the abomination of desolation. The words of the prophecy of Daniel make it most plain where he says "In the middle of the week he will cause the sacrifice and oblation to cease, and for the overspreading of the abomination he shall make it desolate" (Daniel 9.27). In agreement with this prophecy is Revelation 11 where it is said, the two witnesses of God (which are the spirit of truth and the word of truth in the testimony of apostles (John 15.26.27; Acts 5.32) which are "two olive trees, and two candlesticks standing before the God of the earth. They have power to shut heaven so that it will not rain, turn the waters to blood, and smite the earth with all manners of plagues as often as they will. Their corpses will lie in the streets of the great city that are spiritually called Sodom and Egypt three and a half days. And after three and a half days, the spirit of life from God will enter into them and they will stand on their feet." And these two prophecies agree with the prophesy [sic] of (Revelation 12.14) of "the woman fleeing into the wilderness into her place where she is nourished for a time, and times, and half a time." Let us compare these prophecies together. Daniel says the sacrifices and oblations cease in the middle of the week, which are three and a half days. John says (Revelation 11)[6] that the two witnesses (the word and the spirit of truth) lie killed in the streets after three and a half days. In Revelation 12 the woman, which is the kingdom of Christ, "the heavenly Jerusalem, the mother of all the faithful"[7] (Galatians 4) flees into the wilderness for a time, times, and half a time, which may with good warrant according to these prophecies be expounded to a day, two days, and a half. Thus then we conclude, the true sacrifices and oblations of the people of God, the word and spirit, and the heavenly Jerusalem, the spouse of Christ, ceasing, lying dead in the streets and are fleeing into the wilderness. It must follow that there was an utter desolation of all the holy things and all the means of salvation.

For further confirmation of this, see the words of the apostle (2 Thessalonians 2.3) speaking of the last day where he says "That day will not

---

[6] Revelation 11.9
[7] Galatians 4.26

come unless a departing comes first." It shows much weakness in any to think that this is not spoken of a general departing in that there were many particular departures in the apostles' times. But here he is speaking of a departing of the truth and an exalting of an adversary, the "man of sin, to sit in the temple of God, as God, showing himself that he is God,"[8] "whom the Lord will consume with the spirit of his mouth, and abolish with the brightness of his coming."[9] These words show to the understanding of the most simple that there is an utter departing in that there must be a coming again to abolish this wicked man. And here may be discovered the damnable heresy of those men who are twice dead, and are plucked up by the roots, and those are the ones who have fallen from grace, which were once dead and have been quickened by the word and spirit of God and are dead again. These are those who now hold and say that the man of sin sits and rules in the church of Christ. In this place it is shown that the Lord's mouth consumes the man of sin and the brightness of Christ's coming abolishes him. Now we confess, if there can be a church of Christ where the spirit of the Lord's mouth is not present, and where his brightness does not shine, in such a church the man of sin may sit and rule as God and these men are the only fit subjects for such a kingdom. Let the children of God learn to know and profess that in the church of Christ there is the spirit of the Lord's mouth and his shining brightness which consumes and utterly abolishes the man of sin. Therefore, they cannot both rule in one house. Now, for the bare words of which they contend, this much we say (not to them, but to those who may be in danger of being seduced by them). These are the words. The apostle (speaking of the man of sin who exalted himself against all that is called God, or that is worshipped) says "So that he does sit as God in the temple of God, showing himself that he is God."[10] Now as it is said, he sits as God showing himself that he is God, even so he sits in the temple of God, showing it to be the temple of God. This exposition is agreeable to the ground of the scriptures, and according to the proportion of faith, for the scriptures teach us everywhere, and we believe, that Christ is the head of the church, and as he "walks in the midst of the seven golden candlesticks,"[11] and as he sits in his church being God. The man of sin cannot

---

[8] 2 Thessalonians 2.4
[9] 2 Thessalonians 2.8
[10] 2 Thessalonians 2.4
[11] Revelation 2.1

sit with God, as God, in the temple of God. Therefore we say to these men as our Savior Christ said to Satan, leave from us. It is written, (2 Corinthians 9.15.16)[12] "What concord has Christ with Belial? And what agreement does the temple of God have with idols, etc.?" And in 1 Corinthians 10.21, "You cannot drink the cup of the Lord, and the cup of devils. You cannot be partakers of the table of the Lord, and the table of devils." But seeing that these men can find no better pretense to follow, and to help heal the deadly head wound of the beast's head, than by pretending that they have found him sitting in the temple of God. If they look with the same eye they may also find in the same place that he shows himself that he is God. If they will abide by this letter of scripture, then they have found a new temple and new God most fitting to them, because that is their temple and God, and they will all perish together. We only mean those who have been enlightened with this truth that Christ and the man of sin cannot rule and reign or dwell together in one house. Now they have found (as they most blasphemously affirm) that Christ and the man of sin are both exalted in one Temple.

In all of this we have not digressed from the matter in hand, in that we have shown that by the departing that the man of sin was exalted, and therefore the departing was general. The man of sin in his general exaltation further appears by the words of Daniel 9.27 where he says (speaking of the sacrifice) "and for overspreading of the abominations, he will make it desolate." Answerable to this prophecy is that prophecy in the book of Revelation 13.7 where it is written, "And it was given to him (speaking of the beast that had seven heads and ten horns) to make war with the saints and to overcome them. Power was given to him over every kindred and tongue and nation." Who can deny but this is general, even a general desolation when the saints are overcome, "and when all who dwell upon the earth (as follows verse 8) will worship the beast"? All our particular knowledge of the fulfilling of this prophecy will make it more evident. And who does not know and see that this prophecy is fulfilled in that Romish mystery of iniquity "who yet sits upon many waters, with whom the kings of the earth have committed fornication and the inhabitants of the earth are drunken with wine of her fornication?" (Revelation 17.2). We do not doubt that many will agree with us in this understanding. We wish unfeignedly for the salvation of all and that they would come to the knowledge of the truth. We do earnestly desire that those

---

[12] 2 Corinthians 6.15–16

who are overwhelmed in this mystery of iniquity and are under the power of
this deceivableness of unrighteousness would but consider which way it can be
avoided, but that this prophecy is fulfilled in that great exaltation of the man
of sin in that Romish profession. If they would but come to the scriptures,
and particularly to the book of Revelation, they should be forced either to deny
the book's prophecies are true or else they must yield that they are fulfilled in
their profession. For how will they be able to point out upon the face of the
whole earth any one part of this prophecy that is fulfilled, but it will be found
in and from them? For which way should they go about to show the man of
sin, being the mystery of iniquity (in the deceivableness of unrighteousness),
to be exalted, sitting as God, and in the temple of God, sitting upon seven
kings, and ten kings, giving their power thereunto? If these prophecies are not
fulfilled in their Romish professions then it was not nor was it ever begun,
nor fulfilled in any false profession of Christ upon the earth, which cannot be
because we see the apostle to the Thessalonians say, "The mystery of iniquity is
already at work."[13] And in that prophecy of Christ that has already come to
pass (Matthew 24) where he says, "Many will come in my name saying 'Lo
here is Christ, etc.'" This proves that the abomination of desolation is already
set up in the high places. With this prophecy fulfilled, it must be fulfilled
according its due proportion in exaltation and power which must of necessity
be in that Romish church. If they were not altogether blind they might see
that by looking upon the church of Rome which the apostle Paul wrote, and
by comparing that church in Rome and this church of Rome together they
will see a strange exhalation of power and pomp, such as there is no prophecy
in scripture to be found in the church of Christ of a spiritual power setting up
a pope or bishop by virtue of his office with a triple crown, kings and princes
bowing to him, and serving him, and (by virtue of his office) carrying a
bloody sword, and his hands full of blood. This is part of his outward pomp
and power. He bears spiritual names of blasphemy, as to be head of the
church and bishop of the universal flock. He takes upon himself the power to
cast soul and body to hell and to send to heaven whoever he will, to make
spiritual laws and decrees as he will, and to bind men's consciences to the
obedience thereof.

    If this is not he that sits as God, showing himself to be God, if this is not
the abomination of desolation set up where it should not be, where should it

---

[13] 2 Thessalonians 2.7

be found? Can the earth afford a greater exaltation of the man of sin than this? Does it not reach from hell to heaven? What heart would not tremble to see and hear of such high blasphemy and sin against God? If it were not the Lord of hosts that will judge these things, there could not be enough great judgment found. These sins are of the highest pride towards God and greatest cruelty towards his saints "who will go up to heaven and God will remember all these iniquities, and reward them doubly."[14] Although the spirit of God bids the heaven "rejoice, and the holy apostles, and prophets, because God has punished and revenged for your sakes" (Revelation 18.20). Yet, who can with compassionate hearts but lament to see so many souls perish daily and continually under this destruction? All the souls on the earth that exalt, give power, and submit themselves to this man of sin, and so to die, they perish to everlasting destruction, although they do it ignorantly. This will seem to be a hard doctrine to most, but the mouth of the Lord has spoken it. The apostle in 2 Thessalonians 2 proves it without contradiction, where it is said (verse 10) "that the man of sin in his coming will use all his deceivableness and unrighteousness on those that perish." First, it is here proven that the mystery of iniquity prevails by deceivableness. Now, men are deceived by being ignorant of the deceit. They that are deceived through ignorance are those that will perish, for (says the apostle) this deceivableness is effectual or prevails among those that perish. And (verse 12) "That they all might be damned who do not believe the truth, but had pleasure in unrighteousness," speaking of this deceivableness of unrighteousness by the man of sin. For further proof take the voice from heaven (Revelation 18.4), which says "Go out of her, my people, so that you will not be partakers of her sins, and you will not receive her plagues." Here there is no exception, whether one is ignorant or not. If they do not come forth at the voice of the Lord's call, but still remain and abide there, they will surely be partakers of her plagues, "and her plagues come on one day, and they are death, and sorrow, and famine, burning with fire," and "in one hour will she be made desolate" (verses 8 and 19). Whose soul would not mourn to hear of so many great princes and states, and people abroad, and to see nobility, gentry, and people at home perish, and ready to perish daily under this so great and swift destruction? It were to be wished that all good and holy means were used for their information and instruction in this matter, with love and meekness, by the sword of the spirit which is the

---

[14] Revelation 18.5.6

only sword to be used to compel men's consciences to submit to the truth that is in the spirit of the Lord's mouth, by which he will consume the man of sin.

If by this we have said that we can neither persuade them to be careful of their own estates (which is fearful) nor persuade any other to be more careful of them and more compassionate of their estates. Yet this much we have gained toward the cause at hand, that it is being proven that the mystery of iniquity and the abomination of desolation are exalted to the highest in the Romish profession. We do not doubt but it will be yielded that all nations (who acknowledge Christ) have been cast over and are under the power of that Romish profession. So, all these prophecies have been fulfilled in our eyes. They have been produced to prove that there has been an utter desolation of Christ's power and authority while the power and authority of the man of sin has been exalted. It has been proven that all who submit themselves to that power of the man of sin, do, and must perish, unless they repent. Therefore, according to our first words we exhort all peoples and nations, and tongues to take heed and beware, unless they are under the words of everlasting destruction prophesied of in the book of Revelation, and they themselves are not aware of it.

Seeing it proven that all peoples, nations, and tongues have been under it, let them who think they are come forth. Look how they are coming forth, unless they are deceived, or unless by coming forth they have looked back again to whom our Savior Christ says, "Remember Lot's wife" (Luke 17.32). We do not doubt but that we will have the ready consent of diverse nations and peoples who approve of our understandings and applications of this prophecy of the exaltation of the man of sin's fulfillment in the See of Rome. We have no need to make question, but in this we are of one in judgment in the truth. It is impossible that the heart of man should devise a mystery of iniquity or deceivableness of unrighteousness above it, in that there is in it the height and power of all pride and cruelty, reigning and ruling over men's consciences as God under a most glorious show of godliness by which all nations have been made drunk with the wine of the fornication cup, and by which the whole power of Christ (in his laws, statutes, and ordinances) have been and are utterly abolished. In the streets of this great city (we mean no particular place, but the whole mystery of iniquity, spiritually called Sodom and Egypt) are the dead corpses of the two witnesses of the Lord (his word and spirit, in the doctrine of the apostles). For who does not know that they have altogether taken the word of God from the people that they might not have it so much as in their own language, neither may they meddle with the spirit of knowledge and understanding of it, but from ...[15] as they thought (and still think) it was good to deliver it to them, and that must stand for the word and the spirit of God without trying. This may suffice for a plain and general discovery of Babylon, Sodom, and Egypt (spiritually so-called), and of that beast with seven heads and ten horns, and the...[16], seeing there are so many excellent discoveries written about it.

Will we now sit down as though our danger had past in finding out the first beast, and so make the prophecy of God (Revelation 13.11) of no effect, which it so plainly sets forth and describes a second beast of no less danger than the first beast? Will we betray the cause of God, and the souls of thousands and ten thousands of men? God forbid. Will any of you who freely approve of all the findings out and discoveries of the first beast not with willingness consent to the finding out of the second? Far be it for you to have so little concern for God's truth and the salvation of men. Well, we will endeavor to discover the second beast leaving it to the consciences of whomsoever it may most concern to judge whether we deal faithfully or not, and we will forejudge ourselves to deal with it most weakly. In Revelation 13.11–18 it is written, "I saw another beast coming up out of the earth, which had two horns like the lamb, but he spoke like the dragon and exercises the power of the first beast. He says to those who dwell on the earth that they should make an image of the first beast, and causes as many as who would not worship the image of the beast to be killed, and all are made to receive a mark on their right hand, or on their foreheads, and that no man may buy or sell unless he has the mark or the name of the beast or the number of his name."

Which way now (in finding out the second beast) are we able to look other than the great hierarchy of archbishops and lord bishops? Are you not those that pretend (in meekness and humility) to speak the word and power of the Lamb, who says, "Learn of me that I am meek and lowly, etc"[17] but exercises the power of the beast and speaks like the dragon? Have you not made and set up the image of the beast? Is your pomp and power not his? Has there not been much similar cruelty used by that power? Does the blood of the dead not cry? Have the imprisoned not groaned under that cruelty? Do

---

[15] The original text is illegible at this point.
[16] The original text is illegible at this point.
[17] Matthew 11.29

not the silenced at home and the banished abroad daily complain? May not all of these cry out, "How long, Lord, how long? When will you take revenge?"[18] Are not your canons and consistories, and all the power that belongs to them, with all the rest of your courts, offices, and officers, not parts of this image? Are they not like the beast? Will you say they are like the Lamb, or his apostles? It cannot be that you say they are. The fear of the Almighty would astonish you. If you cannot possibly prove that power, that pomp, that cruelty of those canons and courts with the belongings and belongers are like the Lamb, then let the terror of the Almighty possess you and make you afraid to use and possess all those things under the pretense of power of the Lamb. Do you not have souls to save? Pity yourselves and do not perish. There is mercy with the Lord if you will fear him. What will it profit you to enjoy these things for a little while (as many as your predecessors have done before you), even a little while, and then be condemned and fall under the fierce wrath of God? Would you not be much better, a thousand times better, yes, ten thousand times better, and more, to be ministers of Christ abounding in labors, in weariness and painfulness, in often watching, in hunger and thirst, in often fasting, in cold and nakedness,[19] that you may say (at your last ends) not as apostles but as the apostles say, "We have fought a good fight, and have finished our course. And we have kept the faith. Henceforth a crown of righteousness has been laid up for us."[20] But if this is your fight (as it has been the fight of a diverse number of your predecessors), to cause as many as would not worship the image of the beast (your hierarchy) to be killed, and to make all, both small and great, rich and poor, bond and free, receive a mark on their right hand or on their forehead and that no man may buy or sell unless he has the mark of the beast, or the number of his name. If this is your fight it is evidently the fight of the second beast, and not the fight of the apostle Paul. There is no crown of righteousness laid up for such a fight.

Do you not do all these things when you force and compel men to submit to your whole conformity, which is the perfect image of the beast? Not to speak of your surplice, cross, churchings, burials, coops, chantings, and organs in your cathedrals. How many more abominations we cannot reckon up, which we have no need to do, seeing so many writings are full of them.

---

[18] Habakkuk 1.2
[19] 2 Corinthians 6.5
[20] 2 Timothy 4.7.8

But whoever will look upon them with an eye of less than half uprightness will easily see that they come out of the bowels of the beast and are the deformed image of his ugly shape.

To let all these pass (the beast will be called to account in the day of the Lord), we come to your *Common Book*, not meddling with every particular of it, but only the most general. By what power do you make prayers and bind men to them and appoint the order of them in time and place, of which you also appoint what it is to be read every evening without alteration, some prayers are to be said after the curate has been paid his due, some on the north side of the table, some in one place, and some in another? Do you see a special ground of these four abominations in appointing what your priests are to pray, when to pray, where to pray, and what to put on when they pray? This is because you made so many priests and have so many still among you that do not know what to pray, where to pray, nor when to pray, nor what put on when they pray, in as much as if you did not allow them a sum of made prayers, they have been and still would be altogether without prayers. This hides the mystery of iniquity with the deceivableness of unrighteousness from the simple and from the great and wise, by your made order of prayers. Take your *Common Book* from them and then the impudent would be ashamed of such a ministry. O that ten of the best and chief of a thousand of your priests might be debarred from your book and be set in a congregation of very partial hearers of their side to show their best abilities for the office of the ministry. Baal's priests were no more discovered (1 Kings 18) than they would be. Their fault was in their God in that he had no ear to hear. Your priests' fault would be found in themselves because they would not have one word to speak of God's glory or to his edification. How can you not know this as well as you know your right hand from your left? How will you answer this when you come before the righteous judge? Will you be able to stand in his presence? May the Lord give you hearts to repent, otherwise how can you think you will escape the fierce wrath of the Lord? Did the Lord bring evil upon the house of Jeroboam—"and swept it away, as a man sweeps away dung until it is all gone," and "the dogs ate those of Jeroboam's house that died in the city and the fowls of the air ate those that died in the field" because he set up calves to worship and made priests of the meanest people who were not the sons of Levi? (1 Kings 14.10.11; 12.31). Do you think you will escape with less a judgment than those that set up the image of the beast and such a blind priesthood to support it? You know that it is blind ignorance that supports the mystery of iniquity. Therefore, the Lord will by the brightness of his coming abolish it. What will we say of your bareheaded and barefooted white penance sheet, to which (to mock the Almighty) is joined a written repentance?

Thus you devise men's prayers and repentance and they must pray and repent as you by your power have appointed them. Do you have the power also to appoint the Lord to accept these prayers and repentance? Or do you not care whether the Lord accepts them or not as long as you are submitted to? Do you then seek your own worship and not the Lord's? Judge yourselves and let all judge between the most holy Lamb and the most polluted beast, and confess and testify whether these things are of the Lamb or of the image of the beast.

The like of these things cannot be numbered and there would be no end to them if we should follow them. But we will now draw this to an end hoping that those who see these things will see it all.

Yet, let us now speak to some things concerning your excommunication of which power are cast out those that most seek to serve God in sincerity. If the most wicked fall under it, they may be remitted (submitting to the power) by paying large fees, especially if they are rich and simple or have means of degree. Whosoever withstands the power of the forty days, then with a writ of signification he is cast into prison without bail or mainprise.[21] Is this learned from the Lamb or any of his apostles? We read that the apostles suffered such violences and tyrannies. But the word of God teaches the disciples of Christ no such administrations. This is not the meekness of the Lamb, but the image of the cruel power of the beast.

The power of this excommunication is of another special use for profit, in that by the power of it is brought in all duties, tithes, and court fees. What a horrible profanation of Christ's holy ordinance is this to make it an instrument to compel men to bring in exacted fees and duties and tithes. We read (1 Corinthians 16)[22] that Paul appointed in the churches gatherings for the saints, and (1 Timothy 5)[23] gave direction for the relief of widows. He also gave a special charge for providing for the elders and especially for those who labor the most. "The elders," says the apostle, "that lead, go before, or rule

---

[21] A pledge verifying that the accused would show up at court on a later date. The letter issuing this writ and given to the sheriff was known as mainprise.

[22] 1 Corinthians 16.1–4

[23] 1 Timothy 5.3–16

well, let them be held in double honor, especially those that labor in the word and doctrine."[24] First, here it is shown that the power by which they must lead, go before, or rule, that is, by the word and doctrine. The apostle proves by two reasons from the scriptures that such elders are worthy of double honor, because the scriptures say: 1. "You will not muzzle the mouth of the ox that treads the corn."[25] "The laborer is worthy of his wages."[26] Here it is shown what the apostle means by honor, that is, maintenance. But all this is from a voluntary, liberal distribution, as shown in 2 Corinthians 9.13. How unlike this is to your ruling power and to your double honor and maintenance? Here there is no imprisoning by power, nor excommunication for fee, tithes and duties. We confess our lord the king may give you what is his pleasure, but it is wished that all those goodly palaces and possessions with all the privileges and prerogatives which belong to them were to be preserved for the king's state and dignity. They were more befitting for the king and his posterity to support them in their due pomp and royalty than to support the pride and pomp of those who pretend to be ministers of the gospel. The apostle Paul was more worthy of a double maintenance than you and all the priests in all your provinces and dioceses. Yet he labored with his hands, although he had the care of more and more worthy churches than are now on earth. These churches would have willingly administered to him, but he would make the gospel free. O, that we might live to see all those that preach the gospel (if they stand in need) to live off the gospel, that is, off the free liberality of the saints. Those pastors would not devour the flock, but feed it. We may pray that the Lord would put into the heart of the king to take into his own hands all those possessions and tithes, by which those devouring shepherds (that destroy the flock) feed themselves. That day will be the happiest day to the whole land that ever was since it was a...[27]land. It will involve these four things. First, it would overthrow that high pride and cruelty of the image of the beast and the mystery of iniquity. Secondly, it would make a way for the advancement of the kingdom of Jesus Christ in its sincere and humble profession. Thirdly, it would enrich the crown and fill the king's coffers, upheaped with such yearly revenue as no peace nor war would ever be able to make them half empty. All

---

[24] 1 Timothy 5.17
[25] Deuteronomy 25.4
[26] Luke 10.7
[27] The original text is illegible at this point.

this may be done by holy, good, just, and lawful means. Fourthly, it would enrich the whole land above measure by disbursing the land of all those courts with all the suits and services that belong to them, the taxations, fees, and penalties of which are without number. The king would have no need of taxes or subsidies, although we would not wish the king's people to withdraw the showing of their loyal love to our lord the king in those things.

O, what a full and ready consent there would be in the king's people for these things. How profitable it would be for them. May the Lord persuade his heart to it, seeing it would be for God's glory, his own benefit, and the so great good of his whole land. It would be the greatest and chief benefit of all them to whom it may seem the greatest loss. They should be disburdened of those things which although they are pleasant for a season yet they will be most bitter in the day of account, which will come, let them be sure. It would make them live moderately off that which they have, and use good and honest endeavors to support themselves. There would be true comfort in such gain.

Lastly, to make it appear plainly enough that this hierarchy of archbishops and lord bishops are the image of the beast, let all behold the names of blasphemy which it bears, and they are these, so far as we know the number of them:

Archbishops
Primates
Metropolitans
Lords Spiritual
Reverend Fathers
Lords Grace

What names of blasphemy are here. They are the titles and names of our God and of our Christ. What words of detestation were sufficient to be uttered against such blasphemous abomination? Who is able to keep silent? If men (professing Christ) will not speak, the stones will speak rather than the Lord be without a witness.[28] Will men be afraid to speak for loss of goods, of lands, or for fear of imprisonment, banishment, or death? No, no, let them take it all, life and all. Let them shed blood until they have enough. Let the servants of God rejoice in the saying of the angel of the waters, "Lord, you are just,

---

[28] Luke 19.40

which are and which was and which will be, because you have judged these things, for they shed the blood of saints and prophets. Therefore, you have given them blood to drink, for they are worthy" (Revelation 16.5.6). The Lord has fulfilled this upon all those that are dead and have not repented of this abomination. The Lord will fulfill this upon all that are alive if they do not repent. Is it not sufficient to despoil and rob Christ of all his power? But you will also take him the titles of honor due to his name. To pass by your derived Grecian names, which we (to speak the truth) are not able to declare the interpretation of to our own satisfaction (and that no way lessens the iniquity of them, but rather it shows it more that you should get names of hidden blasphemy that simple men cannot understand without an interpreter). Let us speak with fearfulness of that name, so that you might all tremble to hear of, and that is the lord spiritual, the very attribute of the God of all spirits. He is the only Lord spiritual and the spiritual Lord. And give us leave to show you how you are hedged in, that all subtle sophistry will not help you out. Do you not bear this title by reason of your spiritual power and authority? Do you not by your own spiritual power and authority make canons and decrees? Are not all your courts spiritual courts? Do you not require spiritual obedience in all these things? Is your title and power not a different title and power from all other lords? See how the style hedges you in, which goes this way, "All the lords spiritual and temporal," so that you cannot say you are spiritual lords because of your profession as much you will not deny but the temporal lords are spiritual lords in profession as well as you. Therefore, it must be that you are spiritual lords because of your spiritual power, and your spiritual power is over the spirits of men. As temporal lords have power over men's bodies, so must spiritual lords have power over men's spirits. But there is only one spiritual Lord, who is the Father of Spirits, and therefore whoever takes this title and this power upon themselves, they take upon themselves the name, title, and power of God. This is the man of sin who sits as God, showing himself to be God, which the second beast does according to or in the image of the first.

Do you think that God has forgotten to be just and his judgments have gone forever? Can you see and condemn in your words and writings the exaltation of the man of sin in the Romish profession? Can you not see and condemn it on your own? To such the apostle Paul says, "O you who condemns those that do such things and does the same, do you think you will escape the judgment of God?" (Romans 2.3).

And now for that double degree of Reverend-fatherhood which you take for yourselves. Some of you are called Most Reverend and some Right Reverend Fathers. How can we find out more about what condition you bear this name? It is plain that you do not bear the name because you have begotten all people in Christ. Most commonly you are the Reverend Fathers in God before the people even heard your voice. It must be your inspired name seeing it is not by your operation or work. So you are inspired with a Reverend Fatherhood upon the instant time of your entrance before you have wrought any work among that people. When you meet Christ in his coming what will you answer him for the breach of his straight commandment that says, "Call no man father upon the earth, for there is but one, your Father which is in heaven"?[29] Are you not exalted above your brethren by this name? Then you are they who Christ speaks of in this place, and whom he will bring fallow (Matthew 23.9–11) for taking upon yourselves the name of God and exalting yourselves above the brethren. If you have not sold yourselves to work wickedness (which God forbid) and if you think it is robbery to make yourselves equal with God,[30] let your hearts tremble and your hands shake to subscribe to such names of blasphemy. Let your ears tingle when you hear them uttered and read in your presence. Observe what magnificence is placed on you when you sit upon your high places and hear yourselves thus entitled. Remember that he who sits over you will tread you under foot for robbing him of his honor, if, by repentance you do not make peace with him.

Now we will discuss the next name of blasphemy (that is within you capacity to speak of) it is the title of Lords Grace. This is your household title. We mean that it is a title that may not be omitted in all ordinary occasions. Does this attribute not belong only to the Lord of Grace? Will you share this prerogative with him? Now, although this title is used (in what sense we do not know) in the styles of some civil magistrates, of which we do not meddle, but we know all your titles of degree you bear by a spiritual prerogative. The mystery of iniquity consists of this. Therefore all your names and honors and prerogatives (whereby you challenge superiority) are names of blasphemy, and are directly against the express commandment of Christ, who by his commandment (are worthy to be obeyed) charged his disciples that they

---

[29] Matthew 23.9
[30] Philippians 2.6

should in no way seek superiority in his kingdom, neither in name nor in power.

"The lords of the Gentiles bear rule one over another, and are called gracious lords and bear names of honor, but it will not be so among you. He that will be the greatest will be the least in my kingdom" (Luke 22.25.26). That is, he that will be exalted in name or power by being a disciple of my kingdom, he will be the least.

The words of our Savior Christ, however, are not regarded at all. The man of sin will have a kingdom where there will be mighty power and authority one over another's conscience. He appoints and compels men how they will worship their God, and imprisons, banishes, and causes to die all those who resist. The man of sin will have in his kingdom names of the highest honor. Yes, even the names, titles, and attributes of God. Thus he sits as God does in name, title, and power. This prophecy is now fulfilled, as he that has an eye may see and he that has an ear may hear. Let any man but hear the prophecy of this book of Revelation and he may see it fulfilled in the first beast and second beast as evidently as if Christ should send one from the dead and declare it to him and say this is the first beast and this is the second. They would not believe him in his word and they would not believe him if he should send one from the dead (Luke 16.31). Now all agree with us in judgment concerning the first beast, that is plainly seen in the Romish profession, and that it is impossible that the man of sin should be exalted in a higher measure of exaltation. We call all of you forth as witnesses before God and men, whether it is not plainly seen that the second beast, that has two horns like the Lamb, pretending or making show of the word and power of the Lamb in humbleness and meekness, but speaking like the dragon, and exercising the power of the first beast and is made in the image of the first beast. We call you all to witness whether the second beast is not as plainly seen in the hierarchy of archbishops and lord bishops and whether it is possible that there should be made so lively an image of the first beast as is in the hierarchy in all titles and names of blasphemy, in all pomp, and in all power throughout. It beings with their book worship, with the conformity belonging to it, and so going through all their offices, and officers, courts, canons, and decrees. If all these things are not the image of the first beast, conceived in his bowels, and brought out of his bosom, let heaven and earth witness and let all the men on the earth deny if they can, and show any other image of the first beast. Therefore all of you who this may most concern, either deny this prophecy of God and wipe it out (which if you do, God will deny you, and wipe you out of the book of life), or else confess that it is fulfilled in and among you and give glory to God, and cast away your abominations, and take heed of the hardness of hearts that cannot repent which heap up as treasure to themselves wrath against the day of wrath. O, why should you for the pleasure of unrighteousness (for a very few days and little do you know how few) utterly destroy your own souls and perish, yes, and destroy the souls of all that submit to you in the least of these things unless they repent?

If you will yet justify yourselves in these things and make show of yourselves to be the servants of the Lamb and not the servants of the beast then stand forth and defend your kingdom and cause with the spiritual sword of the Lamb, which is the word of God, and convince your gainsayers and stop their mouths, and so you will approve your bishops in deed. If you can prove by God's word that we should say prayers as you command us, we will both sing and say as you bid us. If you can prove your names of blasphemy and titles of degree, your pomp, and all your cruel spiritual power, good. By that warrant, we will yield it all to you and not diminish you of the least of these titles. What fear do you have to bring it to trial? You have enough learning. You have enough partakers. If you had but half a good cause, if you will fight this battle, we say to you as Michaiah said to Ahab, when he would go up to Ramoth Gilead: "Take it in hand, go by and prosper."[31] But we will tell you also with the same prophet that if you stand in this cause, "The Lord has determined evil against you"[32] (2 Chronicles 18.16.22).

In all this let us persuade you in the fear of God and the shame of men to cast away all these courses we will now mention. Do not, when a poor soul by violence is brought before you to speak his conscience in the profession of his religion to his God, do not first impose the Oath *Ex Officio*. O, this is a most wicked course. If he will not yield to that, then imprison him close. O, the horrible severity. If he will not be forced by imprisonment then examine him upon diverse articles without oath to see if he may be entrapped in any way. O, this is a grievous impiety. If any piece of advantage (either in word or writing, or by witness) can be gotten, the magistrate's sword is turned on him and his life is taken. O, the bloody cruelty. If no advantage can be found, get him banished out his natural country, and from his father's house. Let him

---

[31] 2 Chronicles 18.14
[32] 2 Chronicles 18.22

live or starve, it does not matter. O unnatural compassion without pity. Let these courses be far from you. There is no show of grace, religion, or humanity in these courses. This is so they may lie in wait for blood, and to lay snares secretly to take the simple to slay him.

To conclude this point in hand, let it be truly observed whether those that are of the Romish profession (servants of the first beast, coming in question before this hierarchy) have not found much more favor than those that have stood most for reformation. Has there not been gnashing of teeth and gnawing of tongues, with all extreme perverseness and contempt against the one, when there has been good, mild, and even carriage towards the other? We do not disapprove of that good carriage towards them, nor do we envy it, but we could wish that the wholesome word of doctrine with all the cords of love were applied and used on them for their information and drawing them from their blind errors. We mention to this end to show what uprightness there can be to God or the king in this. First, it is not possible that this whole hierarchy will confess that those who seek reformation have much more light of truth and gifts of knowledge for the building up of a people to God than the other. The first and they are all of one judgment concerning the doctrines of the scriptures in the fundamental points of religion (as they speak). Yet, there is no comparison between their patient enduring of those of the Romish profession and their impatient lack of enduring of the other. Is this uprightness to God? Secondly, touching the king and state, the children in the streets know the treachery and the infidelity that has been found in the diversities of the one profession. They themselves know the ever untouched fidelity of the other. What uprightness is this to the king and state? The evident reason of this may appear to the wise. Does this not appear to be it, that the Romish profession is but chiefly an enemy to the kingdom of Christ and dangerous to the kingdom of the king by approving of archbishops and lord bishops, and wishing they were cardinals. But those of all sorts that seek reformation are the most chief enemies to the kingdom of archbishops and lord bishops and would have them be humble and faithful pastors to feed the flock and therefore in no way are to be suffered howsoever true they are to God and their king. Does all this not show the affinity and nearness between the first and second beast?

If any one should stumble at this first part of the prophecy (Revelation 13.12), where it is spoken that the second beast causes the earth and those that dwell on it to worship the first beast, and therefore the Romish beast being the first, this hierarchy cannot be the second, because it does not cause men to worship the pope of Rome. We pray it may be observed how it is shown (2 Thessalonians 2.7.9.10) that the mystery of iniquity is a working power of Satan. His working power (according to its degrees) is set forth for us in the book of Revelation after diverse manners and described for us in diverse shapes and similitudes and named for us after diverse names. In the height of its exaltation this power is set forth and described to us under the two names and similitudes of the first and second beast, both of which exercise one power and (though in diverse likenesses) do bring all, both small and great, under the subjection of that one power, "both their hearts are set to do mischief and talking of deceit at one table" (Daniel 11.27). And so the second beast causes all to worship the first, in that it is all one power building up one kingdom. The pope's person is not the mystery of iniquity, for then, when the pope is dead, they mystery of iniquity and the beast would be dead until another pope was set up. If the pope's person was the man of sin then the Lord (by the spirit of his mouth) should abolish and consume the pope's person, but there is no such prophecy in scripture. Should then the prophecies concerning the fall of Babylon be understood as the overthrow and consuming of the earthen or stone walls, and timber houses of a city? But this is too carnal an understanding, to conceive that the spirit of God's mouth which will consume the man of sin, spoken of in 2 Thessalonians 2, and will shake asunder the city, "which spiritually is called Sodom and Egypt."[33] It is too carnal to understand this as earthly houses and cities and fleshly persons. They are not the matter and substance that will be abolished by the brightness of his coming, here spoken of, as we do not doubt but will easily appear to the wise, though some have been, and are, much mistaken in this matter.

So that we may come to the true understanding of this part of the prophecy, "and he did great wonders (speaking of the second beast) so that he made fire come down from heaven in the sight of men" (Revelation 13.13). In order to see how it is fulfilled in the second beast we must remember (as we have formerly said) that this is a spiritual prophecy of a spiritual mystery of iniquity, which none may deny. It then appears that these wonders that were wrought (by making fire come down from heaven) are lying spiritual wonders and the fire is a false spiritual fire, which (even as the true spiritual fire, which is the Holy Ghost) does truly work wonderfully and powerfully upon the

---

[33] Revelation 11.8

hearts and affections of those that believe the truth, even so this false fire (which is the spirit and power of Satan) does work effectually upon the hearts and affections of those that do not receive the love of truth. This occurs after a wonderful manner of deceivableness of unrighteousness, so that men are strongly persuaded and believe that it is the true fire from heaven, even the spirit of God. The hierarchy of archbishops and lord bishops has made this fire come down from heaven, especially in their former times when men had their word and power, with their prayer book, and all their cathedral abominations in such admiration and with such zeal were...[34] to them. Yet, as some are to this day zealously persuaded of the holiness and goodly order of these things, all of which (in the beast that has two horns like the Lamb) made such a glorious show being compared to the former things, as men were ravished in their spirits and thoughts (and yet some...[35] do think) that their hearts and affections were kindled with fire from heaven. By this false fire (which is by an effectual working power in all deceivableness by unrighteousness) even in this the first and second beast have and do work all their signs and lying wonders, and these men (through great ignorance) have and do look for some strange signs from heaven to know the two beasts by. Their hearts have been and are (with the pleasures of unrighteousness) stolen away. For all of those (that have any understanding) who remain under the power of the second beast, they may easily discern how by a wonderful fiery blind zeal all those that are under the power of the first beast are misled. But they cannot discern their own estates, which are one and the same under the second beast, who is more deceivable because of his two horns like the Lamb. Therefore men should look more carefully at themselves lest they are still deceived, as men will rest in security and perish to destruction, which all must do that obey the power of either the first or second beast, as is with all evidence is plainly shown (Revelation 14.9–11) where it is written, "If any man worships the beast and his image and receives his mark on his forehead or on his hand and whosoever receives the print of his name, he will drink (says the spirit of the Lord) of the wine of the wrath of God, which is poured into the cup of his wrath, and will be tormented with fire and brimstone and they will have no rest day or night."

---

[34] The original text is illegible at this point.
[35] The original text is illegible at this point.

What will prevail with men if neither the forewarning prophecies nor the threatening judgments of the Lord will move them to consider and flee the fierce vengeance that is already here? Does our Savior Christ say that the abomination of desolation will be set up in the holy places? Does the apostle Paul show that the man of sin exalts himself and sits as God in the temple God? Does the prophecy of Revelation so duly set down and declare the manner of working of the mystery of iniquity according to it several decrees until it comes to that height of exaltation before spoken of by Christ, and by the apostle in the similitude of the first and second beast, who bears the names of blasphemy in taking upon themselves the names and attributes of God, as shown before causing all that dwell upon the earth to worship the beast and his image, and so sits as God in the high places, and in the temple of God, which is in the hearts of men? (1 Corinthians 3.16; 2 Corinthians 6.19).[36] Do we see all these things fulfilled before our eyes and will the reader not consider it? Does our Savior Christ show the greatest judgments of the Lord to be upon men in those days, in so much as no flesh will be saved, and unless those days are shortened no flesh will ever be saved? Does the apostle Paul show that because men will not receive the love of truth the Lord will send them strange delusions so that they will believe lies so that all might be damned who do not believe the truth, but have pleasure in unrighteousness? Does the spirit of God in John's Revelation say that all who worship the beast and bear the least mark of the beast and his image will drink of the mere wine of God's wrath out of the cup of his wrath? Will all of this not move the hardened hearts of men to look about and carefully search out the prophecies of scripture concerning these things and compare them with these times, and seek and find out how they are fulfilled, which (through the grace of God) every faithful heart, seeking, will now easily discern, seeing the first angel (Revelation 16)[37] has poured out his vial so that noisome and grievous sores do appear upon the men which have the mark of the beast upon them that worship his image? Yes, (glory and honor and praise be given to our God) the first angel has also poured his vial upon the throne of the beast, and his kingdom does already war dark. Who does not see this that looks but with any seeing eye after religion? Do you not now more than ever see that the noisome botches of many gross absurdities appear in the bewitched understanding of

---

[36] No such reference in 2 Corinthians
[37] Revelation 16.2

those men that bear the mark and worship the beast and his image? Is it not the palpable darkness of blind ignorance openly discovered on the throne of the beast? Does the beauty of this image not fade? Has the baptizing by midwives not vanished? Is the bishoping of the young and old not in much decay? Have the daily reading of injunctions and homilies not grown to forgetfulness? Are not the profane perambulations well laid aside? Have the holy evens and days and ember weeks almost passed out of mind? Has this book itself not become much out of use? Has the whole conformity not received a blow? Will any halting subscription not serve the turn? O that the spiritual lords of this spiritual kingdom could see the smoke of the burning that has already deeply begun and does highly ascend that they themselves might help to heap coals upon the throne and flee from its burning.

Do not let them forecast to preserve it nor seek to deliver it out of the hand of the Almighty. They may more easily pull the prey out of the lion's mouth, or "draw out a leviathan with a hook"[38] than prevent the mighty One that has judged these things (Revelation 18), "who is clothed with a garment dipped in blood and his name is called the word of God and who has upon his garment and upon his thigh a name written, the King of Kings and the Lord of Lords" (Revelation 19.13.16).

Thus we have (according as we foretold ourselves) set down these things with great inability, but yet with all fidelity according to our consciences in the best measure of understanding concerning the second beast, which has been made in the image of the first. We desire that the godly wise who seek salvation by the Lamb will compare the beast (which we all agree to be the Romish hierarchy) and his image (how can it be imagined, but it must be the hierarchy of archbishops and lord bishops). Compare them together in their spiritual pomp, spiritual names of blasphemy, spiritual power, and cruelty, and cast but a partly indifferent eye upon their administrations in their offices, officers, courts, canon and decrees. Then let the word and spirit of God direct them to judge righteously of the beast and his image to know them so that you will not submit to the spiritual power of the beast and his image and not receive his mark on your forehead or on your hand or the least print of his name. If you do, your portion is to "drink of the cup and wine of God's wrath and be tormented with fire and brimstone before the holy angels and in the

---

[38] Job 41.1

sight of the Lamb."[39] The word of the Lord has spoken it and his word is true and not lying.

---

[39] Revelation 14.10

BOOK 2

B ut will we know think that we have fully discharged ourselves to God and
men in speaking generally to all? Will we not in humility particularly call
upon those servants of the Lord of whom he has especially prophesied that
they will "hate the whore and make her desolate and naked and will eat her
flesh and burn her with fire"?[1] And this will be done, said the Lord, by the
kings of the earth (Revelation 17.16) of whom we could not be content once to
speak of for fear of offending, but there is infirmity in us and no faithfulness
to God or them. The wise king (that knew right well the power and authority
of a king) advises, "not to stand in an evil thing before the king because he will
do whatsoever pleases him" (Ecclesiastes 8.3). But in a good cause why should
we fear to stand before kings seeing their thrones are established by justice?
(Proverbs 16.12). Our cause is then good for it is the cause of God as all will
confess, thus we do in all reverent humility beseech of all kings and princes
that they will perform this service to the Lord according to this prophecy
prophesied to them, in the performance of which the Lord requires their
fervent zeal, which they should show by their perfect hatred and detesting of
the whore, by whose zealous hate they are provoked to "make her desolate and
naked, and to eat her flesh and burn her with fire."[2] After this manner and
with these great and fervent affections these kings will obey the Lord in this
work and serve him. In all this we beseech that we may not be understood as
though we mean the kings should do this by their temporal sword of justice,
no, nothing less. The Lord requires no such means in this business. He has
testified by prophecy, as we have formerly shown (2 Thessalonians 2), that
"he will abolish and consume the man of sin, the mystery of iniquity," which
is this beast and whore and city, "by the spirit of his mouth and by the
brightness of his coming."[3] Therefore this prophecy may not be understood
that kings should do this by their temporal power, but by the word and spirit
of the Lord in their testimony, with all holy zeal. This cannot be done unless
they first take all their power and authority from the beast. "No man can serve

---

[1] Revelation 17.16
[2] Revelation 17.16
[3] 2 Thessalonians 2.8

two masters, but he will please the one and displease the other."[4] Kings cannot serve the Lamb and beast, but they must hate the one and love the other. This is the most plainly set down in the prophecy (Revelation 17) because in verse 13 and 17, it is said of kings that they will have "all one mind and be of one consent with the beast and will give their power and authority to the beast and will fight with the Lamb until the words of God are fulfilled." (Verse 16) "They will hate the whore and make her desolate"[5] for God has put it in their hearts to fulfill his decree. Thus we see these kings prophesied of by the spirit of the Lord to do this great work of God. When they will take it in hand they will not halt between two opinions,[6] they will be neither hot nor cold,[7] but they will be most zealous for the glory of God and will no longer retain any friendship with the beast (our meaning is always spiritual). Now then those kings and princes that will in this service obey the most high God and advance his glory that has so greatly advanced them to high honor and dignity, let them take all their power and authority from the beast and withdraw all the affections of their hearts and souls and turn again to hatred and an utter abhorring of the beast and whore. And so they will make it manifest to all the world that they are true lovers of the Lamb and perfect haters of the beast and they are the ones in whom this prophecy is fulfilled. O that kings and princes would strive to go one before another in giving honor to God in this.

Among all the rest of these great and mighty kings and princes of the earth, loyalty, nature, and grace does bind us with desires of exceeding dutiful and reverent affections to wish and desire that our lord and king might be the foremost in this great and acceptable service of the King of Kings and Lord of Lords, which is a worthy service most well beseeming of our lord the king for whom the king of heaven has done such great things. If our lord the king will do this service for his God then he must not by his power support the beast or his image which are one and the same power. And seeing our lord and king has seen the deep iniquity of the peremptory ruling presbytery, let him much more see the high iniquity of the proud, ambitious, cruel, ruling prelacy, which is a power set up in the place of God, bearing the names of blasphemy.

---

[4] Matthew 6.24
[5] Revelation 17.16
[6] 1 Kings 18.21
[7] Revelation 3.15

O, let it be far from our lord the king to give his power "which God has given him to punish evildoers and to reward those that do well" (1 Peter 2.14). Let it be far from our lord the king to give this power to the beast or his image for this advances the mystery of iniquity and smites down the mystery of godliness. God has not communicated his own power to kings and princes for this end.

Since we have begun to speak to our lord the king, let us declare what power and authority God has given to him and his subjects that they should out of conscience obey.

Our lord the king has power to take our sons and our daughters to do all his services of war and of peace, yes, and all his servile service whatsoever. He has the power to take our lands and goods of whatsoever sort or kind, or the tenth of it to use at his will. He has power to take our "men servants and maid servants and the chief of our young men and cattle," and put them to his work and we are to be his servants (1 Samuel 8.11–18). In all these things our lord the king is to be submitted to and obeyed.

Also, he has the power to make all manner of governors, laws and ordinances of man (1 Peter 2.13–14). God gives our lord the king power to demand and take what he will of his subjects and it is to be yielded to him and to command what ordinances of man he will and we are to obey it. In all these things we acknowledge before God and men that we should be subject "not for fear only but also for conscience'[SIC OR TYPO?] sake" (Romans 13.5). We do not meddle with any conditions or contracts made between the kings and his people, of which our lord the king (in favor) may or does abridge himself of his prerogative and so makes himself subject to his own covenants or conditions, which our lord the king should keep, though it is to his disadvantage if they are not merely unlawful. But we speak only of that power which God has given to the king all of which our lord the king should use lawfully. If he should do otherwise (which God forbid), he is in these things to be submitted to (Ecclesiastes 8.3.4; 1 Peter 2.18–24). "Whosoever resists, resists the ordinance of God and will receive to themselves condemnation" (Romans 13.2). Thus, God has given our lord the king all the worldly power that extends to all the goods and bodies of his servants. Does our lord the king require any more? We know he does not. Then do not let our lord the king now be angry that we, his servants, speak a second time to him. Does the king not know that the God of Gods and Lord of Lords has under him made our lord the king an earthly king and given him all earthly power and that he has reserved to himself a heavenly kingdom, "a kingdom that is not of this world" [8] (John 18.36.37) and "neither are the subjects of his kingdom of this world"? (John 17.14). Yet this king was in the world and his subjects are in the world (verse 12)[9] and that with this kingdom our lord the king has nothing to do (by his kingly power) but as a subject himself. Christ alone is King and he is the only high priest and chief bishop. There is no king, no primate, metropolitan, archbishop, and lord spiritual, but Christ only, nor may there be any either in name or power to exercise authority one over another (Luke 22.25.26; Matthew 23.11.12). Will our lord the king, not withstanding all that Christ has done for him in giving him such a kingdom with such great dignity and power, will the king not withstanding, enter upon Christ's kingdom and appoint (or by his power suffer to be appointed) laws, lords, and lawmaker over or in this kingdom of Christ, who (we may be bold to say with warrant) if he were upon earth in the flesh, he would be subject to our lord the king in his earthly kingdom. So he was to Caesar. He paid him tribute and he commanded to "give to Caesar things that were Caesar's."[10] Yes, he would not meddle with anything that belonged to the king, not so much as to command the two brothers to "divide the inheritance,"[11] nor to judge the woman "taken in adultery."[12] Far be it from the heart of our lord the king to give his earthly power to any to rule as lords over the kingdom and heritage of Christ which he has reserved to himself to rule and govern only by his word and spirit where no earthly power may be admitted in that it is no earthly kingdom.

Behold now we have begun to speak to our lord the king, and we are but dust and ashes and our lord the king is but dust and ashes as well. Therefore, do not let our lord the king be angry that his servants speak a third time to him. We know our lord the king may do "whatsoever pleases him and who will say to him, what are you doing?" (Ecclesiastes 8.3.4). Yet, though he should kill us, we will speak the truth to him. "It is the king's honor to search out a thing" (Proverbs 25.2). We know the king is a wise man and a man of understanding. Thus, we then speak to him. Will the king challenge to

---

[8] John 18.36
[9] John 17.11
[10] Matthew 22.21
[11] Luke 12.14
[12] John 8.1

himself to sit upon the throne of David and judge Israel? We, the king's servants, mean will the king have the same power over the church and house of God that the kings of Israel had under the law who sat on David's throne? Will and should the king make a covenant and stand to it? Does everyone have to stand to it? Will and should the king compel all that are found in his dominions serve the lord as the king commands? (2 Chronicles 34.32.33). Will and should the king slay all that do not come to the Passover? (Numbers 9.13). If our lord the king has this power then he should execute it, and then he sits on David's throne. If so, then the king of Spain has similar power to compel all in his dominions to serve God as he commands. So every king sits upon David's throne, and all kings are for this reason to be obeyed. Will our lord the king that is a man of understanding not yield that Queen Mary, the king's noble predecessor, had the same power and authority by her sword of justice over her subjects that the lord our king has? Her subjects were bound to obey her in all things and submit to her sword of justice as well as our lord the king's subject are to obey him and submit to his sword of justice, for all earthly kings have one manner of power and sword (Romans 13). If our lord the king by his discerning judgment sees this, then our lord the king will easily see that as Queen Mary by her sword of justice had no power over her subjects consciences (for then she had the power to make them all papists, and all that resisted her suffered justly as evil doers). Neither does our lord the king have power by the sword of justice over his subject's consciences. All earthly powers are one and the same in their several dominions. If our lord the king will have any other power it must be a spiritual power and then that must be with another sword, even a spiritual sword. For an earthly sword is ordained by God only for an earthly power and a spiritual sword for a spiritual power. Offenses against the earthly power must be punished with the earthly sword and offenses against the spiritual power with the spiritual sword. With this sword the King of King makes our lord the king mighty through him "to cast down holds, casting down the imaginations and every high thing that is exalted against the knowledge of God and brings into captivity every thought to the obedience of Christ" (2 Corinthians 10.4.5), who is "the fruit of David's loins concerning the flesh," and only "sits upon David's throne forever,"[13] (Acts 2.30; Luke 1.32.33; Isaiah 9.7) and upon his kingdom to order it and to establish it with judgment and with justice, "the rod of whose

---

[13] Isaiah 9.7

power is sent out of Zion, who is ruler in the midst of his enemies, whose people will come willingly" (Psalm 110.2.3). He does not require any earthly power to build up his church. This is shown when he declared that "all power was given to him in heaven and in earth." He bids his disciples, "Go therefore and teach all nations, baptizing them in the name of the Father, etc" (Matthew 28.18.19). "He that will believe and be baptized will be saved, but he that will not believe will be damned" (Mark 16.16). "When he ascended upon high he led captivity captive and gave gifts to men. He gave some to be Apostles, etc., for the repairing or gathering of the saints" (Ephesians 4.5.12).[14] Here it is shown to our lord the king that which we know he is not ignorant of, that Christ only sits upon David's throne to order it. We the king's servants show it so that the king might not be deceived by deceivers who would persuade the king that he has the same power over the church of Christ that the kings of Israel had over the church of the Old Testament. To this end, they that might use the king's earthly power to rule over and build up (as they pretend) the spiritual tabernacle, temple and church of Christ, which if the king will suffer them to do, he will sin against God in entering upon the kingdom of Christ, who is the only king of Israel (John 12.15), "whose power and sword are spiritual, whose tabernacle, temple and house is holy, made without hands,"[15] (2 Corinthians 3.17; 1 Peter 2.5; Hebrews 9.11) and therefore he has given spiritual "gifts to men, for the gathering together of the saints for the work of the ministry and for the building up of the body which is his Church." He does not nor will he require that people be commanded and compelled by an earthly sword or power as in the days of Hezekiah and Josiah, kings of Israel. That was an earthly or "carnal commandment" (Hebrews 7.16). They had a worldly tabernacle made with hands and worldly ordinances and carnal rites (Hebrews 9.1.2.10). Therefore the ordinances or laws were commanded to be kept by a worldly power, and the tabernacles were to be built by hands. But now we have a tabernacle "which the light pitched and not man" (Hebrews 8.2) and that carnal commandment is changed (Hebrews 7.12). We have a commandment "after the power of endless life" (verse 16) to the obedience of which law no earthly king's power can cause or bring any man to obey in any one thing. The tabernacle was not made with hands. No earthly power which consists only of

---

[14] Ephesians 4.8.11.12
[15] Hebrews 9.11

the strength of hands can cause any one part of it to be built. But all this is to be done only by the King of Israel's power who has all power given to him in heaven and in earth, whose power is all-sufficient to bring under obedience all his subjects of which no earthly power can be helpful, whose sword is his word, "which is lively and mighty in operation and sharper than any two-edged sword," (Hebrews 4.12) and therefore does not need the help of any king's sword. If his sword will not prevail to bring men under obedience to his own laws, what can our lord the king's sword do? It is spiritual obedience that the Lord requires and the king's sword cannot smite the spirits of men. If our lord the king will force and compel men to worship and eat the Lord's Supper against their consciences, he will make his poor subjects worship and eat unworthily. In doing so, he compels them to sin against God, and increase their own judgments.

O, do not let our lord the king suffer such evil to be done by his power. Little does our lord the king know how many thousands of his people have been compelled through trouble and fear of trouble to worship and to eat the Lord's Supper unworthily and in so doing worship and eat and drink to their own damnation. Although they perish in their own sins, yet their blood will be required at the hands of those that compelled them to sin against their consciences. The Lord in mercy give the king a heart to look into it so that it will not be laid to our lord the king's charge if he will suffer those to exercise such power by his authority.

We bow ourselves to the earth before our lord the king in greatest humbleness. We beseech the king to judge righteous judgment in this matter, whether there is so unjust a thing and such a great a cruel tyranny under the sun as to force men's consciences in their religion to God, seeing that they err, they must pay the price of their transgressions with the loss of their souls. O, let the king judge, is it not most equal that men should choose their religion themselves, seeing that they only must stand before the judgment seat of God to answer for themselves? It will be no excuse for them to say we were commanded or compelled to be of this religion by the king or by those that had authority from him. Let our lord the king who is a man of knowledge yet further consider if the king should by his power bring his people to the truth, and they walk in the truth and die in the profession of it in obedience to the king's power, either for fear or love, will they be saved? The king knows they will not. They that obey the truth in love, whom the love of God constrains, their obedience will only be acceptable to God (1 Corinthians 13). Thus our

lord the king may see that by his kingly power he cannot cause or make men
bring an acceptable sacrifice to God. Will the king make men (whether they
will or not) bring an unacceptable sacrifice to God? Does the king think he
pleases God? God forbid. If the king will please God in such service, then he
must seek to "convert sinners from going astray" (James 5.20), "and turn men
to righteousness" (Daniel 12.3) not with his sword of justice but "by the
foolishness of preaching" (1 Corinthians 1.21). For that is the means by
which God has appointed to save those that believe. (1 Corinthians 1.27.28)
"For God has chosen and appointed the foolish things of the world, the weak
things, the vile things, the things that are despised, and the things that are
not, to confound and bring to naught the things that are." These things God
has chosen to set forth in Christ, the power of God, and the wisdom of God.
Here is the absolute authentic word of command. The mighty, powerful,
punishing sword of our lord the king is not required to this work of the
publishing of the gospel of Jesus Christ. Let the king call to mind that which
no doubt the king has often read in the Gospel according to Luke (9.54.56),
that when the Samaritans would not receive Christ, his disciples said, "Will
you command fire to come down from heaven and consume them?" Jesus
rebuked them and said, "You do not know of what spirit you are. The Son of
Man has not come to destroy men's lives but to save them." By this the king
sees that Christ will have no man's life touched for his cause. If the Samaritans
will not receive him, he passes by them. If the Gadarenes pray for him to
depart, he leaves them.[16] If any refuse to be his disciples, he only bids them
"shake off the dust of their feet for a witness against them."[17] Here there is no
sword of justice at all required or permitted to smite any for refusing Christ.
Then do not let our lord the king suffer his sword of justice, which God has
given to him with his own power to defend and rule with authority, and keep
in all obedience his own people, the people of God, to the king's own laws and
statutes, which appertain to the well-governing and ruling of the king's state
and kingdom which is worldly and must fade away. Do not let our lord the
king suffer this sword to be used to rule and keep in obedience the people of
God and of the king to the laws, statutes, and ordinances of Christ, which
appertain to the well-governing and ruling of the kingdom of Christ which is
heavenly and endures forever. The sword of this kingdom is spiritual and by

[16] Luke 8.37
[17] Luke 9.5

the power of this sword only are Christ's subjects to be ruled and kept in obedience to himself. By this sword our lord the king must be kept in obedience himself, if he is a disciple of Christ and subject of Christ's kingdom. This takes away (without gainsaying) all the kingly power and authority of our lord the king in the kingdom of Christ. He cannot be both a king and a subject in one and the same kingdom. The king's understanding heart will easily discern this.

Let our lord the king in all happiness and prosperity sit on his own princely throne of that mighty kingdom of Great Britain, which God has given to the king and to his posterity. May the Lord give the king a most wise heart to rule and judge his people. May the Lord give all his people faithful hearts to love and obey him. Let all those who are the king's enemies that do not want him to reign over them be slain before him.

Let our Lord Jesus Christ in power and majesty sit upon David's throne, the throne of the kingdom of Israel, which his Father has given to him. Let Christ according to his own wisdom judge his people Israel. Let our lord the king be his subject, which our lord the king yields himself to be. The king must grant that as he as an earthly king he can have no power to rule in the spiritual kingdom of Christ, nor can he compel any to be subjects of it (as a king) while the king is but a subject himself. There may only be but one king in Israel.

Do not let our lord the king be angry, and his servants will speak of this but once. Will our lord the king, being himself but a subject of Christ's kingdom, take upon himself by his kingly power to make primates, metropolitans, archbishops, and lord bishops to be lords in the kingdom of Christ and over the heritage of God? Will our lord the king do this against the whole rule of God's word, in which there is not one tittle to warrant our lord the king to do this? Will our lord the king not be supplicated by the humble petition of his servants to examine his power and authority in this matter? Far is it from the hearts of us, the king's servants, to move the king to depart from the least tittle of his right that belongs to his royal crown and dignity. And far be it for the king to take from Christ Jesus any one part of that power and honor which belongs to Christ in his kingdom. Let our lord the king pardon his servants for meddling in this matter. For we profess ourselves bound upon the peril of our souls to be faithful subjects both to Jesus Christ our King and to our lord and king. Therefore, it stands upon us to know what belongs to Christ our heavenly king and to our earthly king. Christ our spiritual King has freely spoken to us and commanded us to "give to our king that which is our king's."[18] Will our lord the king not say as freely to us, "Give to God that which is God's?"[19] We do not doubt but our lord the king will say so. Why do we then appeal to our lord the king that is our earthly king? Let the king speak according to the true judgment of his heart. Will the king say that it belongs to him to make spiritual lords over the house of God? Will the king warrant his saying to be good? If the king's warrant is only of his princely prerogative, may we give to the king this power in submitting ourselves to such spiritual lords and to their power? Would this not take from our spiritual Lord and King that which is even his own name, title, and power, and give it to another? What greater evil can be committed against Christ than to take his honor and power from him and give it to earthly men, who should fear and tremble before him in giving to him glory and honor and not taking it from him? Do not let our lord the king be a partaker in such a great evil to suffer a power and name of blasphemy to be set up so directly against the express commandment of Christ who forbids all lordly titles and ruling power one over another in his kingdom. We do not dare but to think that it is done ignorantly, both by our lord the king who suffers it, and by those that administer in this greatest evil. We the king's servants say this greatest evil because it is the abomination of desolation set in the high places which are the days of "greatest tribulation that ever was or will be, of which days, unless they be shortened, no flesh will be saved."[20]

If it will not appear yet to our lord (the king) that this hierarchy of archbishops and lord bishops is this abomination of desolation set in the high places, then we beseech the king upon our knees, by his highest honor and renown, by his truest justice and most righteous judgment, by his most godly prince-like care of the salvation of his subjects, and lastly and above all, by his chiefest love of God and to his holy truth, that our lord the king will with his royal consent give way that this cause may come to an equal trial. But only thus far, that the king will take and hold his sword of justice from this hierarchy so that they may not smite the faithful, true, and loyal subjects of the king neither to death, nor to imprisonment, nor to banishment, for speaking or writing only against their kingdom. Let our lord the king (by his humble

---

[18] Matthew 22.21
[19] Matthew 22.21
[20] Matthew 24.22

supplication of us his servants) be entreated to leave them to defend their spiritual power and names by the sword of the spirit, which should be the weapon of their warfare if they are spiritual lords as they pretend. Our lord the king will then see this cause truly decided to the king's honor and great comfort. The king knows that this hierarchy with all their learned dependency, if their cause is good, they cannot lose it for a want of learning, in that they have wisdom and learning, if it is according to godliness, sufficient to convince the whole earth. If they can with all that mass of learning maintain their primacy and prelacy, archbishopry and spiritual lordships, then may our lord the king let them enjoy it with comfort. If they cannot, with all the spiritual weapons and armor they have uphold it, then let it fall and go into the bottomless pit from where it came (Revelation 9.2) and where it must go, though all the kings on earth should strive to uphold it (Revelation 20.1.2.10). Do not let our lord the king, therefore, give the least support of it by the power of the sword. May the Lord grant that we may find favor in the king's eyes in this so just and equal a cause which is that we may but try the power of these (called) spiritual lords and that by the earthly power they may not force men to yield to their spiritual authority. How can it but seem equal in the king's sight that spiritual lords should have no more spiritual authority than they can get and maintain by spiritual power? If those of the hierarchy think it is unequal that the doctrine of their power should be tried and be most unwilling and ready to do so, but will by policy and secret intimations shift it off, then will our lord the king who is wise easily discern that their "deeds are evil" and "they hate the light nor do they come to the light unless their deeds should be reproved" (John 3.20). "But they that do the truth come to the light so that their deeds may be made manifest that they are according to God."[21] Thus our lord the king and the entire world will have a full trial of them and see whether their deeds are wrought according to God or not. If they will now come to the light of God's word in the sight of all men and manifest their deeds to be wrought according to God, then they have approved themselves. But if they do not our Savior Christ has condemned them with his own mouth. Let our lord the king also condemn them in his own wisdom. Will we need to be importunate with our lord the king in this cause of his poor people which concerns the condemnation of all their souls? What need do we have, seeing our lord the king knows that "a king that judges

---

[21] John 3.21

the cause of the poor rightly, his throne will be established forever" (Proverbs 29.14). Then let our lord the king hear the cause of the poor, and rather notice that the king's most noble predecessor has before justly adjudged the same cause and freed his people so far of the bondage in which they were held. King Henry VIII, that prince of great renown, freed his people from the bondage of the first beast, especially in these two great and main particulars. In causing the scripture to be set over and printed for the people in their own language so they might hear the word with their own ears; and also that their worship should be in their own tongue, that they might speak to God with their own tongue and not in a strange tongue, as they did.

Let heaven and earth judge, and let our lord the king judge, and let all the king's people judge, whether this was not the depth of all darkness, when men might now know what God speaks to them, nor know in their public worship what they speak to God. Let our lord the king judge whether there was ever such spiritual cruelty upon the earth, when the poor people of God for whom Christ died were debarred from the presence of God in their public worship, and might neither hear God nor speak to God with their own outward ears and tongues, but as the ministers of the man of sin appointed and in a strange tongue as they taught them. We know our lord the king sees that here the abomination of desolation was set up in the high places, as also the corpses of the two witnesses of God prophesied of in Revelation 11.8 (which are the word and Spirit of God) lay dead in the streets of that great city. There is no longer any true use at all for them. The people are deprived of the life of them, for the word was a dead letter to them, and the spirit a dead spirit.

The king's predecessor of famous renown freed his people from that bondage of the first beast. But there has risen up a second beast which exercises the power of the first beast, and now our lord the king's people cry to the king with the sighs and groans of their spirits (and would also cry with a loud voice but for fear of the beast) and humbly beseech the king that he would put his helping hand out to free his people from the bondage of the second beast so their souls many not perish to everlasting perdition, which all must do that are under the bondage of the same, and so we continue. Now let the king hear with an ear of compassion, and see with an eye of pity, the cruel spiritual bondage that his poor people are kept under by the second beast in these particulars.

The king's people have the word in their own language and may pray in their own tongue. But they must understand the word as the lord bishop will have it understood. They must not pray nor administer in the holy things but as they appoint. Now let the king with a godly, wise heart consider in what woeful spiritual bondage God's people and the king's are kept by this hierarchy. How plainly would our lord the king see this cruel spiritual tyranny, if the king but would make it his own cause. Would the king think it is not a most cruel tyranny if the king should be by force compelled to understand and believe the scriptures as the hierarchy of Rome would have him, and to worship God and administer the holy things as the hierarchy would appoint? If the king would not do so, would that hierarchy then have the power to put the king in prison? If that would not serve the turn, could that hierarchy procure or cause the king's life to be taken from him, or at least banish the king from his kingdom and nation. Would the lord our king not think this was a great tyranny and cruel bondage? We know the king would, for which cause the king and his predecessor have cast off this bondage. Then let the king see that the king's people are under the same bondage. If they will not understand the scriptures and worship God as the hierarchy of archbishops and lord bishops command and appoint, they will straight send a pursuivant [sic] to apprehend them by violence and force, imprison them, sometimes for diverse years, many times not suffering so much as their wives to come to them, and if their lives cannot be gotten, then procure their exile or banishment. May the Lord give the king a heart to pity his people for this matter. The king is ignorant of these dealings, and none dare to tell the king that the prelacy has been so mighty and so cruel.

Will it please the king to view the cause of his people (who are true and faithful subjects) yet further? What does it profit the king's people to have the word of God to hear, and read it, seeing that they are debarred of the spirit of God to understand it, but according to private interpretation, by the lord bishops as though they had the spirit and could not err? O, that our lord the king who is a man of excellent wisdom would bend his wisdom to behold how (of which the whole power of the beast consists) this hierarchy of archbishops and lord bishops does nothing different than the first beast. The first beast keeps both the word and spirit from the people. They keep the spirit of God in bondage and the word of God has no effect, debarring the people of God from it, tying them to their spirits in the understanding of the scriptures which none may try whether they are of God or not. But they must believe and obey, or else go to prison, and if then if they will not yield be either hanged or banished.

Judge, O king, is this a rule of direction and ordinance of the Lamb who commands bishops to be "gentle, towards all men, apt to teach, suffering evil men patiently, instructing them with meekness that are contrary minded, proving if God at any time will give them repentance, they may acknowledge the truth, and come to amendment?" (2 Timothy 2.24–26). By these fruits may our lord the king and his people know the bishops of the Lamb, who are lowly and meek, and bids them to learn so that they may to be of him (Matthew 11.29). To pull men that are contrary-minded out of their houses by pursuivants [sic], to cast them into prison and cause them to be there at an excessive charge, utterly undoing them, their wives, and children, and bringing them all to outward misery, and causing them to be banished from under their natural prince (to whom they are most true subjects), cast forth from native country, and from their father's homes and all their friends and familiars, will not our lord the king say that these are the bishops of the beast, who is "like a leopard, and his feet like a bear's, and his mouth as the mouth of a lion,"[22] (Revelation 13) of whom they learn to be proud and cruel? All these evils and many more have come upon the king's people because they will not understand the scripture by the spirit of the lord bishops and pray in their worship to God by the direction of their spirit.

Will our lord the king hear the earnest complaint of his people and grant redress that as the king's people, by the means of the king's most noble predecessor enjoy that blessed liberty to read and hear the word of God in their own language and to pray in their public worship in their own tongue, so that by our lord the king's means people may enjoy this blessed liberty to understand the scriptures with their own understanding and pray in their public worship with their own spirits? If men then err, their sin will be upon their own heads and the king's hand will be innocent and clear from their transgression, which it cannot be if the king will willingly suffer his power to be used to compel men to pray and understand by the direction of the lord bishop's spirit. If the king will give his power to the lord bishops to compel men to eat meats "which through our Lord Jesus Christ are all clean, yet to him that judges them unclean to them they are unclean" (Romans 14.14), in which case if a man freely of his own accord does eat and doubt "he is

---

[22] Revelation 13.2

condemned, because he eats not of faith."[23] Why then, if a man in this case is forced by the king's power (whether he will or not) to eat when he doubts, and so he is condemned (verse 24), is this not "to wound the weak conscience, and to sin against Christ?" (1 Corinthians 8.12). Can our lord the king's hand be innocent in this matter when by the king's power men will be compelled to sin? O, that the king would then see that he may not give his power to rule men's consciences in the least things that are indifferent, much less has the king power to command men's consciences in the greatest things between God and men.

This being so, we the king's servants (with all the humility and reverence that can or may be given to any earthly prince) do out of our true loyalty, obedience, and the faithfulness of our hearts, thus speak to the king. Let it suffice our lord the king and let it not seem a small thing that the God of Gods has made our lord the king a mighty earthly king over diverse nations and has given our lord the king an earthly power to make laws and ordinances (such as the king in his own wisdom will think best, and to change them and alter them at his own pleasure) to rule and govern his people by, and to appoint governors and officers to execute the king's will. All the king's people are bound of conscience to God and duty to the king to obey the king with their goods, bodies and lives in all service of peace and war. Whosoever will resist the king in this matter, they resist the ordinance of God and will receive judgment from God, besides the punishment with the sword of justice which God has given to the king to punish evil doers that transgress the king's laws. God has also honored the king with titles and names of majesty that are due but to himself (Psalm 82.1.6; Daniel 5.18) and has commanded honor to be given to the king (1 Peter 2.17). God has commanded all his people specially to pray for the king (1 Timothy 2.1.2). Let this kingdom, power and honor fully satisfy our lord the king's heart, and let it suffice the king to have all rule over people's bodies and goods, and do not let our lord the king give his power to be executed over the spirits of his people. For they belong to another kingdom which cannot be shaken (Hebrews 12.22.23.28), differing from all earthly kingdoms. For our lord the king knows that the chief of earthly kingdoms are compared to "gold, silver, brass, iron" (Daniel 5.23). But this is the kingdom which the God of heaven has set up, which will "never be destroyed and this kingdom will not be given to another people, but to the

---

[23] Romans 14.23

holy people of the most high God and all powers will serve and obey him."[24]
(Daniel 2.44; 7.27) Therefore in this kingdom let our lord the king give us
his servants leave again to tell the king that he must be a subject in this
kingdom, and that our lord the king has no power nor prerogative (as a king)
to make laws. For in this kingdom, "there is but one lawgiver, who is able to
save and to destroy" (James 4.12). Neither does our lord the king have the
power to appoint officers in this kingdom and much less to make spiritual
lords over this kingdom to bring all men's spirits into subjection to their
spirits in the understanding of the scriptures and worshiping God.

Unless we may seem to speak untruly to the king, we humbly beseech
our lord the king that it may be lawful for his servants, with his princely
favor, to show the king some few particulars out of a multitude. And first, we
show the king that whereas our Savior Christ (Matthew 18.15.20) gives a rule
of direction to admonish a brother, if he sins, not speaking particularly of
some sins, but generally of all or any one sin, as we the king's servants
understand with all the understanding that God has given us. The lord
bishops say this is not to be understood generally of every sin against God but
particularly of some and must be subject to the spirit of their understanding
and that rule of Christ must be no sure nor perfect rule. Next, let us show the
king that if there is such a sin committed as the bishops judge to be a sin,
according to their rule (which let the king give his servants leave to suppose to
be adultery) and that it proceeds or comes to this degree, it must be told to the
church, which we understand to be the whole congregation, more or less, the
lord bishops by their spirit of understanding say, "Tell the church,"[25] that is
to be understood, tell the ordinary, which is either the bishop's chancellor, or
the archbishop's official. They are those that have power to bind on earth, and
it will also be bound in heaven. Their fees being paid to them, they have
power to loose on earth and it will be loosed in heaven.[26] O that the king's ear
would but hear half of the depth of this iniquity. The king's servants know the
king's heart would never endure that his people's consciences should be thus
wounded and their souls destroyed by being compelled to submit to such
spirits of understanding. Furthermore, let our lord the king know that the
Holy Ghost testifies (Acts 14.23) saying that "they had ordained elders by

---

[24] Daniel 2.44
[25] Matthew 18.17
[26] Matthew 16.19

election in every church, and prayed and fasted." This we understand was the whole congregation's fasting and praying, and election, and that the church has power to appoint or ordain or lay on hands, if there are no elders, as they did (Acts 13.2.3). But all this (say the lord bishops, by the spirit of our understandings) does belong to us, and the patron. The people have nothing to do with it, but must be content to have such a pastor as appointed to them, though they never heard him, knew him, nor saw him, and although the congregation afterward should never like him so well. Yet the lord bishops have power to take him away from them, and to deprive him, and silence him, and punish them if they hear him, although he was never so well approved among them. Thus the king's people must be compelled to understand the scriptures, for the abandonment of their power of ordination, and deprivation. We the king's servants understand, according to the best understanding that God has given us, that the apostle Paul, giving a rule of direction for the people of God on how to worship God when they come together (1 Corinthians 14.26.33) that "everyone as he has a Psalm or a doctrine or a tongue, may speak to edification and if anything is revealed to another that sits by, the first is to hold his peace, for all that have gifts may prophecy one by one."[27] In all this, God is not the God of confusion, but of order. Thus, we do hold that the disciples of Christ should come together to worship God and edify one another in the liberty of the spirit, according to the gifts and graces that are given to everyone (Romans 12.6) and that "every man as he has received the gift may administer the same to one another" (1 Peter 4.10). The lord bishops utterly deny the substance of all this understanding. Their spirit of understanding directs that when the congregation comes together, the priest or the curate that is licensed by them must only perform the worship, and must begin their worship with their book, strictly tying them to such sentences, and then to that which is written after, then a confession, then an absolution, with versicles [sic] and answers, and Psalms, and lessons, and *Te Deum*,[28] and the litany, three days a week, and at other times when the ordinary will command.

Thus may our lord the king see how his people's spirits are in bondage to the lord bishop's spirit in the understanding of the scriptures. They must

---

[27] 1 Corinthians 14.26.27
[28] A hymn of praise sung as part of a liturgy

of force and against their consciences understand them as they are commanded or else go to prison.

Our lord the king may also see that neither Christ nor his apostles ever commanded or practiced any set form of worship, whose spirit had been most fit to have ordained such an order, yet the lord bishops (in the perfect image of the first beast) have composed a proportion, and framed an order of prayers and readings for the worship of God, commanding absolutely the observation of it, forcing the spirits of the king's people to be subject to their limitations and so deliver God's people their "bread by weight" and their "water by measure,"[29] not suffering the hungry to be satisfied with the bread of life, nor the thirsty to be quenched from the rivers of waters, but forcing the unwilling to "drink stolen waters" out of their cisterns and eat "hidden bread" out of their storehouses. But the simple that eat and drink of it "know not that the dead are there, and that their guests are in the depths of hell" (Proverbs 9.17–18). Let not our lord the king be displeased, seeing his servants speak but the words of sobriety. If the king thinks we misapply them, that is the thing which we so humbly and earnestly beseech the king that it may come to trial by the king's free consent, and that the king's hand of power may not be against the just and the due trial of it.

Now when we the king's servants do sue for a trial, we desire our lord the king not to conceive that his servants mean a day of dispute, and so to handle the cause of the lord as men that contend for prizes, who submit their cause to private censure. For that it is private and concerns none but themselves. But our humble and most equal suit to our lord the king is that seeing this hierarchy of archbishops and lord bishops challenges such power and prerogative over our consciences, that all who cannot of conscience yield it to them may walk according to their consciences and publish their defense against them, that those that bear the names of the spiritual lords may by spiritual power only convince their gainsayers, and not pretend to be spiritual bishops and use only the king's temporal sword to rule and convince men with, that our lord the king would suffer us his servants to demand of them that take it upon themselves to be lord bishops of whom they have learned to rule by such power and who has taught them to put the contrary-minded in prison. How will they answer to Him (that will bring the greatest of them to answer) who taught all his disciples to "instruct the contrary-minded with

---

[29] Ezekiel 4.16

meekness, proving that at any time God will give them repentance," and has taught them "to be gentle suffering the evil?" (2 Timothy 2.24–25). Let our lord the king give us his servants leave to ask their lord bishops whether they think that God has forgotten this his commandment? Or will he quite forget to put it in their account because they have altogether forgotten to keep it?

O, that our lord the king would but take his sword out of these lord bishops' hands, to whose office it does in no sort appertain if they were Christ's bishops, and that the king would let them use only that sword which is sharper than any two-edged sword,[30] which belongs only to Christ's bishops in their office. Let the king turn them out. Let them, if there be any manner of uprightness in them, come forth with that sword and armor only which the Holy Ghost has appointed them, if they are Christ's disciples (Ephesians 6.11.17). We will come to them through God's grace in the spirit of love and meekness. But when they smite us with the king's sword of justice and maintain their authority only by that power, and yet will they be spiritual lords, how can we with faithfulness to the cause of God but shoot them through with the arrows of the Almighty, and doubly filling them, (Revelation 18.6) and discover by the word of truth the height of their iniquity? For it may please our lord the king to consider that there is no other way to try and discover whether they are spiritual or not but to apply the word of God to them, to examine and compare them by it, as the church of Ephesus did to those "who said they were apostles but were not and found them liars" (Revelation 2.2). If this hierarchy of archbishops and lord bishops will not nor may not be tried by the word of God, but will still cause (by all the means they can) as many as will not worship in their manner to be killed. None may speak or write against it but they will be put to death, imprisoned, or by banishment destroyed, then our lord the king know the practice of the first beast in all these things, that where the first beast has full power, none may write nor speak nor look amiss, but they die. The king can judge whether this hierarchy of archbishops and lord bishops are not the second beast who has been made in the image of the first beast. If the king's people may not say and write and by the word of God prove this hierarchy to be so, but must without gainsaying believe the scriptures and worship God as they command, then they are the lords over faith. The people of God have no power from God to

---

[30] Hebrews 4.12

understand the scriptures, but all power is given to them. Then, we must believe that they cannot err.

We beseech our lord the king (who is a man of wisdom) to give righteous judgment to whether the lord bishops do not challenge only to themselves all power to understand the scriptures and not to err when they will by force and violence of imprisonment, banishment, or death, compel the king's people to yield obedience only to their understanding. If the king's people must not believe that they only have the power of the spirit and cannot err, how can it be that the king's people must be compelled to obey them in all understandings and practices, unless the king's people must obey them though they err? If our lord the king will not altogether turn his ear from the deep complaints of his servants, then let the king hear his servants on this point which is so hateful to the king, and is of all estates (that have any understanding in the mystery of godliness) so much detested. Yes, the lord bishops themselves do in words profess great detestation and that is the presumptuous sin of blasphemy of that Romish beast who holds that he cannot err and therefore "thinks that he may change times and laws," as is prophesied of him (Daniel 7.25). He does this, as our lord the king well knows, appointing or commanding laws, days and times, and forcing obedience, and saying he cannot err, so that whatsoever he does must be obeyed as holy and good. O, that our lord the king and all his people would see that the hierarchy of archbishops and lord bishops do no less, although in word they deny it. Yet in deeds they practice and hold the same thing; that they cannot err. This can never be denied. Neither will they ever be able to open their mouths to deny it if they might be brought to answer. For will they ever be able to answer it, that they should expound on the scriptures and make spiritual laws, canons, and decrees, and command absolute obedience and in diverse interpretations of their canons, decreeing excommunication *ipso facto*,[31] but they will be forced to show by their deeds that they cannot err. Men must obey them on that ground, because they cannot err, or else on this ground, they must be obeyed although they do err. They must be obeyed, upon this last ground thousands do obey them. But we beseech our lord the king that it may be lawful, without offense to the king, to try the hierarchy on the first ground, which is, that as the hierarchy of Rome says in words they cannot err, that so in their deeds this hierarchy do absolutely profess they cannot err. We,

---

[31] By the fact itself

with the best of our ability, have made this plain to our lord the king and to every eye and ear.

The hierarchy of Rome expounds the scriptures, makes laws, canons, and decrees, and binds all men's consciences to obey, forcing them by excommunication, imprisonment, banishment, and death. None may examine their power, authority, or warrant by way of the scriptures, but all must be received as holy and good because the hierarchy of Rome says in words that they cannot err. We beseech our lord the king to see that the hierarchy of archbishops and lord bishops do all the same things. They expound the scriptures, make laws, canons, and decrees, and bind all men's consciences to their obedience, forcing the king's true obedient servants, by means of excommunication, imprisonment, and banishment (the king in mercy and justice refraining them of blood). None may examine the power and authority of any of their decrees by the scriptures, but all must be received as holy and good. Does the king not in the wisdom of his heart see, and may not all the king's people see, that this hierarchy of archbishops and lord bishops in all their deeds do show that they challenge to have the same power not to err which the hierarchy in Rome say in words they have? Thus, they absolutely do in deeds profess they cannot err. In this the hierarchy of arch bishops [sic] and lord bishops are the more deceitful deceivableness of unrighteousness.

We now beseech the creator of hearts to give our lord the king a new heart to consider all the exalted abomination of desolations executed and practiced by this hierarchy of archbishops and lord bishops. Let our lord the king know that it concerns the king highly to consider it, in that it is set up and supported, and all its cruelty executed by the king's power, by which they make our lord the king guilty of all the imprisonment, banishment, and persecution which by the king's power they impose on all the faithful subjects of the king who withstand their abominations. But above all let our lord the king (for the glory of God and for the salvation of the king's own soul) suffer us the king's servants to prevail with the king that our lord the king would but search the scriptures (which the king knows he must be directed if he will be saved), and let the king see with his own eye what show of warrant can be found that the king should take to himself power to elect bishops. O, we beseech the king that the successive possession and the goodly appearance of this power may not sway with our lord the king in this matter. Let the king set before his eyes the worthy recorded remembrance (by the spirit of God) of Cyrus king of Persia, who "brought forth the vessels of the house of David which Nebuchadnezzar had taken out of Jerusalem, and had put them in the house of his gods"[32] (Ezra 1.7.11) not regarding the monuments of his predecessor's great conquests, nor the despoiling of his gods of such beautiful ornaments, nor the departing with treasure of so great a value. All these respects could not hinder this king from restoring the vessels of the house of the Lord. Let our lord the king be no less minded to the house and church of God. Let our lord the king freely restore at once the church and house of God to the whole glorious power of Christ, its only king, and particularly that the most beautiful ornament of the election and ordination of bishops and deacons, who ought to be elected and ordained according to the rule of the Holy Ghost (Acts 14.23; 6.3), and who ought to be qualified with all and everyone of those gifts and graces set down by the apostle (1Timothy 3; Titus 1). Yes, and their wives and children also, or else it is a grievous iniquity to choose them. Who must only by their office bear those names and titles which the Holy Ghost has given them, and lead or rule by that power which Christ has appointed and by those laws and ordinances, and live by those maintenances, if they stand in need. Will our lord the king change all these and many more laws, statues, and ordinances which Christ Jesus the Mediator and King of the New Testament has appointed and ordained in his church? Will the king take this power to himself to elect in such a manner and such men as the king thinks good, and gives names, titles, and power such as best pleases the king? Has Jesus Christ with his blood purchased to himself this honor to be the head of his church? (Ephesians 5). Has he shown himself a faithful mediator? Has he been accounted worthy of more glory than Moses? Has he built his own house himself? (Hebrews 3).[33] Will he be despoiled of all his honor? Will our lord the king be enticed by evil men to enter upon the inheritance of the Son of God in appointing and by the king's power suffering to be appointed lords and laws in and over the house of God which are not according to the pattern? Which lords, because Christ is not their buckler, nor the faith of their shield, nor the sword of the Spirit the weapon of their warfare,[34] they have deceitfully seduced our lord the king and brought themselves under his protection for their defense, and getting the king's sword into their hands to destroy all that speak or write against them. They prefer

---

[32] Ezra 1.7
[33] Hebrews 3.1–6
[34] Ephesians 6.16.17

their own kingdom before either Christ's kingdom or the kingdom and state of our lord the king as we have already shown the king in that they with such loving patience suffer and permit so many thousands of Romists, who by their profession, and the practices of some of them are dangerously opposite to the kingdom of Christ and to the king and state. But these lord bishops cannot in any way endure those that do faithfully seek a reformation, because they are the only such adversaries to the kingdom.

We still pray our lord the king that we may be free from suspicion for having any thoughts of provoking evil against those of the Romish religion in regard of their profession, if they are true and faithful subjects to the king. For we do freely profess that our lord the king has no more power over their consciences than over ours, and that is none at all. For our lord the king is but an earthly king, and he has no authority as a king but in earthly causes. If the king's people are obedient and true subjects, obeying all human laws made by the king, our lord the king can require no more. For men's religion to God is between God and themselves. The king will not answer for it. Neither may the king be judge between God and man. Let them be heretics, Turks, Jews, or whatsoever, it does not appertain to the earthly power to punish them in the least measure. This is made evident to our lord the king by scriptures. When Paul was brought before Gallio, deputy of Achaia, and accused by the Jews because he was persuading men to worship God contrary to the law, Gallio said to the Jews, "If it were a matter of wrong or evil deed, O you Jews, I would according to the right maintain you. And he drove them from the judgment hall," [35] (Acts 18.12.17) showing them that matters of wrong and evil deeds, which were between man and man appertained only to the judgment seat, and not questions of religion. The like is shown by the town clerk of Ephesus in Acts 19.38.39. And furthermore Paul, being in like case accused of many things (Acts 24), in the twenty-fifth chapter appealed to Caesar's judgment seat where he said he ought to be judged, approving and justifying that Caesar's power and judgment seat was the holy ordinance of God. And our Savior Christ is himself obedient and commands and teaches his disciples obedience. But this judgment seat and power which was of God had nothing to do with the causes of the religion of God, as our lord the king may see. If it had, could then our Savior Christ not have commanded obedience? But he would have utterly overthrown his own kingdom and

---

[35] Acts 18.14.16

power. Neither could the apostle Paul say he should be judged at Caesar's judgment seat if Caesar had, or might have judged in causes of religion to God. For then he would have utterly overthrown the office of apostleship. If he had submitted his apostleship wholly to the judgment of Caesar, and so had the power and authority of it been altogether destroyed and made no effect, this may in no way be.

Now let our lord the king (whose honor it is wisely to judge in things that differ) judge whether there is in these days any other earthly power or any other spiritual power but the same that was in Christ and his apostles' times, in which times all earthly power was in the hands of earthly kings and princes and those that were in authority under them. Christ and his apostles did not diminish the kings and princes of the least of their titles. All spiritual power was in the hands of Christ and his apostles that were in authority under him, of which spiritual power and authority neither Christ nor his apostles would suffer any earthly king to diminish them of the least title, but rather give them their lives. If then our lord the king discerns that earthly kings and princes had the same power that kings and princes have now, and their kings and princes had no power over men's religion, which was spiritual and belonged to Christ, men were then to give to God that which was God's and to Caesar and so to all earthly princes only that which appertained to them.[36] Then let our lord the king judge by what warrant of God's word the king can now take to himself a spiritual power and set up a hierarchy of archbishops and lord bishops, and give authority to them to make laws and canons of religion, and to give them power to compel men to their obedience by such severe courses as they have done. Let our lord the king consider (and may the Lord give the king wisdom in this matter) that if no king nor prince could have set up such a hierarchy with such power and titles then, but they would have utterly trodden under foot all the dignity and power of Christ and his apostles (for Christ and his apostles must have been subjects to it), then neither may any king set up a hierarchy now, because it does utterly tread under foot all the dignity and power of Christ and his apostles, as well now as it did then. For now we have Christ and his apostles in all their power and dignity as well as they had in those days, according to that saying of our Savior Christ in the parable: "They have Moses and the prophets."[37]

---

[36] Matthew 22.21
[37] Luke 16.29

We humbly beseech our lord the king to suffer a little of the foolishness of his servants, although we may seem as fools to the king in this matter. If there had been such a strange hierarchy set up in Christ's and the apostles' days, would the hierarchy have suffered us (that are thousands of the king of Great Britain's subjects) to have gone to Christ and his apostles to have asked them whether we should have obeyed them or not in all their canons and ordinances and whether we should have given them those titles of superiority and all that ruling power which they challenge over us the king's subjects? Surely, they will say, they would not have denied us that liberty to have gone in so weighty a cause and being so many to have asked counsel of Christ and his apostles what we should have done. Twenty thousand being ignorant and ten thousand being doubtful whether any such power might be submitted to or not and thousands being of doubt that it might not be submitted to, so they will say they would not have denied us. But we know what their canons would have made of it. We may justly suspect that they would have informed the king that it was very dangerous to suffer so many to go to Christ and his apostles for counsel, and that it was not fit to suffer such giddy heads to have that liberty for making rents and divisions. It was much more...[38]for the king to suffer them to make all whole by their power, and to subdue such busy refractory spirits. Let the king with favor suffer his servants to speak by the way, unless peradventure or any such things come in the way. And we the king's servants now take it for granted that archbishops and lord bishops (that profess such great holiness) would not have denied us to have gone to Jesus Christ and his apostles for direction. If Christ and his apostles had (in the hearing of all our own ears, being so many witnesses) commanded us absolutely not to yield to the archbishops and lord bishops any such power or names, could we yield it to them, although the archbishops and lord bishops should (with twenty thousand witnesses) affirm that Christ and his apostles speak otherwise to their hearing? Would our lord the king think that it is equal that we should be forced to believe their hearing because they are lord bishops, contrary to our own ears and there being so many witnesses of one nation and tongue besides hundreds of thousands of witnesses of other nations and tongues? We know our lord the king would not think it no more equal (if the case were so) that we should be forced to believe the lord bishops hearing than that they should be forced to believe our hearing.

---

[38] The original text is unclear at this point.

Then judge, O king for the case is all one and the same. For we have Christ and his apostles in their writings, and they do absolutely speak to our understanding that in no way there should be any such hierarchy of archbishops and lord bishops in Christ's church. The lord bishops say that Christ and his apostles speak to their understandings, that their power and names are not contrary to Christ's words. Can our lord the king (who is accounted a most wise and just prince in his judgment) judge that we are all bound to cast away our own understandings of Christ's speaking and are to be compelled to believe and understand Christ to speak as the lord bishops understand Christ's speaking? O, let our lord the king with compassion consider whether ever since the heavens and earth were created there was a more unequal extreme cruelty than this, that the king's people should be compelled (in a cause that concerns the everlasting condemnation of their souls and bodies to hell) of force to submit their souls and bodies to the understanding of the lord bishops who are not able to direct themselves from the ways of death, but every man has perished that ever bore that office with those names and power, if they did not repent of it, although they had no other sin. They also that now bear that office with those titles and powers will likewise perish to everlasting destruction, if they do not repent and cast it away. The spirit of the Lord has spoken it: "The beast was taken, and with him that false prophet that wrought miracles before him, by which he deceived those that received the beast's mark, and those that worshiped his image, both of these were cast alive into a lake of fire, burning with brimstone," (Revelation 19.20) and thus manifesting to our lord the king that Jesus Christ is the only King of Israel, that sits upon David's throne, and therefore only has the power of the king of Israel. None may partake with him in that kingdom and power who had the spirit without measure. Yet, neither he nor his apostles that had the spirit without error to deliver the counsels of God did ever by example, practice, or by rule command nor give power that any should be compelled by any bodily punishment to obey their laws and ordinances, which were infallibly true, holy, and good. How much less should our lord the king command or give power to archbishops or lord bishops (men full of the spirit of error) to make laws and canons with authority from the king to compel by imprisonment and sharp persecutions of the king's true subjects and people of God to the obedience of it, who for their religion to God (although they are contrary-minded to the king) should not (seeing they do not discern) be punished either with death or bonds? This is confirmed to the king by the testimony of King Agrippa and noble Festus the governor, who adjudged Paul to have done nothing "worthy of death or bonds,"[39] but that he would have been loosed if he had not appealed to Caesar. Yet, Paul was contrary-minded to Caesar and to the Jews in his religion to God. But they judged him by the law of nations, by the power of which law the kings of the nations are to rule and judge, according to their own several laws, and against the law which Paul had not transgressed, for his cause was concerning the faith of Jesus Christ which could not be judged by that law.

Let our lord the king give his servants leave to commend this to the king's best observation, which is worthy to be observed, that wherever throughout the New Testament the professors of the faith of Jesus were adjudged by earthly rulers and governors for any thing that they did or held of conscience to God and of faith to Jesus Christ, if earthly rulers and governors took the cause in hand by their power, the judgment was always wicked and abominable. If our lord the king will but begin his observation with the forerunner of Christ, John the Baptist, whom Herod put in prison and beheaded. Then let the king come to Jesus Christ, whom they judged and crucified, "finding no evil he had done."[40] And so if it pleases the king to look throughout the whole book of Acts, there the king knows how the disciples of Christ were imprisoned, threatened, beaten, and stoned. Then "Saul made havoc" with his letters of commission, "and entered into every house and drew out both men and women and put them in prison."[41] Then "Herod stretched forth his hand and vexed certain of the church, and killed James the brother of John with the sword" and caught Peter and put him in prison."[42] Then Paul and Silas were taken at Philippi by the governors and people and were sore beaten and cast into prison, and the jailer who was commanded to keep them...[43]being charged to preach ordinances which were not lawful for the Romans to receive or observe.[44] Here may our lord the king see a true pattern of how the people of God are persecuted when the civil power judges their cause of faith and profession in their religion to God. Thus worldly governors

---

[39] Acts 26.32
[40] John 18.38
[41] Acts 8.3
[42] Acts 12.1–4
[43] The original text is unclear at this point.
[44] Acts 16.21–24

have dealt with the church of Christ when the disciples fell under their censure for their faith to God. And all these sentences of death, bonds, and persecutions the king can judge to be unjust and unlawful in that their rulers and governors had no lawful power nor authority to judge Christ nor his disciples for matters of faith, being in all other things obedient to their laws. But men will say all this is answered in one word. They were heathen rulers. Now, if our lord the king will challenge a prerogative or power because he professes Christ, then let it be lawful for the king's servants to tell the king that if he will profess to be a disciple of Christ, that gives the king no power to do any or all of these things to imprison, to banish, to put to death, that belongs only to his earthly kingdom. Christ and his apostles had no such power given to them. Neither were the disciples taught to take upon themselves any such power and to execute it upon the contrary-minded, but taught them to instruct the contrary with meekness, and by preaching the word, seek their conversion, with all longsuffering, and not to destroy them by severe punishments. Yes, the disciples of Christ must wait and labor for the "grafting in again,"[45] according to the prophecies of the scriptures (Romans 11.24–27). Therefore, the king knows they may not be destroyed, although they are the greatest enemies of Christ that are upon the earth, and have, and yet do cast the greatest reproach and contempt upon Christ with such words that are most fearful to utter. Yet the disciples of Christ must wait for their conversion and not work to their own destruction. Let our lord the king call to mind how the apostle Paul taught all the disciples of Christ how to be minded toward all infidels, where he says, "I am debtor both to the Grecian and to the barbarian, both to the wise and the unwise"[46] (Romans 1.14–15). The same apostle says, "To the Jews I became a Jew, to those that are under the law, as though I were under the law and to those that are without the law, as though I was without the law. To the weak I become as weak, that I may win the weak. I am made," says the apostle, "all things to all men that I might by all means save some" (1 Corinthians 9.20–22). All these instructions and directions are for our lord the king, to direct the king how he should go in and out with holiness and all meekness before his people to win them to Christ, and not to set up a cruel hierarchy to make havoc of the king's people (as Saul did), pulling them out of their houses, both men and women, casting them into

---

[45] Romans 11.23
[46] Romans 1.14

prisons, forcing them to flee the land, and persecuting them with all cruelty. May the king suffer all this to be done by his power upon this ground of being a Christian king? The king's servants show the king once again in all humility that Christ the King did not do so himself. He never appointed any one man to be punished for disobeying the gospel with the least bodily punishment. Therefore, we instantly exhort our lord the king that the king would no longer be seduced by those most dangerous deceivers that have received the king's power to punish those that Christ, the King of Israel, would not punish, and that persuade the king that the king has the same power in the kingdom and over the house and people of Christ that the kings of Israel had in that kingdom and over the house and people of God as it was the church of God.

We (according to our great weakness) have shown to our lord the king before that the king cannot challenge that power, meaning only in respect of religion. We will by the king's favor, repeat the substance of the whole ground in a few words. We beseech the king that we may do it, in that the whole cause depends on it. We repeat it to the king in these few words, which will never be disannulled or made void while the heavens and earth endure, this is because they are not our words, God forbid any such arrogance should possess our hearts, but they will never be made void, neither will any ever be able to gainsay them with any of truth, because they are the words of the everlasting God of truth. We show the king that the king cannot have that power (in respect of religion to God) in the kingdom and over the house of Israel or people of Christ now that the kings of Israel had in the Old Testament or in the time of the law. The ground we repeat to the king is that the kingdom of Israel was an earthly or worldly kingdom, an earthly or worldly temple, tabernacle or house, an earthly or worldly people, and the king an earthly king, who in and over all that kingdom, temple, and people could require only earthly obedience. The kingdom of Christ is a heavenly kingdom, not of this world. His temple, tabernacle, or house, is a heavenly temple, tabernacle or house. His people are a heavenly or spiritual people and are not of this world. The King Christ Jesus is a heavenly, spiritual, king who requires spiritual obedience.

Therefore, our lord the king cannot as king have any power over this kingdom, temple, tabernacle, house, and people of God in respect of the religion of God because our lord the king's kingdom is an earthly kingdom. To our lord the king belongs only all earthly obedience, service, and duty, which ought to suffice any earthly man. May the God of all grace give our lord the king a gracious heart to be satisfied fully and contented with that great honor, power, and dignity that belongs to the king, and to give glory and honor to God for it, that it may go well with the king and his posterity forever. And may the God of heaven deliver the king from all such enchanters of Egypt as will persuade the king to take upon him the power of the kings of Israel over the church of Christ only for setting up and support of their high priesthood with urim and thummim, with pomp and power, and the Levitical revenues of Israel, which they challenge and hold as appertaining to them forcing the king's people by cruelty to obey them as though with them only remained the oracles of God.

Now if they will show any manner of uprightness to God or faithfulness to the king or any regard to God's people, let them not maintain their kingdom which they have obtained by deceit and flattering the king, as is prophesied in Daniel 11.21. Do not let them maintain it by the king's sword and power, but let them come forth with that sword and power that they glory so much and use so little and maintain their names, power, and cruelty with it. We profess before God, and the whole host of heaven, and before our lord the king and his people, that if they can prove evidently to our consciences by the holy word of God that we may obey them in all their canons and decrees, and give them those names and titles without the everlasting destruction of their souls and bodies in hell, yes, if they can just prove that we should rest or depend upon their judgments and understandings in the exposition of any one part of God's word, or that they have power to ordain and appoint any one ordinance, or the manner of administering any one ordinance in the worship of God and church of Christ, we profess to our lord the king that we will yield to them all the obedience they require. If they will prove these things only by convocation canons, how can our lord the king require that the king's servants should dishonor God by casting his holy truth away and with it the salvation of our souls and depend upon their canons and yield to them obedience and perish, both in souls and bodies? We have rather chosen to lay down our lives at the feet of our lord the king in presenting the cause in the king's presence, saying with Esther, "If we perish, we perish,"[47] for coming so boldly uncalled into the king's presence. We will wait with hope and expectation that through the gracious work of our lord the king that he will hold out his golden rod that we may live. Not this only, but also that that by

---

[47] Esther 4.16

the king's means, comfort, and deliverance will appear to Israel, and that our lord the king will say, as the great king of Persia said, "The Lord God of heaven has given me many kingdoms of the earth, and has commanded me to build him a house in Jerusalem. Who is he among you of all his people with whom his God is, let him go to Jerusalem and build the house of the Lord God of Israel?" (Ezra 1.2.3) As King Darius said, (Ezra 6.7.16) "Suffer the work of the house of God, that the Israelites may build this house of God in his place that they may offer sweet odors to the God of heaven, and pray for the king's life and for his sons."[48] As Artaxerxes, king of Persia, said, "Whatsoever is by the commandment of the God of heaven, let it be done speedily for the house of the God of heaven. For why should he bring wrath against the realm of the king and his children?" (Ezra 7.23).

Beseeching the director of all hearts to direct the king's heart in these things, we continue to pray for the king and his son, and the king's realms and children, that the king and his seed, to God's glory, may sit upon the throne of Great Britain while the earth endures, possessing from God wisdom, and riches, and honor befitting the dignity of their high renown and that they may walk in the ways of God that God, according to his promise, may prolong their days. May the Lord give all the king's people faithful, upright, and honest hearts, that they may all with one heart as of one man, fear God and honor and obey the king, with all the honor and obedience that he has or can be due to any earthly king or prince, which is, all earthly and worldly obedience with lands, goods, body, and life.

We most humbly supplicate our lord the king and all the honorable and worthy governors under the king that they will not suffer themselves to be misled in judgment in condemning us as movers of sedition, and our books for the seditious books, because we differ from the received profession of religion in the land, but that they will, according to the great gravity and wisdom that is upon them, weigh what sedition is. They will easily find that to profess and teach a differing judgment in religion to the state cannot be proven as sedition. For then our Savior Christ and all his apostles would have been found seditious, which never could be proven against them, neither could Tertullus with all his oratory prove Paul a mover of sedition to Felix the governor "who was willing to pleasure the Jews in this matter,"[49] (Acts 24) if

---

[48] Ezra 6.7.10
[49] Acts 24.27

he could have found any advantage against Paul. But under all that excellent and mighty government of Caesar, under whom there was so many wise kings and noble governors, difference in religion could never be proven as seditious against the state. It could neither be proven as sedition in all or any of those that differed from the profession of religion established in Queen Mary's days, although they taught and professed the same as even the lord bishops themselves will confess.

It is neither accounted nor found seditious in the diverse, excellent, well-governed nations round about to profess and teach a differing judgment in religion from the profession generally established, as our lord the king and all his worthy governors see and know. It is but the false surmise and accusation of the scribes and Pharisees who feared their own kingdom, and of Demetrius, the silversmith with the craftsmen, whose craft was in danger, by which they got their goods (Acts 19).[50] They raised tumults and moved sedition and ever laid the blame upon the disciples. Even so it is now and ever will be that those who fear their own kingdom and desire private gain, do, and will falsely accuse the disciples as Christ as being movers of sedition against the state. If the lord bishops will not be found false accusers here, as their predecessors have been, then let them (if they can) forbear to accuse before they have cause.

Let them take heed lest when they will see "five in one house divided, three against two, and two against three, the father divided against the son, and the son against the father, etc.,"[51] let them take heed that they do not call that sedition. If they do, they will call Christ a sower of sedition, for what was his desire but that the fire of such sedition should be kindled (Luke 12.49.52.53). May it please our lord the king and all that are in authority in government under the king, with their wise judgment to consider that it will be a strange thing to condemn men for sedition who profess and teach that in all earthly things the king's power is to be submitted to, and in heavenly or spiritual things, if the king or any in authority under him will exercise their power against any, they are not to resist, by any way or means although it were in their power, but rather submit to give their lives, as Christ and his disciples did, and yet keep their consciences to God. They that teach any other doctrine let them be accursed.

---

[50] Acts 19.24
[51] Luke 12.52.53

BOOK 3

We, being yet (through the help of our God) most desirous to awaken all of you of our own nation out of that dead security and spiritual slumber, of which, as in the sea, you are all overwhelmed and finding no better nor any so fit portion of God's word to effect these our unfeigned desires as this prophecy of our Savior Christ (Matthew 24.15) who prophesied of days of so great a tribulation, and it is repeated in Mark 13 and Luke 17 and Luke 21. All of these places the evangelists must be most carefully and diligently compared together, because the wise reader will find (by good observation) that there are four prophecies of our Savior Christ, set down together by the evangelists, which are: first, the destruction of Jerusalem; secondly, the days of the exaltation of the man of sin, seen and discovered; thirdly, the days of the Son of Man in the brightness of his coming for the consuming and abolishing of the mystery of iniquity, the abomination of desolation, the man of sin; and lastly, the day of Christ's coming to judgment.

Every one of these prophecies must be diversely considered with their proper appertainings for the true and holy understanding of them, and not confounded together. Two of which, we have, and will (by the grace of God) speak of, as God will enable us—first, the exaltation seen and discovered, and the dangers of those days; second, of the days of the Son of Man in the brightness of his coming for the consuming of the man of sin—as being the most fit scriptures to stir you up to the consideration of your spiritual estates and standings, and to direct you in these matters (the scriptures we mean, not us), if you will not harden your necks and perish in the ways of death and sin.

We have endeavored to provoke you to look up that you might see "the abomination of desolation set up in the holy place,"[1] and how the kingdom of the man of sin is even within you all that submit yourselves in any obedience to the power of the first or second beast, "bearing the beast's mark or the print of his name,"[2] so we will also be willing, with the help of our God, to stir you up to consider the great danger that our Savior Christ has foreshown of what will occur in these days, when men see the abomination of desolation set up,

---

[1] Matthew 24.15
[2] Revelation 14.11

and according to the Savior's exhortation begin to flee, as all that have eyes may see men are now beginning to do. The danger that Christ foretold is that in those days (which are these days) "many will come (who are now coming) in Christ's name, and say, Lo, here is Christ. Lo, there is Christ. Many false Christs will arise, and many false prophets and they will show great signs and wonders so as if it was possible, they would deceive the very elect."[3] Weigh then within yourselves whether you should consider it when the days are so dangerous and perilous, as "if it were possible the very elect should be deceived." Such is the danger of these days, by reason of the false professions of Christ, and false prophets that do arise. Seeing the false prophets are the teachers and maintainers of false professions, we will endeavor to discover them both under one, and will only speak of such false prophets and professions that are among you and are known to you, not burdening you with the multitude of strange and foreign false prophets and false professions that are in the world, of which we generally admonish you to beware. It is full time that you look to those false professions and false prophets that are among you, if you have any regard at all of God's glory, or of the salvation of your own souls.

Seeing that we cannot speak of the false Christ, or false professions of Christ that are among you, but we must name them. We pray that it may not be offensive that we term them by such names and titles as men distinguish them.

The first is that great and so much applauded profession of Puritanism. We will prove that the profession is a false profession. Yes and such a false profession as we do not know the like of in any another upon the earth. We will not need to produce any testimony but your own. In your so many books you cry out about the things that are amiss among you, and sue and supplicate, and yet still continue in your former ways. By this you testify against yourselves that you are unreformed, and that there is a way of reformation, of which you would be, if you might have leave or license to enter into it. Seeing that you cannot obtain it, you justify that it is lawful to walk in an unreformed profession of religion upon this ground because you may not have leave by act of Parliament to reform. What more false a profession can be found on earth than this of yours, who profess that you know a way of much

---

[3] Matthew 24.23

truth in which you would walk, but you do not, because you cannot by superior power be permitted.

Let this suffice in this place to prove that you walk in a false profession of Christ by your own acknowledgment, calling daily for liberty that you might reform yourselves, but seeing it will not be granted, you go on in the false way that you disapprove of. Your grounds and reasons we will hereafter (by God's assistance) try. But in the meantime let God's people know that there will never be found warrant to give men liberty at any time to defer to eschew evil, or to refrain to do good, for fear of men, or in obedience to men, or under any pretense whatsoever. That profession is most wicked and false. Most false prophets are all those that profess and teach such a doctrine that men are not bound without any delay, all respects laid aside, with all speed to eschew evil and do good, as the true prophet David did, and taught and said, "I made haste and did not delay, to keep your commandments" (Psalm 119.60). So we proceed to show that all your Puritan prophets (so called) are false prophets, and such as our Savior Christ foretells of those who say, "Lo, here is Christ," but commands, "Believe them not."[4]

Although we might prove that you are all false prophets because you teach many false doctrines, yet we hold it the most easy and plain way for the understanding of all to show that you are false prophets. This is because you are not sent, nor called by God, and thus you will have the least deceivable show for yourselves.

Before we speak of your not being called and sent by God (which must appear by your election and ordination to the office or work of a bishop or pastor, for other prophets we know none among you), we will set down the gifts and graces, of which they are to be qualified that are to be elected, ordained, and undertake that office, and also as to how their wives and children are to be qualified. These are the words of him that said, "Let there be light, and there was light,"[5] and of him that said, "You will have no other gods before my face,"[6] and of the lawgiver, all of whose laws are perfect laws.

These are his words, and this is his law. "Let a bishop or pastor be the husband of one wife; watching, temperate, modest, harborous, apt to teach, and able to exhort with wholesome doctrine and to convince them that say

---

[4] Matthew 24.23
[5] Genesis 1.3
[6] Exodus 20.3

against it, not given to wine, no striker, not given to filthy lucre, but gentle, no fighter, not covetous, one that can rule his own house honestly, having children under obedience with all reverence. Do not let him be a young disciple, or newly planted in. Let him be well reported of, even of them that are without. Let his wife be honest, no evil speaker, sober, faithful in all things" (1 Timothy 3; Titus 1). This is the law of God. According to this law, in every particular a bishop or pastor, and his wife and children, must be qualified. It is the law of the perfect lawgiver. You will have no other bishop or pastor before his face. This we set down to put you and the people of God in mind to look first that you, their bishops, or pastors are qualified. For all that are not so qualified, both in themselves and their wives and children, are not sent of God to be pastors of his flock, but are false prophets in the first degree. God sends none but those that are according to his own rule. By this you may see that every holy man and excellent preacher may not be a bishop and pastor over the house of God.

And now we turn to election and ordination, which is the door and way where the true bishops and pastors of the flock enter. The Holy Ghost does teach (Acts 14.23) that election and ordination were performed in and by the church or congregation with fasting and prayer. This is the door and way, "and all that have entered by any other way are thieves and robbers,"[7] as our Savior Christ testifies (John 10). Are you all not now at once convinced? Must all of you not be forced to confess that you have no such election or ordination? Is your purchased election of patrons, either particular men, or of dean and chapter, or of some college, or the private election of some friend, unlike this holy order of election, which Christ has appointed to his church to be made with the gracious free and full consent of every heart and tongue in the whole congregation? How woeful and wretched is the estate of you all (if you do not repent) that join in this great wickedness to deprive the church of Christ of such a blessed and comfortable ordinance of Christ. How blessed and comfortable a thing it would be for a holy people to elect their pastor that should lead them, and feed them with the wholesome word of doctrine and exhortation and watch over their souls in the Lord.

What a blessed comfort it would be for a holy man to be so elected by a holy people. A godly people should have holy pastors over them, whom they would all love and revere. Godly pastors should have a holy people follow

---

[7] John 10.1

them of whom they would carefully feed and cherish. This is the ordinance of God and law of election. But to get an election for money, either of a man's own, or his friends, or by private favor or friendship or beholdings to men, and so corruptly become a pastor over a flock of people diversely affected, and many who are openly profane and wicked, here is an unholy election of an unholy pastor over a corrupt and unholy flock. This is not to enter in by the door but to come by another way, which seeing you all do, none of you entering by that holy election which Christ has appointed. Christ himself has adjudged you all, not to be shepherds of the sheep, but to be thieves and robbers.

Thus, you are all false prophets. How will you be able to stand before the Lord in this matter? How can you justify yourselves before men? Will you make the word of the Lord of no effect and bless yourselves in your own ways? If you still do so, as you have done for a long time, you will not be blessed by the Lord, in that you violate and utterly abolish that holy law of election, which Christ has ordained in his church for the choosing of the true shepherds of his sheep, and for the keeping of thieves and robbers out of his sheepfold.

Next in order to be spoken of is ordination, a holy ordinance of God commanded by the Holy Ghost (Titus 1.5), and the example of its administration was given to us by the apostles in the church of Christ (Acts 6.6), and practiced by the disciples (Acts 13.1.3), and taught to us to be a doctrine of the beginnings of Christ, and of the foundation (Hebrews 6.1.2), being called the doctrine of laying on of hands. This ordinance was performed and done in the presence of the church or congregation by fasting and prayer and the laying on of hands, ordaining, and appointing and separating those that were elected and chosen to office (Acts 6.6; 13.2.3; 14.23). All this was performed and done by and in that congregation where they were chosen officers. The church or congregation being in this holy manner will assemble together to perform this ordinance, all fasting and praying to the Lord with one heart and soul to give a blessing to that which is his own ordinance.

Is your ordination like this? The best of you are all fain to get your ordination by suit and service, by riding and running, by attending and waiting, by capping and curtseying, and at last by prostrating yourselves on your knees at the feet of an archbishop or lord bishop, receiving your ordination from him who exalts himself above God, exercising the power of the beast, despoiling Christ and his church of this holy ordinance, taking it wholly into their own power, and disposing of it only to those who promise faithful obedience to the hierarchy and archbishop and lord bishop. Is this not the second beast which you say, both in words and writings, is an antichristian hierarchy? May the Lord give you eyes to see how you have broken the covenant of the Lord in polluting and abolishing this his holy ordinance, and be ashamed to remember the covenant you have made with this hierarchy by which covenant of obedience you have gotten your ordination, and so you are the prophets of the beast. For "to whomsoever you give yourselves to obey, his servants you are to whom you obey," (Romans 6.6)[8] although you deny him in words as you do. Have you gotten an office from the hierarchy, and under the hierarchy, and will you in words and writings protest against the hierarchy, and yet retain your office which you have gotten by promising obedience to it? Do you think you serve Christ with this your stolen office? Do not halt between Christ and the man of sin. If you will deny your lords that have preferred you to office, deny your office also. In both you will do well. But if you will retain your office, retain your lords also that have preferred you. In both of these you will do well. What conscionable answer will you make to these things? Does any dare affirm that Christ has appointed such an ordination, either in the manner of administration or in the means of coming by it? Has Christ appointed you to sue, and make means to a prelate, and ride many miles with letters of recommendations, and pay all fees that are due (we speak within our compass) to get ordination? Did the apostles ever ordain a pastor but before or in the presence of the flock? Did any ever go and sue or seek ordination from the apostles? When any were ordained, did they kneel down at the apostle's feet? Did the apostles bid them receive the Holy Ghost? Is this the manner and means set down in the scriptures of coming by ordination? If it is not so, how dare you seek and submit yourself to it. Will you say that Christ has appointed no certain due order and means of ordination? Then you blaspheme in saying the rules and examples of the New Testament are uncertain rules of direction, and so you make Christ not as faithful as Moses. Is the holy ordinance of the laying on of hands one of the doctrines of the foundation (Hebrews 6.1.2), and may it come by any means, or from any persons, yes, even from the pope? You approve of it as you do, seeing you have no ministry but from Rome. It is the root from which your entire ministry is sprung and the wild olive that you are

---

[8] Romans 6.16

all by your ordination engrafted. Therefore as the root is, such are the branches. The root you all confess is most unholy. So the Lord judges you. You evil spirits, out of your own mouths you are all most unholy, and false prophets, prophets of the beast, and not of Christ in that you are not elected and ordained by the rules of Christ and do not have the word of God nor the testimony of your flocks for your true entrance.

What can you now say of this your office that is unjustly come by, unless you will plead possession (however so unjustly you came by it) for a good title, and so you justify Ahab's possession of Naboth's vineyard when Jezebel had slain the right owner of it. As the Lord lives, no less but much more is the wickedness of your possession, in that the beast has trodden under foot and "crucified the Son of God" (Revelation 11.8) and "sits as God in the temple of God,"[9] and has appointed you his priests to serve at the altar. Thus you have consented together in evil, and trample under foot the testament which Christ has purchased with his blood, and have broken into the sheepfold of the Lord like thieves and robbers, and do nothing but steal, kill, and destroy. You destroy all the people that submit to your ministry in that you bring them under the power of the beast. You having fallen down on your knees and worshipped the beast, receiving your spirit and office from the beast. The people are partakers of this sin in that they accept you in your office, and yield that power which Christ has reserved in his own body (which is his church) to the beast. So you are all despisers of the law of God and have given away his holy ordinance of election and ordination, which he has by his own word and spirit appointed in his church. You have given Christ's honor to the beast. So all are, both priests and people, worshippers of the beast and his image, and have received his mark. Therefore, "you all will drink of the mere wine of the wrath of God, if you do not repent" (Revelation 14.9.10).

And thus much to the ministry of the Puritan profession, to prove them all false prophets, as those that run and God has not sent them, their election and ordination to their office, and their possession of their office are most unholy and unjust. They are not elected according to the exact rule of the law of Christ Jesus distinctly and most perfectly set down in the New Testament forever. Whosoever adds or takes away either in word or action, by doctrine or example, the Lord will add to them all his judgments and take away his mercies (Revelation 22.18.19).

---

[9] 2 Thessalonians 2.4

Thus you have by the word of truth all been declared and proven to be false prophets who have not entered into the sheepfold by the door. It must follow according to the words of the Lord that all the great signs and wonders that you show in this your false ministry are lying signs and wonders.

Let it not be grievous for you to hear of these things to provoke you to wrath, but let it be grievous to you that you sin and so are provoked to indignation against yourselves that you may come to repentance.

Here is all your zeal of wonder, and signs of so great fervency, by which you work on the blind consciences and ignorant affections of the simple deceived souls, proven false and deceivable. All your fire which you kindle the hearts of men and seduce simple women, making them believe you have brought it from heaven. All this is but the false enlightening and heat of a false spirit, even of that spirit which your spiritual lord breathed on you when you knelt on your knees before him. He laid his hands on you, and most blasphemously, even in the high dishonor of the spirit of grace, and had you receive the Holy Ghost. By and in the power of this spirit you preach and pray, and do all your great wonders. You have no other spirit. This is the spirit to which you have submitted and by this spirit only are you sent. Therefore you are all false prophets, and you do not have the spirit of God abiding in you. "You are gone out of the way. You have caused many to fall. You have broken the covenant of Levi,"[10] in that you are admitted to the order of the priesthood by the man of sin, who is an adversary of God. This blasphemous consecrating of priests is directly contrary and opposite to the holy established ordinance of Jesus Christ in the gospel, of which the spirit of God can give neither approbation [unclear], nor admit of such to be the prophets of God (that have not entered by Christ the true door and way, but have entered by he who sits as God in the temple of God) but judges you all to be false prophets.

Therefore leave off your great days of humiliation by fasting and prayer, where sometimes you make the people cover the altar with tears and some of you have taken upon yourselves to cast out many devils. You go to great heights in showing signs and lying wonders, to deceive if it were possible the very elect according to the prophecy of Christ which is fulfilled in you. "Kindle fire upon the altar of the Lord no more in vain. The Lord has no pleasure in you, neither will he accept an offering at your hand, but will curse

---

[10] Malachi 2.8

you as deceivers who vow a holy offering by bringing a corrupt sacrifice to the Lord" (Malachi 1.10.14). All this you do, and will do, as long as you serve in your office and ministry, received by the power and authority of the man of sin, contrary to the holy ordinance of election and ordination appointed by Christ in the New Testament.

Now all these things we dare not but think you have done, and do through ignorance. Amend your lives therefore and turn, that these your great and grievous sins may be put away, when the times of refreshing will come from the presence of the Lord. Take heed, both you and all the people that do with such admiration run after you, as we ourselves have done (we speak it to our own shame). Take heed lest that now your ignorant zeal and fiery spirits of error by which you have enflamed the hearts of the simple, is discovered, take heed lest you "boil in great heat, and gnaw your tongues for sorrow, and blaspheme the God of heaven for your pains, and for your sores, and do not repent of your works, as is prophesied men will do," (Revelation 16.9–11) from which the highest measure of sin the Lord for his Christ's sake will deliver you. Through God's grace we will hope better things of you, which may the Lord grant that we may find in you. The Lord knows our unfeigned heart's desire is that you might also be saved. We exhort the people of God no longer to "hearken to the voice of strangers," but that they would flee from them, according to the counsel of our Savior Jesus Christ (John 10.5). Let the people see with their own eyes how you have all shown yourselves to be hirelings, who are neither the shepherds nor are the sheep your own, in seeing the wolf coming you have fled and left the sheep. Nay, many of you even of those that are accounted most faithful and holy, have, and do go yourselves and lead your flocks to hear the voice of strangers that are set up and stand by in that office and public place, which you challenge for your own, and are glad to preach in corners. Others of you make a secret composition with the hierarchy (which you profess to abhor), and then hire some wretched man under you to surplice and cross and sin for you. O, how hateful and abominable are the works of darkness of this kind, which are done to you in the light. All this under a great seeming show of holiness, but it is mere hypocrisy and dissimulation, because you are hirelings and not good shepherds who would lay down their lives for their sheep rather than lead them into the hand of the destroyer. If you deny them to be thieves and robbers that come into your places and are made pastors over your flocks against your wills, and against the mind of the flock, then you must acknowledge them as the true shepherds over the flock and that they have come in by the door, and acknowledge yourselves justly thrust out, seeing you in your judgments hold but one pastor over a flock.

We will not follow you in these particulars, unless further occasion is offered. But remember how you compare your fellow priests to bishops to Circumcellions or friars, going up and down with the bishop's bulls like beggars to see where they can get entertainment. Do you not see this all yourselves? Yes, some of your chief spirits at working lying wonders stand in the marketplace to be hired from the east to the west and to be transported from north to south wherever you can get a good town pulpit, or a privileged chapel, a great chamber or dining parlor to administer in. How so ever profane the town or household is, will you not let them all be made partakers of the holy things at first, before you know your sheep or your sheep know you, contrary to Christ's own word (John 10.14)? All the power you have to administer is by the authority of the bishop's bull, which you hold in so great contempt. Yet it is all the seal of admittance to your ministry, and warrant for your administration, a most fit warrant for such administrations. O, that you could see these things. If you have any love of God in you, cast off all these abominations and become disciples of Christ and preach Christ in his own ordinance as his disciples did (Acts 11.19). If you will not but run on in the heat of your blind zeal in your false ministry, then you will be found to be those false prophets that come in sheep's clothing of whom our Savior Christ has foretold (Matthew 7.22), that will say, "Lord, Lord, have we not by your name prophesied, and by your name cast out devils, and by your name done many great works?" To whom he will answer, "I never knew you. Depart from me, you that work iniquity."[11] Let this suffice to have proven by God's word that your election and ordination to the office of your ministries is not of God, and that you have not "entered in by the door, but have climbed up another way," and therefore are "thieves and robbers, false prophets, hirelings, strangers,"[12] whose voice Christ's sheep do not know. They flee from you and will not follow you (John 10.5). By this all that hear and follow you are most plainly proven by the most evident words of Christ not to be his sheep, none of them, for he says, "His sheep know his voice and follow him and they will

---

[11] Matthew 7.23
[12] John 10.1.5.12

not follow a stranger because they do not know his voice."[13] This is all the comfort that God's word does afford any of you and your flocks that follow you. They are not Christ's sheep. This is all the comfort that the people can have in you. You are not Christ's shepherds. So you are like people, like priests, like shepherds, like sheep. You will perish every man for teaching and drawing them after you, because you are false prophets and are not sent from God. The people will perish every one of them for hearing and following you because you are strangers and hirelings, if you and they do not repent (Luke 13.3). This is the word of the Lord which you will neither all nor any one of you be able to gainsay. You will never be able while heaven and earth endure to make any show from God's word for your entrance into your office of ministry. You are then utterly confounded in all your ways, and all the people that follow you.

We have spoken sharply to you, as it may be thought. If we have not, we had need, seeing that you have so often spoken of this your false ministry with excellent words. Yet you have not regarded our words, which might discomfort us in you and discourage us in our own simple plans. But it is the love of God's glory which (through his grace) we hold most precious and the longing desire of our souls after your salvation, and the salvation of this whole land which is so dear to us which we so much wish and pray for. By the hope and assurance we have of God's mercy and power to prevail by weak means, these causes have stirred us up, driven us on, and encouraged us to speak to you. We pray that you, by the name of Jesus, if there is any purpose of heart in you to fear God and walk in his ways, or any love in you for these people with whom you are bound so much to regard with all faithful carefulness, make haste to reform your own ways, and to inform this people in the way to life, and salvation, according to the strict rule of God's word. Do not continue to lead them on in the way to death and condemnation, according to the new inventions of your own hearts and the old traditions of other men.

We will now return to speak a few words of your ground and reasons (or rather excuses) that cause you to undergo these things of which you cry out so much for reformation. One is because it is under a Christian king. We demand of you, how, if the king should bid you to truly inform him whether it is more lawful for a Christian king to restrain the church of some of the ordinances which Christ has appointed than for a heathen king? It cannot be

---

[13] John 10.5.6

that you would tell the king that a Christian king might more lawfully do such evil than a heathen king. If you would, you would make Christianity a liberty to sin, which it may not be. Why then, if a Christian king may not more lawfully do such evil, (as you hold it to be evil or else why cry out so much for reformation) neither may you more lawfully obey him in such than a heathen king. Leave off such deceitful pretenses and vain imaginations, for which if you should be required warrant out of God's word, you would easily see that it is but an excuse of a false show. The disciples of Christ, who were most obedient subjects, taught you and us all obedience to our king. Yet they would not be restrained in the causes of God, but chose rather to obey God than men, and rather to suffer imprisonment and beating than to be restrained either of preaching or practicing any of the ways of God. Although they were commanded, imprisoned, and beaten up by the high priest, the council, and all the elders of Israel that were not heathen governors, (Acts 5) those who were faithful disciples were content to obey in all sufferings. Such obedience you would have submitted to if your hearts had been upright to God and the king. But you have all been found deceitful upon the weights and lighter than vanity itself in these things when you came to trial and you have daubed with untempered mortar. It is no marvel that you fell because the Lord was not your strength, in that you did not seek the right way, but would have established a presbytery, hierarchy, and a decreeing synod, which would have been no more pleasing to God than a hierarchy of archbishops and lord bishops and a canonical convocation house. They both have one mind with the beast and give the right hand of fellowship one to another, seeking and exercising one power, which is, to rule over men's consciences by their own laws and decrees. Therefore, do not strive any more for your way. The Lord will ever be against you in it. For if a ruling presbytery by their synodal decrees and ordinances is lawful, why then is a ruling prelacy by convocation canons not lawful? Why not have a ruling pope? These are all one condition in their degrees and none of them are more pleasing to God than another. Although they are every one more sinful in their degrees than the others, yet they all abolish Christ's ruling power. If they do not repent, Christ will "crush them with a scepter of iron, and break them in pieces like a potter's wheel,"[14] and will rule his people with a scepter of righteousness.

---

[14] Psalm 2.9

Your next ground and cause of undergoing these things you so much dislike is because you are loath to break the peace of the church. Where you have learned to undergo sin for the sake of peace we do not know, but we are sure that you did not learn it from God. Paul and Barnabas had not learned your lesson, for if they had they would not have made such a great dissension in the church at Antioch as they did about the doctrine of circumcision. If Paul had been of your peaceable minds, he would (seeing he had suffered Timothy to be circumcised for the sake of peace) also have suffered a little of the doctrine of crucifixion, but he would not. Furthermore, the apostle commands the church (Romans 16.17) to avoid, or to not have fellowship with those that cause division and offenses that are contrary to the doctrine which they had learned. The same apostle warns the Thessalonians (2 Thessalonians 3.6) in the name of the Lord Jesus Christ that they must withdraw themselves from every brother that walks inordinately and not after the instruction which they had received. Now, if there is in you any conscience of the religion of God, see how corruptly you walk in these things, making a show of godliness but denying its power. Do your brethren, the archbishops and lord bishops with archdeacons, chancellors, and the rest, not cause divisions and offenses contrary to the doctrine which you have learned? Do they not walk inordinately and work, too, and not after the instructions that both you and they have received from the apostles? How then is it that you will not (according to the apostles' commandment, exhortation, and so straight warning) avoid them, and have no fellowship with them, and withdraw yourselves from them? Is your peace a godly peace, which is so contrary to the whole word of God? Besides this we must tell you (bear it patiently) that it is but ignorant dissimulation in you to say you undergo all these things because you would not break the peace of the church. For if you did so much tender the peace of the church as you pretend, and that you would not have your beloved stirred up, nor wakened before she pleases, why then have you written so many books of open contempt? Why have you fought so much and made challenge for disputations? Why do you make so many loud outcries and daily complaints and tedious Parliament suits? How can you possibly devise more unpeaceable courses? Unless you should raise tumults contrary to the law of God and of the king (which we know is not in your thoughts), you can in no way devise anything to be more unpeaceable. Had it not been a much more peaceable course to have separated quietly with love and humility rather than to have stirred up so much bitter strife in the bosom of the church whose peace you pretend so much to regard? O, that you could see that it is your own peace that you respect in all of this. What breach of peace would it have been in the church if you all had peaceably withdrawn yourselves, and lovingly admonished the church, holding it a true church as you do? Would it not have been much more peaceable and much less trouble for the church if you had done so? There is no question that it would have. But whether your peace and profit would have followed is the question. You must take heed that this is not the cause of your (for peace as you call it) undergoing of these things. We could speak largely of this point, but we spare you, only wishing that you do not persuade yourselves, nor make the people think that you have suffered great things, while you eat the fat of the land. Know this, all you who eat any bread from whosoever hands, by, or in respect of your office ministry, that you feed off the portion of his meat of whom you seek to destroy, fulfilling the prophecy of Daniel 11.26, where he prophesies of the destruction of the man of sin, saying, "They that feed off the portion of his meat will destroy him." Do the simple not understand that you are getting bread by the office, which office (as is proven) you have and execute by the power and under the authority of the man of sin? You feed off the portion of his meat and serve at his altar, and so you eat of the things that appertain to that altar, gaining them by that office. Let all the people know, of all estates and degrees whatsoever, that give you any maintenance or entertainment in respect of that office, entertaining you as prophets, they will never receive a prophet's reward, but you sin against God in maintaining and entertaining false prophets, although they are as full of good meanings as the papists are in entertaining their priests. We do not have the least intent to dissuade any from doing good for you, but they should not receive you, nor give you a cup of cold water in the name of the prophets. All their liberality bestowed upon you in that regard will never receive recompense of rewards at God's hands, seeing you are all false prophets, and so adjudged by Christ himself in that you have not entered by Christ into the sheepfold. If any of you will open your mouths to defend yourselves in this matter, the word of the Lord will convince you, and stop your mouths, so that you will not be able to speak with any understanding. Now we advise you to be ashamed to plead that you do undergo these things for the peace of the church, unless you will hold your peace. For you are wise enough to know that there is no other way to break the inward peace of the church, whose peace you must mean, for it is not in your powers nor hearts to break the outward peace of the church. There is no other way to break the inward peace of the church, but by words and writings of opposition and contention, and making division, all of which you have practiced to the uttermost of your own powers. When, for fear of your own peace, you durst go no further, then you have set out your books of unknown authors (which are no better than libels), and you have no regard what troubles and dissensions you make in the church, so you can preserve your own peace. Thus, you maintain by all force and violence of contention a most troublesome civil war, which of all is most dangerous in church and commonwealth. Yet, you profess you suffer and undergo all these evils of which you complain because you tender the peace of the church. So, through ignorance you fall into great dissimulation and hypocrisy, it is (if you could see) only your own peace you seek. Therefore it is you who undergo these things that you disapprove of. Would you not, if you might (without danger or loss), reform yourselves and as many as you could, according to that reformation you sue for? Your own consciences can tell you that you would, if the king at first had made a law that all should have been in subjection to the bishop's power and government in the church, but he would have no man punished by imprisonment nor put out of their livings that should refuse, would you all that have any conscience of your ways not have reformed? If you would not, then the reformation you plead for is not useful, unless the king approves it. So you have striven all this while about needless things, if the king's commandment may disannul the necessity of them. Then are they needful, if the king will permit them? If not, your reformation may be spared, and so you should not have gainsaid it, as you have done.

In this your iniquity greatly abounds in that you make so small a matter of those things where you in judgment differ from the lord bishops, seeing that the difference is no less than for the whole government of Christ in his church. May the Lord give you and all his people grace to duly consider how greatly you dishonor Christ, and make a mockery of him, when you profess him to be your king, and yet say his government is not of absolute necessity. So you hold it of absolute necessity to give him the name of a king, but not to give him the power of a king. What a great impiety of high contempt is this? What earthly king would endure this at his subjects' hands? If you should do so by our lord the king of Great Britain, acknowledge him to be your lord and king, and call him by that name and title, and bend and bow to him with words and all reverence, but wholly submit yourselves to be governed by the laws and officers of a foreign power, and by rebellious subjects who should be obedient to the king, and yet set themselves up as kings and take the king's power from him, were you not all worthy to be accounted traitors and rebels? Would the king not have cast you all out of his kingdom, or destroy you all in it? Would the king be satisfied with all your words of flattery that you could use in acknowledging him, and calling him by the name of your king, when he should see he had no power to govern you by his laws and officers but that you did submit to be ruled by the laws and officers of his rebellious subjects and enemies? Would our lord the king endure this? Having power in his hand to avenge himself of you, would he not, after his often proclamations made [sic] and his many messengers sent to you, command you to come out from under those governors, and that government, lest you will be destroyed with them, and you submit yourselves to him, and he will be your king and your defense? If for all this you would not hearken and obey, would the king not come with his power according to his word, and destroy you all together who would not suffer him to rule over you? Certainly, the king would do it in justice, and for his own honor, and having protested it with his word. Even so, be sure, Christ Jesus your king will do by all of you, if you still stand in rebellion against him, submitting yourselves to that rebellious hierarchy of archbishops and lord bishops who should be his subjects, but are his enemies, and exalt themselves above him, governing you by foreign power and government, and not by Christ's power and government. The king's proclamations are meant for you, commanding you to "come out from among them, and separate yourselves, and be his children and people. He will receive you, and be your God and Father"[15] (2 Corinthians 6). "Go out of her, my people, that you will not be partakers of her sins, and that you do not receive her plagues"[16] (Revelation 18). Thus Christ Jesus your king calls to you. If you will not yet hearken to his voice, but flatter with your tongues, and say you acknowledge him to be your king, but you do not submit to be governed by his power, he will certainly in his justice for his honor, having protested it by the word of his mouth, come against you all, and give you the "cup of the wine of the fierceness of his wrath." (Revelation 16.19) O, you people destitute of understanding. O, nation not worthy to be loved. Can you think in your minds that God has given all earthly kings power to make good laws, to rule and govern their people by, and commanded their subjects to be

---

[15] 2 Corinthians 6.16–18
[16] Revelation 18.4

obedient to them? Has he not given Christ Jesus his beloved Son (whom he has set upon David's throne forever and made king over his people Israel) power to make true laws and good ordinances to govern and rule his people by? Has he not commanded all his subjects to be obedient to them? No king of power will suffer his subjects to submit themselves to be governed by the government of any other, and to be deprived of that government which God has given them over their subjects. Can you be so unwise to think that Christ Jesus, who is a king of greater power, will suffer it in his subjects? Can you not see that a king is no king if his government over his people is taken away? Can you think that Christ may be a king without his government? What vanity possess your minds that you would make so small a matter of Christ's government, saying you differ with the bishop's in no fundamental point, but only in matters of government. See (if there is any fight in you) if the lord bishop's power of government was taken away, where would their kingdoms be? Their names and titles would not support their kingdom. This they see and you find by their Canon 7 Anno. 1603, which they have made for the firm establishing of their government, knowing it to be fundamental, without which their kingdom would presently come to naught even in one hour. Even so they have brought Christ's kingdom to naught among you by taking his government from him. Who has bewitched you to say and teach, and seduce the simple as though government was not a fundamental point? Do you not know what government is? Can you divide Christ's government (as he is a king) from his power, or his power from his government? Will you make him a king without a government? Is he then a king other than in name? If the lord bishops should compel you to deny Christ of the name of a king in or over his church, would you not then say they overthrow a fundamental point of faith? Do you not have the understanding to discern that the power or government of a king is of far greater authority than the name of a king? Would it be a much less matter for a king to be deprived of the name and title of a king than of the power and government of a king? Let the simple judge which is greater, a king of great power and government, or a king of great name and title. Let them contend and see who will get the victory. All this we set down to show you how greatly you err through an ignorance that cannot discern that power and government in earthly kings is much greater than name and title and therefore you err in common judgment. But you err much more in spiritual judgment in that you cannot discern Christ's name and the power of government to be of equal estimation. For if you do not hold all things in Christ, and all things of Christ to be equal, and of like condition or proportion, you overthrow the nature and property of God. Thus, all the graces of Christ himself are equally alike, and all his works are equally alike. It was all one with God to make a behemoth as spoken of in Job 40, and the pismire (Proverbs 30)[17] and God esteemed them both alike. All the word of God is alike and of like power and authority, as Christ himself showed when an expounder of the law asked him, "Which is the first and greater commandment?" Jesus answered, "You will love the Lord thy God with all thy heart, soul, and mind. This is the first and greatest commandment." The second is, "Love thy neighbor as thyself."[18] The apostle James makes it most plain that the commandments of God are all of like power and authority and all of like necessity to be obeyed. The Holy Ghost shows and provides evident reason that every commandment is alike and to be obeyed, and why the breaking of one is the breaking of all, because (says the Holy Ghost by the apostle) he that commanded one commanded all (James 2.10.11). From this ground of truth we speak to you in the words of the Holy Ghost. He that has commanded in the church the true preaching of the word, true baptism, and true administration of the Lord's Supper, the same God has also commanded true government in the church. Therefore, although you should have the word of God truly preached, and baptism and the supper of the Lord truly administered, yet if you have a false government, you are transgressors of the whole law of God, and guilty of all.

Thus the word of God disapproves and utterly condemns that blasphemous doctrine of yours as you fearfully deceive yourselves and the people of God, which you hold and teach that Christ's government in his church is not fundamental. Besides the word of God we have endeavored to show you that in all common sense and understanding, a king that does not have the power of government over his subjects, but submits to the government of strange lords, they are disobedient and rebellious, and give their king only the name of king. You are such subjects, giving Christ only the name of a king, but give his power of government to strange lords, your lord bishops, your archbishops and bishops, who enlarge you by their spirit, and you are enlarged. They restrain you by their power, and you are restrained. They set you up as shepherds when you please them, and put you

---

[17] Proverbs 30.25
[18] Matthew 22.35–39

down like hirelings when you offend them. If they destroy your flock before your faces you stand by and dare not aid them, but give counsel for peace, to submit to their cruelty, although they condemn your most innocent, and justify the most guilty. All this evil and much more you justly bring upon yourselves and the people in teaching and professing that you do not differ from the lord bishops on any fundamental point, making and accounting that the government which Christ has appointed in his church not to be fundamental. By doing so you sin against God with a high hand and make Christ Jesus a vain lawgiver, while by your practice and profession, both in deeds and words, you declare that the ordinances of Christ, which he has appointed for the whole government of his church, are not of absolute necessity, and fundamental. If the Jews had so said and practiced against the ordinances they received from the government of the temple and tabernacle, and appointing the officers by the mouth of Moses, it would have made an utter confusion of all, and they must die. Behold one greater than Moses is here giving ordinances for the government of his temple and tabernacle, and for the ordaining of officers, against which if you resist and admit of any other you must die, unless you repent (Hebrews 10.28.29; 12.25). You make an utter confusion of it all. O that you would but look with your eyes and see what a confusion it would have brought into the temple and tabernacle, if any other officers and any other government had been brought in other than Moses appointed. Would not all their sacrifices and services been polluted and most abominable to the Lord? Would Moses ever have endured it? Would Aaron have consented to this? They would not. If all the people had, they all would have been destroyed with Korah, Dathan, and Abiram,[19] who would have overthrown the government and officers of the temple, for the Lord would have been as just in his judgment upon all as upon some. O that you would consider this, "and not forget God, lest he tears you into pieces, and there are none that can deliver you."[20] Are the laws and ordinances given by Jesus Christ for the government of his temple and tabernacle, and appointing of his officers, not so perfect as those that were given by Moses? Will not the bringing in of any other officers and government to the church of Christ than he has appointed cause as great confusion as it would have done in the temple? Will not all the sacrifices and services be polluted and most abominable as

---

[19] Numbers 16
[20] Psalm 50.22

theirs would have been? Will Christ Jesus the Mediator and High Priest endure it or consent to it any more than Moses and Aaron would have done? If you say he would, then you make Christ less faithful than Moses and make his church less holy than the temple and his laws and ordinances not as perfect as those that were given by Moses, and so the transgression against them deserves less punishment. But all the prophets and apostles, and Christ Jesus himself testified to the contrary, as you know right well. Most especially the author to the Hebrews handled these things at large, showing that the temple, tabernacle, and all the officers, and offices, and ordinances of administration for government and service given by Moses, were but a pattern, shadow, and similitude of the heavenly temple and ordinances established and given by Christ, who is "the mediator of a better testament, established upon better promises," and is "the high priest of a more perfect tabernacle," and has purified all the ordinances with a better blood. He is as faithful as Moses, and is worthy of more glory and honor (Hebrews 8.5.6; 9.11.23; 3.2.3), and he will punish with sorer punishment those that despise his law than Moses could (Hebrews 10.28.29). Therefore, take heed to yourselves for you have brought utter confusion upon the house of God by submitting to another government and other officers than Christ has appointed in his church. All your sacrifices and services are polluted, just as theirs would have been in the temple if they had permitted such a thing. If the government of the temple was fundamental, how much more is the government of the church of Christ? Be wise in spiritual wisdom, and then you will yield that true government is an absolute necessity in the church of Christ under the gospel as it was in the temple under the law. If you will be of understanding according to all the understanding of men, you will confess that a king's own government, by his own laws and ordinances, is fundamental and of absolute necessity, and must be over his own subjects in his own kingdom or else you make him but a king in name and not in power. Then you must confess that Christ's government is of absolute necessity and fundamental in his kingdom or else you make him but a king in name. How can you in all true judgment but acknowledge that it is much better to have the power and government of a king without the name of a king than to have the name of a king and not the power and government of a king? Therefore you might as well submit to the lord bishops the right to take away Christ's name as a king as submit to take away from him the power and government of a king. Here lies the depth of the mystery of iniquity in the man of sin, in taking wholly from him his power, and yet professing his name. By this all the nations of the earth are deceived and it blinds you all because you have the profession of Christ's name among you, saying he is your king. This makes you rest satisfied, although you do not yield to him one thing that appertains to his kingly office, but only the name and title of a king. We may make this plain to you (for you do not see it) that you give Christ only the name of a king in your church, thus, we show it to you. All that can be given to a king by his subjects is to give him all the titles of honor due to his name and to submit in obedience to his power. This is all that God requires to himself in the first, second, third, and fourth commandments. This every king must have, their name and power, and especially Christ our king. Now, the name of a king you give to Christ, but not the power of a king. So that it may evidently appear to the simple, we pray that you will consider that all the power of a king consists in punishing evildoers and rewarding the well doers, as is proven in Romans 13.1–4, where the apostle shows that all the powers that are, they are of God. They are to this end only to punish the evil and reward the good. Now, speak uprightly before God and men, does Christ have power in your church? Are his officers and people permitted to execute it? Are the good by Christ's kingly power cherished, comforted, and rewarded, and are the evil by the power of Christ corrected and punished? Does Christ have the power by his own ordinances, laws, and officers to receive and keep in the good, and to cast out and keep the bad out of the church? If you should say, Christ has his power in your church, you all (called Puritans) are condemned at once as the most evil doers in the whole church because you above all are the most evil spoken of, mocked, condemned, hated, cited, silenced, excommunicated, and imprisoned. Is all this done by the holy kingly power of Christ? Then you are the most evil doers. Then all the proud boasters, cursed speakers, malicious, covetous, and flatterers, who have peace and preferment in the church, are the well doers. Is this power of Christ? If it is not, as we know you will all confess it is not, then you must confess that Christ does not have the power of a king in the church. For if he has no power to punish evil doers, and reward the well doers, then he has no manner of power by his kingly office among you, then you give him only the name of a king. So you give him no more than Pilate gave him, when he wrote a title and put it on the cross, "This is Jesus the king of the Jews."[21] But in all this you think to excuse yourselves in that you are innocent of these

---

[21] John 19.19

things and protest and seek much to have it otherwise. Even so was Pilate. He washed his hands, and would be innocent from the blood of that just man. He protested that he saw no evil in him. He sought to loose him, but when could not avail, he delivered him to the high priests and elders to be crucified. Thus, you do, the best of you all, that when you cannot prevail that Christ might have his power set up, (as you pretend) you deliver it to their hands that destroy it, and submit yourselves to them also. Will you yet say Christ is your king, when it is evident that he has no power to rule over you? Will Christ be such a king? "Do not be deceived, God is not mocked."[22] He will command you, his enemies, who would not have him reign over you to be slain before him if you do not repent. No pretense or excuse will be admitted for the committing of evil, neither excuse of fear nor ignorance. The Lord does, teach all men everywhere to repent, and they that believe and obey will be saved. They that do not believe will be damned,[23] which you will all be, everyone of you that submit to any other government than that most holy and blessed government which Christ has established in his church, where he is the head and king. Therefore, the church of Christ is "in subjection in everything" (Ephesians 5.24). Our Savior Christ will no more be the head nor savior of such a church that submits itself to the power of a stranger, his enemy, than any godly wise husband will be the head of a wife that submits her body to the power of another man, although she never makes so many fair pretenses of excuses. For this end and to show all others the love and duties the Holy Ghost, by the apostle, has compared Christ and his church and a husband and a wife together, to teach all the love and duties of a husband and wife one to another, and to declare to all Christ's love for his church and the duties of his church to him again.[24] How can the Holy Ghost make a more fit and plain comparison to the capacity of man than to show and declare the power and love of Christ, over and to his church, and the subjection that the church is to yield to him in everything, which subjection seeing your church will not yield to Christ, but denies him the whole power of government over it? Christ cannot be the head of such a church, neither can your church be his body, for everybody is guided and governed by its own head, and none of you that are members of that body are members of the body of Christ. But the

---

[22] Galatians 6.7
[23] Mark 16.16
[24] Ephesians 5.22–33

spiritual lord archbishop and the lord bishop are the head of your church, in
that it is in subjection to them in everything, as you well know. Therefore, it is
their body, for every head has its own body. You are all members of their
body, of which Christ is not the Savior. "But he is the Savior of his own body,
which is the church, of which he is the head" (Ephesians 5.23). May the God
of grace give you grace to consider your fearful estate and standings and deliver
you from that dangerous, delightful security where your hearts are so
[unclear], all your senses and affections are bewitched and ravished by that
"ware of gold and silver, and all excellent metals of pearls, and all precious
stones, of silk, and scarlet, and all costly vestures of vessels of ivory, and of all
most precious wood, and of cinnamon, and odors, and ointments, and
frankincense, and wine, and oil, and fine flour, and wheat, and beasts, and
sheep, and horses, and chariots, and servants, and souls of men, and apples
that your souls lust after."[25] All these things the Holy Ghost has set down
most largely (Revelation 18) to discover the deceivableness of unrighteousness
in all the precious delightful sweet and pleasant spiritual baits and snares that
are in that your glorious profession of Puritanism, by which your souls are
bewitched and ravished, as also in all other professions among those people
that are the waters, where the women arrayed in purple and scarlet does sit
(Revelation 17).[26] You are these people in that you are in subjection to the
power of the beast and his image, and therefore all your sacrifices, oblations,
and incense are in vain, your prophesying or preachings, your prayers and
prayings to God are an abomination to the Lord. "Your silver has become
dross. Your wine is mixed with water."[27] The Lord has "covered you with a
spirit of slumber,"[28] and has shut up your eyes. Your prophets and chief seers
he has covered, because you "come near to him with your mouth, and honor
him with you lips,"[29] in calling Christ your king, but you have taken
"government from his shoulder, who is called wonderful, counselor, the
mighty God, the everlasting Father, the Prince of Peace, the increase of whose
government and peace will have no end" (Isaiah 9.6.7). Here the prophet
shows likewise that he sits upon David's throne and upon his kingdom to

---

[25] Revelation 18.11–14
[26] Revelation 17.1–4
[27] Isaiah 1.22
[28] Isaiah 29.10; Romans 11.8
[29] Isaiah 29.13; Matthew 15.8

order it. But all this power you give to your strange lords, and you cry and say that Christ is your king. Thus you do flatter, "with your lips and dissemble with your tongues,"[30] and your ways are not upright before the Lord.

What might we say to provoke you to set your hearts to seek the Lord and turn your feet to walk in his paths, and your ears to hearken to his voice? Seeing that you will all with earnestness profess to do so, do it with faithfulness and cast away all ignorant hypocrisy. Now that the abomination of desolation is set up before your eyes, hear this voice of the Lord: "Flee into the mountains and come out of her my people, and do not turn back to that which is left behind. Remember Lot's wife"[31] (Matthew 24.15.16; Revelation 18.4; Luke 17.31.32). We will not use any more reasons to prove that you did not come out of Babylon, but your own confession will witness against you, in that you daily complain of your bondage. Therefore, you may see you are in the house of bondage. But there is no bondage in the house of God, where the children of the free woman stand fast in liberty, as Christ has made them free (Galatians 4.31; 5.1). Why are you still in bondage under all those ceremonial traditions (which you say your souls abhor), if you are one of those that Christ has made free? We will entreat you with godly advice to consider what the bondage is and see how you can look to be delivered. Is your bondage that you complain of not a spiritual bondage in that you are restrained of spiritual liberty in the holy things, having ceremonies and ecclesiastical laws and canons pressed upon you, which of conscience you cannot obey? So it is plain that your bondage is spiritual. How would you be delivered from your spiritual bondage, and who should be your deliverer? Can you be delivered but by a spiritual power? Can you have any deliverer but a spiritual Lord? If you seek to and depend on any other lord to be delivered from spiritual bondage, you take to yourselves another God, and set up a spiritual power against the power of God. You should "put on the whole armor of God," and "wrestle against principalities and powers, and spiritual wickedness which are in the high places and stand fast."[32] You have shrunk in the day of battle and have not faithfully "contended for the maintenance of the faith given to the saints,"[33] but you have and do yield to the spiritual

---

[30] Isaiah 59.3
[31] Luke 17.32
[32] Ephesians 6.11.12
[33] Jude 3

wickedness that are under the power of those spiritual lords, the archbishops and lord bishops, and have cast off the armor and sword of the spirit by which you should resist and overcome, and those with spiritual wickedness will be consumed and abolished. You have taken to yourselves a direction after the device of your own hearts, seeking and suing, by petitions not to God, but to men, that you might have leave (as you pretend) to set up Christ as your king and governor. If you could get leave, you make a show as though you would reform matters that are greatly amiss. But seeing you cannot, you are content to let them alone and groan under them (for so you speak) and not to be too busy or you should make matters worse. The people of Israel were of this same condition when Moses was sent to bring them out of Egypt. For when they saw that their leave would not be granted, but that more work was laid upon them, and that there was a danger and trouble, they would have made their peace and have groaned still under their burdens as they had done and so have continued in that their bondage, as you do in your spiritual bondage. But the Lord was merciful to them according to his own promise, and brought them out by a mighty hand, and with great signs and wonders. Even so the Lord has promised to bring his elect (which are those that hearken to the voice of his call) out of this spiritual bondage of Babylon, Egypt, and Sodom (where you are), by great and marvelous signs and wonders, as the spirit of God has declared (Revelation 15; 16) by the seven angels, which pour out the seven vials of the wrath of God upon the earth.[34] But you must know that this is a spiritual prophesy [sic] and all these are spiritual signs and wonders, which the Lord has graciously promised to show upon Babylon, Egypt, and Sodom (spiritually so-called), to the destruction and everlasting overthrow of the scarlet colored beast, and the woman who sits upon him who is that great city of Babylon, and upon all the people that did not come forth at the call of his voice (Revelation 17.18). But take heed that you are not deceived by looking for these things with carnal eyes as the Jews did, who looked for an earthly king to deliver them, so that when the spiritual king came they did not know him, but hated him, despised him, persecuted him, killed him, and cast him out, and so remain in transgression and under condemnation to this day, by the just judgment of God. Take heed lest you do so in suing after and seeking by earthly means to be delivered out of your spiritual bondage. When the spiritual means and way is shown to you, you

---

[34] Revelation 16.1

condemn it, despise it, hate it, persecute it, speak all manner of evil against it, oppose it, reject it, and condemn it, and so you still remain in your transgression and under the condemnation of the just judgment of God, which the Lord has pronounced against all those that do not come forth of Babylon, partaking with her in her sins, and so will be made partakers of her plagues, whose plagues you cannot escape if you do not come forth, but believed those false prophets whose prophesy [sic] lies to you. Do not be deceived by your good intents and meanings and good desires of which you are full, nor by your great affections of zeal where you abound above all people that we know or have heard of, that have any knowledge of the gospel. We do not speak of the ignorant, zealous papists that go before you and all the earth (that know the name of Jesus) in these things, which make them think their estates are most happy. Take heed or you will still be deceived as well. We confess that these are excellent things, if knowledge and faith go with them. Furthermore, your obedience to the second and great commandment, which is, "Love thy neighbor as thyself,"[35] and all the particular duties of it, such as "Honor parents, do not commit adultery, kill, steal, bear false witness, covet nothing that is your neighbors,"[36] in these excellent duties very many of you greatly abound, and we cannot but with great affections look upon you and love you for them, yet know that many papists are not far behind you in these things. Therefore, do not let these things deceive you as though you had all things, because you have these. You see it testified by our Savior Christ that a man may have, or do all these things, and still not follow Christ, as it is shown in the example of that excellent ruler whom Christ "looked upon and loved" for those excellent things in him (Mark 10.21). Therefore do not please yourselves so much in those things, although we acknowledge they are worthy of great commendations in you, and our souls are much affected to you for them. But if you do not follow Christ in regeneration, that is, if you are not "born again of water and of spirit, and so enter into the kingdom of heaven,"[37] all is nothing, as you see by the example of this ruler. Cornelius (Acts 10), if he had not been baptized with the Holy Ghost and with water, for all his prayers and alms he had not, nor could he have entered into the kingdom of heaven.

---

[35] Matthew 22.39
[36] Exodus 20.3–17
[37] John 3.5

Thus entered all the people of God of whose entrance the scriptures give testimony, either by rule or by example, and if there is any other entrance found out, it is not, nor cannot be of God. This is the only door which Jesus Christ has set open for all to enter in at, that enter into his kingdom (John 3.5). May the Lord sanctify all your hearts with grace so that you may enter in. Christ has appointed no other way of salvation but that men first believe and be baptized (Mark 16.16).

Thus, we have spoken the truth freely to you from our hearts. Do not suspect us of the least contempt or spite, if we seem sharp. There are multitudes of you of that Puritan profession (so called) that know our love is most true and unfeigned to you all, and that we cannot but love and have reverence for you. Therefore we could not any more seek your reformation, wish it and pray for it. We will not give the Lord rest until he hears us, that we may see your salvation accomplished.

BOOK 4

The next false profession of Christ and false prophets among you that we will (by God's assistance) speak of is that false profession and those false prophets who are usually called Brownists. You are the ones who say you are Jews, but are not. You have made yourselves a name to be the Separation and are falsely so-called, but are not, as through the help of God we will make it plain by the word of the Lord both to your own consciences (if you will not always resist the truth) and also to the consciences of all others. This we will do by those grounds of truth which you acknowledge, which you must be forced either to forsake, or else be convinced by them.

The first ground is this, in your book called *The Apology*, the first part of your third position stands thus set down: "A true visible church is a company of people called and separated from the world by the word of God, and joined together by a voluntary profession of the faith of Christ in the fellowship of God."[1] By this means, that is, by the word of God, and by doing this, that is, separating themselves from the world and joining together, (you say) they become a true visible church. Now, we come to a full discovery of your false profession of Christ. Let it be observed that you confess you were of the world before you separated, which when you were, then you were enemies of Christ, for Christ testifies the world hates him (John 7.7). None of you were then Christ's, for those that are Christ's or of Christ, "are not of this world" (John 17.14). Now to become Christ's you say you are called and separated from the world by the word of God and joined together by a voluntary profession of the faith of Christ in the fellowship of the gospel. This is your constitution, in which you have erred, as it plainly appears. For when you were called, and (as you say) separated, you should have joined to Christ, and have entered into his kingdom, which seeing you have not done, you are not separated from the world, nor do you have any fellowship in the gospel. We confess the Lord has called to you, and you have joined yourselves together in a voluntary profession, but you have not joined yourselves to Christ. Therefore your profession is a false profession, and you have a false Christ that is no Christ,

---

[1] Henry Ainsworth, *An Apologie or Defense of Such True Christians as are Commonly Called Brownists* (Amsterdam: Theatrum Orbis Terrarum, 1603).

as will be hereafter be plainly proven. To show you that you are not joined to Christ, you were of the world before you constituted or set up your church by your own confessions, the word of the Lord does evidently declare that there is no way for those that are of the world, who are not in Christ, but are enemies to Christ, as all that are of the world are, there is no way to join and come to Christ, but only to "amend their lives, and be baptized" (Acts 2.38). And "all of you that are baptized into Christ have put on Christ" (Galatians 3.27). Let us now entreat you on God's behalf so that you will no longer be fighters against God in contending against his truth, from that which we trust through the mercy of God, you will no longer be able to hide yourselves. If all men that know God and his Son will not confess that infidels and unbelievers have no other way to come and be joined to Christ, but only by believing and being baptized, then you that confess that you were of the world before you set up your church, must also confess that you were infidels and unbelievers. You will be ashamed to say that there are any believers of the world, seeing our Savior Christ say, "The world cannot receive the spirit of truth" (John 14.17). Moreover (John 16.8–9) "The Comforter will reprove the world of sin, because they did not believe in me." And (John 17.25) "O righteous father, the world has not known you." And John in his first Epistle, chapter 5.18–19, speaks, "We know that we are of God, and this whole world lies in wickedness."[2] This is the condition of those that are of the world: 1. They cannot receive the spirit of truth. 2. They do not believe in Christ. 3. They do not know God. 4. They all lie in wickedness. You confess yourselves to be of the world before you joined yourselves together in your voluntary profession, by a covenant of your own devising (you being of the world), your condition was the same. Then you were without the spirit of truth, unbelievers, not knowing God, and lying in all wickedness. So you are all infidels, and there was, nor is, no way for you to join to Christ, but to "amend your lives and be baptized," and by baptism "to put on Christ," which seeing you have not done, you are still of the world. The spirit of truth is not in you. You are infidels and unbelievers. You do not know God and you remain in your wickedness. So your profession is a false profession of Christ and you do not have the true Christ, but a false Christ. So your baptism is a worldly baptism brought out of the world, an ordinance of the world, and not the baptism and

---

[2] 1 John 5.19

ordinance of Christ, whose baptism is not of the world, as he is not of the world.

Do we need to lay down any other ground to convince you, and stop all your mouths? Is this not easy, plain and evident enough? What can be more plain? You confess (yourselves) that you were of the world before you made you separation from England. Our Savior Christ says those who are of the world do not believe in him. Who will not grant that they who do not believe in Christ are infidels and unbelievers? Then you, being of the world, were infidels or unbelievers, and the Holy Ghost teaches that infidels or unbelievers must amend their lives and be baptized and by baptism put on Christ. Our Savior Christ, giving a general direction to his disciples to preach the gospel to all, gives likewise a general direction of what all unbelievers must do if they are to be saved. "They must believe and be baptized" (Mark 16.16). You are now driven to this straight either to confess that before your separation you were infidels or unbelievers, and then you must believe and be baptized, or else that you were believers and faithful, and you have separated from a faithful and believing people, and not from the world. You must return to your vomit with that false prophet, your first and chief shepherd, that has misled you upon these false grounds, who is not able (through his infidelity) to keep his face towards Jerusalem and the land of Canaan, has fainted on the way, and rebelled in the wilderness, and is returned to his so much formerly detested Babylon and Egypt.

Next let us show to you that your prophets are all false prophets. Although it is a fully sufficient proof that they are false prophets because they are elected and ordained to their office by a congregation of infidels or unbelievers that are not joined to Christ and have not put on Christ by baptism. Yet, we will further show them to be false prophets, because they prophesy lies and by their lying wonders would if it were possible deceive the very elect. These are deceitful workers and transform themselves into the prophets of Christ, as though they were the ministers of righteousness, whose end (says the apostle) will be according to their works (2 Corinthians 11.13.15). Yet, they doing it ignorantly through unbelief, if they repent, may be received to mercy (1 Timothy 1.13). But they must repent as Paul did, who left off being a persecutor, a blasphemer, and an oppressor, or else he could never have been saved. So they must leave off being false prophets, seducers, and deceivers, or else they will all be damned (Revelation 19.20).

We first want to show you how your false prophets transform themselves and how they are the most dangerous deceivers and tempters. In the forefront they cry come with a main ground of truth, and this they utter with a loud voice, "It is fallen, it is fallen, Babylon, that great city. Go out of her, my people, etc.,"[3] and separate yourselves and come out. This is all their cry to bring the people from the assemblies of England. Then they run upon England and prove it is Babel, and Babylon, we confess, with enough proof that when they have finished working a just distaste in the hearts of some people of the spiritual abominations in those assemblies, so far as they themselves dislike. Yet being both loath to cast Babylon clean on the ground, and utterly to make her naked and desolate, and to lay all her honor in the dust, and not being willing, through hardness of heart, and want of true zeal and holiness to run the race to the end and to separate themselves from all uncleanness, they still teach you to retain your first and chief badge or mark of Babylon, which is your baptism, where you receive the seal of the covenant of grace, as they say, and teach you. This you may not part with upon any condition. Is there any false prophets like these prophets that will teach you to separate and, "Come out from Babylon and to touch no unclean things,"[4] and when they have done so, you teach them to retain the baptism received there, which they teach, and you profess to be the seal of the covenant of grace? So you are sealed into the covenant of grace by Babylon. So you are made Christians and members of Christ by Babylon, for without this baptism you are not Christians. O, how you cry out against the sweetness of the stolen waters of Babylon, and yet you cannot beware of it, but are bewitched by it, of which you retain with as little understanding as when you received it and were washed or baptized into it. But your false prophets, to make good the retaining of your Babylonish baptism, like deep deceivers with the turning of devices, plead that your baptism must be retained, and is not to be repeated, no more than Israel's circumcision when they came to the Passover in Hezekiah's time. O, that all men would see your deceivableness of unrighteousness in this, that to draw simple people after you, and to build yourselves up a kingdom, you cry against the assemblies of England, they are Babylon, Egypt, and Sodom. Separate yourselves. "Do not be unequally yoked with infidels. What

---

[3] Revelation 14.8; 18.4
[4] Isaiah 52.11; 2 Corinthians 6.17

fellowship has light with darkness? What concord has Christ with Belial?"[5] Therefore, all must be cast away. No communion is to be kept. But when you are urged or called on for the retaining of your baptism you received in Babylon, then Israel's circumcision is your hold. So you make England Israel and yourselves Judah, pretending as though you came out of Israel. What deceitful deceiving is this? What turning of devices to cry, "Come out of Babylon, and touch no unclean thing," and to show and declare in all words and writings, that if any man worships the beast and his image, and receives his mark on his forehead or on his hand, he will drink of the cup of God's wrath, applying this particularly to England. When you have done this, you come forth sealed in on the forehead with the seal of baptism (as you call it) having no other seal for your whole Christianity. We hope you will not say that there may be a church of unbaptized Christians. All this you prove good, because Israel's circumcision was good under Jeroboam. So you make a show in this particular as though you came out of Israel. But, if your first cry had been, "Come out of Israel, and separate yourselves from Israel," you might have cried long enough before any that had feared God, or had any understanding of his truth, would have followed you to have built new churches, and set up a hierarchy of ruling elders, as they and you (brethren in evil also) have done. We draw this point to an end. If you come from Israel, then you were true Israelites before. Then all that you have left behind you are true Israelites, as well as you. For all the ten tribes under Jeroboam were true Israelites. You and the assemblies of England from which you came were all in one estate and condition of profession before you separated. They still remain as you left them and as you daily leave them. They are not Samaritans, if they were not before. Therefore, if you like to stand on the ground that you have brought your baptism from rebellious Israel, then you, Judah, must necessarily acknowledge Israel to be your sister. The Lord testifies that Israel was Judah's sister. Neither did Judah ever deny Israel to be her sister. Therefore, you may not utterly cast off England that is your sister Israel.

As you acknowledge in your book called, *The Apology* (page 113), through ignorant dissimulation and flattery, that you never doubted but "there are thousands in the Romish apostasy in England who have not received the beast's mark on their forehead or hand, but are careful to keep the commandments of God and faith of Jesus." Must you not then acknowledge,

---

[5] 2 Corinthians 6.14.15

unless you are destitute of all understanding, that these thousands that are baptized with the same baptism that you are, and that do not receive the mark of the beast, and are careful to keep the commandments of God, and faith of Jesus, must you not then acknowledge that these thousands are a true church, or are true churches as well as you? Dare you say more of yourselves? You cannot challenge any preeminence. Are you anymore (if you were so much) truly baptized, free from the mark of the beast, or careful to keep the commandments of God and faith of Jesus? What dark blindness is this, and palpable words of flattery, to confess in words that there are thousands in England's apostasy in as holy and blessed estate as any people of God can be? When you have done so, both by practice, writing and teaching, you deny all spiritual communion with any one of them, and do not to suffer any one of them to have communion with you, unless they make and submit to a new covenant with you, which is a covenant you have made according to the devising of your own heart. What Zion have you built that will not open her gates to men (as you confess) that are truly baptized, have no mark of the beast, and keep the commandments of God and faith of Jesus? How woefully you are overtaken in these things. How can we think less of this other than that it is ignorant dissimulation and flattery, with such fair words to stop the mouths, and blind the eyes of Mr. Bilson and the Oxford doctors? When you had walled up that breach and daubed it with the mortar of a deceitful temper, you then profess and practice the contrary. You do this when it will serve your turn, make England Israel, and when you please, it is Babylon, Sodom, and Egypt. You have for a long time, and still do, like most subtle charmers, charm the simple and ignorant, so that they do no receive the love of the truth that they might be saved. Instead you build and hold up your kingdom and throne. If any have inclination to leave you and return to England again, then England is Sodom, Egypt, Babylon, and worse if it could be worse. If any question the casting away of that baptism or washing they received there, then England is but rebellious Israel, and let her take away her fornications out of her sight, and her adulteries from between her breasts, and she may still be a wife. What can be said to this your deceitful double dealing? We must be forced to leave a simple double answer. If you were Babylonians, and have Babylon's baptism upon you, then you have no rule or example that the Babylonian's circumcision could be accepted and admitted to the Passover. If you were true Israelites before you separated, and have Israel's baptism upon you, and so became Judah, then you must acknowledge Israel, from whence you came (which is England), as your sister. So you may go again and follow the voice of that old deceiver, who has so long bewitched you, who lies in wait for you, knowing that you cannot stand upon these grounds, but you must be forced either to cast away your baptism or else return from where you received it, unless you will be the most willfully blind people upon the whole earth that have the knowledge of Christ, of which you give just cause of jealousy. Therefore, in God's fear, take heed, and do not perish in your stiff-necked perverseness.

To show yet further that you are false prophets and prophesy lies, we produce out of your book subscribed with general subscription, your *Apology* (page 110), where you gainsay Mr. Bilson for saying you affirm by consequence their sacraments are not sacraments, and their church is no church. To clear yourselves of this imputation, you teach that "we must be careful in all such causes and always discern and distinguish between a true church, a false church, and no church, between true sacraments, false sacraments, and no sacraments." Your proof and example is: "Judah, a true church; the ten tribes of Israel, a false church; the Philistines and others the like, no church. And so on this day, the Turks and pagans may be reputed as no true churches, the Romish synagogue and all her daughters are false churches, the Christians who are set apart in the true faith and order are true churches." Thus, you say the difference may be put. But you are all false prophets and teach lies. These are but the devices of your own hearts. These are your school distinctions where you pervert the holy word of truth. We exhort all the people of God to take heed of you when you distinguish, and when you bring your matters about "in a respect and in a double respect," not because we hold it unlawful to use distinctions, and to show respects, but because you usually use it to deceive. There is no truth of God so evident, but with your distinctions, respects, and twofold respects, you will pervert it. When you are not able with evidence of truth to maintain you false wares, then your distinctions and respects must make it good. By this you ensnare the simple and compass them about as with a thick mist, so they cannot see which way to go, but are fain through hardness of heart and infidelity (which are causes of their ignorance and blindness) to give their hearts to you to be led. You, like deceitful blind guides, lead them into the pit, as in this particular in hand, where if you are overthrown and discovered, your whole cause is thus far destroyed, as you are all yet once again proven to be infidels and unbelievers. We do not doubt but by the gracious aid and help of our God, we will be able by his word to convince you all in this matter, without whose great help and aid, we in humility confess, we are not able to withstand such strange and wise adversaries of his truth as you are, who do exercise yourselves to deceive. Our own experiences and knowledge of you causes us to speak. We hope you do it ignorantly, or else there is no hope of your repentance and salvation.

To the point in hand we say and prove by the word of God that you can in no ordinance of God distinguish or put difference by the warrant of God's word between false and none, and your vain distinction will hold only in worldly things, and you are carnal in this and sold under sin. Do not blame us, though we reprove you sharply for this, because you have deceived yourselves and the whole world, so far as your voices have sounded and you have and do daily destroy the faith of many.

We proceed to prove that you cannot by God's word distinguish nor put difference between false and none in God's ordinances. The eternal word of truth shows (Revelation 2.2) where the Holy Ghost speaking of false apostles commends the church of Ephesus for "examining them those who said they were apostles, but were not and found out to be liars." And (verse nine) "know the blasphemy of those who say they are Jews but are not, but are the synagogue of Satan." In Revelation 3.9 the same words are uttered by the Holy Ghost. Thus the spirit of God teaches us that a false church is no church, but a synagogue of Satan and false apostles are no apostles, so then false sacraments are no sacraments. So false and none in God's ordinances are all one and you cannot distinguish or make a difference between them. For further manifestation of the truth, let us refer to the things that are of God to God and so will it appear to all but those who will not see that there is no difference nor distinction to be made in God's ordinances between false and none. As thus: a true church of Christ; a false church; and no church. If a false church cannot be a church of Christ, then it is a false church of Christ. So there are two sorts or kinds of church of Christ, and so should Christ have two bodies, a true body, and a false body? What blasphemy this is, when the apostle says, "There is but one body." So likewise if you say, there is a true faith of Christ, a false faith, and no faith of Christ, if a false faith and no faith are not all one, then there are two faiths of Christ, a true faith, and a false faith of Christ. But the apostle says, "There is but one faith." In like manner, if you will say, as you do, that there is a true baptism, a false baptism, and no baptism, if a false baptism and no baptism are not the all one then there are two baptisms. But the apostle says, "There is but on baptism." And of all these there is but one, as "there is but one God and Father of all, which is above all, and through all" (Ephesians 4.4–6) who if he were in you all you would submit to his truth, and never open your mouths any more against it. Cast away your logical distinctions, which are fit to distinguish between a false hour glass and no hour glass, and a false looking glass and no looking glass, and not fit to distinguish between a false baptism and no baptism, a false church and no church, between which the Holy Ghost admits of no distinction nor difference. We conclude, therefore, with the word of truth against all these your deceitful distinctions and lying prophecies that a false church is no church of Christ at all, for Christ has no false church. Therefore, you hold England as a false church, it is no church of Christ, and so your false baptism is no baptism of Christ. So you are infidels, unbelievers, and false Christians, that is, no Christians, and you are they that say, "You are Jews and are not, but are the synagogue of Satan."[6] Let this suffice for the overthrow of your most false and deceitful distinction.

You bring for your proof of a true church, a false church, and no church, and say, Judah was a true church, Israel a false church, and the Philistines no church. These are but your own sayings and devisings without proof, by which you have and do mightily deceive, although your words are without understanding. Israel was a true church as Judah was a true church. The Israelites were the true seed of Abraham, separated from the world under the covenant of God, which was the covenant of circumcision (Genesis 17.7–15), as well as Judah in Hezekiah's time, when they came to the Passover. If they had been false Israelites, then their circumcision had been false and they then were a false church. So they were no seed of Abraham, no Israelites, their circumcision no circumcision, and so no church. For a full conclusion and a certain rule of direction from the word of God by which the people of God may try all your deceitful distinctions of this kind when you put differences between true, false, and none, in or of any ordinance of God, let all observe, and we wish to God you would be informed, that God and his laws and ordinances are one, (John 14.6) of equal power, authority, and truth, and therefore you can no more say, a true church, a false church, and no church, a true baptism, a false baptism, and no baptism, which are holy ordinances of God, than you can say a true God, a false God, and no God. And your

---

[6] Revelation 3.9

distinction will hold no more between a false church and no church, a false baptism and no baptism, than between a false God and no God. If a false God is no God, then a false church is no church of God, and a false baptism is no baptism of Christ. Your false church then, being as it shown and proven to be no church of God, then it is the synagogue of Satan. Your false baptism is no baptism of Christ then it is the baptism of Satan. May the Lord give you to consider your estates and standings in this matter, that although your contempt of us is, and has been great, yet you may not still contienne[7] Christ and his truth which is the means of your salvation, though witnessed by us, who are so despised in your eyes.

Having shown you by evidence of truth that you by bringing your false baptism out of a false church (both of which you confess), your baptism is no baptism, and that a false church is no church, this has been made plain as the indifferent may judge. We will try Mr. Robinson's ground for this retained baptism, who will been found to make haste to deceive with as many windings and turnings as any, and not be altogether trusting to bring his baptism from Israel. He strives with all deceitful skill to prove that their baptism is true in one respect, though brought from Babylon. This matter he undertakes after this manner, in his book of justification of separation (pp. 184–85). He commends to the reader a distinction of a two-fold respect. "Baptism," says Mr. Robinson, "is to be considered first nakedly, and in the essential causes: the matter, water, form, washing with water into the name of the Father, etc." These are the essential causes of Mr. Robinson's naked baptism. In this respect, he confesses true baptism in both England and Rome. Mr. Robinson, we will speak angrily to you and mourn for the hardness of your heart and your great blindness and ignorance. Have you lost the beginnings of knowledge in the mystery of godliness? Is all light shut from your eyes and all truth debarred from your understanding that you should write that water, and washing, and words are the essential causes or matter of baptism? If you had known Christ, of whose baptism you pretend to speak, you would never have written this. Do you know that Christ's kingdom is a spiritual kingdom and that his ordinances are spiritual ordinances? Will you confess this with your tongue, and with your tongue and deeds deny it? So that it may appear plainly that you do, consider it yourself, and let all that seek the Lord in spirit and truth consider with what understanding you can say that naked water,

---

[7] French word meaning "to contain"

washing, and words are the essential causes of spiritual baptism. You spoil men through philosophy and vain deceit,[8] in which iniquity you abound. Away with your naked respect and be counseled to buy "white raiment that you may be clothed, that your vile nakedness does not appear."[9] Do you not know that "all that are baptized into Christ have put on Christ?"[10] Do you come with your philosophy to teach simple souls a naked baptism and make it good with respects? May the Lord give you grace to see your greatest evil in this. May the Lord deliver his poor people from your deceitful ways. May the Lord give them to learn to know from the word of God that there is but one baptism of Christ, (Ephesians 4.5) and that whosoever is baptized into Christ has put on Christ, or is clothed with Christ (Galatians 3.27). Therefore, whosoever will walk with your naked baptism will be found naked at the day of Christ's appearing though you piece it and patch it with green leaves. For your essential causes lay down plainly what baptism you speak of and you will be convinced in it yourself. And thus, if you say of Christ's baptism, which is spiritual, that its essential matter is earthly water, would your ignorance not easily, appear? The like of your form, if you should say that the form of spiritual baptism is bodily washing with only bare words, your own understanding would reprove you. This is what we wish. You often have been required to lay away your school terms in the causes of God, by which you do for the most part but hide the truth and blind the eyes of the simple. Now do you think the simple should understand you in the essential causes, and matter, and form of baptism? Do the scriptures show that any of the holy men of God ever did make this distinction? If your art had been good or profitable, could not our Savior Christ have used it for the manifestation of his truth? Would he not have endowed his apostles with that gift? Yes, the Lord endowed them with the most excellent gifts for the evident declaration of his truth of which logic and philosophy had no part. If you had not used vain sciences you could never have forged so many deceits as you have in your book. Now we desire for you to know that the scriptures do not teach any baptism that is in one respect true and in another respect false. There is no such thing in the whole word of God. These are but your own devices by which you divide Christ to serve your own turns to deceive and persuade men

---

[8] Colossians 2.8
[9] Revelation 3.18
[10] Galatians 3.27

that they are in one respect truly baptized and in another respect falsely baptized. If they will come and walk in your way and join to your societies, you can make that part which was false, true. What popery is this you take upon yourself to dispense with the false administrations in the ordinances of Christ? Thus you run into dark places while you forsake the lantern that should light your paths, which the light of truth teaches you, and all men, that the baptism of Christ is "the baptism of the amendment of life, for the remission of sins" (Mark 1.4). Our Savior Christ says, "Unless a man is born of water and of the Spirit, he cannot enter into the kingdom of God"[11] (John 3). And (Hebrews 10.22) "Let us draw near with a true heart in assurance of faith, our hearts being pure from evil confidence, and washed in our bodies with pure water."

Here is the true baptism set down, which is the baptism of amendment of life for the remission of sins. Here is the true matter where men must be washed, which is water and the Holy Ghost that is pure from an evil conscience, and washed with water. Therefore you cannot divide the water and the spirit in this baptism. Christ has joined them together and he that denies washing, or is not washed with the spirit is not baptized, and he that denies washing, or is not washed with water is not baptized, because we see the baptism of Christ is the washing with water and the Holy Ghost. To take away a subtle exception, if a man is in prison, or any place and is converted by the Lord, and would be baptized with water but cannot, he is accepted with God, "who accepts the will for the deed" (2 Corinthians 8.12), and in this the Lord's mercy is equal with his justice. If a man's heart consents to evil he is guilty, although he did not do it (Matthew 5.27–28).

Thus we have discovered much in this great deceitfulness of your way in the first respect of your false distinction, in which you would prove only the essential matter, water, and washing with water, and words, the essential form. We pass by your form of words because we think you will not stand upon it, in that you see there is no certain form of words that are held (Acts 10.48; 19.5). Take this with you to consider, that if there were any truth in your distinction and respect, then were any of these washings with water, with those words, the true matter and form of Christ's baptism? If so, any child who has baptized another with water and those words, it is a true baptism in that respect. Let the child come and join to you and you can make it good in all

---

[11] John 3.5

The Life and Writings of Thomas HelwysThe Life and Writings of Thomas Helwys

respects. Do not pass these things over as you have done, for you are not able to answer them with any true understanding from God's word. So we will now address your second respect.

Secondly, you say, "Baptism is to be considered clothed with such appurtenances as which the Lord has appointed it to be administered. For example, a lawful person may perform it on a right subject, in a true communion, where it may be administered and dispensed." In which regard you say you do not "approve it to be a true baptism either in Rome or England." If this darkest error did not possess your heart, you could never have written such things. But we know your stiffness in your false ways and we should have pity to point out your palpable ignorance in these things. Did ever a man of any understanding in religion write such a thing? You are lighter than vanity. Will any man that has any knowledge of God be so blind as not to see how the spirit of error leads you to justify that a baptism where there is neither the spirit of God, lawful minister, right subject, nor true communion is the true baptism and ordinance of Christ in its essential parts?

Has any like ignorance appeared in these days, especially among men that will cry out for proof of scripture in all things? If your ground were true, then a Turk baptizing a Turk with water and those words in any assembly whatsoever is the true baptism of Christ in the essential parts. See what rocks you run upon while you forsake the way of truth. It may now appear no marvel, though you would have baptism be nakedly considered, that you have made a most naked baptism an ordinance of Christ. First, where there is no spirit of God, no lawful minister, no right party to be baptized, no true communion, it may well be called a naked baptism, and you a naked man of all grace and godly understanding to maintain it for a true baptism and ordinance of Christ, in any respect. If all this will not serve to convince you, we will yet smite you with the rod of iron, and break you like the potter's vessel in this point. You profess and acknowledge that baptism comes in the head of circumcision. Then let all men judge whether if circumcision is administered by an unlawful person, upon no right subject, and in no true communion, could it ever have been approved as the true ordinance of God in its essential causes? Could one so circumcised upon any conditions have been admitted to the Passover? You will (we hope) be destitute of all devices to answer this. All those that are in any way indifferent between you and us will see your great error, that if a Babylonian had circumcised a Babylonian in their Babylonish assemblies, that circumcision had not been in any respect the ordinance of God, and such a one could upon no condition have been admitted to the Passover by that circumcision. Now to show that you hold England Babylon in your book, throughout it appears, but we especially hold you to these (pp. 277 and 338) where you affirm "that Rome and England were never within the covenants of God, as Judah was." So you have debarred yourself from bringing your circumcision and so your baptism from apostate Israel. Therefore you must hold yourself to this, to prove circumcision administered in Babylon by an unlawful person, upon a wrong subject, and not in true communion, you must prove such a circumcision is an ordinance of God in any respect, and so that one so circumcised might be admitted to the Passover. Prove this, and we will confess that your skill is above all men's, and Ezra and Nehemiah will be reproved by you for causing the people to put away the children that were born of strange wives in Babylon, (Ezra 10.3; Nehemiah 13.23–25) of whom if you make question over whether they were circumcised, you cavil[12] and are without cullor.[13] For then the Israelites had been guilty of the breach of Lord's covenant, in which they were commanded to circumcise all their males in their household. But we will leave you to prove your Babylonian circumcision is in any respect the ordinance of God. Prove it by scripture and by sound reasoning from the ground of scripture, and not by logic and natural philosophy, showing things in nature to be true, which in the spirit will not be proven true. Thus you deceive natural men, and yourself, as in this point at hand, because with you carnal eyes and ears you see and hear water, and washing, with such words to be used in the administration of the Lord's baptism. Therefore, you, according to your natural understanding, judge these things to be the essential causes of spiritual baptism. You teach simple souls that these things being once truly done, they are not to be repeated or done again when they are wholly natural actions, and profanely done, as you confess. Therefore, it can in no respect be said to be the baptism of Christ, which is wholly a spiritual action, and should be performed in a holy manner. Thus you make the ignorant believe that you can put the spirit of grace into natural actions formerly profanely done, and make the same actions spiritual and acceptable to God.

Thus you make the midwives' baptism a good and holy ordinance of God in the essential causes. So you can make all the profane waters and

---

[12] To raise a trivial objection

[13] Under a pretext, pretense, or mask of something with alleged authority

sermons in plays (which are usual) holy, and good actions, and the ordinances of God. This is then your rule (deny it if you can), every washing with water in the name of the Father, etc., is the true baptism and ordinance of Christ, in its essential causes, by whomsoever administered it, and upon whatsoever person or thing. This may be good in logic and philosophy, but this is a blasphemous, cursed doctrine in divinity. Woe are we for you that ever such abominations should be uttered by you. We are ashamed to follow you in the particular application of these things, which if they should be urged to the full, it would make every heart that had any grace, and knows you, tremble, and grieve for you. This is what your logic and philosophy has brought you. By this you have confounded many simple hearted and those weak in understanding, by which (you think) you have a privilege to understand the meaning of God in the scriptures before those that are ignorant of these arts. Now the Lord has confounded you in them. (Glory be his name.) May the Lord give you a heart to acknowledge it, and to repent, and deny yourself, and give glory to God. We will omit to speak of your improper speech, saying that baptism must be "clothed with a right person upon whom it must be administered." Thus to make your matters agree, you speak preposterous things, for the party must put on and be clothed with baptism, and not baptism clothed with the party.

The next thing that (by the help of our God) we will endeavor to discover is that you are a false prophet and a deceiver in your strong grounds. Upon which you often reply and repeat it in your book and that is this. You say, "Baptism is the vessel of the Lord, and as when the house of the Lord was destroyed, and the vessels thereof, together with the people were carried into Babylon, they still remained vessels of the Lord's house in nature, and right, though profaned by Belshazzar and made quaffing bowls, and being brought again out of Babylon to the house of the Lord were not to be newly cast, but (being purified) might again be used for holy use. So this holy vessel of baptism though profaned in Babylon, being brought again to the house of the Lord, remains still the holy vessel of the Lord." This is a strong doctrine from example both with you and all the rest of the false prophets of your profession. It is no marvel though that you have greatly deceived many in this matter, because the doctrine and example is good, but most deceitfully misapplied by you. You pretend as though your baptism were brought from the house of the Lord, as the holy vessels were. Will you, if there is any uprightness in you, show how and from what house of the Lord your holy vessel of baptism was brought? You show us plainly from where you have brought it again out of Babylon, that is England. But out of what house of God did it come, before it came into Babylon (that is England), that is not shown. How deceitfully you feign these things. These are the imaginations of your own vain hearts. Have any of you brought your baptism from the house of the Lord into England? Do you have any other root or foundation for your baptism than England? Do not all men know that your vessel of Babylon was composed, formed, framed, and made there? How will any man be able to open his mouth to deny this? Why then, was your holy vessel (so falsely called) made in Babylon? Thus you are found to be false disassemblers to say and feign that your baptism is a vessel brought out of the house of the Lord into Babylon, as the vessels of the temple were, when it is more evident that it was molded and made in the Church of England, which you confess is Babylon. Mr. Robinson, have you and all your congregation not received the true matter (as you call it) and true form of your baptism in England? Was it not administered upon all of you in the assemblies of England? Then your vessel of baptism was made there. See your deceit in this matter, if there is any grace or understanding in you, and how Satan has seduced you and your own heart has deceived you. Now may the Lord Jesus give you a heart to repent, and in the name of the Lord, we beseech you to repent, for you have been and are a malicious adversary of God's truth and you lead many souls in the way of destruction. May the Lord, for his Christ's sake, deliver you out of these and all the snares of Satan. May the Lord deliver his people out of the net in which you have like a cunning fowler taken them and overcome them.

We pray that you will with patience suffer us to show you how you are all deceived in this point, in saying baptism is the vessel of the Lord's house brought with you. Clearly it applies to your own baptism, which you may see, if you do not both wink and cover your eyes, never came out of the house of the Lord, unless you will say, the Church of England is the house of the Lord, which we hope the Lord's word has convinced to all your consciences that it is not. Therefore your baptism cannot be the vessel of the Lord's house, but it is the true doctrine or ordinance of baptism that may be said or called by way of comparison the vessel of the Lord's house. This we and all must confess is the vessel of the Lord's house, whether it is carried either to Rome or England, and though it is polluted and profaned there, as both it and many other doctrines and ordinances of the Lord are. Yet having been purged from those errors and abuses, by which both they and you have and do pollute them, they may, and should be brought into the house of the Lord again, and remain holy vessels to the Lord forever. But the corrupt pollutions and administrations in this holy vessel or ordinance of baptism, which has been defiled and profaned, these may no more be brought into the house of God than Balshazzar's quaffings, or any other profane administrations where he did abuse and pollute those holy vessels. Yes, although he had used them for the same uses which they had been used in the house of the Lord, as if he had set shew bread upon the vessels and had kindled and made the same lights for the candlesticks. All of this must be cast away as abominable, with all the uses that he has used them for, and the vessels must be purified and brought again into the house of the Lord only as they were carried forth. Therefore, even so this holy vessel must, the true doctrine or ordinance of baptism, be brought again into the houses of the Lord only as it was carried forth, and all the corrupt uses and abuses of which it has been used and all the profane administrations in this holy ordinance must be cast away as all being abominable before the Lord. None of those uses and profane and false administrations may be admitted into the house of the Lord. This now is the sum of all that we have spoken of on this ground. The vessels of the Lord's house are carried into Babylon, and Belshazzar and his princes, his wives and concubines drunk from them and profaned them. The vessels of the Lord are brought again to the house of the Lord and are sanctified, but Belshazzar drinking from them and profaning of them is cast away as abominable.

So the like may be said, following your own example of comparison. The vessel of the Lord's house, the holy ordinance of baptism, is carried into Babylon and the Babylonians, they wash or baptize in this ordinance, and profane it. The vessel of the Lord, the holy ordinance of baptism, is brought again into the house of the Lord, but the Babylonians washing, or baptizing, and profaning it must be cast away as abominable. Thus your baptizing must be cast away and may not be permitted in the house of the Lord, you confessing England to be Babylon where you received it, unless you will also admit Belshazzar's drinking and quaffings. Do not continue to deceive yourself and delude others in saying baptism is the vessel of the Lord making a deceitful show, as though your baptism was the vessel of the Lord. You make an example of the vessels of the Lord that were brought forth out of the house of the Lord and carried into Babylon and polluted there in use only, and after being sanctified from that polluted use, they were brought again into the house of the Lord. By this example you bring in an imagination, as though your baptism were brought out of the house of the Lord, when it is brought forth from the assemblies of England, with whom you justify God never made a covenant and that they were never his people, nor God their God. (Page 338) You err by not knowing the scriptures, or else you fully misapply them for your purpose (which God forbid). It is the ordinance of baptism that is the vessel of the Lord's house which has been, and is carried into Babylon, and has been polluted in your use in baptism and all of your profession. This vessel or ordinance of the Lord is to be brought again into the house of the Lord and to be sanctified from that polluted use of your baptizing. It cannot be if you bring that polluted use which is your baptizing into the house of the Lord with it, no more than the vessels of the Lord could have been sanctified if Belshazzar quaffings had been brought into the house of the Lord with them. This is a due proportion according to your own example of comparison.

We will pass by many things in your book where there is great falsehood and deceit. We do this because it would be an endless work to follow you. You are so intricate, tedious, and full of turnings and windings, losing yourself and losing such simple readers as we are. The one hope that we have in your book is that the simple will not read it, because they are not capable of understanding you. Among those that are as full of art as you, we think it will do small harm. We cannot deny but that there are many worthy truths in it, but they are mixed with so much falsehood that the reader must be wise-hearted. In that you and all the false prophets of your profession do mix your falsehood with divers truths, all God's people have need to be aware of you. That is your sheep's clothing. By this fair show you ensnare and work your lying wonders, as when you smite men's hearts to the ground by laying out the deformities of Babylon, and ravish their affections with the description of your Zion (which is falsely so-called), declaring the beauty and supposed comely order of it, and setting forth the communion of saints, as with the tongue of an angel of light. Thus, you deck your bed with ornaments, carpets, laces, and perfume it with myrrh, aloes, and cinnamon. With your great craft you cause men to yield and with flattering lips you entice many to follow you as an ox that goes to the slaughter and as a fool to the stocks for correction. They are stricken through as a bird that hastens to the snare not knowing he is in danger. Of such hearts the wise man has by the wisdom of the spirit forewarned us (Proverbs 7).[14]

---

[14] Proverbs 7.16.17.21.23

We have endeavored to show you your halting between Babylon and Israel. We exhort you to tread straight steps before the Lord so that men may see that your paths are straight. Show us the writing of your genealogy so that we may certainly see from where you came. If you came from, Israel, and are Judah, then do not war against England as against the Babylonians, but remember they are the ten tribes, your brethren (1 Kings 12.24). These ten tribes were not false Israelites, but the true seed of Abraham and so they are true Israelites. The two calves set up at Dan and Bethel did no more than make them false Israelites than the calf which they made at Horeb. This wickedness of Jeroboam did no more make Israel a false church than Solomon's wickedness made Judah a false church when he followed Ashtaroth, the god of the Zidonians, and Milcom the abomination of the Amorites, and built the high places for Chemosh, the abomination of Moab, and to Molech, the abomination of Ammon, in the mountain over against Jerusalem. Who does not know that reads the scriptures that Judah abounded in abominations, in so much as the Lord by the prophet Ezekiel (chapter 16) says of Judah, "Samaria has not committed half their sins but you have exceeded them in all their abominations."[15] And in verse 15 the Lord by the prophet called Judah a harlot because of the greatness of her fornications. Yet all this did not make Judah a false church. Therefore, if you hold or account England as Israel, then you must hold and account England a true church. It is by your devisings you say Israel was a false church. If England is as Israel, a true church, then all your sins are exceedingly great, who have made such as separation as you have. If you are from Babylon, then look throughout the whole book of God and you will find that no Babylonian circumcision could be admitted into the house of the Lord. Let all behold in the book of Revelation what the estate and condition of Babylon is, and of all those that are in her, and how the voice of the Lord says, "Come out of her, my people." And, "if any will worship the beast and his image, and receive his mark on his forehead or on his hand or receive the print of his name, he will drink of the wine of the wrath of God."[16] Therefore nothing may be retained that is brought from Babylon, no mark, nor any print of the name. Will you bring the print, seal, and name of Christianity from there? What veil of darkness overspreads your hearts in this? You are deceived through the vain imaginations of your own hearts,

---

[15] Ezekiel 16.51
[16] Revelation 14.9

supposing that although you come out of Babylon, you were not Babylonians. But if you hold the assemblies of England to be Babylon (as you declare you do), then unless you can show in your genealogy that you, with your vessel of baptism (which is your baptizing), was brought from Jerusalem, and out of the house of the Lord, if you cannot prove this (which is double folly to go about), then you must be content to know that you were Babylonians, and yet [unclear] that your seal of Christianity is the seal of Babylon. So you are but Babylonian Christians, and servants of the beast, bearing the beast's mark, title, and name on your foreheads. You and all the rest of the false prophets of your profession do in flattery and dissimulations, not knowing the mystery of godliness, affirm and acknowledge that in the assemblies of England there are thousands of them that truly fear God, alluding to the seven thousand in Israel. You make them believe that they stand in the state of grace and salvation. So you prophecy [sic] peace and salvation where the Lord prophecies [sic] destruction. The Lord prophecies [sic] that all who do not come forth from Babylon will be partakers of her plagues and whoever yields in obedience or bears the mark of the beast "will be tormented with fire and brimstone"[17] (Revelation 14). But you prophecy [sic] that there are thousands in England (which you acknowledge to be Babylon) who did not receive the beast's mark and who are careful to keep the commandments of God and faith of Jesus, and that truly fear God. If these are not in the estate of salvation then no flesh is or can be. But this cannot be the estate of anyone in Babylon, which (if you understand the mystery of godliness) you might easily see. The bondage of Babylon is spiritual bondage, and all that are in Babylon are in spiritual bondage, and none that are in spiritual bondage can be in the estate of grace and salvation. All that are in the estate of grace and salvation must "stand fast in the liberty by which Christ has made them free," and may not "be entangled with the yoke of bondage" (Galatians 5.1). "And where the spirit of the Lord is, there is liberty" (2 Corinthians 3.17). Add to this that which was formerly shown that all that do not come forth out of Babylon must perish with Babylon. Do not deceive yourselves and do not flatter those in England. There is not one person either of them or you (we speak of persons of understanding) that are in the state of grace or salvation, or will ever be saved, if they do not come forth out of Babylon and cast away the mark of the beast of which you are all marked (Revelation 19.20–21). We exhort you all that by

---

[17] Revelation 14.10

grace in Christ you work out your own salvation with fear and trembling, or else you will perish from the highest to the lowest. The King of Kings, the Lord of Lords has said it, that Babylon will be destroyed with all that are found in her (Jeremiah 51.6; Revelation 18.4).

We will now conclude with you and put you in remembrance as you see no distinction nor difference can be made between a false and no church, but they are both one. A false church are those that say and make a show that they are a true church but are not. False apostles are they that say and make a show that they are apostles and are not (2 Corinthians 11.13). False Jews are those that say and make a show that they are Jews when they are not (Revelation 2). Thus your distinction has been utterly overthrown so as you will never be able to open your mouths to maintain it, but the simplest soul among you will be able to discover your deceit, your whole false building is at once fallen to the ground. A false church is no church, and then England being judged by you to be a false church is no church. So your baptism is brought out of no church, and your false baptism is no baptism. Thus, the simplest among you will be able to say to you, is our baptism that we had in England a false baptism? Then, it is no baptism. Then are we not baptized? To this you will never answer them, although you should set your souls to [unclear] God's truth and their souls. So likewise if you tell them that England is a false church, they will say to you, then it is no church. You will not know which way to contradict them, in that the scriptures teach that a false church is no church, as a false God is no God, a false Christ no Christ, a false apostle no apostle, a false ordinance of Christ no ordinance of Christ, a false baptism of Christ no baptism of Christ. Thus we do not doubt but (through the grace of God) we will see by the brightness of Christ's coming that your dark deceitful ways will be discovered by the simplest, and you will be ashamed to speak of a false baptism, and to say, it is partly the true baptism of Christ, and partly the baptism of the devil, and so join Christ and Beelzebub together, and make them partners in one baptism. We hope the fear of God will teach you better wisdom than to still blaspheme for the supporting of your kingdom of darkness. If you were not a "stiff-necked people, and of uncircumcised hearts and ears,"[18] you would not have resisted the truth of God this long with contempt and violence, as you have done and do, persecuting it with bitter envying and railings, for which the Lord may justly give you up to the

---

[18] Acts 7.51

hardness of your hearts. But the Lord in great mercy will show mercy on all of you that do it ignorantly. We have shown you from the word of God all the evidence of truth that we are for the present able to do, that your distinction between the false church and no church is vain and feigned, and that the word of God admits of no such distinction in the Lord's ordinances, but that which is a false ordinance of God is no ordinance of God, because God has no false ordinances. You must, therefore, be forced to hold and say of the assemblies of England that they are either true churches of Christ or no churches of Christ. If you hold them to be no churches of Christ, then you cannot in any manner of show of [unclear] say that you may retain your baptism which you have received in no church of Christ, but in a church or congregation of infidels and unbelievers, which you must necessarily account them if they are no true church of Christ. Now all people in the world are either of the world, or chosen out of the world, and those are Christ's disciples (John 15.19). All people are either with Christ or against Christ. "He that is not with me is against me," says Christ (Matthew 12.30). It is now high time to leave off halting between opinions and [unclear] one another in their sins. It is now time to leave off talking of separation, and to separate indeed, and to tell the people of God their sins, and show them their transgressions, and not to account them Christians that by the hearing of the word they become almost Christians as King Agrippa did, but to show them that if they do not become altogether Christians they must be content to be accounted as infidels as Agrippa was. The entire world is either believers or infidels. If there is any knowledge of God in men they will grant us this. Who will not grant that all that believe in Christ Jesus are holy and elect, and will be saved if they continue to the end? Concerning England therefore, you must "either make the tree good and the fruit good or the tree evil and the fruit evil."[19] If the faith of the Church of England is a true faith, then is the Church of England a true church? If the faith is a false faith, then it is a false church, that is, no faith in Christ and no church of Christ. If their faith is no faith in Christ, then they are all infidels and unbelievers, of whom, although you have so accounted by your working toward them, yet by your words you declare them to be otherwise when you are urged to speak plainly. In your writings, though, you show them to be infidels when you affirm that God never made a covenant with them. But you have walked deceitfully too long in this point. Therefore,

---

[19] Matthew 12.33

we must press you to it, if you profess uprightness either to God or men, to manifest in all plainness whether you hold the assemblies of England as believers of Christ. Let us have no respects, no double respects, and no putting of differences of persons. All the Church of England is one body, "seeing they all drink of one cup,"[20] (1 Corinthians 12) and if you hold them as believers in Christ, and truly baptized into his name, then they are your brethren. You may not "account them as enemies but admonish them as brethren" (2 Thessalonians 3.14.15). Then your separation is most wicked, and your building of new churches is contrary to all rule of scripture and you have falsely applied the voice of the angel, crying against England, "Babylon is fallen, she has fallen. Come out of her."[21] If they are believers in Christ Jesus, the voice of this angel cannot be applied to them. You must walk toward them by another rule, even by that rule which Christ has appointed, that all should walk by toward their brethren if they sin, (Matthew 18)[22] and not separate from them and build churches upon new foundations. If this in our writing concerning you who are called Brownists, we are judged to convince sharply, we hold it lawfully done because you are a froward[23] generation, and great deceivers of minds, making a glorious vain show to come out of Babylon, but do not. Not withstanding that we have written sharply in some things, we could desire to be freed from froward suspicions, from which you might free us. Because there are many of you both near and dear to us whom we require in love (as we all do) to apply the sharpest reproofs to themselves, for they had need. And touching on you, Mr. Robinson, remember that you have a letter of most loving respect in your hands concerning these things to which you have not answered, which could have prevented the publishing of this which especially concerns you.

Now, as we have said to you called Brownists in this point, so we say to England, and to the presbytery. If the pope and they of that profession are believers in Christ Jesus, and are truly baptized into his name, then you of England and all the nations of the earth have sinned greatly to separate from Rome in that you were all of one body, and members one of another. Being believers in Christ Jesus, they are your brethren. You should walk toward

---

[20] 1 Corinthians 12.13
[21] Revelation 18.2.4
[22] Matthew 18.15–20
[23] Stubborn or obstinate

them as brethren, and you should not have separated from Rome as you have done, and do, and build new churches everyone upon several foundations. If you of England, and the presbytery, and you called Brownists, did make any conscience effort to walk by the rule of Christ, you would not walk towards Rome as you do. If you hold them to be believers in Christ Jesus, and truly baptized into his name, which if they are then are all the scriptures that are applied against Rome to prove she is Babylon, and that great whore that sits upon many waters, and upon the scarlet colored beast, and Antichrist, have all these scriptures been misapplied to Rome? These cannot be applied to any persons or people that are believers in Christ Jesus and have put on Christ by baptism. There is no voice of the Lord that calls believers to come out from Christ Jesus. The scriptures do not teach any such thing. Therefore, Brownists must return to the Church of England, and the Church of England and the presbytery must return to Rome, and be all sheep of one sheepfold, and repent of your unjust separation form the body of which you were, and all are members. We say, all are members because by one spirit you are all baptized into one body, and though you say you are not of the body with the church of Rome, are you not of the body? (1 Corinthians 12.13–15). You have and all do by one baptism put on Christ and you all have brought that baptism from Rome. So you are all Christians and believers by succession from Rome. You all account Rome believers in Christ. Therefore, though you say you are not of one body with Rome, yet you are all members of one body with Rome.

Furthermore, if Rome be believers in Christ Jesus, then these prophecies of scripture are nowhere to be found fulfilled upon the whole earth. First, the prophecy of Christ (Matthew 24) "of the abomination of desolation set in the holy place,"[24] is not to be seen. The "days of such great tribulation as was never seen from the beginning of the world, in which days no flesh will be saved, unless they should be shortened, all flesh should be condemned."[25] These days have not yet been heard of. The prophecy of Daniel the prophet (9.2.7; 12.11) who prophesied and said that "the sacrifices and the oblations will cease, and the daily sacrifices will be taken away."[26] This prophecy cannot yet have come to pass, if Rome be believers in Christ, and their sacrifices and

---

[24] Matthew 24.15
[25] Matthew 24.21.22
[26] Daniel 12.11

oblations are true sacrifices and oblations. For Rome's sacrifices and oblations have never ceased. Thus the prophecy of the apostle (2 Thessalonians 2) who prophesies that there will come a departing is in no part fulfilled if Rome be believers, unless it is fulfilled in them that have departed from Rome. Then the Church of England and the entire presbytery must look to those who first departed. If Rome and England and the presbytery, and the Brownists are all believers, and of the faith of England, then there has been no departing from the faith, but a great increasing far beyond the primitive times. The scriptures nowhere show of whole nations, kingdoms, and countries that are of the faith of Jesus as they are now. Yes, a great whole part of the world, the like that was never heard of, nor prophesied of, if you are all believers, as you are all either believers or infidels, for you are all of one faith and baptism. But if you are believers, there is no departing yet heard of, neither is the man of sin yet disclosed or revealed, nor exalted, nor sits or has sat as God in the temple of God, showing himself that he is God. There is no such prophecy that has yet come to pass. If Rome is all believers in Christ, that prophecy (Revelation 11) where it is prophesied "that the people, and kindreds, and tongues, and Gentiles, will see the corpses of the two witnesses of the Lord, killed and lying in the streets of the great city which is spiritually called Sodom and Egypt, and the inhabitants of the earth will rejoice over them,"[27] this prophesy [sic] cannot yet be accomplished nor begun. If Rome be believers then that prophesy [sic] of the first beast to who is given "a mouth to speak great things and blasphemies, and to make war with the saints, and to overcome them, and to whom power is given over to every kindred and tongue and nation, so that all that dwell on the earth shall worship him"[28] and the prophesy [sic] of the whore that sits upon many waters, who has "committed fornication with kings of the earth, and all the inhabitants of the earth are made drunk with the wine of fornication,"[29] all these prophecies and many more cannot in any measure be fulfilled, or begun, if the church of Rome be believers and of the faith of Jesus.

If these prophesies [sic] are not fulfilled, nor begun then the mystery of iniquity that began to work in the apostles' days, to the exaltation of the man of sin, given he is ever-working, was contrary to the prophecy of scripture, and

---

[27] Revelation 11.8–11
[28] Revelation 13.5.7.8
[29] Revelation 18.3

that may not be. Let Rome, therefore, and all that profession see and consider that all these prophecies of exaltations are fulfilled in that profession. Thus, their glory is their shame. They glory in nothing more than in their exaltation, and great power, authority, and the magnificence of their church, and all that is true. This is also true, that all these prophecies are fulfilled in their exaltation, which you of the Church of England, and the whole presbytery confessing, and protesting against them for the same, you must hold them all as infidels and unbelievers unless you will fall into great blasphemy and say that they are believers who execute the power of the man of sin. They cause the sacrifices and oblations to cease, and so are taken away from the altar of the Lord, so as there are no sacrifices to be daily offered to him. Will any say that these are believers who take from the Lord's altar his daily sacrifices causing none to be offered to him? If these are believers that utterly overthrow the worship of the Lord, then there can be no infidels.

Further, you cannot say the church of Rome are believers, unless you will say they are believers that depart away from the faith, and are ministers of the man of sin exalting a power above the power of God. They set up his power (the ministers of which they are) to sit as God in the temple of God, making a show of that power that it is the power of God, when it is the effectual working of Satan, with all his power and signs and lying wonders. They that are subject to this power are such as the Holy Ghost testifies, "receive not the love of truth, and who do not believe the truth."[30] Can you of the Church of England, and you of the presbytery and you that are called the Brownists that hold this prophesy [sic] is fulfilled in that exaltation of the Romish profession, can you hold that these as believers in Christ of whom the Lord says, "They receive not the truth, nor believe not the truth, but have pleasure in unrighteousness,"[31] and exalt a power against God, to be worshipped as God? What wickedness and blasphemy is this to say they are Christians and believers in Christ?

Moreover, you cannot say that the Romish professors are believers unless you will say they are the believers who set up the first beast, and are the ministers of that power of the beast, which beast or power has "seven heads and ten horns, and upon his horns ten crowns, and he is like a leopard, and his feet like a bear, and his mouth as the mouth of a lion, to whom the dragon

---

[30] 2 Thessalonians 2.10.12
[31] 2 Thessalonians 2.12

gives his power, throne, and authority."[32] All this they do of that profession, and not only this, but "they also worship the dragon which gives power to the beast, and they worship the beast, saying, who is like the beast, who is able to fight with him?"[33] They, being ministers of this beast or power, do in their ministration open their mouths to blaspheme against God, to blaspheme his name and his tabernacle, and those that dwell there. By his power they have made war with the saints and overcome them. Can you with great blasphemy against the Holy One of Israel, the most high God, say that these are believers in Christ Jesus and Christians that do these fearful things, seeking to destroy God, and the faith of Jesus, and all his saints that hold the truth of Jesus? If you cannot say those who do such things are believers and Christians, then you cannot say that those of the Romish profession are believers or Christians, but that they are infidels and unbelievers, seeing that you confess this prophecy is fulfilled in the Romish profession. So all these things are done by them. Moreover, to these the prophecy (Revelation 17) of the woman, and the beast, and the ten kings that give their power and authority to the beast, these fight with the Lamb. Can you say that any of these are believers and Christians that fight against the Lamb? No, the spirit of God testifies in this place that they who are called, and chosen, and are faithful are on the Lamb's side. They then that fight against the Lamb are those that are not called, nor chosen, nor faithful. Therefore, they must be infidels and unbelievers. All these prophecies that have been confessed you believe have already been accomplished by and under that Roman profession. How will you of the Church of England and presbytery be able to say that they of the Church of Rome are believers and Christians? If they are not believers and Christians, they are then infidels and unbelievers, and so is your baptism and ministry of England, and the baptism of the presbytery, and all the ordinances that you have received from Rome. They are to be cast away as the marks of the beast and are most abominable to the Lord.

But it will not be amiss, seeing there arises so just an occasion to show (the Lord directing us) the ground and root of all this evil and sin against the majesty and holiness of God, against all which you of England and the presbytery commit sin in accounting Rome and all of them of that profession Christians. Although all these abominations which we have shown in all these

---

[32] Revelation 13.1.3
[33] Revelation 13.4

prophesies [sic] (and might be shown in many more) are committed and to this day are maintained by them to the highest dishonor of God in exalting the man of sin to sit as God in the temple of God, and to the utter polluting of all the holy ordinances of God, in abolishing the witness of the Lord, his word and spirit, and in the killing of the saints, fighting against the Lamb, making all the nations of the earth worship the beast, and to drink of the wine of her fornications that sits upon many waters. Not withstanding all this, these who you account as Christians, upon this ground and from this root because when they are infants, they are washed with water in the name of the Father, etc., and you approve when they are baptized as infants because they are the seed of Christians and the faithful.

What words might we take to ourselves to make this madness and the madness of all the world appear, who pretend that all the seed of Christians and of the faithful are to be baptized only under this pretense, and approve of baptism of the seed of all the wicked and ungodly in these parts of the world? Yes, those have been wicked to the third and fourth generation, and to the tenth generation enemies of God, and blood persecutors of his truth, destroying the faith of Jesus, and advancing the man of sin. The seed of all these that are baptized, and by reason of this baptism they are all held and accounted as Christians by you, although they walk in the steps of their forefathers. Is there any knowledge of God in these things? Or do men think that now under the gospel they may do and approve of what they will? Will men neither walk by the law of God nor by the law they propounded to themselves? Do you set down a law to yourselves that the infants of the faithful are to be baptized, and do you approve of the baptizing of the infants of the enemies of God, that fight against the Lamb and the infants of Rome, also, that do not have as much faith as the devils, who believe and tremble?[34] In the word of the unspeakable wisdom the Holy Ghost has said that the "nations will be drunk with the wine of her fornications."[35] Who may not see this prophesy [sic] has been fulfilled? If men were not so drunk that they can neither see their way, nor tell what they say, they would not walk and speak like drunken men.

The Church of England and the presbytery do allow the baptizing of all the infants of Rome, whose pope and cardinals and all their whole ministry

---

[34] James 2.19
[35] Revelation 17.2

who administer the baptism, and parents of the infants that are baptized, and those infants that have already become men of years, would destroy their kings, princes, countries, and all of them for professing Christ as they do. Are these the seed of the faithful? Is this to baptize and to allow of the baptism of the seed of the faithful? Weigh within yourselves what truth there is in this. The Brownists approve of the baptism and baptizing of those whose parents persecute their own children for walking in their way. Are these the seed of the faithful? What blindness and inuprightness is this to profess a ground and walk by no ground. You must agree (if you can) among yourselves and make a new law. This (you see) will not serve your turn, for if you allow none to be baptized but the seed of the faithful, you will not have whole countries and nations who are all Christians, as you have. It is apparent that whatever you say, that you hold that all infants, whether their parents are faithful or unbelievers, will be baptized. Your rule then is that both the seed of the faithful and the unfaithful will be baptized, and this is your practice. What warrant can be found for this? Or does it not matter whether there is warrant or not? You allege circumcision for your ground, that because infants were circumcised, therefore, infants must be baptized. But yet you cannot find that the infants of any people were to be circumcised. If any were circumcised but those that God commanded, neither the Lord nor his faithful subjects ever approved it. Will you now approve of any baptism, and make it good, and yet make circumcision your example? May the Lord persuade your hearts and the hearts of all men to begin while it is still the day to examine the ground of your practice in this, so that you may stand before the Lord on the last day, and through Christ be able prove that you have walked by the strict rule of God's word, and not by the vain inventions of men, which God hates, and let all of God's people hate. But his law let them love, "which is a perfect love, and converts the soul, and it is pure and gives light to the eyes"[36] (Psalm 19). By your practice it is made a most imperfect law when you say that the infants of the faithful are to be baptized only, and when you have laid that down for your law, you both baptize and approve as good the baptism of the infants of the unfaithful and unbelievers, and the enemies of God and his truth. This is neither perfect nor pure law. Therefore, it is not the law of God. You who wait for salvation by Christ Jesus may not walk by that imperfect and impure law, but must seek diligently with your whole hearts the law and statutes of the

---

[36] Psalm 19.8

Lord that you may keep them. This law when you will diligently and faithfully search into and throughout it you will find it nowhere mentioned that any infants are to be baptized. Therefore, it is but the mere vain invention and tradition of men, which whosoever follows, can never have favor or acceptance with God, because they make the law of God of no authority (Mark 7.13). In this great and weighty cause, we will not (through the grace of God) burden you with many grounds or arguments, but lay down before you some few things with all the plainness and evidence of truth that God will make us able.

First, we pray that all those whose hearts God has inclined to seek his truth, and who desire in uprightness to walk in the light, that they will duly consider what the covenant of the gospel is and with whom it is made. Thus has the Lord set it down: "This is the covenant, says the Lord, I will make with the house of Israel. I will put my law in their inward parts, and write it in their hearts, and I will be their God, and they will be my people" (Jeremiah 31.33; Hebrews 8.10). Our Savior Christ declares this more fully (Mark 16.16)[37] where he says, "Go into the entire world and preach the gospel to every creature. He that will believe and is baptized will be saved." Thus the Lord by his spirit in the preaching of the gospel put and wrote this law in the hearts of men according to the parable of the sower (Matthew 13.1–9). They will believe in him and be baptized. Thus, they will be his people. He will save them, and so he is their God. Here is the new covenant set down by the Holy Ghost, both on God's behalf, and on their behalf with whom it is made, and here it is plainly declared and expounded by Christ himself. The Lord on his behalf does covenant that he will put and write his law in men's hearts by the power of the spirit in the preaching of the gospel. He will be their God and save them. The covenant on his people's behalf, which they are to keep and perform, is to believe the gospel and be baptized. Let all men now that have any willingness of heart to be informed by the word of God, and whose hearts are not willingly set to go on in their ignorant [unclear] ways, without trying their ways whether they are of God or not, let them, we say, search, examine, and try by what show of truth it can possibly be conceived that under, or by this covenant of the New Testament infants should be baptized. The Lord requires no such thing in this covenant of men to baptize their infants. If you will but see and consider with wise and gracious hearts, how

---

[37] Mark 16.15.16

the Lord sets down the covenant which he made with Abraham (Genesis 17), you will see with what evidence the Lord in mercy sets it down. Thus the Lord says to Abraham, "I will establish my covenant between you and me, and your seed after you in their generation for an everlasting covenant to be your God and your to seed after you. And I will give to you and to your seed after you, all the land of Canaan for an everlasting covenant. And I will be their God."[38] This is on the Lord's behalf. The Lord says, "This is the covenant that you and your seed after you will keep. Let every man-child among you be circumcised. You will circumcise the foreskin of your flesh, and every man-child at eight days old, as well as he that is born in the house and he that is bought with money."[39] This is the covenant on Abraham's behalf and his seed. Thus the Lord declares in every particular aspect of his covenant with his people, as well as what he will do for them as well and what he requires them to do in obedience to him. Here we see God has commanded Abraham, and his seed to circumcise all the males in their house. Now this covenant is disannulled, and all its ordinances as shown in Hebrews 7.18. The Lord says he will make a new covenant with the house of Israel, not like the old, teaching us that we should not form and frame it according to the old, but that we should receive it, according to the new form and frame of which he delivered it. Under this covenant the Lord does not command or require of his people that they should baptize all their household and infants, both born in their house and bought with money, according as under the old covenant he commanded that they should circumcise them. How dare you then contend against the Lord. Where he says he will make a new covenant not according to the old, you will say and have it according to the old. You will have it that according to the circumcision of infants under the old covenant, so you will have infants baptized under the new. Is this not to set yourselves against the Lord and to change his covenant, which he has sealed with his blood, and after your own wills in what you think is good, to make it according to the old covenant, directly contrary to the Lord's own word and saying? You have no way to maintain the baptizing of infants, but by saying the new covenant is according to the old. This is directly contrary to the saying of the Lord, who is the covenant maker, and who says in plain words, the new covenant which I will make with Israel will not be according to the old. Here it is made evident

---

[38] Genesis 17.7.8
[39] Genesis 17.10–12

to all that will not resist the truth that your baptizing of infants is contrary to the new covenant of the Lord. Thus you make your own tradition good, make the new covenant like the old, which the Lord says is not like the old. How can you possibly oppose the word of the Lord more directly? Furthermore, the Holy Ghost, according to the author of Hebrews (chapter 9), endeavored by all evidence to prove that the new covenant is not like the old. He shows that the Old Testament or covenant had a worldly sanctuary, and that the services of the tabernacle only stood in "meats and drinks and diverse washings, and carnal rites,"[40] which purified the flesh, but did not purge the conscience. The Holy Ghost shows that the New Testament or covenant does not have a worldly sanctuary, and that the service of the tabernacle does not stand in carnalities which do not purge the conscience, but it is a perfect tabernacle, the sacrifice of which does "purge the conscience from dead works to worship the living God."[41] Thus, the scripture shows that the ordinances of the new are not according to the ordinances of the old. For this cause the Holy Ghosts says Christ is the mediator of the New Testament. That is because the New Testament or covenant, and tabernacle, and ordinances are not carnal but spiritual. If you will have infants baptized, that is, washed with water and certain words, then you bring in a carnal rite, which does not purge the conscience (for you do not hold that infants' consciences are purged by it), and so you make the new covenant and ordinances carnal, like the old, which may not be, unless you will directly oppose the evident word of the Lord, as you have long done, to your utter destruction, unless you repent. Moreover, we desire that the people of God, whose whole hearts are set to seek his face, that they will search the scriptures to see what the baptism of the New Testament is declared to be. If this is faithfully searched into, it will convince all on the earth that it can not [sic] appertain to infants.

First, in the Gospel According to Mark (1.4), it is preached by John to be the baptism of amendment of life for the remission of sins. The apostle in Romans 6.4 says, "Baptism is a burying into the death of Christ that we should walk in the newness of life." And in Galatians 3.27, the apostle says, "Baptism is the putting on of Christ by faith." How should this baptism belong to infants? Can there be an amendment of life for the remission of sins in infants? Can infants be buried into the death of Christ to walk in newness

---

[40] Hebrews 9.10
[41] Hebrews 9.14

of life? Can infants put on Christ by faith? If they can do none of these things, which are most plain that they cannot, then they may not be baptized. What was sufficient to give satisfaction in this long conceived error of baptizing infants, you may see by the ordinance itself. They are not capable of it. You may see that the Lord by the covenant does not command nor require any such thing at the hands of parents to baptize their infants and all their household. The covenant is that men should believe and be baptized. There is not one word to command them to baptize their infants and all their household. O, that you would be weary of this your great ignorance, to say that baptism is the seal of the covenant. Yet, you will seal those that cannot receive the seal and those that are not mentioned in the covenant, bringing in under the covenant whomever you will, without the will and mind of the Lord. Although the covenant will still overthrow you, because there can be none under the covenant, but those who believe and are baptized. The Lord will admit no other than he has mentioned in his covenant, though you seal ever so many with water and words. Although this might suffice, yet we will endeavor by the Lord's assistance to convince you by your own ground.

You cannot deny but that there is neither rule nor example in all the New Testament for the baptizing of infants, of which you confess that the mediator of the New Testament has not appointed it. Therefore, you are driven to prove it by consequence making yourselves and the simple believe that it must follow by a necessary consequence that as infants were circumcised, so they must also be baptized. If you will have a necessary consequence of this, and then you must make it of the whole matter and not a part, as you think good. As thus, he that will be a proselyte must be circumcised and all the males in his household. So then if your consequence from this ground is necessary, he that will be a disciple of Christ must be baptized and his entire household. It follows then upon your consequence that no man can be admitted a disciple unless all his household will be baptized, for no man could be admitted as a proselyte unless all his males were circumcised. If a Jew then that has a wife, diverse children, and bondmen (as they have) that come to the faith of Jesus, if his wife or any of his children of bondmen will not be baptized, then he cannot be admitted as a disciple of Christ unless you will allow him to do so by his authority to cause them to be baptized whether they believe or not, as they did by their authority circumcise their household. Thus, your consequence must stand if you will not be willing to deceive yourselves in the means of your salvation.

Deal faithfully, therefore, with God and his truth and his people. You that take it upon yourselves to be guides do not lead God's people to destruction by such deceit as this, when you have neither rule nor example to prove that infants must be baptized. Yes and when the covenant of the Lord does evidently debar them from the ordinance of baptism considered in itself also, yet you will bring in and maintain the tradition of your elders, prove it by a consequence from the covenant of the Old Testament, and make the new like the old, when the Lord says it is not like nor will be according to the old. If the people of God would but with upright hearts read diligently the whole Epistle to the Hebrews, they should (through the grace of God) find to their full satisfaction the difference between the old covenant and the new, and the priesthood, and the tabernacle, and the ordinances, services, and sacrifices set down so plainly as it would make an end of this controversy and many more, to the advancement of God's truth and the salvation of the souls of his people that will follow him in the regeneration or new birth, which is to be born again of water and of the spirit. In this regeneration or new birth whosoever does not follow him cannot enter into the kingdom of heaven. In the Epistle to the Hebrews, they that read will find (as we have formerly shown) that the old covenant was a carnal covenant and commandment (Hebrews 7.16). As the Lord spoke to Abraham (Genesis 17.13) speaking of the covenant of circumcision, said, "My covenant will be in your flesh for an everlasting covenant." As the covenant was, so was the priesthood, and the tabernacle, and the sacrifices, and service, all carnal and worldly, as is with all evidence and plainness set down in that epistle. But the new covenant is not a covenant in the flesh. It is a new covenant in the spirit, a spiritual covenant written in the hearts and minds of God's people, established upon better promises than the first covenant. All this is evident by the words of the covenant, which are, "They that believe and are baptized will be saved."[42] As this covenant is spiritual, so is the priesthood, so is the tabernacle, all the ordinances, sacrifices, and the services. All this is most plainly set down in that Epistle to the Hebrews. The differences between the old and new covenant, if it were carefully searched into and found out, it would overthrow your deceitful consequence, which you draw from covenants that are dislike, or not like in substance, contrary to all understanding. It would make you cast away your carnal baptizing of infants and baptize no infants, but such infants as were

---

[42] Mark 16.16

babes in Christ, such as are begotten by the immortal seed of the word. It would show you your carnal ignorance and blindness in holding that Israelites beget Israelites now, as under the law, or that Christians beget Christians by generation, which has brought in such madness among men, as the Brownists hold and profess that no infants that die are under the covenant of grace and salvation, but such as they beget. Thus, they only beget infants that are heirs of salvation. All this and much more evil comes from making the new covenant like the old, and so it makes them both carnal, which you do in holding that parents beget children to be under the spiritual covenant by carnal generation.

But because some through the weakness of their judgment and understanding cannot see the old covenant to be a carnal covenant, we will in short yet further endeavor to show how it is a carnal or worldly covenant. First, it was a carnal covenant in that all the promises that God made to Abraham in the covenant of circumcision were of worldly things, as we see (Genesis 17.6.8) where the Lord says, "I will make you exceedingly fruitful. I will make nations of you, yes, kings will proceed from you. And I will give you and your seed after you all the land of Canaan for an everlasting possession." Here is the whole covenant of circumcision which God makes, in which there is no promise but of worldly things. Secondly, in his covenant of circumcision the Lord requires a carnal obedience, that is, "Let every man-child be circumcised in the foreskin of the flesh."[43] Thirdly, the judgment for the breach of this covenant is a worldly judgment. (Verse 14) "The uncircumcised man-child in whose flesh the foreskin is not circumcised, that person will be cut off from this people, because he has broken my covenant." Moreover verse 13, where the Lord says, "This is my covenant in your flesh." Who will be so blind as not to see that this is a carnal covenant? Will men be so void of all understanding, as to say that God makes a spiritual covenant with a people in their flesh? Though men have been so ignorant, let them still not be so ignorant.

After the like manner as has been spoken of, the covenant may be spoken of, the tabernacle, priesthood, and all those services and carnal rites, all in which covenant and worldly ordinances there is no promise of salvation for the keeping of them, nor cannot be, because they do not make the conscience holy (Hebrews 9.9). "Neither sanctify they that come thereto" (Hebrews 10.1).

---

[43] Genesis 17.10.11

There is no judgment of condemnation pronounced against any, although they should presumptuously break them, but in bodily death (Numbers 15.30; Hebrews 13.28, etc.).[44] Yet they might be saved through repentance. But now they are under the new covenant, which is spiritual. There is a promise of salvation to those that keep it. "He that believes and is baptized will be saved."[45] And there is a condemnation pronounced against those that do not keep it. "He that will not believe will be damned."[46] He that sins presumptuously or willingly of knowledge against this covenant, or any of the ordinances in it, will never be forgiven (Hebrews 20.29).[47] Thus all may see that will not wink their eyes that the new covenant is not like the old. It is a covenant established upon better promises, and the first covenant was established upon worldly or earthly promises. But the new covenant is established upon spiritual or heavenly promises, even of life and salvation. The difference of these two covenants is that with a spiritual eye one may discern that it will easily overthrow that most false and improper consequence from which it is drawn from the old covenant to the new, for the baptism of infants, the consequence of it if it were rightly laid down, the darkness of it would easily appear. And thus, under the old covenant infants were circumcised in the flesh, so under the new covenant, infants must be baptized in the flesh. What ignorance is this? What wine of fornication is this that has made all the nations drunk? There is no such baptism in the New Testament as baptism in the flesh. God forbid that men should remain still so ignorant as to think that Christ Jesus in his heavenly kingdom and new covenant has established any carnal rite, or ceremonial ordinance, the "handwriting of which he has put out and abolished" (Colossians 2.14). Therefore, the baptism of the New Testament must be a spiritual baptism of water and the spirit (John 3.5) of such a baptism infants cannot be baptized. Its great wickedness is a profanation of the holy and divine ordinance of God to use such administration upon infants, making the ordinance of God of no effect, there is no benefit or advantage, end, or use of it. You will all confess that all infants must be regenerate and born again, or else they cannot enter into the kingdom of heaven. Our Savior Christ, the Savior of us all, says that they that are born

---

[44] No such reference in Hebrews
[45] Mark 16.16
[46] Mark 16.16
[47] No such reference in Hebrews

again must be born of water and the spirit. To what end then is the baptizing of infants since they are not regenerate?

Furthermore, you frame your consequence with these words as infants were sealed with the seal of the covenant under the law, so they must be sealed with the seal of the covenant under the gospel. We demand of you, is washing with water a seal? If it is a seal, it is a seal in the flesh. Where then is the print or impression of it? It has none, therefore, it cannot be a seal. O, how blindly the wise men of the world are carried away in these things, contrary to all understanding, to be brought to imagine that washing an infant with water is a seal. Are these not vain inventions, without ground of scripture, reason, or common sense? Can you walk in this way and think that it pleases God? Will God be pleased with you when you walk in those ways that best please your own minds? Do not be deceived. God will not hold you guiltless for using his name and ordinance in vain. If you will examine the New Testament throughout, you will find no seal, nor none sealed, but those that believe, "who are sealed with the Holy Spirit of promise," (Ephesians 1.13) by which in the Holy Spirit "we are all baptized into one body" (1 Corinthians 12.13). There is but "one spirit, one baptism, and one body," (Ephesians 4.4.5) whose holy seal of the spirit infants cannot have. They cannot be baptized with that one baptism into that one body. So your consequence for the baptizing of infants is directly contrary to the covenant and ordinance of God. The covenant of the Lord is that "they which believe and are baptized will be saved,"[48] and the ordinance is the "baptism of repentance for the remission of sins."[49]

To conclude this point with a ground that all who have any knowledge of the word of God will confess, which is this: the covenant of the New Testament is a covenant of life and salvation only to all that believe and are baptized (Mark 16.16). The seal of the covenant must necessarily be answerable to that holy covenant, a seal of life and salvation only to those that believe and are baptized (Ephesians 1.13.14; Revelation 2.17.18). The apostle here to the Ephesians shows that "after they believed they were sealed with the Holy Spirit of promise." Let all those who confess with whom there is any uprightness that infants who cannot believe (for "faith comes by hearing, and hearing by the word of God," Romans 10.17) cannot be sealed with the

---

[48] Mark 16.16
[49] Mark 1.4

seal of the covenant. It is not in the power of parents to set this seal upon their infants, as it was in their power to set the sign of circumcision upon their flesh. Therefore, it is not required of them by the Lord. It is altogether impiety and wickedness, and a profanation of the holy ordinance of God to take in hand to administer it upon infants. The Lord will revenge himself for such wickedness, if it is not repented of. But against this ground of truth that the covenant of life and salvation is made only with those that believe and are baptized, it is objected that the covenant is made with them and their seed. Though many writers write of such matters, and most affirm it, yet Mr. Robinson, being next at hand, we will produce his warrant for this ground, being as good as any others and as he has unadvisedly overseen in the setting of it down. Thus, he speaks in his book (page 282): "The scriptures everywhere teach that parents by their faith bring their children into the covenant of the church, and entitle them to the promises." Little does Mr. Robinson think how suddenly in his accustomed haste he has brought in a meritorious faith. It is wished that he and all men did see and feel that their faith is little enough to bring themselves under the covenant of God, if it were not for the gracious and most merciful acceptance of God in Christ. But God has not promised anywhere to accept to salvation on the parents' faith for their children, nor to condemn them for their parents' infidelity. This is but one among many of Mr. Robinson's doctrines of the devils which he has heaped up in his tedious book. His proof for his doctrine is Genesis 17. We prove this doctrine most false by Genesis 17, where Abraham, his faith, and earnest prayer to God could not bring Ishmael his child of thirteen years old under that covenant (Verses 18–21).

Thus, Mr. Robinson has altogether overseen in the scripture that he himself alleges. Add moreover to this Genesis 25.23, where Isaac's faith could not bring Esau under the covenant. Thus all may see that Mr. Robinson does but quote scripture for his proof, and does not show how it proves his ground. The next proof for this ground is Acts 2.39, where the apostle speaking to all the unbelieving Jews and Gentiles says, "The promise is made to you and to your children, even as many as the Lord your God will call." How Mr. Robinson will apply this to his purpose we do not know, but we confess that this promise ("They that believe and are baptized will be saved"[50]) is made to all unbelieving Jews and Gentiles, and their children to this day.

---

[50] Mark 16.16

But this in no way proves that the faith of the parents entitles children to the promise, nor that the promise of salvation is made to the unbelieving Jews and Gentiles, or to their children, unless they and their children amend their lives and are baptized. Since, Mr. Robinson, as it should seem, understands children in this place to be infants, we will first leave that to him to prove what the apostle speaks here concerning infants. We will then require of him how he proves that the inheritance of the kingdom of heaven goes by succession of generation, as did the land of Canaan.

The second part of his unjust and ungodly affirmation is that God takes occasion by the sins of the parents to execute his justice to the condemnation upon the children. Here, Mr. Robinson doubles his sin, in that as he has before made the parents' faith the cause of blessing to salvation, which (he says) is everywhere to be found in the scriptures but shows it nowhere. So, he now affirms that the parents' infidelity is the cause of God's judgment to condemnation upon their children. Mr. Robinson propounds his doctrine and rule for a general rule and doctrine. To prove that he is a false prophet in this, we also refer the godly reader to 1 Kings 14 where it is shown that Abijah, the son of the most wicked Rehoboam, being very young, was not cursed for his father's sins. Josiah being but eight years old when his father died, the Lord blessed him abundantly in his infancy, notwithstanding all the grievous transgressions of his father Ammon (2 Chronicles 33–34). Neither did the Lord punish the people of Israel's children for their great transgression (Numbers 14.27–39) when they murmured because of the spies, by which sin, although they so provoked the Lord's wrath as he caused all there carcasses to fall, to be wasted and consumed in the entire wilderness. He did not suffer anyone of them to go to the land of Canaan except Joshua and Caleb. Yet, even then in his anger, he declared his mercy to all their children and promised to bring them into the land. Now we confess with Mr. Robinson that we are all by nature the children of wrath, conceived and born in sin. But we desire to know of Mr. Robinson whether he does not hold that all children alike are the children of wrath and alike begotten in sin? Or have some parents conferred grace by generation more than others, and if they do not (as we assure ourselves you will confess), but that all infants are alike in themselves the children of wrath. Let us then see, not after a sort, but directly, but what evidence of scripture it can be proven (their sins are all alike in themselves) that God should execute his justice to condemnation upon some children for the sins of the parents, and show mercy to salvation upon others for the faith of their parents, seeing the just God has said that everyone will receive salvation or condemnation according to that which he has done in the flesh and not according to that which his parents have done. Let all see Mr. Robinson's great iniquity in this his affirmation, in that he blasphemously charges the most holy and just God to punish infants to condemnation for the actual sins of the parents when they themselves have not sinned after the same manner of transgression (Romans 5.13). We pray Mr. Robinson and all men to consider the words of the Lord (Exodus 20)[51] who says he will "visit the sins of the fathers upon the children of them that hate him" whose hatred is shown by the breach of his commandments. But do infants hate God and break the commandments? You all confess with the prophet in Ezekiel 18.14.17 (not withstanding these words in Exodus 20) that "if a wicked man begat a son that sees all his father's sins which he has done, and fears, and does not do them, he will surely live." You must then grant the infants of wicked parents that do not sin as their parents do, will not die. This should stop Mr. Robinson for the present in his speedy course who runs his race as though he were strong and none could stay him. But the Lord and his word will overthrow him in these ways if he does not repent, whose repentance we much desire for God's glory, and for his own good.

And now let the covenant of the Lord stand firm and good against all the adversaries. The Lord's covenant is "they which believe and are baptized will be saved."[52] The words being spoken by him who made it were with authority and were to convince the consciences of all that will hear them that this covenant is made with only those that believe and are baptized, who are those that are of the faith of Abraham, (Romans 4.12–16) and not those that are of the flesh of Abraham. "There are," says the apostle, "children of the flesh and children of the promise. The children of the promise are counted for the seed" (Romans 9.8). How ignorant and obstinate have men become, to whom no word of God can persuade. They will have the children of the flesh be the children of the promise and the seed. They will have the seed of the faithful, that is, all the children begotten from their bodies, be the children of the promise, and the seed with whom the covenant is made, saying, "The covenant is made with the faithful and their seed," meaning all the children begotten of the flesh. Yet the apostle says the children of the flesh are not seed. But the

---

[51] Exodus 20.5
[52] Mark 16.16

apostle's testimony will not serve their turn. The pope says it is not so. The bishops and the presbytery (having learned it from the pope) say it is not so. The Brownists (having learned it form the bishop) say it is not so. Here are many witnesses, and they have a long and ancient custom, and the fruit is fair to look upon and pleasant to the eye and mind, that infants are begotten and born Christians. The most wicked and profane parents that are like this, they may be accounted to begat Christians, and that their children may be made members of the body of Christ when they are newborn. The best men like this well. The worst like it well. This pleases all flesh in these parts of the world. There was never any doctrine of Christ nor of the apostles that ever was so acceptable to all men. It must be acceptable because such a good thing is so easily to come by. What a grievous thing it would be if one might not be a Christian and a member of Christ's body before they had learned of Christ and to believe in him. This would trouble children if they should be forced to know Christ before they could be admitted to be his disciples and be baptized. This would be a great trouble to parents that their children should not be baptized before they had carefully brought them up in the instruction and information of the Lord. This would be a great burden to bishops and priests, if they should have none admitted as members of their church until by their diligent and faithful preaching of the gospel they were brought to knowledge, faith, and repentance, and to amend their lives and be baptized. If these old doctrines of Christ and his apostles should be put into practice it would trouble and offend all the world, being so contrary to all custom, and counsels, and affections of men. O, crooked and foolish generation[53] how long will the Lord bear you? How long will he suffer you? Will you make the way broad and wide which he has made straight and narrow? Will you still walk in the traditions of men after the lust of your own hearts, and tread his statues under your feet? Will the long evil custom and false testimony of men, agreeable to your own affections, overthrow the divine and true witness of our Lord Christ and his apostles? Does our Savior Christ say that those with whom he has made the new covenant are those in whose minds and hearts he has written, who he declares those that believe are to be baptized? Will you add to the covenant of the Lord, and say it was made with the faithful and their seed before they can believe? Does the apostle say that the seed to whom the promise is made are those who are of the faith of Abraham and not those

---

[53] Deuteronomy 32.5

that are of the flesh of Abraham? Will you say that they who are of the flesh of the faithful are the seed with whom the covenant is made? Can you devise in your hearts more directly a way to oppose the Lord and falsify his truth than you have done in this? Will you contend against the Lord and despise the spirit of grace, and trample under foot the blood of the New Testament? Do you think that you will escape more punishment than those that despise Moses' law? Do not deceive yourselves. Do not think that God does not care for these things, and that he does not regard the breach of his holy ordinances because he seems to hold his peace in that he does not strike you with bodily judgments. Unless you repent he will reprove you, and set all things in order before you, and tear you into pieces, when there will be none that can deliver you. O, consider this and do not forget God. What will it profit you to have your infants washed with water and a few words, in which the name of the Lord is blasphemed, and you perish for so profaning his ordinance? The infant is never the better. It will not be saved by it. There is no such ordinance required at your hands. Let the word of the Lord be your guide in these things, and not the word of man nor long custom, although it is most pleasing to your carnal minds.

We leave you to your remembrance of Abraham's faith that could not bring his children under the covenant. It did not bring Ishmael or any of his six sons that he had by Ketourah, his wife, under the covenant (Genesis 25). Therefore, that is a most deceitful and false ground to say that because they were circumcised because they were under the covenant that they are also under the covenant of Abraham's faith. If so, then all of Abraham's bondmen and household are under the covenant, and Ishmael whom the Lord deigned to be under the covenant, and yet he and all of them were commanded to be circumcised.

****

This then is the ground of truth that cannot be gainsaid, that all the males, free and bond, that were born in Abraham's house or bought with his money, which were not of his seed, were all to be circumcised, because it was the covenant that God commanded Abraham to keep. All his males were to be circumcised, but not because they were under the covenant of circumcision by Abraham's faith. This is but a vain invention of the man of sin, and a mystery of iniquity to deceive those that have pleasure in unrighteousness, having no show, nor warrant of scripture to say they circumcised because they were under the covenant of Abraham's faith. All evidence of scripture is against it in that the Lord plainly declares in his word that they were to be circumcised, even those that were not under the covenant. Even all of Abraham's household, where there was no one under the covenant but himself when the commandment was given. Now then, you having no cullor,[54] show no warrant from the scriptures for the baptizing of infants, but a deceitful consequence from the example of circumcision. We beseech all who hope for salvation by Jesus Christ to see the deceit of your consequence. Thus you say, and this is what you all hold, that as the seed of the faithful were circumcised, so the seed of the faithful must be baptized. You have no proof for your ground other than your strong persuasions and long custom in which not one of you has faith. We will show you again the deceit of your consequence.

First, it is not drawn by due proportion, which is a most deceitful way to deceive the simple. From this your consequence is drawn: as Abraham, who believed, was circumcised and all the males of his household, both men and children of eight days, bond and free, so now any man who believes must be baptized with his entire household, both men and children of eight days old, bond and free. Secondly, the deceit of your consequence is because it is not a necessary consequence. You can prove nothing by consequence but that which must necessarily follow. This does not necessarily follow nor can it follow because infants were circumcised with circumcision in the flesh under the law, therefore, infants must be baptized with the baptism of repentance for the remission of sins under the gospel, with which baptism they cannot be baptized, as all of any understanding must confess. There is but one baptism. Therefore, mostly blindly, ignorantly, and deceitfully this consequence is drawn. It is neither drawn by due proportion nor can the rule possibly be true by consequence. Neither will you be able tell what to say when you will be required to prove it is a necessary consequence. Therefore, if you will not willfully go on in the ways of everlasting destruction, forsake this root of error which overthrows the covenant of the gospel of Jesus Christ in its first foundation, bringing in the seed of the flesh of the faithful by carnal generation for the seed of the promise, instead of the seed of the faith of Abraham by spiritual regeneration. You are making the infants that are

---

[54] Under a pretext or pretenses, under the mask or alleged authority of someone or something

begotten of the faithful after the flesh members of the body of Christ and heirs of the covenant of the New Testament (which is the covenant of faith and repentance) through the faith of their parents. By this means you have and do daily bring all the wicked and ungodly in these parts of the world to become members of Christ's body and heirs of the covenant by natural birth which our Savior Christ says (John 3)[55] can in no way be but by new birth, that is, being born again by water and spirit, which is, by believing and being baptized. Thus you utterly destroy the holy covenant of the Lord, the holy baptism, and the body of Christ. You make them common to all, young and old, wicked and profane, blasphemers, persecutors, murderers, adulterers, and witches, and their children. Let all know this such as the members are, such is the body, and such is the baptism and such is their covenant, the covenant of death and condemnation to all that are under it, and not the covenant of salvation, which is only made with those that believe and are baptized. May the Lord persuade every honest heart to ground their faith upon this rock, that as under the law none were circumcised but those that were expressly commanded by rule or example. So under the gospel none may be baptized, but those that are expressly commanded by rule or example. By keeping to this ground no simple soul will be deceived. So, we leave this point with godly care to be considered and beseeching the Lord to give you understanding hearts.

Thus, we have with our most willing (though most feeble) endeavors, manifested to you, these two false professions of Christ, and the false prophets that maintain them among you with their divers particular errors and strong delusions by which they deceive you, transforming themselves as though they were prophets of God. But they are all deep deceivers, and prophesy [sic] lies, as we have proven. They will never be able to justify themselves neither before God nor his people. We would much rather desire their repentance than that they should go about to approve themselves in their evil as they will heap sin upon their own heads, and bring shame to their own faces, seeing the time has come that the Lord will reprove the foolishness of such false prophets who make a show of godliness, but deny its power "who lead captive simple women, who are learning and never able to come to the knowledge of truth."[56] These are those that the apostles foretold of, (2 Timothy 3) who, like Jannes

---

[55] John 3.5
[56] 2 Timothy 3.7

and Jambres,[57] resist the truth, who are proud boasters and exalting themselves and challenging to themselves special power to know and understand the counsels of God, when they are men of corrupt knowledge and minds, and are to be reproved concerning the faith. But (says the apostle) they will "prevail no longer, for their madness will be evident to all men." We exhort you with the words of the apostle, "turn away from such."[58]

It follows that we speak some few words of the second prophecy, which concerns the days of the son of man in the brightness of his coming for the consuming of the man of sin, spoken of in 2 Thessalonians of which days our Savior says, "will be as the lightning that comes out of the east and is seen in the west"[59] (Matthew 24). This is set forth to us that the Lord will make his truth appear with unspeakable evidence of light, so as his people will plainly see the way and light of it. According to the Lord by the prophet Isaiah who says (42.16), "I will bring the blind a way they do not know, and lead them by paths they have not known. I will make darkness light before them, and crooked things straight." The Lord will not speak in secret, neither in a place of darkness in the earth. And Isaiah 30.26, "The light of the moon will be as the light of the sun, and the light of the sun will be sevenfold and like the light of seven days, in that day the Lord will bind up the breach of his people and heal the stroke of their wound." And Isaiah 33.19, "You will not see a fierce people, a people of dark speech, that you cannot perceive, and of a strange tongue, that you cannot understand." All this teaches the people of God to look for plain paths to walk in, that shine with brightness and also that the witnesses of the Lord will be a people that will speak plainly to the understanding of the simple. Therefore, the Lord's people must not walk in blind and secret ways, nor deserted paths which do not have light and are not plain, nor be seduced by false prophets and deceitful people that speak in their fierce heat of darkness and obscure things, who are full of deceitful distinctions, blind consequences, and all turning of devices to deceive the simple, saying, "Lo, here is Christ, lo, there is Christ."[60] Of such, our Savior forewarns his people that they are not to believe them, although they will show great signs and wonders. But they will set their hearts and turn their eyes to

---

[57] 2 Timothy 3.8
[58] 2 Timothy 3.9
[59] Matthew 24.27
[60] Matthew 24.23

the clear light of truth which is the everlasting gospel that the "angel fleeing through the midst of heaven preached to those that dwell on the earth, and to every nation, and kindred, and tongue, and people" (Revelation 14.6). This is the spirit of the Lord's mouth, with which he will consume the man of sin and abolish him by the brightness of his coming (2 Thessalonians 2)[61] by the ministry of the seventh angel, who when he has poured out his vial, "there will be sounds, and lightnings, and thunders, and a great earthquake such as there never was. The great city will be rent in three parts. The cities of the nations will fall. That great city, Babylon, will come in remembrance before God, and he will give to her the cup of the wine of the fierceness of his wrath"[62] (Revelation 16). Thus, by the glory of the light of the gospel the mystery of iniquity will be abolished.

Our Savior Christ says that his coming will be as the lightning comes out of the east and is seen into the west. This makes it manifest unto us that the glorious overspreading of the gospel again will be as at the first, general over all, and that men will seek after and resort to the light of the truth of God, as eagles do their prey, according to the prophecy of Isaiah 60.4, "Lift up your eyes round about and behold all these are gathered and come to thee. Thy sons will come from afar." And Isaiah 66.18, "The Lord says it will come that I will gather all nations and tongues, and they will come and see my glory." And the Lord by the prophet Amos (9.11) says, "On that day I will raise up the tabernacle of David that has fallen down and close up its breaches, and will raise up its ruins, and I will build it as in the days of old." And Isaiah 11.11.12, "In the same day the Lord will stretch out his hand again the second time to possess the remnant of his people. He will assemble the dispersed of Israel, and gather the scattered of Judah from the four corners of the world." And here agrees the prophecy in Revelation 19.17 when "the angel that stands in the sun cries with a loud voice to all the souls that fly through the midst of heaven, come and gather yourselves together to the supper of the great God." And Revelation 21,[63] the Holy Spirit, speaking of the glorious exaltation of the holy city after the destruction of Babylon, says, "The kings of earth will bring their glory and honor to it, and the glory and honor of the Gentiles will be brought to it." This is yet the hope and comfort of the saints

---

[61] 2 Thessalonians 2.8
[62] Revelation 16.17–19
[63] Revelation 21.24

of God that it will come to pass that which now "comes against Jerusalem will go up from year to year to worship the King, the Lord of Hosts, and to keep the feast of tabernacles" (Zachariah 14.16). Therefore, says the voice out of the throne, "Praise our God, all you his servants and you that fear him both small and great. For the Lord, that Almighty God, does now reign. Let us be glad and rejoice, and give glory to him. For the marriage of the Lamb has come, and his wife has prepared herself" (Revelation 19.5–7). These words are faithful and true, which must shortly be fulfilled, "Blessed is he that observes the words of the prophecy of the book," (Revelation 22.7) but woe, woe, woe, to all that do not mark and observe them, and faithfully and carefully keep the words of the prophecy of this book.

We demand in all these days of tribulation, which are such as never were nor ever will be, where will the ignorant appear? If in the days of so great danger when there will be (as there is now) so many false prophets showing such signs and wonders, so as if it were possible they would deceive the very elect. If in these days the ignorant are seduced through their ignorance, will they drink of the cup of the wine of God's wrath? The word of the Lord is perfect and plain. Those that are ignorant and are deceived will perish because "they do not receive the love of the truth, therefore God will send them strong delusions that they should believe and be damned"[64] (2 Thessalonians 2). It is just with the Lord, their ignorance being declared to be for want of the love of the truth. Thus, then the ground of truth is most evident and plain. They that through grace in Christ receive the love of the truth, they are the elect of God and will not be deceived, but they will be saved. They that through the effectual working of Satan, with all his signs and lying wonders, do not receive the love of truth, they will be deceived, and believe and be damned. Moreover, our Savior Christ says, "If the ignorant lead the ignorant, they will both fall into the pit" (Matthew 15.14). Therefore, let all take heed and learn to know the truth of God, and to love it, and to understand his word themselves, seeing that the Lord has commanded them not to follow those who say, "Lo, here is Christ, lo, there is Christ,"[65] but to look into the shining light of truth, of which, if they are not able to judge and discern of themselves (by the direction of God's spirit) they can never have faith nor assurance in the way they walk. They will run blindfolded to destruction not knowing where they

---

[64] 2 Thessalonians 2.11
[65] Matthew 24.23

are led. False prophets or true prophets are all alike to them. They are ignorant of the scriptures, which they should examine them and find them out and try their doctrine. This must be carried away with every blast of vain doctrine, when they are not able to try the spirits to see whether they are from God. These are the fruits of ignorance, not to know the voice of Christ from the voice of the false prophets. Yet, such men would have their ignorance excuse them, although their ignorance is only for want of their love of truth. If those that are through ignorance are led into false ways will be saved, then they through ignorance are led into false ways will also be saved, and so (almost) all flesh will be saved. Who can plead ignorance for all their transgressions, in all false worship, and all their false ways? But they that are ignorant, let them be ignorant. Let all the disciples of Christ covet spiritual gifts so that they may prophecy[SIC OR TYPO?], and pray with understanding, and sing with understanding, and speak with understanding, so that they may instruct others, and in understanding be of a ripe age (1 Corinthians 14). This knowledge of salvation is required of all the disciples of Christ alike, there is but one law of obedience for all. Christ has not appointed anyone to be more ignorant than another, and to everyone that asks alike, he gives alike, and they that seek alike, will find alike (Matthew 7.7) because "there is no respect of persons with God" (Romans 2.11).

Now there is one ground that is most dangerously perverted to the destruction of many souls. We pray the best advised godly consideration of every reader. If men walk uprightly in the truth, according to what they know, and endeavor to attain to better and more knowledge of God's truth so that they may walk in it, such men, though they commit much sin through ignorance, yet repenting of their sins of ignorance, there is mercy with the Lord for such sins and sinners. We confess that this is a most true ground, or else no flesh could be saved, if the Lord should not accept the willingness of men's minds in truth, according to that which they have. But this ground is most wickedly perverted and brought in to excuse all unwilling minds to be informed who willingly resist the truth and have no willing minds to be directed by God's word no further than stands their good liking. Yet this ground must excuse all their false worship and all their false ways, and all false doctrine, and exposition of the scriptures, and all the profanation of the holy ordinances of God, which they do through ignorance, although they do not repent of it but justify themselves to have done well. Can any godly heart conceive that because God in his mercy pardons the sins of ignorance, men repenting of their ignorance, that therefore God will pardon men that through ignorance commit sin and justify themselves in their sins, either by word or practice? Cannot men see the great difference between the repenting of their sins of ignorance and the justifying of their sins committed through ignorance? But will they make it all one, to confess sin and to justify sin? Can the just God, contrary to his own word and law, forgive any one sin that is not repented of? "If we acknowledge our sins he is faithful and just to forgive us our sins, and to cleanse us from all unrighteousness."[66] But if when we have sinned in any particular thing, we say, "we have not sinned, we make God a liar, and his word in not in us," and we cannot be forgiven or cleansed (1 John 1.10). Can the holy and just God forgive such sinners and sins, as when they have through ignorance sinned in diverse things against the word of God, they will justify themselves that they are not ignorant and that they have not sinned, and so make the word of God a lie? The word of the Lord is plain. Those who are ignorant and sin and say that they are not ignorant, their sin remains with them. These are the words of Christ in John 9.41, "If you were blind, that is, if you did not see and acknowledge your blindness, you should not have sin. But now you say, we see, therefore, your sin remains." Thus our Savior Christ shows in as plain words as the heart of man can desire that all and every sin men commit through ignorance and say that they do not sin, all those sins are not pardoned, but remain upon them. The judgment of the Lord is against them those that so sin, as the wise man further shows in Proverbs 28.13 saying, "He that does not confess and forsake his sin will not have mercy at God's hands, but he that confesses and forsakes them will have mercy." How will men yet vainly persuade themselves that God will pardon their sins of ignorance, which they neither confess nor forsake, but justify themselves in many grievous sins, and saying they have not sinned, and that they do not commit evil in doing them, but they do that which is good and just in the sight of God? What sin will be condemned if this sin is pardoned? Will not the adulterer that confesses he does evil in committing adultery, and the drunkard that confesses he sins in his drunkenness, and the blasphemer that confesses he does evil in blasphemy, will not all of these be much rather pardoned (although they do not forsake their sins in that they confess them) than they that neither confess nor forsake their sins but justify themselves in their sins? Does this cause God to pardon their sins because they are fully

---

[66] 1 John 1.9

persuaded in their minds that they do not sin? Then the adulterer, drunkard, blasphemer, idolater, and covetous man, fully persuaded in their minds that they are not sinning in doing those things, will also be pardoned. Thus the Lord must accept the ignorant, strong persuasions of men's minds in error and disobedience, for true knowledge, faith, and obedience. If they that through ignorance are fully persuaded in their minds or consciences, obey unrighteousness and justify error, will be saved and through Christ be accepted by God, as they that of true knowledge and faith obey righteousness and justify the truth, so then their salvation is by Christ through the ignorant persuasion of mind and disobedience as well as through true knowledge, faith, and obedience. What will men make of God? How has the mystery of iniquity prevailed? First, to take from him his power and government in his kingdom, as we have shown, and then take from him his justice and judgment. If the Lord will not in his justice judge those that ignorantly pervert his laws, statues, and ordinances, who "call the light darkness and darkness light, sour sweet and sweet sour," (Isaiah 5.20) speaking evil of that they do not know, teaching for doctrines men's precepts, overthrowing the doctrines of the foundation of the beginning of Christ, following the imaginations of their own hearts, and setting up the traditions of men instead of the holy ordinances of God, and because in all these things they are ignorant and walk as far as they can see, and do as they are persuaded in their minds, thinking they are doing God a good service, therefore, they will be accepted with God, if the Lord will not in his justice judge those that sin and transgress against him, then the righteous judgment of the Lord is overthrown, and the ordinances of Christ under gospel are made of no effect. If men know them and do them, they will do well. But if they are ignorant and walk in false ways, maintaining diverse errors, they are persuaded in their consciences that it is the truth, they will also be accepted. What use then are the ordinances of Christ? Then is truth and error all one, if men are as well persuaded of the one as the other? This destroys all the religion of God, if everyone may take liberty of themselves to walk according to the persuasion of their minds though it is in error. Yet, if they know better, so long as they confess the name of Jesus, all is well. If they are so persuaded, they will be saved. Then, not only they that walk in the way of life, but those that are persuaded that they walk in the way of life, will also be saved, through they walk in error.

Thus, as you have set open the door of the kingdom of heaven, and let all in that confess the name of Jesus with their infants, making them (as you think) members of the body of Christ, so now, you will also set open the gates of the kingdom of glory, and let in all that confess the name of Christ, though through ignorance they walk in much darkness, and make them, as you imagine in your foolish minds, fellow heirs with Christ in his glorious inheritance. And yet the Holy Ghost says, "If we walk in darkness and say we have fellowship with Christ, we lie and do not do what is true" (1 John 1.6). Therefore, you will all be deceived with the foolish virgins who were overtaken in their foolishness, who, though they hoped and were persuaded that they should have been let in, yet were shut out.[67] This is how all of you justify your false ways through ignorance, although you should begin to say, "We have eaten and drunk in your presence, and you have taught in our streets, and we thought we had done well, and we knew no better."[68] Yet, the Lord will say to you, "I tell you I do not know you. Depart from me, you workers of iniquity."[69] Then you will see (if you will not learn before) that though you should plead that you had done it ignorantly, it will not serve the turn. Yes, though you should say you had sought to enter in at the straight gate, but through your ignorance you were not able, notwithstanding your seeking, in that you have not sought aright, the door will be shut to you. And when you will knock and say, "Lord, Lord, open to us,"[70] the Lord will answer, "I do not know you and where you are from" (Luke 13.27). Then you will see that your deceitful hearts have seduced you, and that your good meanings were not according to godliness, but according to your own minds and persuasions. Then you will see that your casting down, destroying, and rejecting the holy ordinances of God, and setting up the vain inventions and traditions of your elders (as you do), thinking you do God a good service, you will no more be excused from this than those that have rejected and killed the disciples of Christ, and think they that have done a good service for God.[71] Your sins are much greater than theirs. They ignorantly kill, destroy, and reject the disciples of Christ for keeping the ordinances of Christ, and yet ignorantly destroy and reject the ordinances of Christ, so that none should keep them, and set up other ordinances abolishing Christ in it. Do you think the Lord will hold you

---

[67] Matthew 25.1–13
[68] Luke 13.26
[69] Luke 13.27
[70] Luke 13.25
[71] John 16.2

guiltless for these things, although you do them ignorantly, especially you who justify yourselves and say you do that which is good in God's sight, and that you do not sin in these matters? Hear what the Lord says to his own people, who justified themselves in their way of wickedness, saying, they are guiltless. "Behold, says the Lord, I will enter with you into judgment because you say I have not sinned" (Jeremiah 2.35). Even so the Lord will enter into judgment with every one of you that say you see when you are blind, and continue in the works of darkness, and say you do not sin. Hear us with patience and consider what we say. The judge of all hearts knows that we earnestly desire the salvation of your souls. Will the just God forgive any one sin that has not been repented of? Or can he justify those that justify themselves in any one evil? Whosoever knows God knows this cannot be, for he that is guilty of one sin, is guilty of them all (James 2.10; Ezekiel 18.11–13). If God should forgive any one sin that has not been repented of, he must forgive all sins that have not been repented of. But no sin can be pardoned without repentance. Ignorance will not excuse any. For a further full proof take the words of our Savior Christ, who says, "He that is ignorant and does not know his master's will and sins, or does things worthy of stripes will be beaten and receive punishment."[72] Therefore, let the ignorant never plead their ignorance anymore. The Lord has judged them. They will all perish unless they repent and come to the knowledge of truth. Is it not just that the Lord condemns all the ignorant, seeing that the Lord has given them all means of knowledge, and yet they will not seek it, nor ask for it, no further than they think is good?

What do you think of yourselves? If a king makes laws just and good and binds himself by an oath that without respect of persons whoever breaks any one of those laws he will certainly die, unless he acknowledges his faults and repents and whoever will keep them will be advanced to great dignity and honor. These laws the king has caused to be written are so that all men may have them, and yet further the king in his great mercy, because he would have none of his subjects perish for want of the right understanding of his laws. To prevent them of that danger, the king appoints in every place such a one as will always be ready to truly inform his people in the right understanding of every one of those laws and statutes, and charging them to be directed by no other understanding of them. If, not withstanding the commandments and all

---

[72] Luke 12.48

this love and care of their lord and king over them to preserve them from falling under the judgment of death, his people and subjects will either carelessly neglect to be informed or will think themselves wise enough to inform themselves, or go to be informed for the understanding of those laws to any other than the king had appointed, and resting upon their information break any one of those laws of the king, and do not acknowledge their fault and repent, will their ignorance excuse them, when they had one ready at hand always to inform them before they offended, and ready to inform them that they could repent if they would but ask to be informed? They would not be informed before they break the commandment of the king, neither after they have offended will they be informed to repent, but they justify themselves that they have not offended. Can a just king break his oath and pardon and forgive the willful ignorance of such careless subjects, and advance them to the same honor that he advances his dutiful subjects, but he will dishonor himself, and make his oath and law of no effect? No wise and just earthly king would ever dishonor himself.

Now then, will the most glorious King of Kings who is most wise, just, and holy, having made most righteous, holy, and perfect laws, and "to show stableness of his counsel and has bound himself by oath and promise" (Hebrews 6.17) without respect of persons, that whoever will break any one of those laws, he will certainly be damned, unless he confesses his sin and repents (Mark 16.16; Luke 13.3). Whoever keeps them will inherit glory, honor, and immortality. He has caused these laws to be written by inspiration so that all men may have them. Yet to make his mercy further appear so that none of his people should perish for the want of the right understanding, he has sent the "Comforter, and gives the Holy Ghost to everyone who asks, to teach and lead them into all true understanding" (John 14.26; Luke 11.13) charging them to be directed by no other (James 1.5) for the understanding of it. If notwithstanding the commandment and all this love and care of the King of Heaven over his people to preserve them from falling under the just judgment of eternal death, his people and subjects will either carelessly neglect to be informed or they will think they are wise enough to inform themselves or will go to any other to be informed of the understanding of those laws other than someone the Lord appointed, and relying and trusting on their information, break any one of the laws of the King of Heaven, and do not acknowledge their sin and repent, will their ignorance excuse them? They had the Holy Ghost for asking and could have been informed before they offended and also after they have offended that they might repent. Can the most holy and just God and King, contrary to his oath, pardon and forgive the willful ignorance of such careless subjects as break his laws, who will not acknowledge their sin and repent, and give them eternal glory and honor with his servants (who though they have offended yet have repented), but he will dishonor himself and make his oath and law of no effect? O that men would consider that the most holy, wise, and just God cannot do so against his oath, and make himself unjust and untrue. If men would consider what God is, as he declares himself to be, that is, "a jealous God, not making the wicked innocent, visiting iniquity to the third and fourth generation of them that break his commandments,"[73] "a God of severity against those that fall through unbelief," (Romans 11.22) a God that will certainly "take away their part out of the book of life than take anything away from his word, and that will add all the plagues written in his word to those who add anything to his word"[74] (Revelation 22).

If men would believe God to be such a one as he declares himself to be, they could not be so vain as to persuade themselves that God would forgive their sins of ignorance. Their ignorance is because of their own willful neglect. When through such ignorance they overthrow the ordinances of Christ, and abolish the laws of his testament, and do not repent, but justify themselves in their sins and say they have not sinned in the matter.

What is sufficient to say in this great deceivableness of unrighteousness, where men are seduced to think that if through ignorance they justify sin it will be forgiven them, knowing no better, although they do not repent, which they cannot do, in any sin that they justify themselves? Men cannot both justify and repent of one and the same sin at one instant. If men will be so far void of all grace and understanding as to hold and think that any sin committed through ignorance and through ignorance is justified (because they know no better) and they will be pardoned, then it cannot be denied but that they put Christ to death through ignorance, and through ignorance justified that they have not sinned. But rather that they had done well, and according to the word of God, in putting a blasphemer to death that said he was the Son of God. They will also be pardoned, for they did it ignorantly, and knew no better, as our Savior Christ testified, when he said, "Father, forgive them.

---

[73] Exodus 20.5.6
[74] Revelation 22.17.18

They know not what they do."[75] The apostle Peter acknowledges the same (Acts 3.17) saying, "Brethren, I know you did it through ignorance, as also your governors."

Now let us compare these things together, so we will through the grace of God better see the deceit of this ground, as it is misapplied. The ground we are to remember is this, that if men walk conscionably as far as they know, and desire better knowledge, yet through ignorance commit much sin, there is mercy with God, and they, acknowledging and repenting of their ignorances, will be pardoned by grace through faith and repentance (Ephesians 2.8). This ground is misapplied, as we trust will easily appear, being brought to prove that if men walk conscionably as far as they know and commit some sins through ignorance and through ignorance justify the sin, thinking they do well, and knowing no better, their sin will be pardoned, which if it is, it must be by grace through persuasion and not ignorance, for there is no faith in ignorance. Where is there any warrant for such a ground? Who is so blind that he cannot see the grievous error of this ground thus misapplied? This is to excuse sin by sin, that is, by ignorance. We conclude this point by the word of truth that none can deny that have any knowledge of the means of salvation. There is no salvation, but by grace in Christ, through faith and repentance. So there is then no pardon for any sin but by the grace in Christ through faith and repentance. This being an undeniable ground, none then can be saved, nor can have their sin pardoned by grace in Christ through ignorance, if they justify any sin. Therefore no such sin may be pardoned, but all such sinners must be condemned. For this end and purpose we have spoken all that we have spoken in this point to show to all men that if they justify any one sin or evil, though it is of ignorance, they can never be saved, but will perish to everlasting destruction. Such sins cannot come within men's general repentance of all their ignorance seeing they justify themselves in them, and say they do not sin. Therefore, their sin remains and cannot be taken away by Christ. For an example, you will justify the baptizing of infants. Now when you repent of all your sins of ignorance, do you have any thought to repent of that? And if you were asked, would you not with your last breath justify that you have done well in this matter, and that the baptizing of infants is a holy ordinance of Christ? But if it is no ordinance of Christ, and that you continue to sin, can you be as simple as to imagine that this sin will come

---

[75] Luke 23.34

within your general repentance, in which you bless and justify yourselves? You can no more be forgiven at God's hands than those that ignorantly set up a false Christ and justify him to be the true Christ or than they that put the true Christ to death, and justify that he is a false Christ. We know your answer in this will be that if you could see it is your sin to baptize infants and to maintain it to be a holy ordinance of God, you would repent of it, but before you cannot. Will God not answer you that when he sees you repent he will forgive you, but before he cannot? (Ezekiel 18.21–27).

Will the pope not make the same answer for all the bloody persecutions of which he has, and does persecute all Protestants, so called? Will the lord bishop not make this answer for all their wicked and cruel persecutions against the Puritans and Brownists (so called)? But will they be pardoned, they who justify themselves in all these wickedness (in which they think they do God service) because they repent of all their sins of ignorance, of which they justify these as none? Will God pardon them in all their wickedness because they cannot see it to be their sin? You all will grant that they cannot be pardoned for these sins, they who justify themselves in them. Neither can any one be pardoned of any sin, they who justify themselves in them.

If this were duly considered it would make men take heed what they profess or practice in the profession of Christ, seeing if they profess or practice anything that is not according to the word of God, and justify it for the good, they must perish and cannot be saved. It stands, therefore, that all men upon the peril of their souls should look at their ways and be upon a sure ground from God's word as to what they condemn for evil or error, and what they maintain and justify for truth. If "they that justify the wicked, and they that condemn the just are an abomination to the Lord," (Proverbs 17.15) then they that justify error and wickedness, and condemn truth and righteousness, call light darkness and darkness light, this must be an abomination to the Lord. If all the learned Scribes and Pharisees and false prophets in the world had hearts to believe this, and confess it, it would make them heed as to what they justified for truth, and what they condemn for error, and how they taught others to do so. If all the careless professors of Christ that profess him in word would believe this word of the Lord to be true, it would make them look more circumspectly at their own ways, and not think that any profession of Christ is sufficient, and that they may profess Christ after the manner that is best pleasing to their own minds, making the way so large that they can walk in liberty according to vanity and excess of their own hearts. If the simple-hearted, who in many things are weaned from the world and who have many zealous desires in them, did faithfully believe the Lord, that if they justify any false ways, untruth, or error, and condemn any way of light and truth, their sin remains, and they are an abomination to the Lord. If they believe God in this matter, it would make them take heed as to how they went on in their ignorant zeal, being led by teachers, approving and justifying what they teach them, and disapproving and condemning what they teach to them to disapprove and condemn. They forsake the teachings of God's spirit, not thinking it is possible for them to attain to the understanding of the scriptures but by the teaching of their learned and good men (as they falsely call them). But if they did believe this word of the Lord, that they must perish if they justify any one error or false way, and condemn any one truth, it would make them with fear and trembling seek wisdom, knowledge, and the understanding of God, that they who are taught of God might be able of themselves, by the help of the Holy Spirit (the only true teacher and leader into all truth) to discern and judge between good and evil, light and darkness, and truth and error. Unless they, relying upon men, are seduced and led to justify false ways, and condemn the way of truth in any particular, and so fall under the just judgment of the Lord, even the judgment of eternal death and condemnation, a right recompense of reward for all that will of ignorant simplicity out of their good meanings and zealous affections (falsely so called), submit themselves to be led and taught only of men, seeking for knowledge at their mouths, and not wholly depending on the scriptures for instruction, and the spirit of God to teach them the understanding of it, neglecting (of faith) the reading and searching and mediating on the scriptures day and night, and earnest praying without doubting that the Lord would give them the spirit of wisdom to direct them to the true understanding and meaning of God in the scriptures. They might be able to do so, if an angel from heaven should come and teach them any other doctrine than Christ and his apostles taught, to judge him accursed. When this way will be once truly leaned and faithfully practiced of God's people to attain true knowledge, then all that will seek after Christ will strive to enter into his kingdom by repentance and a new birth, being born again of water and the Holy Ghost. Then men will learn to know the true baptism of Christ, which is the "baptism of repentance for the remission of sins,"[76] and be baptized and put on Christ and not satisfy

---

[76] Acts 2.38

themselves with a childish baptism. This baptism they do not have, nor could they put on Christ, and without this baptism of repentance for the remission of sins they cannot put on Christ. Then the elect of God will not be deceived by the multitude of false prophets, with all their lying wonders, that say, "Lo, here is Christ, lo, there is Christ."[77] They who will take heed to the glorious brightness of his coming, which will be in the shining light of his truth, to that which the chosen of God will flee, and come from afar, as eagles to their pray. The Lord has brought you to this clear light of truth and has bought you all with his blood. Raise up your hearts so that you may seek his face and be filled with the fullness of his presence.

Amen

---

[77] Matthew 24.23

APPENDIX

We hold ourselves bound to acknowledge, and so that others might be warned, to manifest how we have been (through our great weakness) misled by deceitful-hearted leaders who have and do seek to save their lives, and will make sure not to lose them for Christ. Therefore, they flee into foreign countries and free states, and draw people after them to support their kingdoms, first seeking their own safeties, and then publishing (as they pretend) the gospel, or seeking the kingdom of heaven, and publishing, as far as they may with their safety. They justify this by perverting and misapplying the words of our Savior Christ, where he says, "When they persecute you, or drive, or thrust you out of one city, flee into another" (Matthew 10.23). These words they have picked for their purpose, casting away or leaving forth diverse rules of Christ going before and following in the same scripture, which cannot permit their exposition and practice. But we will only instance the reason why our Savior Christ bids them, when they are persecuted in one city, go to another, and his reason is this: "For verily, I say to you, you will not go over all the cities of Israel till the Son of Man comes."[1] This shows that our Savior Christ's meaning was that when they were driven or expelled out of one city, they should go to another city in Israel to preach the gospel. But these men flee to cities in which they cannot preach the gospel, being of a strong tongue. They have no intent or meaning to preach the gospel in those cities. Their fleeing is not to that end, but to save themselves, for being as "sheep in the midst of wolves," and for being "delivered up to councils, and for being brought to governors, and kings, for Christ's sake, in witness to them and to the Gentiles."[2] These men do not need the advice of our Savior Christ, who counsels his disciples to "take no thought of what they will speak, or what they will answer"[3] when they are brought before princes and governors. They flee to such places where they make sure they will never come into question before them.

---

[1] Matthew 10.23
[2] Matthew 10.18
[3] Luke 12.11

The disciples of Christ to whom he speaks these words ("when they persecute you or drive you out of one city, flee to another"[4]) did not understand our Savior Christ as these men do. If they had, they would not have believed the angel (Acts 5.19.20) that bade them, when he delivered them out of prison, "Go, and stand in the temple, and speak to the people all the words of this life." They would have said, "We have been imprisoned and persecuted, therefore we are to flee. Our Lord told us so." But they obeyed the voice of the angel, knowing it did not contradict that rule of Christ. Neither would they (if they had understood Christ as these men do), after they had been beaten and commanded to speak no more in the name of Jesus, still have stayed in that city, "daily in the temple and from house to house, teaching and preaching Jesus Christ"[5] (Acts 5.40–42). But these men flee before they feel either strokes or bonds, and teach men to do so. The whole scriptures are against them in their understanding. Acts 8.1 might suffice to satisfy them in this point, and to discover their error fully, where it is shown that there was a great persecution against the church at Jerusalem, and "they were all (except the apostles) scattered abroad through the regions of Judea and Samaria." And Acts 11.12 states, "They that were scattered abroad, went throughout until they came to Phoenicia and Cyprus, and Antioch, preaching the word."[6] Here we see that, notwithstanding the great havoc Saul made of the church, and entered into every house, and drew out both men and women, and put them into prison, yet the apostles did not flee. Those that did flee went to cities where they could and did preach the gospel. But neither the example of the apostles that did not flee, nor of those that were scattered, who went to cities where they preached the gospel, will serve these men's turn, but they flee to cities most commodious for their safety and profit, where they cannot preach the gospel. Furthermore, in Acts 14, although there was an assault made both by the Jews and the Gentiles against Paul and Barnabas, to do them violence at Iconium, and although Paul was stoned and left for dead at Lystra, yet they returned again to Lystra and Iconium to confirm the disciples' hearts, preferring that duty before the fear of persecution.

For the further overthrowing of this misunderstanding of these words of our Savior Christ, "when they persecute you in one city, flee to another," let all

---

[4] Matthew 10.23
[5] Acts 5.42
[6] Acts 11.19

godly hearts consider how the apostle Paul commended and rejoiced in the church of the Thessalonians because of their "patience and faith in all their persecutions and tribulations that they suffered" (2 Thessalonians 1.4). And in 1 Thessalonians 2.14, in condemnation of them he said "Brethren, you are becoming followers of the churches of God in Judea which are in Christ Jesus, because you have also suffered the same things of your own countrymen, even as they have done of the Jews." Thus the apostles commend the churches of Judea, and of Thessalonica, for their constant suffering of persecution in their own countries, not once advising or teaching them to flee out of their countries to avoid persecution. This is a new doctrine of devils brought in by men that was never found in the faith.

Further, hear what the Spirit says to the church of Pergamum. "I know you dwell where Satan's throne is. And you have kept my name and have not denied my faith, even in those days when Antipas, my faithful martyr, was slain among you, where Satan dwells."[7] And to the church of Smyrna the spirit says, "Fear none of those things which you will suffer. Behold, it will come to pass that the devil will cast some of you into prison that you may be tried, and you will have tribulation for ten days. Be faithful to death, and I will give you the crown of life"[8] (Revelation 2). Who will not be blind may see here how the spirit of God commends the saints for holding the faith and dwelling where there was bloody persecution and where Satan dwelled. He does not exhort them to flee, but not to fear what they should do to them. Then let the simple hearted be no more troubled by these men who have rent the words of our Savior Christ ("when they persecute you, or drive you of one city, flee into another"[9]) from the true sense and meaning of which they stand compassed around about in it (Matthew 10). As our Savior Christ in these words gave a rule of direction to his disciples as to how they should proceed in the publishing of the gospel, appointing them, when they were expelled or persecuted in one city that they should go to another to preach, because there were many cities in Israel to go through. These men of corrupt minds, lovers of themselves, utterly pervert the meaning of our Savior Christ in these words, and say, he gave it for a rule to his disciples to teach them to flee to save themselves from persecution. So by this their understanding, when the

---

[7] Revelation 2.13
[8] Revelation 2.10
[9] Matthew 10.23

disciples of Christ had found a most safe city, there they should hide themselves as these men do, and let the publishing of the gospel alone, unless any would follow after them, or come to them where they might be in safety.

Now do the ignorant, blind, corrupt hearts and tongues of these men conceive and speak against God and his truth. They pervert it to their own destruction, overthrowing the whole doctrine and meaning of Christ in this place (Matthew 10.16–39), where Christ with all the wisdom of the spirit sets himself to teach his disciples to suffer persecution. He shows them what persecutions they should suffer and what persecutions they should have, and how far they should suffer persecution, even to the loosing of their lives. Thus our Savior Christ teaches his disciples to suffer persecution, exhorting them not to fear those that kill the body, and declaring to them for their unspeakable comfort his providence and protection over them, telling them that all the hairs of their head are numbered in his sight. These deceivers, they teach their disciples to flee persecution and persecutors and to spare and save themselves that it may not come to them. When the worthy disciple of Christ, Peter, advised his master so, Christ bade him, "Come behind me, Satan. You are an offense to me[10] and taught him saying "if any many will follow me let him forsake himself and take up his cross and follow me"[11] (Matthew 16). Judge then what Christ will say to these false prophets that are the disciples of the man of sin, supporting and perverting his kingdom with their doctrine. The disciples of Christ cannot glorify God and advance his truth better than by suffering all manner of persecution for it and by witnessing it against the man of sin, with the blood of their testimony. We must leave this point to godly consideration. (It would have been much better, we confess, to have been part of a book than such an addition.) We leave these men with all their disciples (if they will not be informed in this matter) to be a reproach to all men who will say to them, "where have you learned to flee into foreign countries and not to suffer persecution for Christ among your own countrymen?" Where have you learned for fear of men to flee from your own country and fathers' houses, to whom you should and where you might best publish the gospel? Where have you learned to draw parents from children and children from parents to whom they are especially bound to witness God's truth and to be lights to them? You have not learned it of Christ, who would not suffer him that had

---

[10] Matthew 16.23
[11] Matthew 16.24

been possessed when he prayed that he might be with him, but Christ said to him, "Go your way to your friends, and show them what great things the Lord has done for you. He went and published them" [12] (Mark 5.18). Yes, all men will say to them, where have you learned to set up your light in secret places? Where have you learned to pull your shoulders from the yoke and to seek to save your lives? Therefore, (says Christ) surely you will lose them, unless you repent.

Furthermore, if Christ gave this as a rule or precept to his disciples to flee persecution to save themselves, then it was an absolute commandment, and so all the apostles and disciples of Christ broke his commandment and sinned, in that that they did not flee to save themselves when they were persecuted. By this, do these men condemn all their brethren that do not flee as they do, unless they will add error to error, and affirm as some of them do, that it is indifferent to flee or not to flee, thereby making this precept of Christ indifferent to be obeyed or not to be obeyed which cannot be affirmed in any one precept of Christ. Nothing can be both commanded and indifferent to be obeyed or done. Those words of Christ will in no way permit such indifference. They are an absolute precept for that end for that which they are given, which is not to flee to save themselves, but to flee or go to another city to preach the gospel. We put these seducers in remembrance that our Savior Christ gives this rule also to his disciples, that if they will "enter into any house or city that will not receive them, nor your words, when they depart from there, they will shake off the dust of their feet as a witness against that house or city." [13] But when will these men, according to this rule of Christ, shake the dust off their feet for a witness against Amsterdam or Leyden, cities which neither receive them nor the word they bring, anymore than they receive Turks and Jews, and all sorts who come only to seek safety and profit? It should seem that this rule of Christ does not appertain to these men. But let them and all men see that this rule appertains to whomsoever the other appertains. They were both given at one time and upon one and the same occasion and to one and the same persons. And when these great deceivers have learned not to divide Christ, they will learn also not to divide his precepts and ordinances by taking what is agreeable to their corrupt minds and forsaking what is contrary to them. We will pass by the lamentable fruits

[12] Mark 5.19.20
[13] Matthew 10.14

and judgments, that we have and see with our own eyes, and discuss what follows this damnable error when many, yes most men that had in a great measure forsaken the love of the world and began to be zealous for some good things, were drawn by this opinion and these seducers into foreign countries, now knowing which way to support their outward estate, have turned again to the world, and are fain to hunt to and fro, far and near, after every occasion. All is too little to satisfy most of their wants and nothing will satisfy some of their desires. All these things and many more, these hirelings, their shepherds, can well bear withal, so that they may return to the hive and their portion may not be reproved. Those of these best hearts, and some of the best quality that cannot run and rove, and set their hearts to seek the world, consume what they have and fall under hard conditions, and by little and little lose their first love also. It is the general judgment that we arrive at in all this, in that by these means, former zeal and the best first beginnings that were in these men do vanish, fade away, and come to nothing, to the unfeigned grief of our souls to see it. How much better would it have been if they had given their lives for that truth that they profess in their own countries. Now as we, through the grace of God, and by the warrant of his word (as we have here manifested), cast away these perverters of the holy scriptures and their doctrines, so we wish all to do that fear God and seek the glory of his name, and come and lay down their lives in their own country for Christ and his truth. Let none think that we are altogether ignorant, what building and warfare we take in hand, and that we have not sat down and in some measure and thoroughly considered what the cost and danger may be. Also, let none think that we are without sense and feeling of our own inability to begin and our weakness to endure to the end, the weight and danger of such a work. But in all these things we hope and wait for wisdom and strength, and help from the Lord, "Who is able to establish us that we may stand, and by weak means confound mighty things"[14] (1 Corinthians 1). Let none therefore "despise the day of small things," (Zechariah 4.10) nor be grieved and say with that scorner (Nehemiah 4.2), "What will these weak Jews do?" Thus commending all our poor endeavors to the best acceptance of every well disposed reader, beseeching the Lord to make his grace to abound to you all, for the glory of his name, and the salvation of everyone of your souls.

Amen

---

[14] 1 Corinthians 1.27

BIBLIOGRAPHY

PRIMARY SOURCES

Ainsworth, Henry. *A Defence of the Holy Scriptures, Worship, and Ministerie, Used in the Christian Churches Separated from Antichrist: against the Challenges, Cavils and Contradiction of M. Smythe: in His Book Tntituled* The Differences of the Churches of the Separation. *Hereunto Are Annexed a Few Observations upon Some of M. Smythe's Censures, in His Answer Made to M. Bernard.* Amsterdam: Giles Thorp, 1609. [Microfilmed].

———. *An Apologie or Defence of Such True Christians as Are Commonly (but Unjustly) Called Brownists: against Such Imputations as Are Layd upon Them by the Heads and Doctors of the University of Oxford, in Their Answer to the Humble Petition of the Ministers of the Church of England, Desiring Reformation of Certayne Ceremonies and Abuses of the Church.* Amsterdam: n.p., 1604. [Microfilmed].

Barrow, Henry. Writings of Henry Barrow, 1587–1590. Edited by L. H. Carlson. London: George Allen and Unwin, 1966.

Bradford, William. *Bradford's History of the Plymouth Settlement 1608–1650.* Edited by Harold Paget. New York: E. P. Dutton & Company, 1909.

Greenwood, John. *The Writings of John Greenwood, 1587–1590.* Edited by L. H. Carlson. London: George Allen and Unwin, 1962.

Harrison, Robert, and Robert Brown. Edited by L. H. Carlson and Albert Peel. *The Writings of Robert Harrison and Robert Browne.* London: George Allen and Unwin, 1953.

Helwys, Thomas. *An Advertisement or Admonition unto the Congregations, Which Men Call the New Fryelers, in the Lowe Countries.* Amsterdam: n.p., 1611. [Microfilmed].

———. *A Declaration of Faith of English People Remaining at Amsterdam in Holland.* Amsterdam: n.p., 1611. [Microfilmed].

———. *A Short Declaration of the Mystery of Iniquity.* Amsterdam: n.p., 1612. [Microfilmed].

———. *A Vindication of the Position Assumed by the English Baptists.* Amsterdam: n.p., 12 March 1610. [Microfilmed].

———. *A Short and Plaine Proofe by the Word and Workes off God and Gods Decree Is Not the Cause of Anye Mans Sinne or Condemnation and That All*

Men Are Redeamed by Christ. As also. That No Infants Are Condemned. Amsterdam: n.p., 1611. [Microfilmed].

————. *Letter on Church Order Dated September 26, 1608?* Amsterdam?: n.p., 1608. [Microfilmed].

————. *Letter to the Consistory of the United Mennonite Church at Amsterdam.* Amsterdam: n.p., 1610. [Microfilmed].

————. *Letter to the Mennonite Church in Amsterdam.* Amsterdam: n.p., 1610. [Microfilmed].

————. *Synopsis Fidei, Verae Christianae Ecclesiae Anglicanae.* [A Latin "synopsis" of faith of the "true English Christian Church" at Amsterdam under the leadership of Thomas Helwys, delivered (probably between February and 12 March 1610) to the Waterlanders there, with thanks for the teaching they had given them.] [Microfilmed].

Johnson, Francis. *A Brief Treatise Conteyning Some Grounds and Reasons against Two Errours of the Anabaptists. 1. The One Concerning Baptisme of Infants. 2. The Other, Concerning Anabaptisme of Elder People.* Amsterdam: Giles Thorp, 1609. [Microfilmed].

Lawne, Christopher. *The Prophane Schisme of the Brownists or Separatists.* London?: W. Stansby f. W. Burre, 1612. [Microfilmed].

Murton, John. *A Description of What God Hath Predestinated Concerning Man, in His Creation, Transgression, & Regeneration, as Also an Answere to John Robinson Touching Baptisme.* London: n.p, 1620. [Microfilmed].

————. *A Most Humble Supplication to Many of the King's Majesty's Loyal Subjects, Ready to Testify All Civil Obedience, by the Oath of Allegiance, or Otherwise, and That of Conscience; Who are Persecuted (Only for Differing in Religion), Contrary to Divine and Human Testimonies.* London: n.p., 1620. [Microfilmed].

————. *Objections Answered by Way of Dialgue, Wherein Is Proved by the Law of God: by the Law of Our Land: and by His Majesties Many Testimonies That No Man Ought to Be Persecuted for His Religion, so He Tesitie His Allegeance by the Oath, Appointed by Law.* [The Netherlands?] 1615. [Microfilmed].

————. *Persecution for Religion Judg'd and Condemn'd: in a Discoure [!], between and Antichristian and a Crhistian [!]. Proving by the Law of God and of the Land, and by King James His Many Testimonies, That No Man Ought to Be Persecuted for His Religion, so He Testifie His Allegiance by the Oath Appointed by Law. Proving Also, That the Spiritual Power in England,*

Is the Image of the Apiritual Cruel Power of Rome, or That Beast Mentioned, Rev. 13...to Which Is Added, a Humble Supplication to the Kings Majesty. London: By the author, 1615.

Robinson, John. *The Works of John Robinson, Pastor of the Pilgrim Fathers. With a Memoir and Annotations by Robert Ashton, Secretary of the Congregation Board, London.* 2 volumes. Boston: Doctrinal Tract and Book Society, 1851.

———. *Of Religious Communion Private, & Publique with the Silenceing of the Clamours Raysed by Mr Thomas Helvvisse agaynst Our Reteyning the Baptism Received in Engl: & Administering of Bapt: vnto Infants. As Also a Survey of the Confession of Fayth Published in Certain Onclusions by the Remainders of Mr Smithes Company.* Amsterdam: n.p., 1614. [Microfilmed].

Simmon, Menno. *The Complete Works of Menno Simons.* Translated by Leonard Verduin. Scottdale PA: Herald Press, 1959.

Smyth, John. *The Works of John Smyth Fellow of Christ's College, 1594–8.* 2 volumes. Edited by W. T. Whitley. Tercentenary edition for the Baptist Historical Society with notes and biography by W. T. Whitley. Cambridge: Cambridge University Press, 1915.

Williams, Roger. *The Bloody Tenet of Persecution for Cause of Conscience Discussed in a Conference between Peace and Truth. Richard Groves.* London: n.p., 1644. Edited and reprinted by Richard Groves. Macon GA: Mercer University Press, 2001.

SECONDARY SOURCES
Books

Armitage, Thomas. *A History of the Baptists, Traced by Their Vital Principles and Practices, from the Time of Our Lord and Savior Jesus Christ to the Present.* New York: Bryan, Taylor and Company, 1887.

Armour, Rollin Stely. *Anabaptist Baptism: A Representative Study.* Scottdale PA: Herald Press, 1966.

Armstrong, O. K., and M. M. Armstrong. *The Indomitable Baptists.* Garden City NY: Doubleday & Company, 1967.

Bainton, Roland H. *The Reformation of the Sixteenth Century.* Boston: Beacon Press, 1952.

Ban, Joseph D. "Were the Earliest English Baptists Anabaptist?" In *In the Great Tradition: In Honor of Winthrop S. Hudson Essays on Pluralism,*

Voluntarism, and Revivalism. Edited by Joseph D. Ban and Paul R. Dekar. Valley Forge PA: Judson Press, 1982.

Bangs, Carl. *Arminius: A Study in the Dutch Reformation.* Nashville: Abingdon Press, 1971.

Benedict, David. *The History of Baptists.* 2 volumes. Boston: Manning and Loring, 1813.

————. *A General History of the Baptist Denomination in America and Other Parts of the World.* New York: Lewis Colby & Company, 1848.

Bender, Harold S. *The Anabaptist Vision.* Scottdale PA: Herald Press, 1944.

Bettenson, Henry. *Documents of the Christian Church.* 2d edition. Oxford: Oxford University Press, 1963.

Brame, Webb. "Baptists' Struggles for Religious Freedom from 1523 to 1789." Unpublished Th.D. dissertation, Southern Baptist Theological Seminary, Louisville, Kentucky, 1914.

Bray, Gerald, editor. *Documents of the English Reformation.* Minneapolis: Fortress, 1994.

Brook, Benjamin. Volume 2 of *The Lives of the Puritans.* Cambridge: Cambridge University Press, 1912.

Burdine, James. "English Baptist Ecclesiology from John Smyth to Robert Hall, 1600–1830." Unpublished Th.D. dissertation, Southern Baptist Theological Seminary, Louisville, Kentucky, 1950.

Burgess, Walter H. *John Robinson, Pastor of the Pilgrim Fathers: Study of His Life and times.* London: Williams & Norgate, 1920.

————. *John Smyth the Se-Baptist and Thomas Helwys and the First Baptist Church in England with Fresh Light upon the Pilgrim Father.* London: James Clarke & Co., 1911.

Burrage, Champlin. Volume 1 of *The Early English Dissenters in the Light of Recent Research (1550–1641).* New York: Russell & Russell, 1912.

————. *The True Story of Robert Browne.* Oxford: Oxford University Press, 1906.

Carroll, J. M. *The Trail of Blood.* Lexington KY: Clarence Walker, 1931.

Cassel, Daniel K. *History of the Mennonites.* Philadelphia: Daniel K. Cassel, 1888.

Cathcart, William, editor. *The Baptist Encyclopedia.* 2 volumes. Philadelphia: Louis H. Everts, 1881.

Chadwick, Owen. *The Reformation.* Baltimore: Penguin Books, Inc., 1964.

Christian, John T. *A History of the Baptists.* 2 volumes. Nashville: Sunday School Board of the Southern Baptist Convention, 1922–1926.

Clapham, Enoch. *Errors on the Right Hand, Against the Several Sects of Protestants in Those Times.* In Joseph Ivimey, volume 1 of *A History of the English Baptists.* 1811. Reprint, Paris AR: Baptist Standard Bearer, 2005.

Clement, A. S., editor. *Baptists Who Made History: A Book about Great Baptists Written by Baptists.* London: The Carey Kingsgate Press, 1955.

Coggins, James R. *John Smyth's Congregation: English Separatism, Mennonite Influence, and the Elect Nation.* Waterloo, Ontario: Herald Press, 1991.

Cook, Henry. *What Baptists Stand For.* 5th edition. London: The Kingsgate Press, 1964.

Cramer, S., and F. Pijper, editors. *Bibliotheca Reformatoria Neerlandica.* 10 volumes. 's-The Hague: Martinus Nijhoff, 1914.

Cramp, J. M. *Baptist History: From the Foundation of the Christian Church to the Close of the Eighteenth Century.* 5th edition. Philadelphia: American Baptist Publication Society, 1868.

Croft, Pauline. *King James.* New York: Palgrave-Macmillan, 2003.

Crosby, Thomas. Volume 1 of *The History of the English Baptists from the Reformation to the Beginning of the Reign of King George I.* London: n.p., 1738–1740.

Cross, F. L., and E. A Livingstone, editors. *The Oxford Dictionary of the Christian Church.* 3rd edition. Oxford: Oxford University Press, 1997.

Davies, Horton. *The English Free Churches.* 2d edition. The Home University Library of Modern Knowledge. London: Oxford University Press, 1963.

Dexter, Henry Martyn. *The Congregationalism of the Last Three Hundred Years.* New York: Harper and Brothers, 1880.

———. *The True Story of John Smith* [sic] *the Se-Baptist.* Boston: Lee and Shepard, 1881.

Dexter, Henry Martyn, and Morton Dexter. *The England and Holland of the Pilgrims.* Boston and New York: Houghton, Mifflin & Co., 1905.

Dickens, A. G. *The English Reformation.* 2d edition. University Park: Pennsylvania State University Press, 1989.

Dillenberger, John, and Claude Welch. *Protestant Christianity.* New York: Charles Scribner's Sons, 1954.

Duncan, Pope Alexander, Jr. "A History of Baptist Thought, 1600–1660." Unpublished Th.D. dissertation, Southern Baptist Theological Seminary, Louisville, Kentucky, 1947.

Duffy, Eamon. *The Stripping of the Altars: Traditional Religion in England, 1400–1580.* New Haven: Yale University Press, 1992.

Dyck, Cornelius J., Jr. "Hans de Ries: Theologian and Churchman: A Study in Second General Dutch Anabaptism." Ph.D. thesis, the Divinity School, University of Chicago, 1962.

Dyck, Cornelius J., Jr., and Dennis D. Martin, editors. *The Mennonite Encyclopedia.* Scottdale PA: Herald Press, 1990.

Estep, William R., editor. Volume 16 of *Anabaptist Beginnings (1523–1533): A Source Book.* Nieuwkoop, Netherlands: B. de Graff, 1976.

————. *The Anabaptist Story: An Introduction to Sixteenth-Century Anabaptism,* 3rd ed. Grand Rapids: Eerdmans Publishing Company, 1996.

————. *Renaissance and Reformation.* Grand Rapids: Wm. B. Eerdmans Publishing Company, 1986.

Evans, Benjamin. *The Early English Baptists.* 2 volumes. London: J. Heaton & Sons, 1862; Greenwood SC: The Attic Press, 1977.

George, Timothy. *John Robinson and the English Separatist Tradition.* Macon GA: Mercer University Press, 1982.

González, Justo L. *The Story of Christianity: The Reformation to the Present.* 2 volumes. San Francisco: Harper Collins Publishers, 1985.

Haller, William. *Foxe's Book of Martyrs and the Elect Nation.* London: Jonathan Cape, 1963.

Himbury, D. Mervyn. *British Baptists. A Short History.* London: The Carey Kingsgate Press, 1962.

Ivimey, Joseph. Volume 1 of *A History of the English Baptists Including an Investigation of the History of Baptism in England from the Earliest Period to Which It Can Be Traced to the Close of the Seventeenth Century. To Which are Prefixed, Testimonies of Ancient Writers in Favour of Adult Baptism: Extracted from Dr. Gill's piece, Entitled "The Divine Right of Infant Baptism Examined and Disproved."* London: By the Author, 1811–1830.

Jordan, W. K. *The Development of Religious Toleration in England.* Volume 2 of *From the Accession of James I to the Convention of the Long Parliament (1603–1640).* Gloucester MA: Peter Smith, 1936, 1965.

Kirkman, Ralph Everett. "The Anabaptists: Their Historical Roots and Relation to the English Baptist Movement." Unpublished M.A. thesis, Baylor University, Waco, Texas, June 1951.

Knappen, M. M. *Tudor Puritanism, a Chapter in the History of Idealism.* Chicago: The University of Chicago Press, 1939.

Krahn, Cornelius. *Dutch Anabaptism: Origin, Spread, Life and Thought (1450–1600).* Hague, Netherlands: Martinus Nijhoff, 1968.

Lee, Jason K. *The Theology of John Smyth: Puritan, Separatist, Baptist, Mennonite.* Macon GA: Mercer University Press, 2003.

Leopold, Richard W., Arthur S. Link, and Stanley Corbin, editors. *Problems in American History.* 2d edition. Englewood Cliffs NJ: Prentice-Hall, 1957.

Lindsay, Thomas M. *A History of the Reformation.* 2 volumes. Edinburgh: T. & T. Clark, 1907.

Littell, Franklin. *The Origin of Sectarian Protestantism.* Revised edition. New York: The Macmillan Company, 1964.

Lofton, G. A. *Defense of the Jessey Records and Kiffin Manuscript.* Nashville: Marshall & Bruce Co., 1899.

———. *English Baptist Reformation from 1609–1641 A.D.* Louisville: Chas. T. Dearing, 1899.

Lumpkin, William L. *Baptist Confessions of Faith.* Philadelphia: Judson Press, 1959.

MacCulloch, Diarmaid. *The Reformation: A History.* New York: Penguin Books, 2003.

Maring, Norman H. *American Baptists: Whence and Whither.* Valley Forge PA: Judson Press, 1968.

Maring, Norman H., and Winthrop S. Hudson. *A Baptist Manual of Polity and Practice.* Valley Forge PA: Judson Press, 1963.

McBeth, Harry Leon. *A Sourcebook for Baptist Heritage.* Nashville: Broadman Press, 1990.

———. *The Baptist Heritage: Four Centuries of Baptist Witness.* Nashville: Broadman Press, 1987.

———. *English Baptist Literature on Religious Liberty to 1689.* New York: Arno Press, 1980.

McGlothlin, W. J. *Baptist Confessions of Faith.* Philadelphia: American Baptist Publication Society, 1911.

Miller, P. Martin. "An Investigation of the Relationship between Mennonite Theology and Mennonite Worship." Unpublished Th.D. dissertation, Southern Baptist Theological Seminary, Louisville, Kentucky, 1961.

Moore, Walter L. "Baptist Teaching and Practice on Baptism in England: 1600–1689." Unpublished Th.D. dissertation, Southern Baptist Theological Seminary, Louisville, Kentucky, 1950.

Moran, John L. "A Study of the Ministry of the English General Baptists, 1600–1770." Unpublished Th.D. dissertation, Southern Baptist Theological Seminary, Louisville, Kentucky, 1949.

Neal, Daniel. *The History of the Puritans.* 2 volumes. New York: Harper and Brothers, 1844–1855.

Newman, Albert Henry. *A Century of Baptist Achievement.* Philadelphia: American Baptist Publication Society, 1901.

————. *A History of Anti Pedobaptism from the Rise of Pedobaptism to A.D. 1609.* Philadelphia: American Baptist Publication Society, 1897.

————. *A History of the Baptist Churches in the United States.* Revised and enlarged edition. New York: Charles Scribner's Sons, 1915.

————. *A Manual of Church History.* 2 volumes. Philadelphia: American Baptist Publication Society, 1900–1903.

Orchard, G. H. *A Concise History of Foreign Baptists.* Lexington KY: Ashland Avenue Baptist Church, 1956. Originally published in London in 1838.

Patterson, W. Morgan. *Baptist Successionism: A Critical View.* Valley Forge PA: Judson Press, 1969.

Payne, Ernest A. *The Baptist Union: A Short History.* London: The Carey Kingsgate Press, 1959.

————. *The Fellowship of Believers.* Enlarged edition. London: The Carey Kingsgate Press, 1952.

————. *The Free Church Tradition in Life of England.* London: SCM Press, 1994.

————. *Free Churchmen, Unrepentant and Repentant.* London: The Carey Kingsgate Press, 1965.

————. *Thomas Helwys and the First Baptist Church in England.* 2d edition. London: The Baptist Union of Great Britain and Ireland, 1966.

Pettegree, Andrew, editor. *The Reformation World.* London: Routledge, 2000.

Ray, D. B. *Baptist Succession: A Hand-Book of Baptist History.* Cincinnati: G. E. Stevens & Company, 1870.

Rippon, John. *The Baptist Annual Register for 1790, 1791, 1792, and Part of 1793.* London: n.p., 1793.

Robinson, H. Wheeler. *The Life and Faith of the Baptists*. London: The Kingsgate Press, 1946.

Robinson, Robert. *Ecclesiastical Researchers*. Cambridge: Johnson, 1792.

———. *The History of Baptism*. London: Thomas Knott, 1790.

Saito, Goki. "An Investigation into the Relationship between the Early English General Baptists and the Dutch Anabaptists." Unpublished Ph.D. dissertation, Southern Baptist Theological Seminary, Louisville, Kentucky, 1974.

Scheffer, J.G. de Hoop. *History of the Free churchmen Called the Brownists, Pilgrim Baptists and Baptists in the Dutch Republic 1581–1701*. Ithaca NY: Andrus & Church, 1922.

Shakespeare, John H. *Baptists and Congregational Pioneers*. London: National Council of Evangelical Free Churches, 1905.

Smith, C. Henry. *The Story of the Mennonites*. Revised edition. Newton KS: Mennonite Publication Office, 1957.

Smithson, R. J. *The Anabaptists: Their Contribution to Our Protestant Heritage*. London: James Clarke and Company, 1935.

Sprunger, Keith L. *Dutch Puritanism: A History of English and Scottish Churches of the Netherlands in the Sixteenth and Seventh Centuries*. Volume 31 of *Studies in the History of Christian Thought*. Leiden: E. J. Brill, 1982.

Starr, Edward C., editor. *A Baptist Bibliography, Being a Register of Printed Material by and About Baptists: Including Works Written Against the Baptists*. 18 volumes. Rochester NY: American Baptist Historical Society, 1947–1973.

Tanner, J. R., editor. *Constitutional Documents of the Reign of James I, A.D. 1603–1625, with an Historical Commentary*. Cambridge: Cambridge University Press, 1930.

Taylor, Adam. *The History of the English General Baptists*. 2 volumes. London: T. Bore, 1818.

Thompson, Bard. *Humanists and Reformers: A History of the Renaissance and Reformation*. Grand Rapids: Eerdmans Publishing Company, 1996.

Torbet, Robert G. *A History of Baptists*. Philadelphia: Judson Press, 1972.

Tull, James E. *Shapers of Baptist Thought*. Valley Forge PA: Judson Press, 1972.

Turner, Charles H. "The Theology of English Baptists to 1800." Unpublished Th.D. dissertation, Southern Baptist Theological Seminary, Louisville, Kentucky, 1925.

Underhill, Edward Bean, editor. *Confessions of Faith and Other Public Documents, Illustrative of the History of the Baptist Churches of England in the 17th Century.* London: The Hanserd Knollys Society, 1854.

―――. *Tracts on Liberty of Conscience and Persecution, 1614–1661.* London: The Hanserd Knollys Society, 1846.

Underwood, A. C. *A History of the English Baptists.* London: Kingsgate Press, 1947.

Vedder, Henry C. *A Short History of Baptists.* New and revised edition. Philadelphia: American Baptist Publication Society, 1907.

Walker, Williston. *A History of the Christian Church.* 3rd edition. New York: Charles Scribner's Sons, 1970.

Wamble, Hugh. "The Concept and Practice of Christian Fellowship: The Connectional and Inter-Denominational Aspects Thereof, among the 17th Century English Baptists." Unpublished Th.D. thesis, Southern Baptist Theological Seminary, Louisville, Kentucky, 1955.

Watts, Michael R. Volume 1 of *The Dissenters: From the Reformation to the French Revolution.* Oxford: Clarendon Press, 1978.

Weir, Alison. *The Six Wives of Henry VIII.* New York: Grove Press, 1991.

Westin, Gunnar. *The Free Church through the Ages.* Translated by Virgil A. Olson. Nashville: Broadman Press, 1958.

White, Barrington R. *The English Baptists of the Seventeenth Century.* Volume 1 of *A History of English Baptists.* London: The Baptist Historical Society, 1983.

―――. *The English Separatist Tradition: From the Marian Martyrs to the Pilgrim Fathers.* London: Oxford University Press, 1971.

Whitley, William T. *A Baptist Bibliography: Being a Register of the Chief Materials for Baptist History, Whether in Manuscript or in Print, Preserved in Great Britain, Ireland, and the Colonies.* 2 volumes. London: The Kingsgate Press, 1916–1922.

―――. *The Baptists of London 1612–1928: Their Fellowship, Their Expansion, with Notes on Their 850 Churches.* London: The Kingsgate Press, 1928.

―――. *Calvinism and Evangelism in England Especially in Baptist Circles.* London: The Kingsgate Press, 1933.

―――. *A History of British Baptists.* Revised edition. London: The Kingsgate Press, 1923, 1931.

————. *Minutes of the General Baptist Church in England.* 2 volumes. London: printed for the society by The Kingsgate Press, 1909–1910.

————. *Thomas Helwys of Gray's Inn and of Broxtowe Hall, Nottingham.* Reprinted from *Transactions of the Baptist Historical Society.* London: The Kingsgate Press, n.d.

Whitsitt, William H. *A Question in Baptist History: Whether the Anabaptists in England Practised Immersion before the Year 1641?* Louisville: Chas. T. Dearing, 1896.

Williams, George Huntston. *The Radical Reformation.* Philadelphia: The Westminster Press, 1962. 3rd revised edition. Kirksville MO: Sixteenth Century Publishers, Inc., 1992.

Periodicals

"Arrival of Smyth's Followers at Amsterdam, by July, 1608." *Transactions of the Baptist Historical Society* 3 (1912): 64.

Bender, Harold. "The Anabaptist Theology of Discipleship." *The Mennonite Quarterly Review* 24/1 (January 1950): 25–32.

Birdwhistell, Ira V. (Jack). "The Continental Anabaptists and the Early English Baptists: A Review and Analysis of Research." *The Quarterly Review* 24 (January 1974): 47–58.

Brachlow, Stephen. "John Smyth and the Ghost of Anabaptism: A Rejoinder." *The Baptist Quarterly* 30/7 (July 1984): 296–300.

Burrage, Champlin. "The Restoration of Immersion by the English Anabaptists and Baptists (1640–1700)." *American Journal of Theology* 16 (January 1912): 70–89.

Burgess, Walter H. "The Helwys Family." *Transactions of the Baptist Historical Society* 3 (1912): 18–30.

Clayton, J. G. "Thomas Helwys: A Baptist Founding Father." *Baptist History and Heritage* (8 January 1973).

Coggins, James R. "A Short Confession of Hans de Ries: Union and Separation in Early Seventeenth Century Holland." *The Mennonite Quarterly Review* 60/2 (April 1986): 128–38.

————. "The Theological Positions of John Smyth." *The Baptist Quarterly* 30/6 (April 1984): 247–64.

Collins, William J. "Dutch Dissenters and English General Baptists." *Translations of the Baptist Historical Society* 4 (1914–1915): 65–68.

Davies, Emlyn. "Our Historic Baptist Distinctives." *The Chronicle* 16 (October 1953): 191–200.

Dyck, Cornelius J. "The First Waterlandian Confession of Faith." *The Mennonite Quarterly Review* 36/1 (January 1962): 5–18.

———. "The Middleburg Confession of Hans de Ries, 1578." *The Mennonite Quarterly Review* 36/2 (April 1962): 147–54, 161.

———. "A Short Confession of Faith by Hans de Ries." *The Mennonite Quarterly Review* 38/1 (January 1964): 5–19.

Estep, William R. "A Baptist Reappraisal of Sixteenth Century Anabaptists." *Review & Expositor* 55/1 (January 1958): 40–58.

———. "Anabaptists and the Rise of English Baptists." *The Quarterly Review* 28 (October–December 1968): 43–53; *The Quarterly Review* 29 (January–March 1969): 50–62.

———. "Thomas Helwys: Bold Architect of Baptist Policy on Church-State Relations." *Baptist History and Heritage* 20/3 (July 1985): 27–28.

Farrer, A. J. D. "The Relation between English Baptists and the Anabaptists of the Continent." *The Baptist Quarterly* 2 (1924–1925): 30–36.

George, Timothy. "Between Pacifism and Coercion: The English Baptist Doctrine of Religious Toleration." *The Mennonite Quarterly Review* 58/1 (January 1984): 30–49.

Gould, George. "The Origin of the Modern Baptist Denomination." *Transactions of the Baptist Historical Society* 2 (1910–1911): 193–216.

Hudson, Winthrop S. "Baptists Were Not Anabaptists." *The Chronicle* 16 (October 1953): 171–79.

———. "The Ecumenical Spirit of Early Baptists." *Review & Expositor* 55/2 (April 1958): 182–95.

———. "Who Were the Baptists?" *The Baptist Quarterly* 17/2 (April 1957): 304.

Kliever, Lonnie D. "General Baptist Origins: The Question of Anabaptist Influence." *The Mennonite Quarterly Review* 36 (October 1962): 291–321.

Kraus, C. Norman. "Anabaptist Influence on English Separatism as Seen in Robert Browne." *The Mennonite Quarterly Review* 34/1 (January 1960): 5–19.

Littell, Franklin F. "The Anabaptist Doctrine of Restitution of the True Church." *The Mennonite Quarterly Review* 24/1 (January 1950): 33–52.

Mosteller, James D. "Baptists and Anabaptists: I. The Genius of Anabaptism." *The Chronicle* 20/1 (January 1957): 3–27.

———. "Baptists and Anabaptists: II. John Smyth and the Dutch Mennonites." *The Chronicle* 20/2 (July 1957): 100–44.

Patterson, W. Morgan. "Baptist Historiography in America in the Eighteenth Century." *Review & Expositor* 52 (October 1955): 483–93.

———. "The Development of the Baptist Successionionist Formula." *Foundations* 5 (October 1962): 331–45.

Payne, Ernest A. "Contacts Between Mennonites and Baptists." *Foundations* 4 (January 1961): 39–55.

———. "Who Were the Baptists?," *The Baptist Quarterly* 16/8 (October 1956): 339.

Sprunger, Keith L. "English Puritans and Anabaptists in Early Seventeenth-Century Amsterdam." *The Mennonite Quarterly Review* 46/2 (April 1972): 113–28.

Stassen, Glen H. "Anabaptist Influence in the Origin of the Particular Baptists." *The Mennonite Quarterly Review* 36/4 (October 1962): 322–43.

Voolstra, Sjouke. "The Word Has Become Flesh: The Melchiorite-Mennonite Teaching on the Incarnation." *The Mennonite Quarterly Review* 57/2 (April 1983): 155–60.

Waite, Gary K. "The Anabaptist Movement in Amsterdam and the Netherlands 1531–1535: An Initial Investigation into Its Genesis and Social Dynamics." *Sixteenth Century Journal* 18/2 (Summer 1987): 249–65.

Walker, Michael J. "The Relation of Infants to Church: Baptism and Gospel in 17th Century Baptist Theology." *The Baptist Quarterly* 21/6 (April 1966): 247.

Wamble, Hugh. "Inter-Relations of Seventeenth Century English Baptists." *Review & Expositor* 54 (1957): 407–25.

Watson, John H. "Baptists and the Bible as Seen in Three Eminent Baptists." *Foundations* 16 (July–September 1973): 239–54.

Westin, Gunnar. "Who Were the Baptists?" *The Baptist Quarterly* 17/2 (April 1957): 55–60.

White, Barrington R. "The English Separatists and John Smyth Revisited." *The Baptist Quarterly* 30/8 (October 1984): 344–47.

————. "The Frontiers of Fellowship Between English Baptists, 1609–1660." *Foundations* 11/3 (July 1968): 244–56.

Whitley, William T. "Continental Anabaptists and Early English Baptists." *The Baptist Quarterly* 2 [VOL/ISSUE #] (January 1924–25): 24–30.

————. "Note: John Smyth and the Dutch Mennonites—A Communication." *The Mennonite Quarterly Review* 4 (October 1930): 306–307.

————. "Thomas Helwys of Grays Inn and of Broxtowe Hall, Nottingham." *The Baptist Quarterly* 7/6 (1934): 241–54.

Zijpp, N. van der. "The Confessions of Faith of the Dutch Mennonites." *The Mennonite Quarterly Review* 29/3 (July 1955): 171–87.

INDEX